Gentlemen in Crisis

THE UNION LEAGUE HOUSE
FROM *Leslie's Illustrated* AUGUST 19, 1865

GENTLEMEN IN CRISIS

The First Century

of

The Union League of Philadelphia

1862-1962

MAXWELL WHITEMAN

PHILADELPHIA, PENNSYLVANIA
1975

To the Memory of Family Patriots

LEVI DELANO, of Abbot, Me., private, Co. M, 1st Maine Cavalry, taken prisoner by the Confederate Army, May 24, 1862 and died of wounds at the age of 20, at Lynchburg, Virginia, July 16, 1862, en route to Belle Isle prison.

EVERETT MARTIN DELANO, his brother, corporal, Co. E, 1st Maine Heavy Artillery, who died of wounds at the age of 19, May 26, 1864.

CHARLES MANVILLE DELANO, of Peru, Me., captain, Co. I, 7th Maine Infantry, who met the same fate fighting for the cause of the Union on September 8, 1862.

Like their forefathers who felled the first trees and tilled the New England soil to build a new nation, who fought in all the colonial wars, who stood by Washington at Valley Forge, they did not live their lives in vain. This book is humbly dedicated to that past that has secured the present.

Introduction

It is with a deep sense of humility that I approach the writing of this introduction to *Gentlemen in Crisis—The First Century of The Union League of Philadelphia*. Few organizations in America can claim one hundred years of existence, and fewer still can show one hundred years of major concern for and continuous contributions to the solution of the social, educational, political, and economic problems of a growing nation, predicated on the high principles of patriotism expressed in the motto *Amor Patriae Ducit*, Love of Country Leads.

Ralph Waldo Emerson in his essay *History* states: "All history becomes subjective; in other words, there is properly no history, only biography." Maxwell Whiteman's *Gentlemen in Crisis* and his mini-biographies of the Founders and other members of The Union League as related to the historic events from 1862 to 1962 substantiate this assertion. One has to be impressed with the extensive scope of the author's research and the scholarly treatment given to achievements of the League and its members. He is to be commended for his sensitive handling of the courage and foresight with which members of the League continually strove for "justice, truth, and integrity" in all areas to which they turned their attention—from the quelling of rebellion to tariff policy, for infant industry, or from civil rights to constitutional reform, both national and state. His treatment of history is not the "view from a remote bridge" but "one that is seen from within". When one has finished the work and reflects upon it, one has the feeling that he has just read an abridged history of our great nation, written by an historian who sat in the corridors and meeting rooms of the League House.

It was Shakespeare who said "What is past is prologue." Without knowledge of what has gone before, one is poorly prepared to deal with the present and the future. We are now well into our second century. Many of the problems we now face in national affairs and in League affairs, have a similarity to those faced in the first hundred years. The need for vigilance to preserve the institutions that have made this country a world power; the need for patriotism—love of country; the need for a strong Union League with a full membership concerned about the sociological, economic, and political

ix

problems of the times as an important adjunct to social activities within our organization—all these needs are just as great today as they were in our first century. It is hoped that each reader will obtain from this book a new insight into the greatness of The Union League of Philadelphia, and be inspired to work to make the history of the next hundred years just as great.

These remarks would be incomplete without a reference to the Committee consisting of Samuel E. Fulton, chairman, Burton H. Etherington, Jr., Norman Joy Greene, and Joseph S. Riebel. They were instrumental in bringing this work to fruition. All of us owe to them a hearty "thank-you" and a rousing "well done" for their tireless effort and their dedication to completing the job with professionalism and understanding.

EDWARD J. DWYER

President, The Union League of Philadelphia
December 10, 1974

Acknowledgments

Late in 1972, Mr. Edward J. Dwyer the incumbent president of The Union League brought to the attention of the Board of Directors the necessity of a history of The Union League of Philadelphia. The idea was favorably received, and a committee consisting of his successor in office, Burton H. Etherington, Jr., and Joseph S. Riebel and Norman Joy Greene was named to review the book. Mr. Dwyer and the committee had the good fortune of having Samuel E. Fulton, a past president of the League and the Chairman of the League's Committee on History and Art, act in an advisory capacity.

All of these gentlemen have my thanks. Not the thanks which is extended as a formal courtesy that authors provide in acknowledgments, but the thanks that springs up when acknowledging the support of a committee who gave me free range to write and interpret events as I saw them. The committee was primarily concerned with an objective picture of the inner life of an outstanding American institution, not a rose-colored image of the history and traditions of the League. Mr. Fulton's insight and patience was matched by the tremendous amount of time and care given to this book by Joseph S. Riebel. I benefited considerably from their suggestions and those of the entire committee. Without their cooperation and without such total freedom, the task of writing would have been more difficult.

Many other past presidents and officers of the League have been as gracious and as cooperative and each added a distinctive contribution to this work. The staff of the League also was supportive in numerous ways. Outstanding was Daniel M. Layman, the League manager, who gave me access to every nook and cranny of the League House and kindly responded to innumerable questions.

A number of the city's institutions, The Historical Society of Pennsylvania, The Library Company of Philadelphia, and the Presbyterian Historical Society were far more helpful than they may ever know.

My wife thoughtfully refrained from becoming a family critic and advisor on matters of history, hence thanking her is a pleasant obligation. Milton Kenin, League librarian, will breathe more freely now that he no longer has to provide me with books from one of the great American club libraries.

Mrs. Lois Given Bobb and Mrs. Evelyn A. Weiman also were gracious in their professional comments, for which I am indebted. The sharpest critic, from whom I learned much, was Dr. Donald H. Kent, Director of the Bureau of History and Archives of the Pennsylvania Historical and Museum Commission. He too will understand my thanks.

MAXWELL WHITEMAN

The Union League of Philadelphia

I

The First Crisis

IN the spring of 1856, following the first National Convention of
the Republican Party, 331 Philadelphians stepped forward to
adopt the principles set forth by the Convention as their own political
creed. These men became members of Philadelphia's first Republican
Club, and committed themselves to the platform of the Party that
opposed the extension of slavery in the territories, in Kansas and
Nebraska, and "those twin relics of barbarism [Mormon] Polygamy
and Slavery."[1] They were eager to see the Fugitive Slave Law repealed, and they naively believed that the power of the government
could peacefully uproot slavery.

Philadelphia's first Republicans came from various sections of the
recently consolidated city, but most of them lived in the original area
laid out for William Penn. They were a minority of accomplished
artisans, craftsmen, shopkeepers and men of professional stature having
little connection with the local political machinery. Many of the men
were members of the well-to-do families who later helped organize The
Union League. Among the better known of these men were William
Rotch Wister, historian of the game of cricket,[2] and Hector Tyndale,
who after the execution of John Brown escorted the body north for
burial.[3] Joseph R. Fry, who helped raise ten regiments of troops for
The Union League during the Civil War,[4] and Charles Gibbons, who
was constantly in the forefront of Republican Party politics and a
League stalwart,[5] were also subscribers to the national party platform
and members of the first Republican organization of southeastern
Pennsylvania. William D. ("Pig-Iron") Kelley, the antislavery orator,
protectionist and congressman, came from a humble background to
the Republican Club.[6] Altogether the names of 51 men who were

1

to become members of The Union League appeared on the rolls of Philadelphia's first Republican organization.[7]

Some men who later became strong supporters of the Party held back from a formal commitment in the beginning. For example, Henry C. Carey, the nation's celebrated economist and delegate to the Convention, where he made known his views on protectionism and slavery, did not immediately join the Republican Club.[8] Morton McMichael, a disillusioned Democrat who was editor of the influential *North American*,[9] and William M. Meredith, Secretary of the Treasury under President Zachary Taylor,[10] both future presidents of The Union League, had not yet emerged as vocal Republicans.

Locally the Democrats were struggling to maintain a coalition while the Republicans were groping to build one. A hopeful enthusiast and founder of the Republican Club who provided much of the inspiration for the Party was William B. Thomas. Motivated by his antislavery convictions, and liberal with his funds for political causes, Thomas ran for mayor of Philadelphia in 1856. The thinly scattered vote he received was a harbinger of the Republican failure in the national election that fall.[11] The continuing effectiveness of the Philadelphia Democrats was evident when victory over Millard Fillmore and John Fremont brought James Buchanan to the White House. In their first bid for office, the Republicans of southeastern Pennsylvania were defeated.

In the four years that followed, Republican Party views were strengthened and unified. When news from Washington reached the city that Preston S. Brooks had cane-whipped Senator Charles Sumner in retaliation for a stinging denunciation of slavery in the Senate, William D. Kelley, Morton McMichael, Charles Gilpin, a mayor of the city before its consolidation, and other future members of the League denounced the incident as typical of the brutality of the Southern slave-power.[12] As a result, they moved closer to the Republican fold, joining a growing number of dissenters who had become a challenge to the Democrats. President Buchanan, in a dispute with John W. Forney arising from a personal quarrel, broke with his strong Pennsylvania supporter, who thereupon switched to the Republicans.[13] One by one, a number of others separated themselves from the established parties. The Democracy, as the Democrats were called, was further weakened by shifting political alliances in Philadelphia; the influence of the anti-immigrant Know-Nothing Party of the city was becoming minimal. Former supporters of President Fillmore, like John P. Veree, relinquished their Know-Nothing Party ties and moved over to the new party.[14] The Whigs, once the chief opponents of the Democrats, were falling apart.[15] A new political coalition was being formed and the coming together of these formerly disparate political interests in the Republican Party helped to contribute to the election of Alexander Henry in 1858, who was Philadelphia's first Republican mayor.

Although the new Republican alignment still lacked political homogeneity, the Philadelphia forces that were soon to consolidate behind Abraham Lincoln were rapidly gathering strength. Various associations moving in this direction adopted such striking names as "Lincoln Defenders," "Wide-Awakes," and "Republican Invincibles" to show that they were politically alert. The Union Party and the Union Republican Party also declared themselves, but the most influential groups were the People's Party and the Republican Invincibles. The People's Party was, in fact, the original Republican Party; under the name of The Republican Invincibles, a separate unit survived the 1850's to recruit younger men to the Party for another three decades. Among its earliest members were the forebears of Presidents Eisenhower and Nixon.[16]

A political tide was rising, and with it a great debate marked by incessant oratory and a wave of pamphleteering. Halls were packed with attentive audiences eager to hear each side expound its causes: Kansas and Nebraska, free or slave, the virtues or faults of a high tariff, and how the victims of the depression of 1857 could be helped. The press became politically exciting. Controversy mushroomed before the public eye, and newspaper editors took their stands on the complex issues of states' rights, slavery, and the Constitution. Evidence of spreading political bitterness and of the lingering vitality of the Democrats was seen most clearly in the public debates of the issues of the political platforms. In the arguments heard throughout the city before the Civil War, Charles Gibbons emerged as an eloquent Republican spokesman whose oratory was as much of a challenge to the Democrats as his political views. He was a descendant of John Gibbons who came to Philadelphia with William Penn. Numerous members of his family had joined the Quaker crusade against slavery. Close family ties with Lucretia Mott, a proponent of women's rights and a leader in the antislavery movement, and with James Miller McKim, editor of *The Pennsylvania Freeman*,[17] brought Gibbons to the forefront of the Philadelphia antislavery movement. A lawyer, Gibbons quickly rose to prominence at the bar. In 1844, he flung himself into the political mainstream and was elected to the State Senate on the Whig ticket. He was a lively supporter of Henry Clay, but in 1856 he deserted the faltering Whig Party to become an early Republican.[18] His career was bound up with the antislavery movement and the Republican Party, and his oratorical ability was outstanding in an age when public speaking had to compete with the press. His appearance on the public platform always guaranteed a large audience.

Gibbons was active in the debate with proSouthern Democrats in 1859, during the months of wild excitement over John Brown's raid at Harpers Ferry, his trial and execution. One of the first men whom Gibbons challenged was William B. Reed. When Reed, Minister Plenipotentiary to China, returned to Philadelphia in 1859, he began at once to expound the principles of the Democratic Party.[19] In the months that followed, he provided Philadelphia's outspoken Democrats with fresh fuel for their arguments. Hector Tyndale, joined by James Miller McKim and his wife, undertook the responsibility for recovering John Brown's body and bringing it to Philadelphia.[20] The Democrats used this association with Brown, in addition to their antislavery views, as further evidence that the local Republicans intended to "subvert the South."

About the same time, Reed delivered a harsh condemnation of Abraham Lincoln, the Illinois candidate for president. Gibbons responded to Reed in a meticulously prepared, two-and-a-half-hour speech which Morton McMichael spread across the front page of the *North American*. Using Reed's biography of his grandfather, Joseph Reed, president of the Pennsylvania Executive Council in 1781, Gibbons shredded Reed's historical views on the subject of slavery. He reminded the younger Reed that his revolutionary grandfather had supported Pennsylvania's Gradual Emancipation Act of 1781. He then gave a biting record of Reed's political career in Pennsylvania, assailing in particular his views on the extension of slavery through the territories. Gibbons' scalding pre-election speech was as much a condemnation of President Buchanan as it was of his spokesman.[21] Gibbons' position on slavery and his deepening interest in the political crisis brought him into the still small and isolated camp of Philadelphia's radical Republicans, whose prime interest was the immediate abolition of the slave system.

The presidential campaign of 1860 also brought forth an ideological division and a personal rivalry within the Republican ranks. Gibbons and his radical associates constituted a faction which was motivated by humane objectives, and specifically, by antislavery. However, Andrew G. Curtin, the Republican gubernatorial candidate, and Alexander K. McClure were political realists and found themselves in opposition to the astute United States Senator Simon Cameron, a former Democrat who had regained his Senate seat in 1857 by a timely conversion. Political ambitions and expediency had separated them as contenders for power. They did not know that The Union League would temper their political differences, but in 1860, all of these men were vying for control of the state Party.[22]

From the ranks of Philadelphia's prominent families whose personal histories were linked with the colonial period and the events that led to the founding of the United States, came the men who stood on opposite sides of the issues of slavery and secession. The regular Democrats represented one tradition in American thought, and the nucleus of Free Soil Democrats, Whigs, and Know-Nothings that was gradually moving into the Republican fold represented another. They had much in common. Since the American Revolution they had advanced as lawyers and merchants, as physicians and men of letters. They had contributed to the city's political leadership, established its scientific and cultural institutions, and promoted its industrial progress. They could proudly boast of their accomplishments. They belonged to the same social clubs, observed similar religious practices, and were unconcerned by those who were of other religious groupings.[23]

In the beginning political diversity did not interfere with the common activities of these men who belonged to such clubs and organizations as the Wistar Party—named after Doctor Caspar Wistar—where the savants of the city, scholars from at home and abroad, had met with faithful regularity since the beginning of the century, to enjoy "a dash of hock or sherry." They were primarily members of the American Philosophical Society, who exchanged information on new scientific developments or discussed a favorite subject of history.[24] The nation's oldest club, the State in Schuylkill, founded in 1732, did not consider politics or religion as an admissible part of its social activities.[25] The Philadelphia Club, where national problems were often a subject for discussion, had completed its first quarter century at the time of Lincoln's election and was earning for itself the reputation of a prestigious private club.[26] In all three associations, the descendants of the city's colonial families were its honored members and constituted the base of Philadelphia social life. The "fathers of Binneys, Ingersolls, Tilghmans, Reeds, Rushes, Cadwaladers, Biddles, met and mingled" at the Wistar Party. And so did the sons.[27] With the exception of the Binneys and Reeds, the same family names appear on the rolls of the Philadelphia Club, while their relatives could be found as members of the State in Schuylkill.

Out of this elite class also came the merchants and entrepreneurs who extended their business interests to the Southern states and the growing Midwest. Philadelphia bankers had established offices in the key areas of Charleston and Savannah, Lexington and New Orleans. Bales of cotton shipped to Liverpool from Charleston were negotiated in the counting houses of Philadelphia; bills of exchange for hogsheads of Virginia tobacco were discounted by the same bankers. Tinware and nonferrous metals were shipped to Southern consumers from warehouses along the Delaware River, and the fine Madeira wines that enhanced the cellars of Southern gentlemen were supplied by the West India traders, whose vessels also were engaged in the coastwise shipping trade and used the port of Philadelphia.[28]

Philadelphia business with the South was often combined with social interests and strengthened by marriage ties. One of the notable examples, in Charles Jared Ingersoll's family, is the marriage of Charles Ingersoll and Susan C. Brown of New Orleans. Another Ingersoll son became a Mississippi planter and his sons fought for the Confederacy. Of Charles Jared Ingersoll's two daughters, one married Sidney George Fisher, a Philadelphia Quaker, and the other married Dr. John Forsyth Meigs of Georgia, who had settled in Philadelphia.

Fisher was a Union man; and Meigs, despite his Southern birth, became an original member of the Union Club, the predecessor of The Union League.[29] Prominent Southern families sent their sons to Philadelphia's medical colleges, and Southerners were frequently seen at elite Philadelphia parties or having lunch at the Philadelphia Club.[30] John Campbell's bookshop was a favorite spot to browse for proslavery literature, and was patronized by sophisticated Democrats, often Southerners.[31] Social splendor and cultural tastes mingled with a comfortable, well established, mercantile tradition.

However, the Philadelphia merchants who had no links to the South and who formerly had been inclined to Whig politics were changing their political allegiances, and were becoming increasingly critical of their proSouthern colleagues. As the arguments of the small clique of Republican radicals, Charles Gibbons and James Miller McKim in particular, became more and more convincing, the social soirées of the Wistar Party and the luncheons at the Philadelphia Club became awkward and tense. Republican sympathizers began to meet informally at the office of the *North American,* thus far their only spokesman, to discuss their views.[32] At their social gatherings, most were still unwilling to disrupt club life by an open confrontation. But club life and the general social affairs for which Philadelphia had come to be known were soon to be turned into a hostile arena.

Outside the offices of the *North American* these men made their political views known and argued for a stronger protective tariff. Henry C. Carey, coming more into public notice, was invited by McMichael to contribute a column to the paper expounding his tariff views. The Gibbons group promoted the antislavery issue in public debates and discussed the likelihood of disunion of the States as the crucial election approached.[33] William M. Meredith implored his listeners not to yield to secessionist threats, and Morton McMichael urged Northerners to hold high the spirit and meaning of the Union when voters were preparing to go to the polls.[34]

When the votes were counted in the 1860 state election, Andrew Curtin had been elected Governor of Pennsylvania. Upstate voters, encouraged by the Republicans who espoused Curtin as a central Pennsylvanian, had assured his success, and their support gave promise of a Republican victory in the November presidential election. The Peoples' Party, which had not officially assumed the Republican title, worked closely in a coalition effort, and contributed to a division among Democrats. Pennsylvania was carried for Lincoln. The decisive electoral vote that brought the lanky Republican to Washington was not won in Philadelphia, however, and the old Pennsylvania Democrats, though divided, retained considerable power.[35]

With the cry of secession echoing throughout the land after the election of Lincoln, the Democrats, both workingmen and businessmen, regardless of their views on Lincoln and slavery, were united in their opposition to the threatened disruption of the Union. Yet their leaders acted otherwise. Their abrasive declarations challenged anti-Southern views, and their positions of influence, especially in Philadelphia, made the challenge a formidable one. They soon came to be known as Copperheads, the Democratic opponents of Lincoln. Subsequently the term was associated with treason. Critics of the war, justly and unjustly, were dubbed Copperheads. Many Democrats, unsure of the course of events, feared a rupture in the commercial ties with the South, and moderation was urged upon the business community. They, too, were to be called Copperheads.

Philadelphians were educated in the fundamentals of the national dilemma in a series of public lectures that followed the Lincoln victory. On the one hand, they listened to arguments favoring concessions to the South, and on the other, they heard protests that government power should be used to crush all hostile opposition. The Republicans were as divided over the alternatives as the Democrats. The issues of partisanship became inflammatory. Some public meetings had to be cancelled, and others were possible only because speakers received heavy police protection. The scent of mob rule was in the air.[36]

Independence Square became the favorite locale of the speechmakers. One of the impressive meetings that revealed the state of political confusion was held on December 13, 1860. Although it was intended to be nonpartisan, concession to the South and preservation of the Union through compromise were strongly advocated as a means of averting secession and war. John B. Myers, a wartime officer of the League, declared that the "misplaced teachings of the pulpit, the unwise rhapsodies of the lecture room, the exciting appeals on the subject of slavery, must be frowned upon by just and law-abiding people" whose first devotion must be to the Union. Myers' careful nonpartisan phraseology could have been voiced as well by a pro-Union Democrat! His speech was followed by a brief conciliatory address by Joseph R. Ingersoll, who did not share the Southern views of his nephews, Charles and Edward. Joseph R. Ingersoll sought compromise by offering secessionist-minded Southerners the opportunity to convene in Philadelphia in order to find a solution to their differences with the Federal government.[37] In neither speech did the Republican views of Myers and Ingersoll emerge with any degree of clarity or force. Later, in his treatise, *Secession as a Folly and Crime*, written in 1862, Joseph Ingersoll revised his position and exerted considerable influence on the founders of the League, with whom he soon joined.[38]

Opposing Myers and Joseph R. Ingersoll was Pennsylvania Justice George Washington Woodward, who upheld the validity of the plantation economy and underlined the interdependence of Southern cotton and Northern mills. Moreover, he argued, while the North had gradually disposed of its slaves without financial loss, the South was expected to liberate its human property without remuneration, regardless of investment, and without "forebearance or moderation." All that his Republican opponents later recalled of his lengthy address was the pronouncement that slavery was "an incalculable blessing."[39] Privately, Woodward was charged with saying that, "If the Union is to be divided, I want the line of separation to run North of Pennsylvania."[40] Both statements were used to help defeat him in the Pennsylvania gubernatorial election of 1863.

Restraint on the subject of war was characteristic of most Philadelphians. Outspoken Democrats and Republicans continued their appeals to avert conflict. In a meeting held on January 4, 1861, men of such importance as Carey, McMichael, and Charles Gilpin[41] repeated this same theme. To the surprise of many who were present, the most vocal spokesman against disunion was the Democrat, Daniel Dougherty, who before the crisis opposed any affiliation with Republicans. Now he urged a resolution to support Major Robert Anderson who had withdrawn his forces to Fort Sumter in Charleston Harbor. Dougherty's demand for strong reinforcement of the beleaguered Fort inflamed the audience, and his joining forces with Republicans led the meeting to an end in wild confusion. Also a founding League member, Dougherty later made effective use of his oratorical skill in winning fellow Democrats to the Union cause.[42]

Two weeks later Charles Ingersoll, a Democrat of a different stripe, addressed a rally denouncing the Republicans for their intransigeance and stubborn refusal to come to terms with the South. At this gathering Pennsylvania was asked with whom she would side, the secessionists or the Unionists, and the hope was expressed that she would "stand by herself, as a distinct community."[43]

Pennsylvania's proSouthern speechmakers had little influence in conciliation efforts, and the Copperheads, those Democrats advocating peace at any price, only inflamed the passions of Philadelphia Unionists. South Carolina had made her choice and ten other states had joined her in withdrawing from their constitutional "contract" with the federal government. On February 8, 1861, the seceded states framed a Confederate constitution, and on April 12, Fort Sumter was fired upon by Confederate guns. One day later the national colors were lowered in defeat. The challenge in Lincoln's first inaugural address that secession would not be countenanced had been accepted. The violence of civil war was "forced upon the national authority."[44]

Philadelphians, concerned above all with preserving the Union, felt an alarm that only a short time earlier would have been inconceivable. The United States was at war with itself. In a flourish of arrogance, Confederate sympathizers in Philadelphia, especially those who held warm feelings for South Carolina, launched a newspaper just at the time when General Pierre G. T. Beauregard was preparing to attack Fort Sumter. In undisguised effrontery, the publisher called it *The Palmetto Flag*, thus identifying it with South Carolina. The paper stated that it did not intend "to adopt sectional views or extreme partisan opinions," but this was precisely what it fostered.[45] It condemned the warlike preparations of the federal government that "subverted the Constitution" and distorted the views of slavery expressed in the Bible. In bigoted terms, its journalism vented the spleen of its supporters upon "Black Republicanism," and charged the federal government with violating the principles of the United States as a Christian nation.[46] This was the "liberal vehicle" that undertook the goal of impartiality in informing Philadelphians on the issues of the war.

However, this kind of antiUnion propaganda met with strong disapproval. Many newspapers, including the religious press, suspected of proSouthern sentiment were forced to fly the flag as an indication of their sympathy with the Union. *The Palmetto Flag* was a sure target, and its office would most certainly have been destroyed by an inflamed public in April, 1861, had it not been for police protection and the intervention of Mayor Alexander Henry. After having a promise that the paper would immediately suspend publication, which it did with its third issue on April 13, a hostile mob withdrew.[47]

On April 27, two weeks later, the President of the United States suspended the writ of *habeas corpus*. Lincoln had resorted to this extralegal measure in order to restrain the threats of Confederate sympathizers in the sensitive, uninvaded area between Washington and Philadelphia. Arrests by State Department operatives produced such a protest that the Supreme Court declared the suspension of *habeas corpus* unconstitutional and without precedent.[48] Those who favored the suspension sought justification by arguing that unusual conditions demanded it. Opinions were divided as to how to deal best with the problems engendered by the war. Many of the Democrats who wanted to support the war for the Union disliked some of the measures taken to wage it. Others were openly disgusted by the local mob action, and opposed every government measure taken to suppress the rebellion. Discussion again moved to the suspension of *habeas corpus,* for Lincoln ignored the judicial ruling, and a prolonged debate on the Constitution ensued. From the pen of the old federalist Judge Horace Binney came a brilliant counterattack defending Lincoln's action.[49] Others joined the fray over constitutional law and the pamphlet war reached new dimensions.

Throughout the summer of 1861, the subject of *habeas corpus* was uppermost in the minds of many Philadelphians. One of them was Sidney George Fisher,[50] a shrewd observer of his day, and the brother-in-law of Charles Ingersoll. Although Fisher lived among influential peace-party Democrats, he sided with proUnion Republicans. He could not abstain from the battle of words, and offered to write an article for the *North American* "that would show clearly the propriety of the conduct of the President."[51] While Fisher was discussing his viewpoints with McMichael in the editor's office, George H. Boker, poet, dramatist, and Philadelphia Club member,[52] and Charles Gibbons joined the informal meeting. Fisher's recounting of this meeting is noteworthy because it shows the mood of Gibbons and Boker. "They were discussing a plan to bring social opinion to bear upon those who expressed sentiments hostile to the government and the war. I disapproved them [his colleagues] as they looked too much like mob law."[53] Fisher's statement is perhaps enigmatic. If he meant that Boker and Gibbons intended to ostracize a segment of influential Democratic Philadelphians who favored the Confederacy, then the idea of a Union League was already anticipated. But as a Philadelphia gentleman, how could he have associated the behavior of his colleagues with mob conduct unless his disdainful view of popular opinion crept into the meaning of "social opinion?" A week after this event, on August 29, 1861, Fisher's article on *habeas corpus* appeared on the front page of the *North American* under his pen name, "Cecil."

Fisher's views supporting the suspension of *habeas corpus* were derived from the fear that judges concurring with secessionist ideology might easily release prisoners. He held that if a prisoner could be denied a trial but the government could provide the court with a reason for his arrest and detention, the principle of the writ would be upheld. Fisher's rationale was easily and amply refuted. Judge Binney, however, who had a national reputation and who presented a more formidable argument in his *The Privilege of the Writ of Habeas Corpus under the Constitution,* became the chief target for attack.

In justifying the President's action, the older Horace Binney argued that Lincoln could exercise the power of his office whether or not Congress was in session and that the executive power could not be abridged. Although the treatise was written in the summer of 1861, its first printing did not appear until a few days before Christmas.[54] William M. Meredith, who was named by Curtin as State Attorney General in the spring of that year, privately opposed the views of his old colleague. Meredith had been associated with Binney ever since the famous Girard Will case of the 1830's. Out of fear of embarrassing President Lincoln, and Governor Curtin, Meredith withheld his disagreement with Binney from the public.[55]

Democratic lawyers fired back at Binney with a barrage of no less than 21 pamphlets, all of which were published in Philadelphia. Some of the rebuttals focused on an analysis of constitutional law; others attacked Binney's doctrine as unsound; while others questioned the very concept of the war. Most of the pamphlets were published anonymously and almost all under the imprint of John Campbell, also an author and bookseller. Campbell, an Irish immigrant and a former Chartist, cast aside his views on the improvement of society to write *Negromania,* a particularly vicious book attacking American Negroes, and used his press to publish the writings of a number of secessionist sympathizers.[56]

The Philadelphia publishers had taken sides in the controversy, establishing a practice which continued throughout the war years. Henry B. Ashmead,[57] Joshua B. Lippincott,[58] the Bairds,[59] and the Leas[60] were all committed to the Union, and the books and pamphlets which issued from their presses took precedence over their commercial interests. It would be extremely difficult to find an antiUnion or proslavery tract that carried their imprint, at least during the term of the war. Within a year they became members of The Union League and pamphlets in the tens of thousands of copies, sponsored by the League, carried their imprint with precisely the same conviction as the prosecessionist publishers.

Philadelphia newspaper editors also committed their papers to the political philosophies they espoused. Unlike the book publishers, they faced the mob if they supported the South. *The Palmetto Flag* suspended publication under threat; the *Argus* perished for lack of funds, and the *Christian Observer,* a New School Presbyterian weekly, was forced from the scene because of its condemnation of the administration[61]. Although its opinions wavered, *The Democratic Evening*

Journal survived a while longer owing to its occasional support of Union issues.[62] The remainder of the Philadelphia press upheld the administration, not out of fear but out of conviction.

In addition to McMichael's *North American*, the Philadelphia *Press* was turned into a paper of major significance.[63] Its editor, the former Democrat John W. Forney, a wholehearted supporter of the administration who later became secretary of the United States Senate, and the publisher of the Washington *Sunday Chronicle*, successfully blended politics with journalism. Following his Washington appointment, Forney placed John Russell Young in charge of the *Press*.[64] At the age of twenty-two, Young was also the youngest member of the newly founded League. The *Press*, as well as being a spokesman of the administration, eventually became the public voice of the League as the war progressed. Other journalists and editors gradually placed their publications at the service of the Union. Louis A. Godey, publisher of *Godey's Lady's Book*, the most popular midnineteenth century women's journal,[65] Charles J. Peterson, known for his equally popular *Peterson's Magazine*,[66] and Gibson Peacock, a friend of George H. Boker and editor of the *Evening Bulletin*,[67] were conspicuous in the patriotic upsurge that preceded the founding of The Union League.

One other influential sector, the Protestant clergy, continued to publicize its opposing positions. In a pulpit debate that had grown hoary with time, since the colonials first preached on the Bible view of slavery, sermonic literature reached new heights of exegesis. But with each new interpretation the subject was further clouded. The last pronouncements by the clergy before the war, in January, 1861, had attempted to rectify the age-old confusion which had used the Bible both to justify and to condemn slavery. Debate followed debate, and sermons eager to refute one another were rushed to the printer. Nothing could repair the cleavage that had taken place between Northern and Southern Protestants; denominations had split theologically and regionally on whether scriptural literature sanctioned or rejected the ownership of human property.[68] The spirit of the antebellum sermon lingered far into the war. In 1863, after The Union League was formed as a secular club, with the Union as its singular theme, an attempt was made to bring clarity to the interpretation of the biblical view of slavery.

Further confusion was spread through the North by the rumor that a new society, the Knights of the Golden Circle, planned to seize Mexico, invade Cuba, and turn the Confederacy into an imperial empire far beyond the South. It was thought to be a secret organization supported by local peace Democrats. However, few were ready to believe that it operated in Philadelphia, and that such a wild plan

CHARLES J. PETERSON

LOUIS A. GODEY

MORTON MCMICHAEL

was in the making. No evidence was available to establish the truth of its existence, but the story spread far beyond Philadelphia that this secret order was growing uncontrolled in the Midwest.[69]

Moving fearlessly into the arena crowded with sermonic literature and rumors of secret societies, Charles Ingersoll cast aside all restraint to challenge the Lincoln administration with his proSouthern views. In a nationally circulated pamphlet, *Letter to a Friend in a Slave State*, Ingersoll repeated a theme he had first discussed in 1856, conciliation and compromise; however, at precisely this time in 1862, the Union army was scoring a series of victories. He wrote, in the hands of the South, "The sword must make our map at last. . . ." The Republicans had to be dismissed from power and, if restored, a Democratic Congress would bring about a just settlement. Peaceable separation of the South was no longer practical. Confusing his less informed readers, he showed how the Union would be kept intact by maintaining Southern institutions. Appealing to Christian friends, he pointed to the New Testament as a source that upheld slavery. The North, furthermore, had to be cleansed of its abolitionists, or any sincere or permanent settlement was unlikely. At times his *Letter* sounded like a call for Union, but as he pursuel his subject, it became clear that his argument lacked the historical foundation and logic which he claimed for it.[70] At this time League authors, like Charles J. Stillé, more skilled in historical method, were drawing upon English and American themes to prove effectively to their readers that the procedures of the federal government were just. It is even possible that Stillé's pamphlet, *How A Free People Conduct A Long War*, was a rejoinder to Ingersoll's.[71] Interest in Stillé's pamphlet was so great that hundreds of thousands of copies were circulated.

A direct "reply" to Ingersoll came from Judge M. Russell Thayer, who, with Stillé, joined the intellectual force of The Union League. "It is too late and too early for conciliation. The time is past. The time has not come. As for compromise, if you intend by it the surrender of the principles of the Constitution, you must determine which is the best—the Constitution maintained and established by war, or peace without the Constitution, and therefore without government, and therefore with war. It is idle to talk about the Constitution, and at the same time to propose to yield it up to traitors by conciliation. The Constitution cannot be preserved by conciliation against bayonets, cannon, and 300,000 soldiers. History teaches that under such circumstances as those in which we now find ourselves, force is the only safe conciliator; numbers, skill, and cannon, the only referees."[72]

Ingersoll's apocalyptic visions of peace and of conquest, of dividing the map with a sword, were wiped out with the brilliant successes of the Union army early in 1862. The military strength of the Confederacy was being reduced. Kentucky and Tennessee were liberated by Commodore Foote and General Ulysses S. Grant. Shiloh was held by the Union in a blood-bath. The descent of the Mississippi River was facilitated by the capture of Island Number Ten. Confederate forces were expelled from New Mexico, and were yielding in Arkansas. A successful drive brought General Mitchell into Alabama, while Fort Pulaski, at the mouth of the Savannah River, was captured. Union forces compelled Roanoke Island to yield, and other key forts and cities of the South fell one by one. By the middle of 1862, victory seemed in sight. General McClellan, after some delay, brought his army within a few miles of Richmond, and the Confederate capital appeared to be doomed. The Northern press glowed with accounts of the impending fall of the Confederacy, whose strategic military centers would soon be encircled and forced to capitulate.

Suddenly, reverses struck the Union Army. The Seven Days' Battles forced a withdrawal from the Peninsula between the James and the York Rivers, and removed the Union threat to Richmond. Pope was defeated at the Second Battle of Bull Run. The bloody sacrifices at Antietam followed. Though not a decisive victory for either army, Antietam became a turning point in the war and had a direct effect on affairs in Philadelphia. Local friends of the South chose this juncture to air their beliefs, as if a Southern triumph had taken place. In a few days, they said, Philadelphia would be taken, and General Lee's headquarters would be in the Dundas mansion at the corner of Broad and Walnut Streets.[73]

In the fall of 1862, when news of successful Southern resistance, stalemates, and lengthy Northern casualty lists were posted prominently on the city's billboards and in telegraph offices, the Copperheads and other proponents of "peace at any cost" were jubilant. They exulted in their condemnation of the war and boasted of the staggering resistance of the South. Most Philadelphians were stunned by the Union reverses, and they had good reason to be, for no other major Northern city had sent so many of its sons to the field of battle.[74] But quietly, and with considerable hesitation, the Copperhead tide was reversed. Former Whigs, disenchanted Democrats, the politically alienated, and a small number of devout Republicans mustered their strength in a movement whose voice would resound throughout the Union and penetrate behind the Southern lines. Its first step was to break away from the old, ordered club life which was dominated by sentiments obnoxious to proUnion men.

"Society," as Civil War America defined it, was an association of clubmen. As gentlemen they met together to enjoy their mutual advantages and tastes and to share their intellectual pursuits. At mid-century, clubmen formed an amicable, self-contained association. With the advent of the war, political dissent gradually penetrated the nation's important clubs from Philadelphia to Boston, until it reached a point of turmoil. Uneasiness was evident in the Forest and Somerset Clubs of Boston and in the old Union Club of New York City. As the war moved into its second year, a process of fragmentation was beginning to take place within established club life.

Philadelphia clubs found themselves in a peculiar situation. They were largely made up of Northerners with strong proSouthern views, and Southerners who had come to dominate Philadelphia society. It was these men who determined who should belong to the city's inner circles, and who should not. Their standards no longer were based on the criteria of previous decades, when family life and cultural achievement with professional or mercantile success helped define the status of a gentleman. Political partisanship and antiUnion sentiments had become overwhelming considerations. This new turn of events was obviously galling to the proUnion clubmen. It is difficult to determine which of the contending groups were more numerous. Judging by the collapse of the Wistar Party in mid 1861, after pro-Union men had withdrawn, it is obvious that both factions had been important to the success of the club, for after 1861 it became inactive for many years.

Many of the same men were also members of the Philadelphia Club. While it did not meet with the same fate, one of its members stated, "this place reeks with Copperheads." Only when officers of the Union Army made their presence known, did Southern sympathizers restrain their antiUnion declaration. On one occasion when Union sentiment was challenged, harsh exchanges resulted, and a fight took place that led to the expulsion of a secessionist exponent.[75] Perhaps the Philadelphia Club was able to count more proUnion members. No full account of its affairs can be reconstructed due to the absence of its wartime records.

In referring to these conflicts, George Henry Boker wrote that "At no period of the struggle was the patriotic spirit so low, or the spirit of the traitors so insultingly hopeful." "Gradually," Boker added, "our secret foes had emerged from their seclusion, taking their wonted social places, and boasting to their foreign visitors that, in what was called 'unmixed society,' they ordered matters, and that all gentlemen would soon be of their way of thinking. The President was vulgar, the administration was vulgar, the war was vulgar, and the people who waged it were of the common sort, who would shortly receive a merited castigation from the gentlemen of the South . . . ."[76]

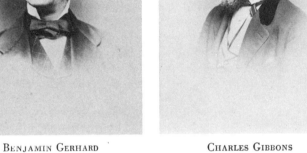

BENJAMIN GERHARD   CHARLES GIBBONS

GEORGE HENRY BOKER

It was because of the defiance, "outspoken treason," and "disagreeable wrangling" prevalent in this segment of Philadelphia "society" that club life reached a state of disruption. The proUnion members of club society who met regularly in McMichael's *North American* office strove to maintain their gentlemanly decorum, but they had grown weary of reiterating their defensive position and of retreating in the face of what they considered to be social arrogance and treason to their country. When reports reached them that other social assemblies consisted of nothing more than "a nice meeting of traitors" led by Charles Ingersoll, the "jackal" at the head of a den of scoundrels, the idea of forming a new club began to take shape.[77]

"In this miserable condition of public and private affairs," Boker recounted, a chance meeting with Judge John I. C. Hare early in November, 1862, led to action. Judge Hare, the son-in-law of the elder Binney and the son of an outstanding American chemist, was possibly the most eminent man on the bench in nineteenth-century Pennsylvania. Hare insisted that disloyal men be excluded from the "society" of the suggested new club, and that articles of association be drawn up to clearly state their views. He had the will and the authority to pursue with Boker the proposition they discussed that day in the heart of old Philadelphia.[78]

After their meeting, Boker hurried back to the office of the *North American* to seek McMichael's support. There they were joined by Benjamin Gerhard, an Episcopalian gravely concerned with the clergy's views on slavery. Gerhard was so favorably disposed toward Boker's idea that he proposed an immediate meeting at his home for loyal and trusted friends of the Union. The meeting was to be limited to 16 men. Everything was done so quietly that an air of secrecy pervaded the initial proceedings held on November 15, 1862. Enthusiasm at this meeting as yet was low; however, those present decided to meet again the following Saturday night at Boker's home. Meanwhile, it was decided to draw up formal rules for their association, and Morton McMichael, Judge Hare, Charles Gibbons, Benjamin Gerhard and Boker were appointed as a standing committee. McMichael acted as chairman, and Boker was named secretary.[79]

At the second meeting on November 22, Charles Gibbons proposed the name The Union Club of Philadelphia, which the association unanimously adopted. The condition of membership was "unqualified loyalty to the Government of the United States, and unwavering support for the suppression of the Rebellion." Two lighter articles, as a token of former days, stipulated that the Club meet every Saturday evening in "the months appointed by the Standing Committee, at the house of a member." Entertainments were to be moderate; three

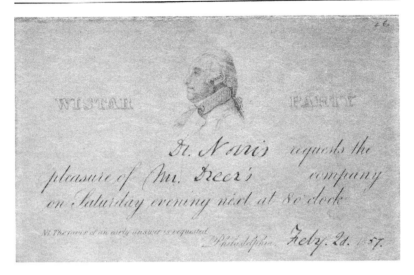

INVITATION CARDS OF THE WISTAR PARTY AND THE
UNION CLUB-ADDRESSED TO FERDINAND J. DREER

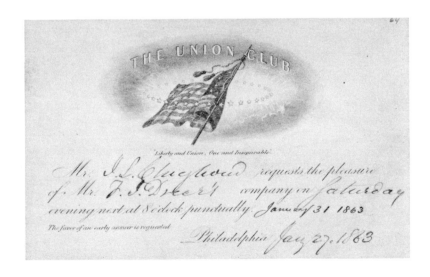

dishes of various kinds and wines "limited to Sherry and Madeira, and to one other." Guests could be invited, provided their opinions were in harmony with the article that spelled out "unqualified loyalty."[80]

The Articles of Association were brief, and reflected the inner commitments of the men who prepared them. It came as no surprise that they were adopted unanimously. Regular Saturday night meetings, actually patriotic festivities, were held in members' homes, and by mid-December the meeting places became so crowded that the Union Club permanently limited its membership to 55. The new club saw itself as a curb to the dominance of Southern sympathizers. News of the founding of The Union Club spread swiftly. The opposition was outraged. "Our Association was regarded by them with hatred and alarm. Our policy of exclusion was vehemently denounced, both in private and in public, by the most able sympathizers of the South," Boker stated. When the names of the Club members became known, one newspaper published a threat that in a matter of days, perhaps, the houses of these gentlemen would be burned to the ground. Although the threat was never carried out, it exposed the passions and frustrations of a middle and upper-class society challenged and divided by its own members. Filling the void left by the Wistar Party and drawing upon members of the Philadelphia Club, the new organization provided a social life free of the rancor of controversy.[81]

The Union Club utilized the format of the Wistar Party invitation, and expressed its proUnion sentiments by using as its emblem a 32 star flag on a slanting staff within a shield of stars.

In the weeks that followed, the enthusiasm of its members soared from a low ebb to unforeseen heights. By mid-December the Club resolved to reorganize itself. If it was to release its forces for the support of Lincoln's program, it no longer could confine itself to Saturday night meetings. It had to be more than a social gathering where men discussed the progress of the war. To be a potent force in national affairs, it had to more deeply involve men willing to take an active part in achieving total victory and restoring the Union. A special meeting was called of men eager to identify themselves publicly with the new movement. With this step, the Club took measures that led to the organization of The Union League of Philadelphia.

II

A Wave of Strength

THREE days before Christmas, 1862, Dr. John Forsyth Meigs addressed invitations to the members and "unconditional friends" of The Union Club, calling for a business meeting on December 27, at his home.[1] Stephen Colwell, presiding at this meeting, read Charles Gibbons' draft of the articles for the new association and led the discussion on the expediency of forming "a social and political organization of loyal citizens" to "counteract the efforts of traitors in the Northern States." Colwell was a trained lawyer who had become a successful ironmaster. He had retired early from business to devote his time to the two themes that fascinated him: Christian ethics and their abuse, and economic thought and its explication. His interpretation of each subject was original, he published widely, and in the area of economics his associates and devotees made up a distinctive school of American economic thinkers. Most of them subsequently became members of the Philadelphia or New York Union Leagues. Colwell was an outstanding protectionist, and was involved in a number of programs to better the status of the Negro. His far flung philanthropic activity, his involvement in the Presbyterian Church, and his other interests all influenced his outlook toward secession and the war, and he was strongly in favor of an organization that would uphold the principles of the federal government.[2]

The meeting began by discussing briefly whether the name The Union Club should be retained or the new name, The Union League, proposed by Charles Gibbons, should be accepted. The latter name was chosen. In contrast to the relatively calm meetings of The Union Club, which had been in existence for some six weeks, the organizational meeting of the new League erupted in unforeseen controversy.

STEPHEN COLWELL   DANIEL DOUGHERTY

Gibbons' articles stated that members were not to conduct any business or maintain social relations with Northerners who had political loyalties to the South. Although neither provision was made obligatory in the articles, an immediate protest was raised. As the course of events unfolded during the war, commercial ties and social contacts with the South were ultimately severed, and there was no need for such a provision. Total support for the Lincoln administration and rejection of Copperheads and their philosophy were emphasized in the other articles. With his customary zeal, Gibbons declared in uncompromising language that the new League would be affiliated with the Republican administration. On this point also, a major clash ensued. Daniel Dougherty, shaking his head defiantly, announced his opposition. "I am for the Union—not for any Republican president." The company was stunned. Colwell looked on with quiet dismay, while Boker murmured something inaudible. Dougherty arose to clarify his statement. He had come into the Union League as a Democrat, recognizing the new association as a powerful agency for a successful outcome of the war. He would support Mr. Lincoln in whatever measures were necessary to save the Union, but no further. In conscience, he stated, he could not support a mere political club having no other aim but the success of the Republican organization. Furthermore, if the provision of the article that called for an association with the Republican administration was eliminated, he was certain that other loyal Democrats would join with him to secure the aims of The Union League.

Gibbons responded in anger to Dougherty's views, which he felt were a desecration of everything sacred to the organization. In his passionate reply he spoke of weak and faltering men, of faint-hearted patriots, and of the thin line that divided loyalty from treason. He then invited Dougherty to leave; the patriotic work of the League would proceed without him. A silence fell on the assembled company. Gibbons and Dougherty, like two warriors, stared at each other angrily. Other former Democrats, Benjamin Harris Brewster and John W. Forney, did not endorse Dougherty's view.

Before Colwell could intervene, Judge Hare broke the silence. Thoughtfully looking about him, he asked if there was not a higher purpose in their assembly than a political alliance? If recognized Democratic League members like Dougherty maintained Union views and endorsed Lincoln's wartime measures, why should they not have the right to differ on other policies? Differences on squatter sovereignty, the tariff, and the Homestead Act were academic in the present crisis; but there was nothing academic about the battlefield or the need to restore the nation. If the new organization was to be purely a social club, or an exclusively political one, he might speak differently. Although personally he held views similar to those of Gibbons, his judgment was on Dougherty's side. Hare insisted that the only condition for admission to a patriotic "social society," borrowing Gibbons' description of a gentlemen's club, should be "to uphold the federal government" and work to suppress the aim of the "traitors."

What was being disputed here was the definition of disloyalty, the definition of treason, and the denigrating use of these words. Any statement that even remotely suggested sympathy with the South, or even vaguely upheld the rights of the seceded states, was considered disloyal. Democrats often were all branded Copperheads without distinguishing between those who were loyal to the Union or those who opposed the war. It was this attitude that Dougherty disapproved of. The men present thought of Judge Woodward, an extreme opposite of Dougherty, whose apologia of slavery and public statements advocating peaceful compromise had been previously attacked by Gibbons as typical antiUnion philosophy. No mention was made of his two sons, both Democrats, who were fighting faithfully against the Confederates in Pennsylvania regiments. The articulate Colonel Charles

DRAFT OF THE ARTICLES OF ASSOCIATION SHOWING WHERE THE
REFERENCE TO THE REPUBLICAN PARTY WAS ELIMINATED.

5. No cards, billiards or other games except chess shall be allowed in the Club House, and no spirituous liquors shall be kept or sold therein.—

6. There shall be a standing committee consisting of nine associates members, who shall have a general supervision of the concerns of the League, who shall be appointed annually, at a meeting of the League in such manner as the meeting may decide.—

7. The standing committee shall prepare such by laws as may be necessary to secure a proper and orderly administration of the affairs of the League, which shall be subject to such amendments from time to time as a majority of the associates may direct.—

Philad^a^ Dec 27. 1862   Stephen Colwell
Fairman Rogers   Jno Ashhurst
Charles Gibbons   J. Forsyth Meigs

Henry D. Moore

B. Gerhard   Wm Henry Rawle
C. I. Antelo   Edwin M. Lewis
Saml L. Reeves   James C. Paul
James L. Claghorn   W. M. Tilghman
W. H. Ashhurst   Henry Pang
John B. Myers   A. J. Lewis
George Trott
Morton McMichael
Jay Cooke

SUBSCRIBERS TO THE LEAGUE'S ARTICLES OF ASSOCIATION

J. Biddle, a former commander of the Pennsylvania Bucktails, a Democratic member of the Congress and a proponent of gradual abolition, also had been dubbed a Copperhead by staunch Unionists, although, as it turned out, Biddle responded in the defense of his native state. What counted in Hare's view was that loyal men, whatever their political background, should be admitted to the new League. The first article was amended to reflect Hare's judgment.[3]

Convinced by Hare's discerning argument, his brother-in-law Horace Binney, Jr., McMichael, and Gerhard accepted the amended article, and many of the men, including Colwell, came up to sign the document. However, when the reference to the Republican organization was snipped out of the manuscript, Gibbons' name, which coincidently was in the precise spot on the opposite side, was also cut away. Gibbons, incensed by this act, stalked out of the room and did not return to the meeting. Only later did he ratify the Articles of Association.[4]

The revised article on membership retained the basic principle of loyalty to the government of the United States, an obligation which has remained unchanged to the present day. It stated that the Association shall "discountenance and rebuke, by moral and social influences, all disloyalty to the federal government; and to that end the Associators will use every proper means, in public and private."[5]

Between December 27, 1862, and January 10, 1863 when the Articles were published listing the names of the Associators, 253 men had subscribed to the document. A contemporary analysis of the political background of the membership showed that of this number there were 135 Democrats, 75 Republicans and 43 whose prior affiliation was undetermined.[6] The proof of Dougherty's objections and Hare's judgment was obvious. The League announced its meetings and made known its intentions through newspaper advertisements, and the names of its members were published. Contrary to the belief of many historians, it was not a secret political society, its members wore no special regalia, and there were no special handshakes by which members identified themselves. As a matter of fact, every effort was made to dispel all suspicion of secrecy. The Union Club did not disband, but continued to hold regular social meetings. It became an autonomous body within the League, adhering to its basic structure, but made no provisions for admitting new members.[7]

To facilitate the operation of the League, an *ad hoc* committee of nine was appointed to find suitable meeting quarters and to prepare the necessary by-laws. Gibbons' hatred for the Democracy did not prevent the committee from choosing him to draft the by-laws, as they had chosen him to prepare the Articles of Association. Further meet-

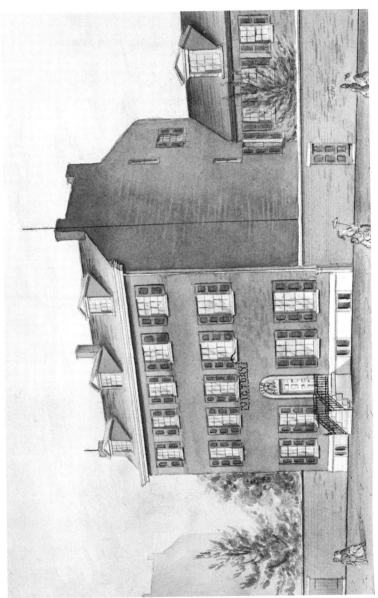

THE FIRST LEAGUE HOUSE AT 1118 CHESTNUT STREET

ings in private homes were ruled out. Continued growth necessitated larger quarters. Furthermore, in one of the few references to a specific program, the Articles called for the publication of patriotic reading matter and implied the establishment of a library facility. Without delay, William H. Ashhurst and James L. Claghorn, both of whose careers from this time on were identified with League endeavors, rented the spacious mansion of Hartmann Kuhn at 1118 Chestnut Street and immediate preparations were made to convert it into a commodious clubhouse. Some members looked upon this move as hasty and extravagant, beyond the reach of what annual dues of $25 per member could defray, but a daily increase in membership allayed their fears.[8]

To make the League house attractive, members contributed choice furniture and objects of art symbolizing the history of the nation. A huge, carved wooden eagle, its wings spread in flight, soared above the eaves of the house. A banner, specially designed for the League, was hung beneath a thirty-two star flag that extended from one of the Chestnut Street windows. For the interior, Thomas Sully made available his huge equestrian portrait of George Washington at the Battle of Trenton, one of the finest paintings of the president as a soldier. Originally painted for Congress in 1842, the commission and its financial terms had not been completed. This major art treasure remains in the permanent collection of the League.[9]

In the meantime, Lincoln issued the Emancipation Proclamation, freeing all the slaves still held in the seceded states. Abolitionist members of the League were overjoyed. Those doubtful on the subject were more eager to support Lincoln than to express disagreement. Reactions to this important measure were reflected in the speeches of Gibbons and Judge M. Russell Thayer, who addressed the first general meeting of the League on January 22, 1863. Elections followed the addresses, and William M. Meredith was unanimously chosen president. Early in 1861, he had been a member of the conciliatory Peace Congress which had acted in the belief that war could be avoided between the North and South. It was thought by some that his election would be regarded as a gesture to wavering men to join the League. The four vice-presidents which the By-Laws called for were William H. Ashhurst, nine of whose relatives also were founding members of the League; John B. Myers and Adolph E. Borie, two of the city's leading merchants, and Horace Binney, Jr., two of whose sons had already tasted the blood and grime of battle.[10] James L. Claghorn, one of the great nineteenth century patrons of American art, was named treasurer, and George H. Boker, secretary. The officers were backed up by nine directors, whose experience at the bench and bar of Philadelphia, in journalism and letters, and in the world of commerce was unprecedented in American club life. With a neatly furnished building, adequate provisions for dining, and a governing body of discerning and indefatigable men, the League was prepared to implement the programs that shaped its wartime activity.

The first step taken by the League was to empower the triumvirate of Gibbons, McMichael and Boker to establish Union Leagues throughout the United States. New York City was the first to emulate the Philadelphia plan, and Boston followed soon thereafter. A printed circular, written by Boker, was sent to the post offices of every city and town not in Confederate hands. Instructions were included for organizing Leagues adapted to rural and urban locales. Philadelphia itself saw the rise of smaller Leagues, these designated by the wards in which they were organized. In a short time southeastern Pennsylvania boasted scores of them, and neighboring states, especially New Jersey and Ohio, followed with a "brood of faithful offspring." Each League was intended to become the focal point of loyalty in its area, and all, including the New York and Boston Leagues, maintained a correspondence with the parent League in Philadelphia.[11]

At the same meeting at which it was resolved to establish other Leagues whose functions would be independent, Benjamin Gerhard,[12] also a founder of The Union Club, proposed that a committee be formed "for the purpose of printing and circulating useful information" to interpret the aims of the war to the broad mass of Americans. In the language of the League, its object was to "disseminate patriotic literature" to a distant and far-flung audience whose only authentic knowledge of Union views was through the medium of the pamphlet and the newspapers. Without hesitation, the Board authorized Gerhard to bring together a group of members to form a Board of Publication, "Provided the fund for that purpose be raised entirely by voluntary subscriptions." This last qualification was dictated by the League's need to conserve its funds for other uses.[13]

In the wartime literature published by the League, the upsurge of American nationalism is apparent. It bolstered Union regiments and propagandized the activity on the homefront. It was an outpouring of pamphlets that occasionally grew to book length, and handbills and broadsides with messages printed in bold letters, and posters as huge and as colorful as those posted on nineteenth century circus billboards. Never before had Americans witnessed such a flood of printed political material sweeping across the nation.

Both the content of the material and the format of presentation varied. Pamphlets with blue, green and pink wrappers contained some of the most brilliant writing of the time. Pamphlets with bold caption

titles designed to catch the eye, like those written by the publisher
and historian Henry Charles Lea, were printed to meet a specific
crisis. They drew upon the history of the American Revolution and the
example of the experiences of the English in successfully conducting a
long war; they were satirical and disdainful in parts, but they were
also mellow, thoughtful, and instructive. They praised the heroism of
the Men in Blue and sought to win the interest of the Men in Gray.
They invoked the Old Testament and the New Testament as divine
proof of the righteousness of the Union cause, and used biblical argument to castigate the evils of slavery and condemn the sinfulness of the
slaveholder. The pamphlets were turned into political weapons aimed
at their opponents, extolling the president of the United States and
condemning the president of the Confederacy. They were both calm
and argumentative as they explored every idea that favored the
Union and discountenanced the South. They lashed out at and refuted
published and spoken statements of the Copperheads.[14]

The network of distribution of the League literature stretched
from the banks of the Aroostook River in Maine to the shores of
San Francisco Bay, and from Northern Minnesota to the cities of
Tennessee held by federal arms. The massive barrage of pamphlets
was a major undertaking that far exceeded the output of all other
independent proUnion publication societies. But the restless Board
of Publication was not content with convincing the Northern public.
It sought to penetrate the lines of the enemy. Stealthily, in the disguise
of an almanac, documents were introduced into the Confederate regiments of Georgia and Alabama with the intent of luring their soldiers
to desert to the Union camp.[15]

Pennsylvania's large immigrant German and Irish population also
required special attention. German League pamphlets inundated southeastern Pennsylvania and their reception was so successful that distribution was extended to the heavy German settlements in Western
Maryland, Ohio, Indiana, and Wisconsin. It was turned into an ethnic
appeal that exceeded previous attempts to win German support in
Pennsylvania where the German American press was born.[16] The
Irish immigrant called for a separate approach. The Democrats had
won them to their side by luring them into the belief that free Negro
labor would compete for the menial jobs that so many Irish held,
particularly after emancipation. To counteract this propaganda, the
antislavery speeches of outstanding Irish leaders from abroad were
sent throughout the land. The magic name of Daniel O'Connell was
invoked to counteract Irish hostility, by reprinting his early addresses
that mingled the cause of Catholic emancipation with the emancipation of the American slave.[17]

LINDLEY SMYTH

EAGLE IN FLIGHT SYMBOL OF THE BOARD OF PUBLICATION

The activity of the Board of Publication was not limited to editing, publishing, and distributing pamphlets. ProUnion newspapers were also an important weapon in the League arsenal. They were supported financially by the League, encouraged to reprint the full text of pamphlet material and in places where newspapers did not exist, they were begun at the expense of the League Board.[18]

The men who undertook this gigantic task, even though they may have lacked the skill of professional propagandists, were so competent in related fields that the machinery of fundraising, publishing, and distribution was soon operating efficiently. Philadelphia's proUnion publishers, together with men of letters, economists, and historians, were soon attracted to the ranks of the Board of Publication.

There were 27 members of the Board presided over by Gerhard, and divided into three units of nine men. Colwell chaired the Publications Committee, in actuality an editorial board; and Ashhurst, placed in charge of distribution, was responsible for overseeing the operations of printing, binding, and sorting, and seeing that publications reached their ultimate destination. Lindley Smyth was responsible for providing the subcommittees with funds. He was an original member of the first Republican Club of Philadelphia and a prominent sugar refiner who, like Claghorn, suspended much of his business activity at this time to devote his energies to The Union League. Each of the 27 members of the Board contributed $250.00 to launch the basic publications fund. Others contributed as liberally. In the first ten months of the Board's work, $35,000 was raised, almost entirely as a result of the energetic solicitations of Lindley Smyth.[19] The generous contributions made by the members of the Board of Publication reveal only their high financial position; their leadership contributions far transcended in importance their monetary support of the League. Moreover, they had the ability to attract literary talent, which, if not as well known as the New England pamphleteers, was politically more sophisticated. Within the corporate context of the League, the Board of Publication pursued its own objectives to "enlighten the public mind."[20]

By the end of February 1863 the work of the Board was so well advanced that its first pamphlet was ready for distribution. Before the first week of March was over, six other pamphlets were considered and approved for immediate publication. Diversity in the selection of material was quickly apparent. Thomas Webster,[21] a fervent champion of Negro rights who led the organization of the first federally sponsored black troops, submitted for consideration a reprint of William Whiting's _War Powers of the President,_ a major defense of Lincoln's stand on _habeas corpus._[22] Matthew H. Messchert presented a summary review of President Washington's and President

Jackson's attitude toward Negro soldiers under their commands,[23] and George M. Conarroe urged a reprint of Charles J. Stillé's *How A Free People Conduct A Long War*, a pamphlet that first appeared in the late fall of 1862. Its encouraging words had immediately attracted national attention. Its comparison of the American Civil War to England's struggle with France gave it a perspective not present in much of the hastily written literature of the war. Its intellectual approach found favor with Stillé's fellow historians, but more important than this, was its warm reception by the men in service who came to realize that sacrifice was a necessity of war and a component force toward achieving victory. Lincoln hailed it as "the best production upon the subject which, it treats," and the United States Sanitary Commission saw that it received the distribution it warranted. Three editions were printed by the League.[24] A series of brief speeches intended to appeal to midwesterners was warmly approved by the Board which issued them under one title, *The Loyalists' Ammunition*. The fourth pamphlet that came to the attention of the Board, also concerned with the Midwest, carried the lengthy title of *Letters from General Rosecrans! To the Democracy of Indiana. Action of the Ohio Regiments at Murfreesboro, Regarding the Copperheads.* It exposed the Knights of the Golden Circle and sister societies that supported the Copperhead movement, and it proudly carried the imprint of The Union League. But it was soon discovered that the reference to the Copperheads in the title hampered its distribution. At the suggestion of Colwell, the term Copperheads was deleted in future printings of the pamphlet. Furthermore, the Board resolved to discontinue the use of the League imprint to avoid possible confiscation of its publications. As a result, many of the League's pamphlets remain unidentified. Corporate literature, however, such as annual reports or resolutions on specific issues, did carry the name of The Union League.[25]

From the beginning of April to the end of October, 1863, when many League policies were determined, the Board of Publication was responsible for issuing 60 pamphlets and numerous handbills designed in bold type that immediately caught the eye. To give the publications a patriotic luster, a woodcut of Columbia, shield in hand and with a spray of stars, appeared on some of the title pages. Their content was frequently related to steps taken by the League to support presidential measures. Among their actions at this time was a vigorous opposition to those who raised a hue and cry over the possible effects of the Emancipation Proclamation. Two sermons from the Presbyterian pulpit spoke explicitly on the issue. One by Reverend Charles S. Porter, a thoughtful and well-reasoned sermon that did not indulge in theological complexities, defended federal policy; the other, by

Reverend William B. Steward, castigated the authors of the American Constitution for their failure to draw upon Christian teaching which, if it had been applied, would have abolished slavery in 1787. This failure, it was observed, was considered the nation's sin. Because of their national appeal, both sermons were published by the League. Four pamphlets with a similar theme gave further evidence of an eagerness of League members to support Emancipation and to counteract hostility to the freedmen.[26]

In the outpouring of pamphlets in the spring of 1863, the most active period of the League's publishing career, the Board approved a second pamphlet by Charles J. Stillé, *Northern Interests and Southern Independence*. It lacked the forceful appeal of his earlier pamphlet, although it argued effectively for an American national homogeneity. The Board would only accept it on the condition that Stillé would delete the lines questioning the practicality of emancipation. Stillé complied, and instead turned to the argument that emancipation would find acceptance as a military measure.[27] In the midst of this discussion, rumors reached Board members of a "disgraceful compromise" with the South by the federal government, which, if substantiated, would force them to discontinue further publication. The rumor was false and a proposed resolution to suspend publication was promptly withdrawn.[28]

Utilizing an old propaganda technique, the Board made available, again in pamphlet form, documents purported to have been sent by Judah P. Benjamin to Lucius Q. C. Lamar, a Mississippi lawyer. At this time Benjamin was the Confederate secretary of state, and in these documents he was alleged to have advocated the reopening of the African slave trade. The pamphlet also contained a number of proUnion statements so carefully woven together that they gave the impression of constituting official Confederate policy.[29] Moving a step further toward artfully using Southern views to further their cause, the Board made available pamphlets with speeches opposing secession that came from the South. They did in fact come from Southerners, but some of the views had been expressed before the war, and others could not be confirmed. Their intent was to show that some Southern leaders had not changed their minds, and, if they contained a grain of truth, this was sufficient. Typical was the *Rebuke of Secession Doctrines by Southern Statesmen* that appeared in two editions with a varying text.[30] Similar publications were circulated among Union troops after crucial battles and attributed to captured Southern generals who admitted to the imminent defeat of the Confederate Army. They boosted Union morale and lowered the spirits of Confederate prisoners.

At the same time, John Pendleton Kennedy, a novelist who ranked in popularity with James Fenimore Cooper, granted permission for the republication of his article *Slavery the Mere Pretext for the Rebellion*. Under the pseudonym of Paul Ambrose, "a Southern man," Kennedy discussed the prewar operations of the Knights of the Golden Circle, secret overtures of the South to France in 1860, and plans to link the Southwest with Mexico with the object of establishing a great Caribbean and Central American empire. He invoked Andrew Jackson's heroic appeal to fight all enemies of "our glorious Union," be they "foreign or domestic traitors."[31]

Propaganda literature that revealed conditions in the South but did not resort to polemics came from the pens of refugees. Southern residents with Northern sympathies fled across the lines and within a short time wrote memoirs and addressed letters that were well suited for publication. Herman Bokum, a German immigrant and long time resident of Tennessee, reached Philadelphia with the aid of a slave, and Frederick A. P. Barnard of the University of Mississippi made his way to New York City. Both wrote accounts of their experiences that were widely circulated. Bokum's narrative was published simultaneously in English and German.[32]

Throughout the crucial summer of 1863, the directors of the League continued to develop policies that required the Board of Publication to move its literature into the national arena. As a private club, the League now chose a course of action that was unprecedented in American history. With the approval of the War Department, it undertook to raise white and black regiments for the army; it also devised a plan to provide for the wounded and ailing discharged veteran and to find employment suitable to his condition. For the families of those who never returned, the League set up a program that provided financial assistance for widows and their orphaned children. To publicize and support each of these humanitarian endeavors, the Board of Publication prepared to make available necessary literature that would appeal both to the common man and to the intellectual.

Once the Board accepted a pamphlet for publication, it recommended the number of copies to be printed, although final determination of the size of the edition was made by the distribution committee. Editions including reprints ranged from a low of 4,000 copies to a high of 100,000; the average edition of a pamphlet consisted of 10,000 copies. As the war continued and demands for literature increased, publication and distribution policies were governed by the issues of the day.[33]

Distribution of League publications was a national undertaking.

Smaller Leagues were an obvious outlet in the cities, but the most reliable center for distribution in sparsely settled areas, especially in the Midwest and Far West, was the local post office, which was usually sympathetic to League endeavors. Not only did it provide greater opportunity to reach a mass of people with whom the League had no direct contact, but there was less danger of confiscation of League literature. Postmasters were federal servants, and many of them were strong Union men who had migrated from New England to the western part of the country prior to the war.[34] This distribution program was accomplished quietly with the approval of Postmaster General Montgomery Blair, who came to Philadelphia to dedicate a post office and pay a special visit to the League when it celebrated George Washington's birthday for the first time in 1863.[35]

Two important groups of men who received the League literature were the intellectuals of New York and Boston. A system of exchange was established with the clubs of these cities which had launched similar publication programs. They were to copy, reprint, and circulate the Philadelphia pamphlets, and from time to time the Philadelphia League drew upon the literature of its fellow societies. It was a task that Ashhurst and his colleagues handled efficiently.

Men in the army had to be reached as well. The Union soldier, as some observers have shown, was no better informed on the aims and conduct of the war than his relatives back home. He needed more than a musket and rations of hardtack, and more than the religious-tract literature that flooded the camps in an effort to save his soul; it was essential to supply the soldier with brief documents expressing the Northern position that he could easily read for himself or to his comrades around the campfire. The League approached its military friends to aid in the distribution of its propaganda.

On February 28, 1863, a historic day for the Board of Publication, distribution of literature to the army was begun. The League committee and its twelve clerks packaged and dispatched 4,700 copies of the *Letters of General Rosecrans!* The method of distribution and the points of destination indicate the geographic range of the committee's program. The Philadelphia office of the United States Sanitary Commission, which actively involved many League members, received 2,000 copies and the New York office, 500; 650 copies went to the Union Volunteer Refreshment Saloon in Philadelphia, and 150 to its sister society, the Cooper Shop, to be handed out to soldiers passing through the city. It was no problem for Ashhurst to forward 500 copies to his brother and fellow League member Adjutant General Richard L. Ashhurst, 150th Regiment Pennsylvania Volunteers, at Falmouth, Virginia. These were for distribution among the I Army,

DATE	NAME OF DOCUMENT	Nº	TO WHOM SENT.
March			
" 16	About the War	250	New. Eng. Aid Society
" "	Rosecrans Letter	250	" " " "
" "	Gen. Washington	400	" " " "
" "	Rosecrans Letter	200	National Union Club. Phila.
" "	Gen. Washington	500	Chs. Eliot Norton } care of
" "	" "	500	Geo. Livermore } Jas. B. Thayer Boston
" "	" "	34	Committee Room
" "	" "	50	Robert Peysert Bethlehem.
" "	" "	50	H. M. Richards Pottstown.
" "	Rosecrans Letter	50	" " " "
" "	" "	50	Robert Peysert Bethlehem
" "	About the War	20	" " "
" "	" " "	20	H. M. Richards Pottstown
" 17	Rosecrans Letter	75	Chicago
" "	Gen. Washington	100	Miss Dorothea L. Dix Washington City
" "	Rosecrans Letter	100	" " " "
" "	About the War	100	" " " "
" "	Handbills of Rep?	150	
" 17	Rosecrans Letter	200	Dr. S. Ashhurst U.S.A. Nashville Tenn.
" "	Gen. Washington	1000	Capt. E. W. Cooper Beaufort, S.C.
" "	About the War	100	Dr. S. Ashhurst W. S. A. Nashville Tenn
" "	Gen. Washington	200	" " " "
" "	" "	50	Mr. Edward Rogers 1713 Locust St.
" "	Rosecrans Letter	50	" " " " "
" "	About the War.	50	" " " " "

DISTRIBUTION RECORDS KEPT BY THE PUBLICATION COMMITTEE

to which a constant flow of literature was directed. Nor was it a problem to dispatch large quantities to another relative, Dr. Samuel Ashhurst, an original signer of the League Articles of Association, stationed with the Army at Nashville, Tennessee. At Murfreesboro, Tennessee, Major General George H. Thomas of the Army of the Cumberland and his associates of the XIV, XX, and XXI Corps each received appropriate bundles of pamphlets. The 5th and 12th Pennsylvania Cavalry, and many of the volunteer regiments, some of whose members joined the League and then went out with their companies, were other recipients of the Philadelphia pamphlets. At sea or at the Union ports on the Atlantic, from Fort Preble overlooking the harbor at Portland, Maine, to the U.S. gunboat *Somerset*, stationed at Apalachicola, Florida, men of the Navy and Marine Corps also received a supply of pamphlets along with their naval supplies.[36]

Ashhurst linked the work of the distribution committee to the efforts of Boker and Gibbons who were establishing Leagues throughout the country, and found the new clubs eager to receive Union documents. Beginning at home, pamphlets were placed in local ward Leagues and in the foreign-language Union Clubs of Philadelphia, each of which was guided by a member of the parent League. Henry Charles Lea organized a Union League branch in West Philadelphia; Nathaniel B. Brown,[37] a prominent attorney, opened one in the 24th ward, and Leonard Myers, a major in the 9th Pennsylvania Militia during the emergency service late in 1862, was an outstanding participant in the 13th ward League.[38] Of even greater importance was the work of Edward M. Davis in founding a League in Cheltenham Township, across the city line in the area where Camp William Penn was soon to open for the training of Negro troops.[39] At this League the Mott and McKim families concentrated much of their work. Each of the local Leagues became a source for the dissemination of Union League literature.

Neighboring New Jersey was inundated with League materials from its most northern point to its southern coastline. Camden, Burlington, Haddonfield, Mount Holly and Pemberton, although small and rural in the 1860's, were significant as points of distribution for other parts of the state.[40] Southeastern Pennsylvania, with its proximity to the seat of war and with its major military and medical installations, welcomed the heavy concentration of handbills, newspapers, and pamphlets. In the circle embracing Philadelphia from York to Easton, heavily populated by recent German immigrants and the older Pennsylvania Dutch, special measures were taken to explain the issues of the war not only through the local postmasters who distributed over 50,000 pamphlets in three months, but through the editors of the German press in Reading, Allentown, and Easton. More than 20 Pennsylvania Union Leagues, other than those in Western Pennsylvania or in the immediate Philadelphia area, are recorded in the Board's distribution records.[41] Using these Leagues for distribution points, 8 pamphlets written in German were addressed and circulated to the people of this area. Popular among the German public was Messchert's tract about Washington and Jackson on the bravery of Negro troops, and George Boker's poem "The Black Regiment," a tribute to the Second Louisiana that suffered over 1,000 casualties. They were translated by Carl Theodore Eben, who later established a reputation for translating the poems of Poe and Lowell into German. When news of the German editions reached midwestern states, requests for this material streamed into the League house. Even though these pamphlets did not carry the name of the League, their source was soon discovered.

In other states, numerous agencies were established by the League in Kentucky, Ohio, Indiana, Illinois, and Wisconsin to counteract Copperhead propaganda. As news of the effectiveness of the counter-propaganda spread westward, requests for literature and advice became a regular occurrence. From San Francisco came a report that the local League had dropped its secrecy and was carrying on its work publicly, and from Chicago came similar news.[42] Pamphlets were pressed into the hands of residents in the border states and welcomed in the territories. In the sensitive area of Louisville, Kentucky, the League was represented by Lewis N. Dembitz, a Jewish scholar and accomplished lawyer. Recognized for his antislavery writing and staunch Republicanism, he was chosen by the League to distribute its publications in both English and German. Dembitz's nephew, Louis D. Brandeis, a future Associate Justice of the United States Supreme Court, recalled his boyhood years in this atmosphere, with patriotic and proUnion literature constantly at hand.[43]

Southern Illinois, rigid in its proslavery attitude, was far more dangerous for proUnion adherents than Louisville, and here Owen Lovejoy performed a similar task for the Philadelphia League. In Alton, Cairo, and in Princeton, Illinois, where he was the minister of the Congregational Church, he showed unflinching determination in distributing Union literature. His brother Elijah, a spirited abolitionist, was killed for publishing antislavery literature in Alton in 1837. On one occasion, Owen Lovejoy undertook the distribution of 1,638 copies of 20 different titles in each of these towns.[44]

Joining the band of devoted League agents in the nation's capital was that remarkable woman, Dorothea Lynde Dix, Superintendent of Women Nurses and a pioneer in the field of mental health. Through

WASHINGTON AND JACKSON

ON

NEGRO SOLDIERS.

GEN. BANKS

ON THE

BRAVERY OF NEGRO TROOPS.

POEM—THE SECOND LOUISIANA,

BY

1863

GEORGE H. BOKER.

PHILADELPHIA:

PRINTED FOR GRATUITOUS DISTRIBUTION.

A Major Pamphlet Used to Recruit Black Troops

her corps of nurses in Washington, countless numbers of soldiers were reached and through them, thousands of others. Her activity was not an isolated example of the work women were doing in behalf of the League, but in this activity she ranked highly with Lucretia Mott, who lived on the outskirts of Philadelphia.[45]

On a broader scale, the distribution committee was successful in working with the governors of several states. No sooner did Governor Oliver Perry Morton of Indiana learn of Robert Dale Owen's *The Future of the North-West, In Connection with the Scheme of Reconstruction without New England,* than he requested a substantial quantity of the pamphlet. Widespread concern over a possible peace compromise with Northern Democrats that would separate New England from the Midwest had been rumored, and Owen's pamphlet was intended to dispel any such fears. Eight thousand copies of the Owen pamphlet were sent to Governor Morton for distribution in Indiana and Southern Illinois. Morton was so impressed by the League's program that he came with members of his family to speak at the new League house in Philadelphia, at which time he requested additional thousands of copies of numerous titles.[46] A package of miscellaneous pamphlets was sent to Governor William Cannon of Delaware, a Democrat who became an active Republican after the bombardment of Fort Sumter. Cannon also addressed the League, and the Board published one of his speeches which was distributed in Delaware.

Distribution records which were kept from the first day[47] pamphlets were sent out show the zeal of the Board in reaching army hospitals and their chaplains, military installations and outposts, antislavery and abolitionist societies (whose work was not suspended after the Emancipation Proclamation) and, above all, thousands and thousands of Americans in their homes, in their houses of worship, in the marketplace, and on their jobs.

The clergy, still grappling with interpreting the biblical view of slavery, was deluged with the League's choice of sermons, antislavery publications, and such literature as the Board thought would be useful. On one day, the Episcopal Diocese, meeting in Philadelphia, received 1,375 copies of different titles; on another day the Presbyterian clergy throughout the state were given twice the amount of similar literature. Only the Methodists of the area, who were strongly committed to the measures taken by the League, sought out the patriotic literature on their own initiative.[48]

By mid-June, 1863, the Board reached a peak in its program with the publication of the Lincoln-Corning correspondence. Erastus Corning, a Democratic member of Congress from New York, had openly rebuked President Lincoln because of the arrest of the Ohio Copperhead, Congressman Clement L. Vallandigham, in an effort to curtail his effective opposition to the war. Lincoln's persuasive response attracted national attention. It came at a time when the desertion rate in the Union army was high, some of it having been attributed to the widespread antiwar declarations. In his rejoinder, Lincoln asked, "Must I shoot a simple-minded soldier boy who deserts, while I must not touch a hair on a wily agitator who induces him to desert?" The publication committee, profoundly stirred by this question, empowered Ashhurst to print as large an edition of the President's reply as he thought necessary, provided it did not exceed 100,000 copies.[49]

Antiwar arguments similar to those advocated by Corning were also being published in Philadelphia by a new Democratic daily, *The Age*. It attacked the suspension of the writ of *habeas corpus*, the conscription act, and the legal tender act, but its main target was the League, which endorsed each of these measures. Democratic leaders complained bitterly that the constitutional rights of the nation were abridged by these acts, and expressed their hostility toward the League in the columns of *The Age*, describing its members as "wolves in sheeps clothing," traitors bent on destroying the Constitution. In spite of its relentless opposition to the government, *The Age* was not threatened in any way throughout the war by the people whom it constantly attacked.[50]

Many of the same men who were busy editing, publishing, and distributing pamphlets were also involved in a program highly abused by *The Age*, the organization and outfitting of white and black regiments. The members of the Board of Publication who also served on the League Military Committee were men who had given up their prewar activities in order to devote themselves completely to the goals of the League. Boker no longer thought of writing another play; Lea gave little time to his book publishing business and less to his historical researches; James L. Claghorn no longer enjoyed perusing art galleries, and Colwell, who had retired early, turned his energies to editing wartime literature. Days and nights merged; vacations were forgotten. Toward the middle of June, 1863, when word reached Philadelphia that General Lee was heading North, there was no time for relaxation. Only in the League House, where provisions for dinner were available, were a few moments of leisure snatched from the tensions of war.

On June 15, President Lincoln called for 100,000 men for six months of service. Governor Curtin issued a similar call, and at a public rally Mayor Alexander Henry of Philadelphia implored 50,000 Philadelphians to augment forces for the defense of the city and state immediately. Governor Curtin hastily appealed to the League, saying "the enemy are over our border in large force destroying property and advancing in this direction via Chambersburg and Gettysburg—arouse our people."[51] Although the population was alarmed by this news, its spirit was raised by the sight of a well-trained regiment of the Grey Reserves led by League member Colonel William B. Thomas, on its way to Harrisburg. At this crucial hour, however, voluntary enlistments were declining. The war industries competed for labor and offered wages superior to a soldier's meager pay. Further the bounty system of the army was unattractive and full of drawbacks.

With a seasoned army of approximately 75,000 Confederate troops moving closer to the Pennsylvania cities, the League's action was prompt and decisive. League members with an average age of 47, whose sons and brothers had already gone to war, drilled with young, raw recruits. Their hectic activity is succinctly described in the diary of Ferdinand J. Dreer, who, at the age of sixty, joined in the daily drills: "met Committee and discussed about postponing the 4th of July celebration by a parade. June 19 Friday met Committee at Sansom Street Hall about recruiting colored soldiers. Monday 22nd went to drill and the Committee at the League at 12 o'clock. Saturday the 27, Great excitement on account of the Rebel invasion into Pennsylvania, in the League House until 3:30 a.m. Monday June 29, all stores and work shops closed, greater portion of the male population that are of age are drilling."[52]

On June 26, during the hours of "great excitement," the League resolved to raise a brigade under its own auspices. A Military Committee was formed. Its purpose was to raise funds for its equipment and a bounty offering from $35 to $300 a recruit, the highest paid in the city. Competition from merchants, associations, and privately organized regiments, some of whom offered only $15, was eliminated. Joseph Reese Fry, one of the early Republicans, chaired the new committee among whose members were Claghorn, Binney, Judge Hare, and McMichael. They were joined by J. Edgar Thomson, president of the Pennsylvania Railroad,[53] and General George H. Crossman of the Frankford Arsenal.[54] Later, Henry Charles Lea who served on the Federal Bounty Commission and was familar with its failure to enlist men in large numbers, divided his energies between the Military committee and the Board of Publication.[55]

On the morning of July 1, men of the League went through their drilling exercises and then paraded along Chestnut Street in a show of strength that they hoped would attract recruits. Lea and a number of others held an emergency conference with Governor Curtin, who

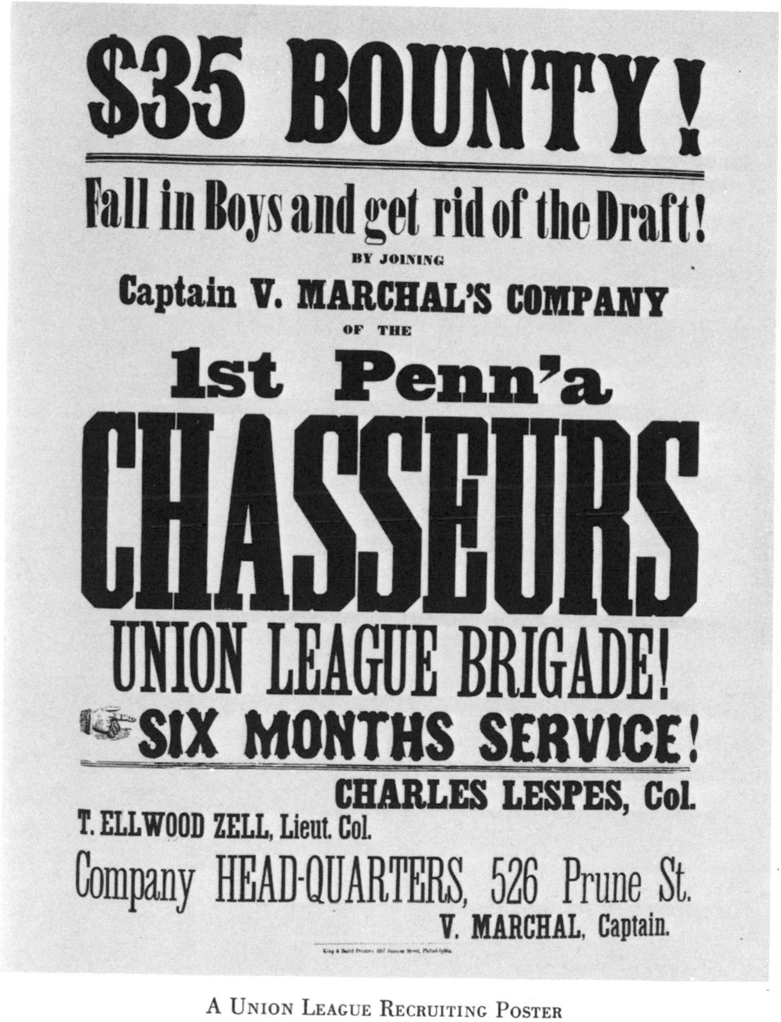

A Union League Recruiting Poster

had come to Philadelphia. He made one of the most stirring public appeals of the war on that day, the busiest day in the brief history of the League. For the second time in two months, Frederick Douglass, the self-educated former slave and abolitionist-orator, addressed League members, this time on the serious issue of training Negroes for the United States Army. On this occasion he came as the guest of Benjamin H. Brewster. Before the war Brewster had been a pro-slavery spokesman, but after its outbreak he became such a vigorous advocate of full equality for Negroes that Lea wrote about his change in attitude in a tone of disbelief. Nothing was more vexing to the proslavery men than Douglass' presence at the League for a purpose they considered despicable.[56] Nor were they any more pleased with the address of Vice-president Hannibal Hamlin when he declared, from the steps of the League, that Union forces were in sight of a long awaited, major victory. On the evening of the same day Senator Zachariah Chandler, the radical Republican from Michigan, also delivered a spirited address.

The speakers achieved their aim of inspiring recruits. Under the imminent threat of General Lee's army, the response to the League's recruiting effort was so great that a first regiment was quickly filled.[57] The League dispensed with its plans for an Independence Day celebration, preferring to use the funds intended for this event toward the organization of the second of its ten regiments. In a circular released jointly by the Military Committee and the Board of Publication, Fry wrote dramatically, "While so many thousands of our brothers are giving the last drop of their blood for the cause, who would hesitate to give any needful part of his fortune?"[58] The response to his appeal was overwhelming; $108,000 was raised by the Military Committee. While the Committee was seeking men for the ranks of a second regiment, Lee had invaded Pennsylvania and one of the great battles of the Civil War was at the height of its fury at Gettysburg.

The menace of a deeper invasion by Confederate forces brought home to Philadelphians the absolute necessity of preparation. On July 5, in the early hours of the morning, news reached prominent League members that General George G. Meade had successfully thrown back the Southern offensive. A special celebration was held the same day at Independence Square. Two days later, the First Union League Regiment, the 45th Pennsylvania, a 90-day militia company under the command of Colonel William D. Whipple, was presented with colors and left for Camp Curtin near Harrisburg. The departing regiment saw an endless series of trains carrying maimed and wounded soldiers eastward to the hospitals of Philadelphia. Long lines of Confederate prisoners marched into the city, along with their wounded, to be imprisoned and hospitalized at Fort Delaware. Over 5,000 Union casualties reached the city, taking up every available hospital bed. Although the major crisis was over and the security of the state established, the Second Union League Regiment, the 52nd Pennsylvania, also received its colors and proceeded to Harrisburg under Colonel William M. Gary's command.[59]

The Board of Publication had already approved one pamphlet which was significant in the military history of Pennsylvania Negroes. It extolled their bravery under fire and their historical role in American wars. In January, 1863, The War Department empowered Governor John Andrew of Massachusetts to raise a regiment of Negro soldiers. Neither Boston's Negroes nor those in the surrounding area were sufficient to fill a regiment and recruits were drawn from other states. At first the sophisticated free Negro was reluctant to join the army, and published arguments against enlistment. But as the war came to involve emancipation, and liberated slaves in South Carolina joined Union combat forces, Negro reaction in the North shifted more favorably to recruitment. As a result, a large contingent of Pennsylvania Negroes, believed to number more than 1,500, enlisted in the 54th and 55th Massachusetts Regiments. Company "B" of the 54th came entirely from Philadelphia.[60] While the New England recruiting was in progress, the League issued another pamphlet containing an address by William D. Kelley advocating the arming of Negroes. Messchert's earlier pamphlet was reprinted with a statement from Major General N. P. Banks, describing the valor of those Negro soldiers under his command at Port Hudson, Louisiana. "They require only good officers, commands of limited numbers and careful discipline, to make them excellent soldiers." Even before the League circulated Banks' statement, George H. Boker had written his poem glorifying their bravery under fire. Douglass' League-sponsored addresses also gave credence to the seriousness of the movement.[61]

For a long time the antislavery element of the League had advocated the organization of Negro regiments, and it became a topic of private discussion and personal correspondence. McKim and Gibbons, recognizing the efficiency of Negro soldiers, found no difficulty in convincing hundreds of League members as well as outsiders of their views. On June 8, 1863, a meeting on the subject of raising black regiments in Philadelphia was held at the League house. Colonel Lafayette Bingham and Major George L. Stearns of Boston who were commissioned by Secretary of War Stanton to launch the recruitment in other states, spoke of their experience in Massachusetts. League member William D. Lewis, whose only son had been killed in combat, chaired the unusual meeting. It was resolved at this time that "no individual, no clique, nor distinct set of politicians be exclusively trusted with this matter. It is the whole people who urge this action, and all classes should be charged with its support."[62]

The 276 men who shortly thereafter formally petitioned the secretary of war for permission to raise Negro regiments included the first Republicans of the city and founders of The Union Club and The Union League. In the spirit of the League's resolution of June 8, many interested Philadelphians threw their weight behind the new undertaking, and assured Stanton that they were willing to contribute the necessary funds not provided by the government. Initially, it was planned to raise three regiments for three years of service, or for the duration of the war. Stanton authorized the request in three days and the machinery was set into motion for the organization of the first black regiments under Federal colors.[63]

Calling itself the Supervisory Committee on Enlistment of Colored Troops—Boker preferred the word black over Negro or colored—this same group worked independently of the League Military Committee, although League men served on both committees. Thirty of the most influential and articulate blacks of Philadelphia, among whom were Octavius V. Catto, Jacob C. White, Jonathan C. Gibbs, and Reverend William J. Alston, arranged for a mass meeting to open recruitment on July 6. Three antislavery champions of diverse backgrounds, Congressman William D. Kelley, Frederick Douglass, and Anna E. Dickinson, who at this time was only 22 years of age, addressed an audience still excited by the news from Gettysburg.[64] Thomas Webster, who became chairman of the Supervisory Committee, was also a member of the Board of Publication, and at his request the proceedings and speeches were published by the Board as one of a series of items that related to the organization of Philadelphia's black troops.[65]

Like the Board of Publication, the Supervisory Committee functioned independently, raising its own funds. William Rotch Wister, the cricketer, and Abraham Barker, a financier whose father had floated government loans in the War of 1812, lost no time in raising over $33,000 that eventually made possible eleven regiments of United States Colored Troops that were recruited throughout Pennsylvania. Barker was particularly influential in securing approval for Negroes of the rights "that had been long denied them." The service of Barker and numerous League associates strengthened the Union Army and elevated Negroes "in their own self-respect and in the esteem of the loyal public; and this service involved more than labor, because, confronting deepseated prejudice, it encountered no little opposition, entailed personal hazard and risked social ostracism." Barker's public "abhorrence of slavery and his deep sympathy for the oppressed" won the admiration of the League.[66]

Many problems had to be faced in training the fresh recruits. Com-

THE RECRUITING OFFICE FOR BLACK TROOPS WAS CLOSE BY TO THE
LEAGUE HOUSE AT 1216 CHESTNUT STREET

missioned Negro officers were few in number and white officers were selected on the basis of their attitude and commitment to the program. One of the circulars issued by the Supervisory Committee defined the kind of officer sought as one who had experience, was not merely seeking higher rank and pay, and would feel equal to training a black regiment. An officer had to see in his recruits the potential of disciplined soldiers fighting in a common cause. To assure the success of this work, the Supervisory Committee opened the Free Military School for Applicants for Commands of Colored Troops. Its headquarters was on Chestnut Street close to the League. Here candidates for the officers' school were interviewed by Colonel John H. Taggart, formerly of the 12th Regiment Pennsylvania Reserves. The headquarters also served as a recruiting station, with another set up in the Negro quarter of South Philadelphia.[67]

There was strong opposition in Philadelphia to the enrollment of Negro troops. *The Age,* the Democratic newspaper, was especially outspoken, and League members were denounced for taking a dangerous step by training blacks in the use of arms.[68] Gradually, the mood changed. Fashionable Chestnut Street, with its many affluent families, became accustomed to the group of black soldiers that stood guard at the offices of the Supervisory Committee beneath recruiting posters which were dramatic appeals to the courage and bravery of Negroes. A new pictorial literature appeared, intended to transform the image of the Negro into a soldier faithful to his country. Brilliant lithographs and sheet music picturing Negro soldiers in colorful uniform gave dignity to the black community, which still struggled under severe prejudice.[69]

It is generally believed that it was this prejudice that led to the choice of the training ground at the northern edge of the city. This is unsubstantiated. The first training camp considered was Fort Mifflin, a Revolutionary War site in an inaccessible section. After the Battle of Gettysburg, however, the Fort was turned into a military prison. Meanwhile, Edward M. Davis, a member of the Supervisory Committee, and Lucretia Mott, part owners of Chelten Hills in Montgomery County, offered their land for the training camp. The land not quite ten miles from central Philadelphia, was served by the North Pennsylvania Railroad, and horse-drawn carriages traveled the Old York Road. Therefore it could be easily reached. The site was named Camp William Penn, after the founder of the colony, and it became the "largest Camp existing for the organization of Colored Troops." Under the keen eye of Lucretia Mott and the Cheltenham Union League, the Camp could only thrive.[70]

To General Louis Wagner, who had been absent from the city with

CAMP WILLIAM PENN

the 88th Regiment Pennsylvania Infantry, fell the task of training the
new regiments. He had returned to Philadelphia because of wounds
received in battle, and then recovered sufficiently to take command
of Camp William Penn, joining the League after it was organized.[71]
The raw recruits were organized into fighting units; officers were
reviewed for their attitudes toward blacks, and their efficiency in
military tactics. Both McClellan's prewar military manual and Casey's
Infantry Tactics were used. Adding a curious touch was an edition of
the tactics with the title page altered to read *for the use of Colored
Troops of the United States.*[72]

In less than three months, Wagner was fully prepared to move
three regiments of black troops from the camp to the battlefield. On
August 13, 1863, Colonel Tilghman's regiment, 3d United States
Colored Troops, embarked for Charleston Harbor; on August 31, a
public review of the troops was held at Camp William Penn. Then
Wagner decided to move the 6th and 8th Regiments through the
city. At first Mayor Henry warned against bringing Negro soldiers
into Philadelphia. Memories of difficulties in Boston when black

GENERAL LOUIS WAGNER   GENERAL GEORGE CADWALADER

troops had to be transported by sea, and fears of antiNegro riots similar to those that took place in New York City, were present in the minds of many. Some thought otherwise. The "admirable discipline shown by the men elicited the approval of the friends of the movement and exhorted praise, even though unwillingly, from its opponents." Nevertheless, anxiety spread through the city when troop movements were begun from Camp William Penn to the Baltimore and Ohio Depot in South Philadelphia.[73]

On October 3, 1863, the first black regiments marched through the city to entrain for the battlefield. The first League historian, George Parsons Lathrop, recalling the historic moment, wrote, "The members of the (Supervisory) Committee and the commander of the troops, however, were at once cautious and confident. They did not believe in the supposed danger; but the officers carried loaded revolvers, to be used in an emergency. The soldiers, on the contrary, were not trusted with any ammunition; those of the Sixth had merely their muskets, and the companies of the Eighth marched entirely without arms. . . . No police escort was present but Colonel Wagner rode at the head of the column, and his stern determined expression convinced those who . . . meditated disturbance that they would be worsted in any attack. The troops followed their route through a number of principal streets, stopped at the Union Volunteer

Refreshment Saloon, and passed in review before General George Cadwalader, who took his station on the steps of the Union League House. Everywhere, the streets were thronged with crowds, anxious, impressed, secretly hostile or openly exultant; but the expected collision did not occur."[74]

Camp William Penn became a site of wonder and disbelief, and curious Philadelphians, impressed by what had taken place, rode out to watch black men drilling and shooting on target. Recruitment had proceeded rapidly. Within ten months after the enlistment drive was begun, ten full regiments were equipped and ready for battle. The first of these, the Third Regiment Infantry, United States Colored Troops, fought at Fort Wagner guarding the entrance to Charleston Harbor when that bastion was forced to surrender; the Sixth Regiment, which had paraded through the city, joined the army at Fortress Monroe and saw more action than any other colored unit from Pennsylvania. It was here that Captain Robert B. Beath, later the first historian of the Grand Army of the Republic, commonly called the GAR, and a prominent League member, lost a leg.[75] The balance of the Eighth Regiment received marching orders on January 12, 1864. It was in excellent condition, and was ordered to leave sooner than expected because recruitment was so successful that the Camp had become overcrowded. The 11 regiments mustered at Camp William Penn were part of the United States Army, and were not credited to the city and state from which they were recruited. The Union League, which made possible their organization, discontinued its work in this area only after the surrender of the Confederacy.

In the midst of this great military undertaking, the League extended its philanthropic work from the sick, wounded, and disabled soldier to the honorably discharged men returning to civilian life and in need of employment. Help for the veteran, whatever it might be, was not looked upon as charity, but as a duty.

In a nationally distributed letter, George Boker outlined the problems of war and of a rapidly changing economy caused in part by the conversion of some industries to military uses and the rise of new industries.

His letter was addressed to state and national Leagues, imploring them to do whatever was possible for the returning soldier and sailor whose factories and workshops had become idle in their absence. The war that turned the artisan into a soldier had also dispossessed the veteran. "In vain he looks around for his old haunts and his old employments; or finding these, he beholds with helpless sorrow his shattered arm, or his amputated leg, or the terrible wound yet aching in his body . . . Shall these men, who have defended our lives, our fortunes, and our national honor return to starve? or to depend on the precarious offerings of individual charity?"[76]

Boker's appeal, judging by the philanthropic records of the League, struck its mark. Members who were engaged in business and industry and they were numerous, responded with all the facilities at their command. In 1863, during the first summer of its work, the Employment Committee provided 320 jobs to veterans in Philadelphia; during the course of the war, thousands of others were found. And like all of the League's wartime committees, this new one functioned independently, even though it was responsible to the corporate body of the League.

The Soldiers' Claim and Pension Agency, housed in the Philadelphia building of the Sanitary Commission, was also in the hands of League members. They engaged counsel to handle legal problems between veterans and the government, and since they did not charge for this service, the door was shut on unconscionable collectors who bilked their clients. In this undertaking the League anticipated the work of the Grand Army of the Republic, the postwar society of Union soldiers, one of whose tasks was to hasten pensions and claim payments.[77]

Another important aspect of the League's humanitarian work was assisting war widows and protecting them from unscrupulous individuals. Proper employment was found for these women whenever necessary, and the League insisted upon fair employment practices for all. In November, 1863, for example, a black widow whose husband had been killed in battle sought employment at the Army Clothing and Equipage Office of the Schuylkill Arsenal, a major center for the employment of widows and orphans. When she was not offered a job, she appealed to the League for help. Boker immediately questioned George H. Crossman, assistant quarter master general of the Arsenal, and was assured that indigent widows and orphans, regardless of color and nationality, received preference. Other employment was found for the distressed Negro widow. Free blacks and Irish immigrants were those most benefited by the League's efforts toward equality in employment. Long before American law insisted upon equal employment practices, the League urged it as a humanitarian concept. There can be no doubt that in the absence of any formal organized body to handle employment problems, either private or governmental, the League filled a void. Moreover, this aspect of its activity was not isolated, and it continued after the war. Employment assistance was a League policy in time of peace and during each military crisis that occurred in the first century of League history.[78]

These costly, time-consuming undertakings did not distract the League from carefully observing the two political party conventions that nominated candidates for the gubernatorial election of 1863. The League believed that if a compromising Peace Democrat was elected to the state's highest office, and yielded to Southern interests, its programs would be shattered. So convinced were its directors of this likelihood, that they determined to defeat any candidate not identified with the Lincoln administration and the aims of the Union.[79]

The League's goal, later formulated in an official document, was the total and complete destruction of the Confederate military machine and the restoration of the Union. Eager to implement this goal, incoming members of the League were attracted to all its committees, but particularly to the Board of Publication, its most vocal department. George McDowell Stroud, the legal historian of slavery and a judge of the Common Pleas Court, and Henry Charles Lea, whose energies up to the summer of 1863 were poured into raising troops and urging a revision of the bounty system, both added brilliant strokes to the new pamphleteering campaign. Stroud's work was far removed from the sober tone of objectivity he assumed while on the bench, and Lea's former interest as a medievalist and historian of the Inquisition remained in a state of suspension. Their efforts were responsible for founding and initially supporting the *Army and Navy Journal*, the unofficial spokesman for the American military forces, and it was distributed by the thousands to the men at the front.[80]

William Elder, an economist, and Lorin Blodget, a statistician, also shared their knowledge and talent with the publication committee.[81] Ellis Yarnall, the American correspondent of the London *Guardian* and a friend of the Wordsworths and Coleridges, urged Lord Coleridge to establish a Union League in London to encourage English sympathy for the Union. He implored the Board of Publication to give more attention to literature that concerned itself with European attitudes to the United States. As a result, three pamphlets on the subject of English neutrality were prepared and distributed in England and France.[82]

Charles Dexter Cleveland, recognized as a man of polite letters and an anthologist, was not an early member of the League but became involved in the publications work that called for skilled writers.[83] Matthew H. Messchert continued to advocate the publication of pamphlets on the Negro, and Charles Izard Maceuen accepted the responsibility of keeping the publication records. A restless man, Maceuen's position with the committee was short-lived. He preferred the field of battle, and died fighting at Quaker Road in the final confrontation at Petersburg, Virginia.[84] In the late spring of 1863, during Maceuen's terms, the Democrats in convention nominated George Washington Woodward of the State Supreme Court as their candidate for governor. Andrew G. Curtin, the incumbent Republican, was chosen again by his party, which was still a loose alignment of diverse groups. Pennsylvania's well-organized Democrats soon revealed considerable strength and a platform consistent with their views of the previous three years. They assailed the suspension of *habeas corpus*, declared that a free press was a guiding beacon for a free government, and denied sympathy with the states in secession. But the party was ambivalent on the terms of securing peace. It has been estimated that 90 per cent of the delegates at the Democratic Convention believed that a compromise with the South was necessary to bring the war to an end. A good number of the delegates were convinced that Congress had extended the war through the influences of the abolitionists, and Democrats as a whole persisted in their claims that Republicans were more concerned with furthering abolitionist aims than with peace or the restoration of the Union. Confident in their platform, and anticipating a victory in the fall election, the Democrats opened their campaign.[85]

The factionalism that divided Pennsylvania Republicans before their convention did not diminish until their candidate was chosen. Simon Cameron's men were not prepared to set aside their differences, and even distrust of Governor Curtin. Alexander McClure worked deftly between the two, although his dislike for Cameron was no political secret.[86] The forces supporting Curtin were sensitive to his accomplishments in providing special needs for Pennsylvania soldiers, but they were not pleased with his opposition to the suspension of *habeas corpus* or arbitrary arrest. Politically, Curtin's position on *habeas corpus* held appeal for the Democrats. Despite inner party strife, manipulation behind the scenes, and Curtin's earlier reluctance to be the standard bearer of the Republicans, his nomination came on the first ballot. It was an important step in strengthening Pennsylvania Republicanism and in cementing the state's Union party. Daniel Agnew, a Beaver County judge, was chosen by acclamation as candidate for chief justice of the state, the position held by Woodward. The gubernatorial campaign of 1863 launched the League on a new chapter in its unique history.

During the party conventions the League had been too occupied with the organization of troops and with providing care for the sick and wounded to consider its political role. Furthermore, its Articles of Association precluded a partisan political stand. In confronting the numerous campaign issues, so many of which were shaped by the conduct of the war, the directors recalled that some of its members had supported Breckenridge, Douglas and Bell in 1860; others had voted for Lincoln; that the League was not committed to any party "and acknowledges no political obligation," but intended to uphold the national government and destroy the "wicked rebellion." It disclaimed all interest in promoting "any man or set of men to office simply because they are the candidate of a particular party." But the candidate who best represented the aims of the national government and of the League was Andrew Curtin, the Republican incumbent. Privately, a vote for Curtin was considered an act of patriotism by League members. The League's official resolution on its political position made little reference to the Democrats, their candidates, or supporters, but reiterated the goal of bringing the war to an end by a decisive military victory.[87]

League members had not forgotten the Democrats' rejoicings during the days when Lee's invasion of Pennsylvania also had threatened Philadelphia. Upper-class Democrats with Southern sympathies, particularly William. B. Reed, Charles Ingersoll, and George Wharton, who had seized control of the party, had lost their political status among Union men and among masses of Democrats, for it was they who were prepared to welcome and find a headquarters in Philadelphia for conquering Confederate generals. Politically, their action was a drawback for the Democrats, and socially, hostility increased between these Democrats and League members. As a result, the League offered its resources to the National Union Party which was in fact the Republican Party. This offer was not looked upon as an act of political partisanship, but as a patriotic necessity. The League also linked its efforts with the Union State Central Committee, the working force of the Party, through Wayne MacVeagh, one of the League's politically active members. In spite of this alignment, every effort was made to preserve its character as a patriotic social club. However, the issues of the election and the clamor for political victory brought the League into the vortex of a wartime election. No state election revolved around such important issues, and few elections had had the benefit of such a concentrated force of intellectual participants.[88]

Wayne MacVeagh, state chairman of the Central Committee, gave to the campaign a viewpoint not customarily associated with this gubernatorial election. He looked upon the pre-secessionist attempts at conciliation and concession as nothing more than appeasing the Southern appetite for power. He countered the secessionist argument for free speech for Southern sympathizers in the North by asking why abolitionist literature had been confiscated or suppressed in the South before the war. Why, he queried further, did the South move from the ballot to the bullet and then declare that bullet to be an assassin's weapon aimed at the Constitution? MacVeagh's official address, delivered on behalf of the Republican Party, also voiced the convictions of the League and helped construct the ideology of the campaign. It was included in the corpus of League pamphlets, and the Board of Publication made available all of its material, including plates of those publications appropriate for the campaign.[89] James Claghorn, art collector and League treasurer, gave the campaign the financial muscle vital for Republican success. Independently, he raised $150,000 and helped underwrite the extensive state-wide pamphleteering movement directed at every literate Pennsylvanian.

The previous six months of selecting, editing, and distributing pamphlets during the war had given the Board of Publication the experience that enabled it to present the issues of slavery, emancipation, the Conscription Act, and new views on the conduct of the war. Its methods were singular and effective against the equally strong and sophisticated propaganda that came from the Democrats. The Democrats allegedly argued for the truth, but on premises so misleading that an uninformed reader could mistakenly believe that all Democrats were proUnion, and that the party strove for a military defeat of the South. Moreover, *The Age*, speaking for the Democrats, attacked the League by spreading the canard that "Union Leagues are merely political, partisan, secret organizations of Abolitionists, the leaders of which are not for the Union and never were, unless it is changed to suit their prejudices."[90]

The Philadelphia League refused to answer these charges, feeling that its public activity was too well-known to require defense, but individual members responded. Rather than become embroiled in controversy, the League writers, particularly Morton McMichael, took a different approach and argued perceptively that "short wars are seldom of much permanent value. The lessons they convey are not severe enough to last long, and in a few years their traces are obliterated and the contest is to go over again. . . . Hence we do not think that there is any need of haste about the close of the war. It must burn out the sore places [slavery and the old regime] and not stop until it has done so."[91] This was precisely what the Union Army eventually did.

In the pre-election months, the League published 17 pamphlets in English and German, and 13 broadsides that examined the history of the Democrats from Jackson to Lincoln and cast Woodward in the role of a traitor. The number of newspaper articles for which the

League was responsible, other than editorials in the *North American* and in Forney's Philadelphia *Press,* is undetermined. A striking fact is that most of the pamphlets, broadsides, and newspaper articles are not identified with the organization responsible for their publication.

With all the controversy that the contest provoked, it was an exciting wartime election. But the bitterness between the parties increased when Democrats revived the argument about the justification of slavery on theological premises. In the spring of 1863, Bishop John Henry Hopkins of the Protestant Episcopal Church of Vermont granted permission to six church laymen in Philadelphia to reissue his pamphlet, *Bible View of Slavery,* originally published in 1851 under a different title. In 1860, after the election of Lincoln, he was asked by a group of New Yorkers to explain the "Scriptural authority for Slavery and the Constitutional position on the contending parties." His answer was published in New York in 1861, and it was this pamphlet that was reprinted with some revision for circulation in the Pennsylvania gubernatorial campaign of 1863. The six men involved were not ordinary laymen, but the Democratic leaders of the state, among whom were George M. Wharton, Charles J. Biddle, and Peter McCall. Hopkins' writing on slavery had influenced a wide audience. Since 1851, when he first defended slavery as an institution ordained by God and upheld by the Constitution, his interpretation had been the subject of considerable debate, and now it became the cause of harsh controversy, even though his writings were neither more nor less a defense of the system than other lectures, sermons, and tracts that pursued the same course. But Hopkins' *View* differed from others in that its proslavery arguments were better reasoned and his ideas were stated with greater conviction. Also, coming from a bishop of the Church, his opinions commanded attention and respect. However, within this same period he altered his views and stated that personally he looked upon the slave system as a moral evil, and that he favored the scheme of returning slaves to Africa under a planned system of colonization. It was his belief that the general acceptance of this proposal, already adopted in a number of states, would preserve the Union and avert a further split of the Church to which he was so devoted. Even though he saw slavery as a moral evil, his proslavery views fundamentally remained unchanged.[92]

Hopkins disclaimed knowledge of the tract's intended use as a political document, although it hardly seems possible that he was unaware of the political position of the men who requested it. However, he was certain that to whatever use it was put, it would contribute to the unity of the Church and the nation.

The Bible View of Slavery exceeded in number and distribution all campaign items sent out by the Pennsylvania Democrats, and because of its content and mass circulation it became the focus of major controversy. Republicans identified the statements of Woodward, an Episcopalian, with the philosophy of the Bishop of Vermont. The Union League, which sought to win the support of the Protestant Episcopal Diocese at its summer convention, looked upon the Democrats' use of Hopkins' tract as an uncalled for introduction of religion into the campaign. And Bishop Alonzo Potter of the Pennsylvania Diocese was provoked by the implication that the Church approved Hopkins' *View* and endorsed the slavery pronouncements of the Pennsylvania Democratic State Central Committee.[93]

Episcopalian members of The Union League were outraged; those on the Board of Publication reacted to Hopkins' *View* with a series of pamphlets designed to undermine the religious campaign literature of the Democrats. They received the broad support of Board members of other denominations. One by one, the arguments of Woodward were tied in with those of Hopkins and successfully blasted. The League attack was launched carefully with the intention of separating the views of the Pennsylvania Diocese from those of the Vermont Bishop. In a series of brief speeches, Nathaniel B. Brown, a prominent attorney and a leader of ward Leagues, lashed away at Colonel Charles J. Biddle, Chairman of the Democratic State Central Committee.[94] These were followed by extracts taken from Woodward's Independence Square speech of 1860 in which he stated that "slavery was an incalculable blessing." This and similar quotations were published under the title, *Opinions of a Man Who Wishes to Be A Governor of Pennsylvania.* Throughout the campaign the Independence Square speech was to haunt Woodward. Immediately after the *Opinions* was published Judge George McDowell Stroud's antislavery tract, *Southern Slavery and the Christian Religion,* made its appearance. To stem any influence that the Democrats had among the immigrant population, Woodward's biased speeches on the foreign-born were printed 26 years after they were made. As a member of the convention to revise the state constitution in 1837, Woodward had introduced an amendment to prevent foreigners "from acquiring the right to vote, or to hold office in the Commonwealth." Although the amendment was not accepted at that time, Woodward's views were resurrected to warn immigrant Germans and Irish of what might be expected if a Democrat was elected.[95]

One of the most popular and effective pamphlets aimed at Woodward and Hopkins came from Judge Stroud. Using as a source book Frances Kemble's *Journal of a Residence on a Georgian Plantation,* a work published the previous year, Stroud linked the ugliest and most barbaric aspects of slavery with selections from the speeches of Woodward and the writings of Hopkins. The annotated extracts from the Kemble *Journal* first appeared in the Philadelphia *Public Ledger* and then as a pamphlet. They took their toll of Democratic votes. On the front of the pamphlet there appeared a woodcut illustration of a badly whipped slave, his bare back exposing stripes of lacerated welts, a picture that graphically refuted Hopkins' contention that slaves were humanely treated.[96]

These pamphlets concentrated on an issue that the Democrats had chosen as a weapon, and they were successful in turning the tide of political sentiment away from Woodward. But they were only the beginning in a major battle of words. Henry Charles Lea's understanding of the issues and his swift reaction to the campaign made him an effective Union pamphleteer. In June, 1863, *A Few Words For Honest Pennsylvanians* made its appearance. Published anonymously, its 16 pages urged Democrats to forsake a party that maintained an alliance with the South. Before the month was out, his *Democratic Opinions on Slavery* came off the press. In it Lea contrasted the views of proslavery Democrats with those of the patriots of the American Revolution. A third pamphlet appeared in August attacking machine politics in Pennsylvania. Here, the historian and social reformer, rather than the polemicist, revealed his incisive style. Lea called for representative and free political institutions which, if they were to succeed, had to eliminate selfish leadership. Lea then turned his attention to Bishop Hopkins. In a brief work which he called *A Bible View of Polygamy*, he satirized the *Bible View of Slavery*. With a biting irony that made Hopkins' distortions seem foolish, and to the consternation of fundamentalists, who held everything in the Bible sacrosanct, Lea foresaw "that the time is not far distant when every citizen may have as many slaves as Abraham, and as many wives as Solomon." Lea was obviously influenced here by the plank in the Republican Party platform of 1856, which looked upon slavery and Mormon polygamy as the "twin evils of barbarism."[97]

Of the many publications that flooded the state and of those that heaped their wrath on Hopkins, none attracted as much attention as the League broadside *The Voice of the Clergy*, which appeared in late September, 1863. Bishop Potter, a friend of the League, rose to defend the Protestant Episcopal Church from those who would use it in support of slavery, and was instrumental in preparing a rebuttal that condemned Hopkins and the Pennsylvania Democrats. First, he obtained the support of 106 rectors and military and hospital chaplains of Philadelphia and the surrounding counties who signed their names to the protest. In a move that broke with tradition, the Negro rector of St. Thomas African Church, William J. Alston, of the first black Episcopal Church in the United States, was invited to add his name to a document which read in part:

"Among the extraordinary incidents of the time is the fact that the Democratic State Central Committee has circulated through Pennsylvania, as a campaign document the Letter of Bishop Hopkins, of Vermont, in which it is maintained that slavery, in the language of Judge Woodward is an incalculable blessing. The sentiments of Bishop Hopkins on this subject are so atrocious, and their adoption and promulgation by men professing to be Christians is so scandalous, that the Episcopal Clergy of Philadelphia' have felt themselves constrained to define their position, as they have done in the following manly and outspoken Protest."[98]

A reprint, broader in scope and endorsed by 164 clergymen throughout the State, was issued under the title *Protest of the Bishop and Clergy of the Diocese of Pennsylvania Against Bishop Hopkins' Letter of African Slavery*. Forty-nine members of the Diocese did not sign the *Protest*, not because they were in disagreement with it, but because they were either absent from the state or unable to be reached. Hopkins was infuriated and responded vehemently. Woodward was incensed, and called upon Peter McCall and George M. Wharton of the Democratic Party to bring legal action against Bishop Potter, but no steps were taken to institute a suit.[99] Any expectations that the Hopkins tract would be an asset in the Democratic campaign were frustrated. The *Protest* had made clear the position of the clergy: "It is not their province to mix in any political canvass. But as Ministers of Christ, in the Protestant Episcopal Church, it becomes them to deny any complicity or sympathy with such a defense."[100]

Many League founders were still dissatisfied with the intrusion of religion into the campaign, and unhappy over the use of the Bible to justify slavery. They associated the unbridled attacks upon abolitionists, whom Philadelphia Democrats held responsible for prolonging the war, with Hopkins' sanctimonious *View*. People were generally confused on the subject and perhaps some League members were, too. Benjamin Gerhard, the spark behind the Board of Publication, believed that despite the League's sharp counterattack, a thorough study based on historical and biblical sources was necessary to edify the public. He convinced his friend Daniel R. Goodwin, provost of the University of Pennsylvania, that such a review was necessary, and Goodwin undertook to write a full length work. *Southern Slavery in its Present Aspects . . . A Reply to a Late Work of the Bishop of Vermont on Slavery* appeared a year after the election was over, amid the tumult of continued unsubsided arguments over slavery and the campaign to re-elect Abraham Lincoln.[101]

Meanwhile, the League reprinted a small edition of Lewis C. Newman's *Bible View of Slavery Reconsidered*. It was the only work that discussed the matter philologically. Newman's knowledge of Hebrew was sufficient to examine the biblical word *ebed*, whose meaning and significance had been abused when translated out of context to describe Southern slavery. Many of the economic misinterpretations that filled proslavery literature revolved around this word. Its proper use, as shown by Newman, helped to expose Hopkins further.[102]

By this time the Democrats had been forced into a defensive position, although their onslaught of newspaper sarcasm continued unabated. Since they were personally embarrassed by Bishop Hopkins' tract, and their subsequent political arguments that rested on the *Bible View* had been discredited, they turned to other issues to try to weaken their opponents. One such issue was the Conscription Act, which made all men between the ages of 25 and 40 liable for military service. This was a convenient target, for the matter, strongly opposed by Democrats, was under review in the State Supreme Court, over which Woodward still presided. Another issue, supported by many Republicans as a wartime measure, was the Legal Tender Act of 1862, which the United States Supreme Court later ruled unconstitutional. A third point was the soldier's right to vote, a subject for debate that had been challenged in the courts a number of times. All three were supported by The Union League. Charles J. Biddle, writing on behalf of the Democrats, used these issues in an effort to weaken Republican charges against Peace Democrats and Copperheads, names he resented and considered undignified. He also linked all Republican activity to the abolitionists, whose aim, he claimed, was to undermine the Constitution in order to achieve Negro equality.

Although the contest was fought over national issues, it was not free from personal scandal and acrimony, which in this case involved Woodward's two sons. In their determination to defeat the Democrats, overzealous Republicans from the western part of the state charged the Democratic candidate with having made an unfortunate statement about one of his sons. Young George A. Woodward had recruited his own company of men in Philadelphia, with all expenses being paid by his father. The company then was absorbed into the Second Pennsylvania Reserves. As a major, George had fought in the Peninsular Campaign where he received a minor wound, but as a lieutenant colonel at Gettysburg he had suffered a crippling wound. It was at this time, shortly before he was nominated, that Judge Woodward was alleged to have told his son that if he had to be wounded, it might have been better if he had been shot through the heart. A rebuttal of the allegations, the public correspondence between father and son, and the excellent military records of both sons were quickly broadcast in a retaliatory campaign pamphlet by the Democratic State Central Committee. Again, the Union Leagues were condemned as secret societies, Know-Nothings in disguise, and as antiMasonic. These charges against the League were as untrue as the alleged statements of Woodward about his son.[103]

Amid the half-truths and charges that came from both sides, The Union League as a body clung to the principle of avoiding the mainstream of machine politics. In the days immediately before the election, it preferred to conduct its own independent torchlight processions, displays of fireworks, and escorts of Union notables, military officers and civilians to Independence Square. Election day, October 13, 1863, was unexpectedly quiet. The war of words was temporarily calmed. ProUnion voters turned out in a larger majority than ever before. Curtin was victorious. Daniel Agnew was elected Justice of the State Supreme Court, and in many local areas the Republicans won unexpected legislative seats.

The impact of the election on the League was manifold. In spite of its nonpartisan convictions, it was brought closer to the Republican Party. Leaders of the Party saw in the League a powerful organization that could move beyond wartime affiliation. Basically, the League's commitment was spurred by patriotic and not by political motivations, but in Curtin's victory the League saw a harbinger of Lincoln's re-election and the need, therefore, to strengthen Republican forces.[104]

Its membership had more than doubled from the original 253 subscribers, and their political views were far from monolithic. And a new class of members, the clergy of many denominations, was introduced as a result of its strong Union position during the gubernatorial campaign. This was the beginning of the League's clerical roll.

For the first time since it was founded, The Union League enjoyed a brief respite from months of hectic activity. Many of its members solemnly observed November 19 as a day of fast, honoring the dedication of the National Cemetery at Gettysburg. Forney, MacVeagh, John Russell Young, and others were present at the ceremony, during which Lincoln expressed the nation's bereavement in that brief but memorable address that outshone the polished rhetoric of other speakers. Young reported the event in Forney's newspapers, MacVeagh still sang praises to the Republican victory, and Governor Curtin was looked upon by those present as a force to be recognized in the nation's capital.

On Thanksgiving Day, a week later, news reached Philadelphia of the fall of Chattanooga to the Union army, and the holiday arranged at the League was turned into a double celebration. Thereafter Thanksgiving was observed annually at the League House. On this first occasion it was informally decided that a year-end report of the League's work be made available for the public record. George H. Boker, as secretary, undertook the task with which his name was to be associated for the next seven years.

The cold, factual style typical of nineteenth-century institutional reports was transformed under Boker's pen. A man who had sacrificed a career in drama and was a prolific author of Civil War poetry had no intention of depriving the League members of his considerable literary talents. Each of his reports expressed the reflective mood that was characteristic of Boker himself. In clear prose he carefully discussed each event and League endeavor as if he were preparing an outline for future historians of the League. Free of flourishes and rhetorical extremes, softened from the first draft which had harsher expressions denouncing Philadelphia's antiUnion elements, and sanguine in its assessment of his colleagues' work, he captured the inner thoughts and motivations of the League membership and their programs.

In his succinct description of the work of the Board of Publication, Boker noted that more than one-million copies of 71 documents had been published and circulated in less than a year, and that the publications of other associations also had been distributed in great numbers. He praised the work of the Committee for Obtaining Employment for Disabled Soldiers and Seamen, the military committees, and others in which the League or its members were involved.[105] Boker took special pride in recounting the presentation of a League medal struck in gold and presented to President Lincoln. The same medal, in silver, was given to each member of the Cabinet and to outstanding military and naval commanders of the Union forces. In addition to these men, a number of English and French notables, who were anxious to wean their governments away from a policy that favored the Confederacy, also had been recipients of the League's award. Such distinguished Frenchmen as the Comté Agenor de Gasparin, a former deputy of the July monarchy, and Edouard de Laboulaye, a prominent intellectual, and the Englishmen, John Bright, Richard Cobden, John Stuart Mill, and others, whose writings in defense of the Union were read on both sides of the Atlantic Ocean, were honored by the gift of The Union League medal and were extended the use of the League House.[106]

Boker reported that every effort was being made to accommodate

First Annual Report of the Board of Directors of the Union League of Philadelphia.

Less than a year has passed since the members of the Union League of Philadelphia assembled in this house for the purpose of organizing their association. Whoever will cast his mind back to the twenty-seventh day of December, 1862, will be able to conjecture what was the state of the country by the condition of his own feelings on that day. The hearts of loyal men were everywhere depressed. The inspiring Battle of Antietam had been followed by a period of military inaction so complete that public spirit sank into hopeless lethargy, and doubt and distrust had crept into the minds of the most sanguine. The rebel pirates were sweeping from the seas the floating fortunes of our merchants; domestic traitors were sneering at our futile efforts to break the power of their Southern brethren, and were predicting a speedy close to the war through the exhaustion of our courage and resources. Upon this state of things was piled the disastrous news which came to us from Fredericksburg and from Vicksburg. Burnside had been repulsed, Sherman had been repulsed. Gold rose to a higher point than it had reached since the war began; the national finances were threatened with ruin. Treason became rampant, almost triumphant in our streets, and loyal men forsook their usual associations rather than encounter its impudent presence. It was at this time and in this threatening posture of affairs that the projectors of the Union

BOKER'S DRAFT OF THE FIRST ANNUAL REPORT OF THE LEAGUE

a membership which had soared to 985 toward the end of the year, and crowded the attractive dining facilities, the library, and the reading rooms. The library received additions on a daily basis, and the League House was gradually becoming a repository for relics and artifacts of the war. In addition to Sully's huge equestrian portrait of Washington, gifts of paintings and other works of art adorned the walls of the House. The League had assumed the bearing and grace of an elegantly appointed social club.

But the Chestnut Street building was no longer suitable for the League's growing membership. The lease on the building was due to expire in August, 1864 and the League saw no advantage of renewing it. There was no building available at that time with ample office space and proper facilities that could be adapted to club needs. A number of members, acting independently, acquired a parcel of ground on the west side of Broad Street at the corner of Sansom, near the former building of the Academy of Natural Sciences and close to the seven-year-old Academy of Music. The trend to Broad Street had become fashionable, and the horse-drawn railroad cars that moved along this main thoroughfare proved no detriment. It was proposed that a new structure be built at an estimated cost of $120,000, which the League could lease for an annual rent and the payment of taxes. This offer basically met with approval, but the Board of Directors devised a plan more protective of the future of the League. Title was to be conveyed to the League upon its incorporation with powers included in its charter to take over the property. Certificates of loan in the amount of $500 would be issued to subscribing members at six per cent annually; the principal was to be paid in 20 years. Upon completion of the loan, the League would become the sole owner of the new house, for which ground was broken on March 1, 1864.[107] While the new house was being built the League rented temporary quarters at 1216 Chestnut Street.

At its first annual meeting, a proposed charter for the League was submitted to the membership, with the request that action be taken immediately. Included among the recommended provisions was an increase in the number of directors from nine to 15, to provide better representation of the membership. The charter was approved, and measures were projected for a club house precisely adapted to the tastes and style of the mid-nineteenth century. In 1865, the charter was granted by the state. Even in relating the technical business steps and the legal aspects of incorporation in his year-end report, Boker reflected on the high purposes of the welding of a social club with a patriotic philosophy, and on the role of the new building. It would be "a monument of the history of that vast loyal movement which began in the gloomiest days of the Great Rebellion, and continued with growing vigor until peace and re-union made at least its public characteristics unnecessary. Some other association, some large comprehensive Club, representing all the different interests of our citizens, might occupy the building, no longer able to contain the universal patriotism of our people; but whatever may be the uses to which it is applied, it would hereafter, to all future generations, be known only as the 'League House' and its history would form a curious and instructive chapter in the annals of our city."[108]

Photo by Gutekunst

THE UNION LEAGUE HOUSE 1865

ABRAHAM LINCOLN

Xanthus Russell Smith

III

ᏊᏔᎧ

From Amnesty to Assassination

S HORTLY before the first annual meeting of The Union League, in December, 1863, the president of the United States delivered his Third Annual Message and announced his Amnesty Proclamation to Congress. The League's response was one of cordial acceptance. No time was lost in reprinting the Proclamation.[1] The presidential election was not far off and Democrats like Daniel Dougherty, who had initially opposed the president as a Republican but had not objected to his wartime policies, were swept into the Republican mainstream by the new issues. Dougherty had worked hard to defeat the Democratic gubernatorial ticket in 1863, and early in January, 1864, he joined in the movement to re-elect Lincoln with others whose political sympathies had lain elsewhere before the war.[2]

January was an exciting month for all departments of the League. The Board of Directors braced itself for an unusual step by unanimously adopting a series of resolutions to secure Lincoln's renomination for a second term. It was the first body in the United States to do so. A committee of 76 was appointed to plan for the renomination and "to use all proper means to aid in his re-election." The following day the full resolution was published in McMichael's *North American,* and a copy in elegant calligraphy was forwarded to President Lincoln. To support the unprecedented move of the Board, which aligned the League with the Republican Party, Boker began work on a preliminary campaign pamphlet, *The Will of the People.* It focused attention on the continuing arguments over slavery, and challenged critics in both parties on their censure of Lincoln for not acting in consonance with their views. Democrats sneered at a war that was converted into a "war against slavery," and radical Republicans still lamented that

Lincoln had not moved swiftly to abolish slavery. He pointed out that those who criticized Lincoln for not using extreme measures immediately after he was first elected were shown that the president was not peremptory in a crisis, and that he did not act independently but allowed public opinion to formulate itself. He followed the "express will of the people." "He has never been forced to retrace his position. Supported by and supporting the popular feeling, he has moved onward in unison with it, and each new development has afforded sure foothold for further progress." In prose that was simple and direct, Boker expressed the official policy of the League and helped clear the path to the Republican Convention that year.[3]

Like Boker, Henry C. Lea knew Lincoln personally. Neither man, however, was so subjective in his feelings about the president that he was unable to write political tracts free of adulation. While Boker undertook to show that Lincoln out of respect for democratic institutions, reflected the popular will, Lea prepared a summary of the first three years of the president's administration. Its convincing tone, its depth of understanding, and its smooth style not only did justice to Lincoln, but elevated Lea above other proLincoln pamphleteers and advocates of a second term.[4]

The Board of Publication was preparing itself for a busy election year. The reprint of the Amnesty Proclamation, Lea on Lincoln, and the Boker pamphlet were all published prior to the Republican convention in Baltimore, and were placed in circulation as precampaign pieces on the assumption that Lincoln would be renominated. Meanwhile, troops leaving Philadelphia—the Eighth Regiment Colored Volunteers left the city on January 16, with others ready to follow—were supplied with copies of current publications. Distribution of League materials continued without interruption. Other League responsibilities continued unabated. The military committees and those engaged in finding employment for disabled and discharged soldiers were faced with a constant stream of homecoming men.

In spite of heavy activities that now involved the entire League membership, the officers and directors looked forward to the celebration of Washington's Birthday. Up until that time, the celebration of national holidays, with the exception of Thanksgiving Day, had had to be canceled because of the Southern military thrust into Pennsylvania. However, nothing interfered on this occasion. The scene on Chestnut Street was both social and patriotic. Visitors appeared at noon and in the course of the day it was estimated that thousands of guests enjoyed League hospitality. The main event was the presentation of a silk flag by the ladies of the city to the League, out of respect for its wartime work in which the ladies were very active. Three of the more impressive responses in the rich oratory of the day were made by McMichael, Boker, and Dougherty, the latter of whom had a superb talent for public speaking. It was a relaxing interlude, and the next day all committees returned to their work refreshed.[5]

A matter of great concern to the Board of Publication and to the military committees was the distribution of the Amnesty Proclamation. The Proclamation, they felt, had to reach the soldiers in gray. But the danger of its confiscation behind Confederate lines was obvious. With many of the Board of Publication as active in the affairs and strategies on the field of battle as they were at their writing desks, a device was found whereby the Proclamation could penetrate the South. In the spring an almanac with the appealing title, *The Planter's Almanac for 1864*, was issued in the typical format of the day. It looked like any almanac from the presses of Charleston or Richmond.

The recto pages of the *Almanac* contained a monthly calendar and the verso pages carried textual material. It opened with an extract from Alexander H. Stephens' "Speech," purportedly delivered at the Georgia State Convention. The *Almanac* was bait to the unsuspecting Confederate soldier, an unmistakable invitation to desert. Mingled with information on the greenhouse calendar, the best time to slaughter animals, and how to prepare lard candles and beer in small quantities were extracts from the Southern press on the perpetuation of slavery. This set the tone for the relevant section on amnesty; while the soldier was still chuckling over some amusing anecdote, he came upon the proclamation, which stated the conditions for receiving refugees and deserters from "rebel lines." A copy of the *Almanac* was a pass to safety.[6] Two copies brought 50 men from various Georgia brigades, and others deserted nightly. Brigadier General William D. Whipple, who had commanded the First Union League Regiment and was now stationed with the Department of the Cumberland near Atlanta, Georgia, together with his aide, Colonel Moses B. Walker, informed the League of the effectiveness of the stratagem. They urged a more liberal distribution of the *Almanac*, but insisted that knowledge of it be kept from the press to prevent publicity from interfering with its success.[7] Some writers for the League, like James Russell Lowell, charged the press and telegraph with "insidious treachery" because of the proConfederate manner in which they reported news.[8] The extent of infiltration of the *Almanac* and other League propaganda cannot be fully estimated, but on the basis of just this account it can be seen that it accomplished in a small way what it had set out to do.

A wave of pleasant excitement spread over the city of Philadelphia in the spring of 1864. Preparations were announced for a fair to

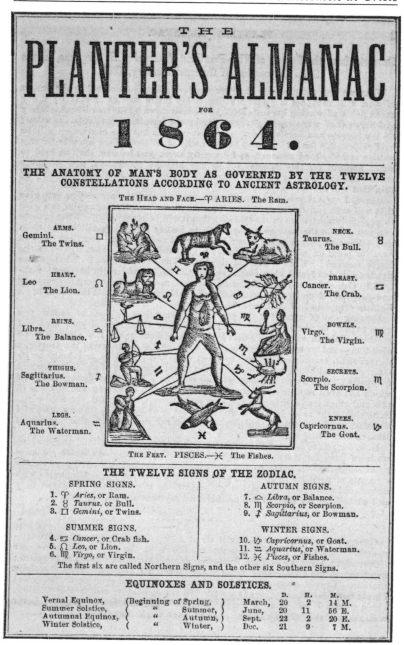

THE PLANTER'S ALMANAC 1864

raise funds for wounded and disabled soldiers. Under the auspices of the United States Sanitary Commission, New Jersey, Delaware, and Pennsylvania became joint participants in the venture. Two of the outstanding men who were to dominate its arrangements and the setting up of the fair grounds, located where Logan Circle is today, were Charles J. Stillé, later the author of the official history of the Sanitary Commission, and Horace Binney, Jr., president of the Philadelphia branch of the Commission and at this time a vice-president of The Union League.[9] They mustered the forces of the League on behalf of the Sanitary Fair. Boker called upon his Princeton classmate Charles Godfrey Leland, an author and translator, to edit *The Daily Fare*, a humorous journal published just for the festival.[10] League men and their ladies made available for sale much of the fine china, silverware, and unusual items that are today sought after as rarities. Books, some hastily written and others the thoughtful products of the war, were sold at the request of the League, while League broadside poems and political pamphlets were distributed without charge. Boker's *Poems of the War* arrived too late for sale at the Fair; but James Murdoch's *Patriotism in Poetry and Prose,* a volume sponsored by individual League members, contained poems by Boker, Thomas B. Reed, Francis Janvier, and other American authors, and found a popular audience. Ten thousand copies of Murdoch's songs were purchased by the Board of Publication for separate distribution on and off the Fair grounds.[11]

The League also attracted other authors eager for its support, and even for the privilege of dedicating their work to the club. Such was the case of Ferdinand L. Sarmiento, a Philadelphia lawyer of Spanish background. Sarmiento produced a small work, *The History of Our Flag,* the second of its kind which is dedicated to the League. In a formal presentation of the book to the League, he wrote: "The history, as well as the origin and meaning of our flag, should be, I contend, a 'household word.' It should be taught in the public schools—It should form the A.B.C. of every American soldier's education, yes—be made the very *alphabet* of glory!"[12]

One of the outstanding items offered for sale at the Fair was a special edition of the Emancipation Proclamation. At the request of Boker, Leland, and the poet Bayard Taylor, whose post as secretary to the Russian legation Boker had helped him obtain, permission was received from President Lincoln to reprint a small edition of the Proclamation. Forty-eight copies were printed, and each was signed by Lincoln, Secretary of State Seward, and Lincoln's secretary, John G. Nicolay. Boker personally defrayed the cost of printing so as not to use the funds of the Board of Publication. A few copies were dis-

tributed privately; the remainder were placed for sale at ten dollars
a copy at Leland's desk at the Fair.[13]

The Copperhead newspaper, *The Age*, petulant over the sale of
a signed edition of the Proclamation, called attention to the original
manuscript which had sold some months before for $3,000 at the
Sanitary Fair in Chicago. "Some Loyal Leaguers hoped it may be
secured for a Historical Society," the editor of *The Age* wrote, and
then proceeded to compare the Emancipation with a forged document
of the notorious English highwayman, Dick Turpin. Turpin's document, quipped *The Age*, was worth "just exactly the price offered
for the Emancipation Proclamation." On this occasion the contempt
of *The Age* evoked no response.[14]

Philadelphians were eager to have Lincoln present at the inauguration of the Fair on May 4, but he was compelled to decline. A second
invitation to the official opening of the Fair on June 7 was turned
down also because the date unfortunately coincided with the Republican convention in Baltimore. Lincoln did consent to be present the
following week as the guest of the Sanitary Commission, the City,
and The Union League.[14a]

At noon on June 16, President Abraham Lincoln arrived in Philadelphia and was escorted to the Continental Hotel, where he was received by Charles Gibbons, one of his ardent Philadelphia supporters.
Boker was present with McMichael, and they tendered the President
the hospitality of the League House upon his return from the Fair.
McMichael presented Sidney George Fisher, who before the day was out
wrote of Lincoln: "Nothing was said beyond the ordinary salutations
and shaking hands. I had all that I wanted, an opportunity to see and
observe the man. Was much pleased by his countenance and manner. He
is tall, slender, not awkward and uncouth as has been represented, well
dressed in black, self-possessed and easy, frank and cordial. The pictures of him do great injustice to his face. His features are irregular and
would be coarse but for their expression, which is genial, animated and
kind. He looked somewhat pale and languid and there is a soft shade
of melancholy in his smile and in his eyes. Altogether an honest,
intelligent, amicable countenance, calculated to inspire respect, confidence and regard. His voice, too, is clear and manly. Am very glad
to have seen him. His whole bearing and aspect confirm the opinion
I had formed of him."[15] Mrs. Lincoln, in the company of eight ladies,
six of whom were the wives of League founders, did not fare as well
in Fisher's diary. "She is stout, by no means handsome, her face had
a sharp look and she is far from thorobred in her appearance."[16]

A few minutes after Lincoln accepted the invitation to visit the
League, he received Mayor Alexander Henry and members of City

Council, some of whom Fisher described as "very coarse, vulgar-looking men." At four o'clock he started for the Fair amid a throng of people who expressed their esteem with outbursts of prolonged cheering. It was impossible for the President to visit the elegant display of exhibits on the Fair grounds because of the intense crowds, the wild greetings, and the magnificent bands. The exuberant clamor was calmed only when Lincoln, in his felicitous manner, responded to the toasts made in his honor. When the time came to return to the League House, the committee of Gibbons, Boker and McMichael, through some inexplicable confusion, lost their distinguished guest. Led by a procession of cheering citizens, Lincoln made his way to the Chestnut Street headquarters in advance of the committee.[17]

Rarely had Chestnut Street east of Broad presented such a gay appearance. The crowd was so thick that the streetcars had to be stopped more than a block away. To add to the excitement and the many blaring bands, a subsidiary Union League contingent from the Tenth Ward arrived with torches, banners, and a band of its own. At the headquarters of the Supervisory Committee for Recruiting Colored Regiments, two companies of black troops presented arms. A band struck up the "Star-Spangled Banner" as the President's carriage rolled by in the direction of the National Union Club. Opposite stood the League House, beautifully decorated with both state and national colors waving from its windows. White streamers floated from the flagstaff each imprinted with the name of a state. The ladies of the League enthusiastically waved their handkerchiefs, and on the League steps stood many cheering members. "The building was illuminated in honor of the occasion and the glow of myriad gas-jets lit up Chestnut Street in front of the League with the brightness of daylight. A series of small gas-jets, on the outside spelled out the League's first motto: 'God and our Country.' "[18]

A grand reception for the President was about to take place in the League. But the welcoming committee having lost him in the throngs of people, there was no one present to greet him officially. In an ironic twist, Daniel Dougherty, the Democrat who had strongly opposed Lincoln at the time of the League's organization, was drawn from the crowd and asked to welcome the President. Dougherty, in a brief welcoming speech, reminded Lincoln that on his first visit to Philadelphia many of those now present had been his opponents, but since then they had flung aside most differences to form the League and dedicate themselves to preserving the Union. The weary President had no intention of giving an address, but at the warm urging of Dougherty he commented briefly on the League as "an organization free from political prejudices and prompted in its formation by motives of the highest patriotism." He expressed his gratitude on the extraordinary efforts made in behalf of the suffering soldiers and sailors, and he graciously offered to shake hands with his hosts.[19]

At midnight the President, after a pleasant dinner and a round of customary handshaking, returned to the Continental Hotel to be greeted by another huge crowd with fireworks, singing, and band-music. In response to the clamor of the crowd, Lincoln appeared on the hotel balcony where Edward C. Knight, an important figure in Pennsylvania railroading and a presidential elector of 1860, introduced him and urged his re-election.[20]

By the time Lincoln returned to Washington, a great naval battle was being waged off the coast of Cherbourg. The U.S.S. *Kearsarge*, under the command of Captain John A. Winslow, arrived at the French port to receive Union prisoners released by Captain Raphael Semmes, commander of the *Alabama* anchored at Cherbourg. The Confederate *Alabama* was notorious for its success as a destroyer, having captured or destroyed 68 United States vessels and virtually driven American commerce from the seas during the war. Now, the *Alabama* deliberately came out to challenge the Union ship. When they met on Sunday morning June 19, the *Kearsarge* was fresh and trim. The *Alabama*, lacking in speed, with a bottom foul with barnacles, fought fiercely but in vain for an hour and twenty-seven minutes before she plunged into the sea. The victorious Winslow was honored by the League by receiving its silver medal for his bravery against Semmes, a former naval roommate to whom he had shown no mercy in battle.[21] Captain Semmes and his surviving men were rescued only through the British ship *Deerhound*, and the compassion of French spectators watching from nearby Normandy. Winslow's personal account of the battle was later published by the League, and as a further tribute to this battle, Xanthus Smith, who had served under Admiral Samuel F. duPont, was commissioned by the League to paint the destruction of the Confederate vessel. Today, this painting hangs in the main hallway of the League House, alongside of a three-quarter portrait of Winslow in the uniform of a rear admiral of the Navy.[22]

In the meantime, amid Union victories at sea and successes on land, Lincoln's opponents were rallying behind the Democratic nominee for president, General George B. McClellan. League committees were busier than ever, and the approaching presidential election commanded their total resources. The directors, the Board of Publication, and the entire membership became immersed in an intensive campaign, separate from that of the Republican Party, to re-elect Lincoln.

The accumulated experience of the Board of Publication had brought

Xanthus Russell Smith

THE KEARSARGE AND THE ALABAMA

its methods of selecting and editing literature to a point of sophisticated refinement. However, because of a continuing fear of confiscation of League publications, its distribution procedures required a
reassessment if its literary operations were to be as effective in the
presidential election as they had been in the gubernatorial campaign.
For one thing, it was necessary to confirm the geographical and political position of its distribution agents, and for another it was essential
to procure correct data on "language and other peculiarities of the
voting population" of the state.[23] Lindley Smyth's suggestion was
adopted: that an agent be employed to canvass every township in
Pennsylvania to obtain this necessary information prior to the beginning of the campaign.

Meanwhile, the Board moved ahead with its publication program,
concentrating on obvious issues. The significance of the Conscription
Act was emphasized, Union soldiers were appealed to, the changing
outlook of Christian denominations toward slavery was noted, and
the Democrats were attacked with unprecedented vigor. Other pamphlets presented Abraham Lincoln as the only man capable of reuniting
the nation. From the date of the close of the Sanitary Fair to the
eve of the election, the Board issued 22 pamphlets and 24 broadsides,
posters, and lithographs. It further published its own campaign newspaper, and acquired for distribution the pamphlets of other societies.

Henry Charles Lea launched the League campaign for Lincoln. Addressing the fighting forces of the Union, he concentrated on George B.
McClellan, not as a former general, but as a "creature of the party
which is to make him president." McClellan was a strong and popular
candidate in Pennsylvania, and Lea felt it especially important to
undermine him and present him as a doubtful choice. In devastatingly
unfavorable language, yet sincere in his characterization of McClellan
who was loyal to the Union but who represented Peace Democrats and
their platform of immediate cessation of hostilities, Lea examined the
nature of such a peace and called it a compromising, inconclusive
peace that could not endure. He called for an overwhelming victory at
the polls which would crush the "fawning tricksters" who had nominated the former general.[24] McClellan's repudiation of the Democratic
platform meant little to Lea, whose appeal to the soldiers was followed
by one to civilians, *Democratic Peace for the Acceptance of Pennsylvania Voters*, in which Lea stressed that support of Lincoln meant
a total, uncompromising defeat of the South, not a "disastrous peace
through negotiation." His unrelenting attack on the Democrats was
just as strong in a third tract of four pages, which constituted elec-
tioneering propaganda at its best. Each plank of the Democratic platform was ruthlessly examined and exposed as an unmistakable con-

viction of the South.[25] Lea's intention was clearly to prevent, if possible, any votes for McClellan or his running mate, George H. Pendleton, who was disposed of in still another pamphlet.[26]

Lea had an uncanny ability to gather facts about antiUnion societies. Two of these organizations whose activities many thought had been exaggerated were exposed by Lea in one pamphlet. The Knights of the Golden Circle, organized in Alabama before secession, still maintained its strength in the Old South; and the Order of the Sons of Liberty, with similar antiUnion motives, was active in Kentucky, Missouri, Ohio, and Indiana. Some of Lea's information was based on documents of the Knights captured in the Peninsular campaign by Colonel Carroll Tevis and forwarded to Boker with the statement that the society's work was "not known to our most prominent government detectives."[27]

German-born Major General Carl Schurz, one of a number of men invited by the League to speak at Philadelphia's Concert Hall during the campaign, described the United States as a "Great Empire of Liberty." Like Lea, he realized that peace was a complex word, and warned that "before using it as a political rallying cry, we ought to be careful to ascertain and define its true significance."[28]

League authors and speakers, including Daniel Dougherty, who toured the state, refused to endorse peace at any price, or accept a political compromise that might undermine the sovereignty of the nation. James Russell Lowell, writing for the Philadelphia League from Boston, while not unsympathetic to the future of the South, was uncompromising in his opposition to a political peace settlement. In a forceful letter to the League, William Whiting, the solicitor of the War Department, warned against the return of the seceded states on terms of equality with the North. The life of the emancipated slave would be endangered, he pointed out, and the new freedom imperiled. Whiting's letter sought to define the terms of reconstruction and was favorably received at the League which published it, but the letter evoked mixed reactions among Republicans outside of the League, who assumed that his sharp statements reflected the policy of the president. More and more, the issue of total Southern defeat was favored. A scorched earth policy was condoned, and an irrevocable surrender was demanded. The arguments of Charles J. Stillé and of Morton McMichael for a long and successful war were well understood by military strategists, to whom full victory was a necessity rather than a concept.[29]

The Board of Publication had no difficulty in enlisting Schurz and other German Americans to write for the preponderantly proUnion German-reading population. In the early years of the war and in the gubernatorial campaign of 1863, the ethnic appeal of the program was very successful. Francis Lieber, German-born political scientist and a member of the New York League, was the editor for the Loyal Publication Society of that city. His address to the Germans, *Lincoln oder McClellan*, although translated into English, was reprinted by the Philadelphia League in its original language. Lieber contrasted for his readers the problems they had had in the duchies and provinces of a disunited Germany and the blessings of a new, undivided homeland. If German immigrants were to reap the lasting benefits of American liberty, it was incumbent upon them to cast their votes for Lincoln.[30]

The importance of the German vote, especially in Pennsylvania, was recognized by both parties. Where a proUnion German press did not exist, or where political views among Germans wavered, the Publication Committee used its energies and funds to either establish a newspaper or win over the editor of an existing paper to the cause of the Union. A sum of $300 to be used for subscriptions went to the *Amerikaner* of Northampton County, "whose editor had lately been converted from Democracy to loyalty." Another newspaper received similar support in Berks County, and when word was received that a German paper in Danville, Kentucky, was in need of funds, an appropriate sum was forwarded. Friends of the League, far removed from the city, kept the Board of Publication so well-informed of publication needs among the Germans of Pennsylvania and the midwestern states that few areas remained untouched by the League's extensive campaign efforts.[31]

On the economic condition of the North, three pamphlets discussed monetary changes, wartime debts, and general financial conditions. Two of the pamphlets, issued anonymously, represented the combined thinking of Carey, Colwell, and William Elder. Their object was to encourage the acceptance of paper money by those Northerners who viewed the Legal Tender Act of 1862 as an enemy far more formidable than the Confederate army. The third pamphlet, by Lorin Blodget, discussed the importance and potential of American commercial, financial, and industrial resources.[32]

While not a direct response to Blodget, one League member, Benjamin Franklin Reimer, addressed the League in a printed circular on the subject of Union weaponry. "In this age of invention and improvement," he wrote, "there is no material improvement in the infantry service in our Army." Soldiers are subjected to "so contemptible a thing as the Springfield rifle." In the heat of the presidential campaign, Reimer urged the League to support his proposal to revise the ordinance by having the army adopt a rapid fire rifle that could fire 15 times in 10 seconds. But other matters occupied the attention of the League, and no action is known to have been taken on Reimer's proposal.[33]

After the Episcopal Church controversy in the election of 1863, the League was eager to avoid another religious conflict. As a gesture of goodwill, it made certain to invite the Methodists who were holding a conference in Philadelphia to meet at the League. The League's clerical friends undertook a survey of religious attitudes toward slavery that appeared under the title *Christianity versus Treason and Slavery: Religion Rebuking Sedition.*[34] It was a united effort to declare Christianity and Judaism the sworn enemies of slavery and secession. In this early ecumenical move, inspired by the circumstances of the war, Episcopalians set aside their differences with Methodists, Northern Presbyterians united in a common front, and Protestant leaders invited Roman Catholics to join them in a public statement. Before the war, the antiCatholic crusade which involved leading Democrats would have defeated such an undertaking. Furthermore, it was the first known occasion when Philadelphia Jews under the vigorous leadership of Reverend Sabato Morais, minister of Congregation Mikveh Israel, were united to join with Christians in issuing a religious and patriotic proclamation.[35] That this proclamation was fostered by a secular institution made it all the more remarkable. The editors were Methodists, Episcopalians, and Presbyterians who solicited statements from Baptists, Lutherans and Congregationalists that they were confirmed opponents of those who would further subjugate Negroes.

Summarizing their findings, the editors stated: "We have not space to exhibit the patriotic testimony of the Friends, the Unitarians, the Universalists, and the Israelites. The Right Rev. Catholic Bishops of Philadelphia, Cincinnati and Buffalo, feebly as they sometimes have been sustained by their Irish Catholic people, have nevertheless, the reputation of standing by the government and the flag of their adopted country."[36]

A pamphlet whose impact was felt quite differently, came from Jeremiah Clemens of Huntsville, Alabama. He had argued against secession in the legislature of his state, but with mixed feelings had voted for it. He had been a major general in the Alabama militia, but left the army because of his opposition to the war. In 1862 he escaped to Philadelphia, where he remained until Huntsville was seized by the Union army. Meanwhile, he addressed the *New York Tribune*, advocating the re-election of Lincoln. His letter was promptly turned into a pamphlet by the League. Clemens returned to Huntsville and under government protection spoke to the citizenry of the town assailing the claims of secessionists and eliciting the loyalty of many of his listeners who were provided with copies of his pamphlet.[37]

The endorsement of Lincoln by so many groups for a second term, so early in the year, and the variety of publications issued in his support before his renomination, were not only unusual but were indicative of the League's careful planning. The introduction of new campaign approaches by the better utilization of nonLeague forces, and more intimate co-operation with the Union Party all placed the League in the national forefront of Lincoln supporters. The fact that it had successfully united men of diverse backgrounds and political views, where the Republican Party could not, won for the League more respect than hostile forces were willing to admit.

One of the men who favored the League, although he remained aloof from membership, was Sidney George Fisher. At McMichael's suggestion, Fisher was asked to prepare what later became the official political statement of The Union League and an important campaign pamphlet. Fisher, always zealous for a literary assignment, approached his topic eagerly. The *Address of the Union League* contained the basic principles of Lincoln's reconstruction views and Fisher's concept of American nationality. "Our enemies are men of our race. They have displayed the valor, constancy and ability that are the attributes of their blood and the fruits of free institutions. It will not be easy to subdue such people . . . and when their military strength is subdued, it may not be easy to convert them from enemies to friends." Fisher understood the necessity of bringing Southerners back to the Union not only politically, but of turning them into contented citizens. But first the Confederacy had to be vanquished, and to accomplish this the re-election of Lincoln was of paramount importance.

In the eyes of Fisher, Lincoln was a man of the forest, a hewer of wood, who had risen to great intellectual heights. The man, the politician and the president were well-described in elegiac terms. Some editions of the *Address* carried a reprint of the original resolutions adopted by the League on January 11, 1864, advocating the renomination of Lincoln, and they were also included in the official campaign biography of Lincoln by David B. Williamson.[38]

Apart from the responsibility of distributing 1,044,904 pamphlets during 1864, the Board of Publication also published a campaign newspaper, the *Union League Gazette*. Suggested by Lindley Smyth, the paper had its own editor and circulation officer and was not limited to Pennsylvania, although the state was heavily deluged with it. In the 10 issues that appeared in the six weeks preceding the election, the *Gazette* published some of the speeches delivered under League auspices, and letters from generals of the Union army, con-

Union League Gazette.

VOL. I. PHILADELPHIA, OCTOBER, 1864. NO. 5.

PATRIOTIC OUTBURST OF ELOQUENCE BY DISTRICT ATTORNEY WM. B. MANN.

Colonel William B. Mann having been officially introduced at an immense meeting at *Union League Hall*, delivered a brief and eloquent off-hand speech, as follows:

He said that if he were addressing an audience in the realms of Jefferson Davis he would be addressing many who could neither read nor write—many who had never heard the truth—and would not feel in the least embarrassed. But his present audience was an intelligent one—composed of those who read and thought on all those great issues important to their political welfare—and he felt embarrassed as to what he should say that would, from its novelty, give them new ideas or more enlarged views. He felt, however, that the only way to redress our ills was to reinforce Sheridan, Sherman and Grant, so that in the heavy blows following those already dealt the rebellion would die finally and forever. [Applause.] It was useless to trouble an intelligent gathering with any recapitulation of events during the last four years. Suffice it to say that the people of Philadelphia had a full knowledge of the South and its people. We were in constant communication with them. Southern students came to our medical colleges; Southern business men came to make purchases; Southern gentlemen came as sojourners, and Southern slave-owners came in pursuit of fugitives from the thraldom of slavery. Many a time these negroes were brought back from their flight, led through our streets, and returned to bondage, whilst their eyes were turned with anxious hope toward the Northern star. Since that time those Southern taskmasters have plunged themselves into a moral hell darker and deeper than that prepared for Satan. [Applause.] All through that time, when these ladies and gentlemen were mingling proudly with us, and receiving our freely-dispensed hospitality; when their students plunged daggers into the backs of Northern mechanics, we were not, as they were, teaching our children how to do deeds of blood; we were not preparing for internal discord. But when their preparations were completed—when they had robbed us of all they required to enable them to defy us—they commenced the war, and that war now continues. During all this time those poor fugitives, who had been dragged back to their tasks in the Southern fields, are dreaming of liberty, to be brought to them by hosts who came from the direction of that Northern star upon which they once gazed so anxiously. But when the war has progressed so far that success is already in our grasp, and even the duration of resistance is measured, a great party rises up and tells us to throw away all the advantages we have gained, and ask an armistice from those who are already in our power, and can bestow no favor on us. What nonsense! A man is attacked by a highwayman in the streets of the city. He calls for help, and policemen hurry to his rescue. He is thrown down by them; one grasps him by the arm, another by the body, another by the throat. What would be thought of the man who at this juncture came up and said to the officers of the law, "Let him up! He is a fellow-man, descended from the same mother Eve! Let him up! He is a brother!" Why, he would be laughed at. Yet this is the very course the malignants wish us to adopt concerning the rebellion. Sheridan has it by the right arm [applause], Sherman has it round the body, and Grant has it by the throat. [Renewed applause.] The malignants come to us and tell us, "Let the rebels up; they are brothers" But we will not! No Republican, no American, no Whig, no patriot, will ever say "let them up." But some really patriotic people really believe it would be the best policy to elect McClellan. Once elected, he would propose his armistice—it would be rejected—and then it would be his policy, as well as the policy of his opponents, to put down the rebellion, as is now being done, by force. But even were such things to come to pass, would not an armistice in itself be a terrible danger? During it blockaded ports would be open, cotton sent out, and arms, gold, everything necessary to a war, be brought in. When this was done, the South would open the war anew, and our work would have to be done over again. And then McClellan, if elected, would have men like Woodward and Vallandigham [laughter] around him—pro-slavery all. The renewed war would be controlled, managed and moulded in its purposes and ends by them. McClellan, when in command of the army, was ruled by a delegation of Philadelphia politicians, who got him to write in his "report" whole pages of advice to the President, putting him right on questions of statesmanship, and pointing out the way in which the war should be conducted. [Laughter.] If controlled once by ordinary ward politicians, what would become of him in the hands of such men as had been mentioned?

Mr. Mann could see nothing in the Chicago platform that could even claim the name of patriotism. There was no praise for our soldiers, or rebuke to the rebels in arms. And McClellan, who had been nominated by the Convention, could no longer be called "Little Mac." [Laughter.] He was the greatest giant in the world, and his stride had never been equalled. [Renewed laughter.] One foot is on the Chicago platform, and the other is on his letter—two things millions of miles apart. [Great laughter.] He exceeds, immeasurably, the Colossus of Rhodes. [Laughter.] The people who nominated him were not Democrats; they were malignants, and by that name the speaker intended always to characterize them. They were Disunionists in heart. Ask any of the numbers to be met every day on the streets, whether they did not wish to have New England out of the Union, and they would always answer "yes." They always took a pleasure in misrepresenting that portion of our country in their conversations, their speeches, and their newspapers. And yet the real Democratic party, when the question of a boundary line between the United States and Canada was being discussed, almost quarrelled with the British Government about what side of a certain piece of woods the line should run. They were for the Union then—every inch of it they were determined to protect and never to part from, and in pursuance of that determination the cry was raised—"54 40, or fight." England's claim was just, however, and a fight was avoided. This spirit of disunion was rendered additionally evident by the persistent use of the term "Yankees," when speaking of the people of New England. The speaker detailed what the new Union would be after it had been regenerated by the war and sanctified by the lives and blood of hundreds of thousands of the flower of our population. The cause of all the bloodshed, ruin and desolation, will have been removed, never again to jeopardize our peace. The day-star of freedom will dispense its calm and gentle light on the country emerging from the darkness now overshadowing it to a new and prosperous career.

The war-cloud will soon pass away; it is becoming thinner and thinner, and the light begins to appear in the horizon. Gentle gales have already come from the patriotic West—Indiana and Ohio—and the streak of light begins to peep in, foretokening renewed brilliancy, to light the people on to that calm peace that can never fail to succeed the storm. [Applause.] The blessings of an honorable peace will falls upon all alike; our swords will be turned into pruning hooks, and the garden of liberty will spring up fresh again in the roseate hues of May, and the nation will become prosperous and happy, and may defy the world. Colonel Mann retired amid great applause.

JUSTICE TO GEO. H. PENDLETON.

HIS PUBLIC RECORD.

A Page of Congressional Impartial History.

Let us Speak of a Man as we find Him.

On January 18th, 1861, South Carolina and three other States having adopted ordinances of secession, George H. Pendleton delivered a speech in Congress, in which he said, in reference to the seceded States:

Sir, I deal in no harsh epithets. I will denounce no State, no body of men. I will not pause to inquire whether they have done all this legally or wisely, or upon sufficient cause. *They have done it, and I recognize the fact.* They have done it with an unanimity of sentiment, with a coincidence of opinion among the people, which is without parallel in the history of revolutions; and the simple question presented to us to-day is this: whether, throughout the limits of those States which thus formally, thus orderly, thus by enactments of representative bodies of highest capacity known to the civilized nations—conventions duly authorized and properly elected to consider this very question—have declared themselves independent of us, are we prepared, by force of arms, to maintain our supremacy and enforce our laws? * * * * * *

Now, sir, what force of arms can compel a State to do that which she has agreed not to do? What force of arms can compel a State to refrain from doing that which her State Government, supported by the sentiment of her people, is determined to persist in doing? It is provided in the Constitution that the citizens of every State shall have all the privileges and immunities of citizens of the several States. What force of this Federal Government can compel the observance of that clause if a State is determined to pass and execute laws whereby citizens of other States shall not have, within its limits, the same privileges as its own citizens?

"Full faith and credit shall be given in each State to the public acts and judicial proceedings of every other State." How will the Federal Government, by armies and arms, enforce the observance of that clause in the Constitution if the judiciary and the executive authorities of a State, supported by the laws, refuse such faith and credit?

"No State, without the consent of Congress, shall lay any imposts or duties on imports." Suppose a State should pass such a law, and the citizens were willing to execute the law, what army could prevent it?

"No State shall, without the consent of Congress, enter into any agreement or compact with a foreign Power." I wish to know from the gentlemen what number of men it would require to annul such an agreement, once made. The General Government is invested with certain powers, necessary to be executed, in order to keep the machinery of the Government in motion. Can any number of troops, or the use of any armed force on the part of the States, compel the General Government to execute those powers if the agents appointed for that purpose deliberately, persistently, refuse to execute them? *Sir, the whole scheme of coercion is impracticable. It is contrary to the genius and spirit of the Constitution.*

The following passage puts Mr. Pendleton in direct antagonism with General McClellan. The letter is for conciliation and compromise; but if the rebels will not hear to such terms as comport with the national honor, then he is for coercing them into obedience to the laws. Now, mark what Mr. Pendleton says:

"My voice to-day is for conciliation; my voice is for compromise, and it is but the echo of the voice of my constituents. I beg you, gentlemen, who with me represent the Northwest; you who with me represent the State of Ohio; you who with me represent the city of Cincinnati—beg you, gentlemen to hear that voice. If you will not; if you find conciliation impossible; if your differences are so great that you cannot or will not reconcile them, *then, gentlemen, let the seceding States depart in peace; let them establish their Government and empire, and work out their destiny according to the wisdom which God has given them.*"

It is not our present purpose to dissect General McClellan's record, but we cannot forego the opportunity to place in juxtaposition the directly antagonistic opinions which he has expressed upon this vital and practical question. In his letter of acceptance he says:

"So soon as it is clear, or even probable, that our present adversaries are ready for peace *upon the basis of the Union*, we should exhaust all the resources of statesmanship practiced by civilized nations and taught by the traditions of the American people consistent with the honor and interests of the country to secure such peace, re-establish the Union, and guarantee for the future the constitutional rights of every State. The Union is the one condition of peace; we ask no more. * * * * *If a frank, earnest, and persistent effort to obtain these objects should fail, the responsibility for ulterior consequences will fall upon those who remain in arms against the Union; but the Union must be preserved at all hazards.*"

So that one of the Chicago nominees is a War Democrat, who is determined to preserve the Union "at all hazards," and the other a Peace Democrat, who stands pledged to acknowledge the independence of the rebel Confederacy, without striking another blow for the Union. But we resume our extracts from Mr. Pendleton's speech. He continues:

"My colleague (Mr. Stanton) said the other day that war seemed inevitable. He said the end of that war was dissolution and disunion. If he said truly, if he judged wisely, in God's name let us leap over the intervening agony of war, and come to the end and conclusion at once.

"If George III. had conciliated his colonies, how much wiser a man history would have proclaimed him! If, failing to conciliate, he had allowed the separation without the disgrace and defeat of the Revolutionary war, how much wiser a man still would he have been!"

Votes and Dodges of George H. Pendleton.

Thus, on the 10th of July, 1861, Mr. Pendleton, with only ten others, including such patriots as Burnett, of Kentucky; Reid, of Missouri; Vallandigham, Voorhees, and Wood, voted against the bill for the collection of the revenue in seceded States. The bill was passed by 136 to 11.

July 15, 1861, he *dodged* a vote upon Mr. McClernand's preamble and resolution declaring that "a portion of the people of the United States, in violation of their constitutional obligations, have taken up arms against the National Government," and pledging the House to vote "any amount of money," and "any number of men which may be necessary to insure a speedy and effectual suppression of such rebellion." Only five members voted against the resolutions. Mr. Pendleton's name appears in the proceedings only a few lines above the record of this vote.

July 18, 1861, Mr. Pendleton voted against the bill providing "increased revenue from imports." The bill was passed—yeas, 82; nays, 48.

July 29, 1861, Mr. Pendleton voted against the bill "to provide additional revenues for defraying the expenses of the Government, and maintaining the public credit." The bill was passed—yeas, 77; nays, 60.

July 30, 1861, Mr. Pendleton voted to lay on the table the "bill to increase the number of cadets in the Military Academy at West Point."

gressmen, and such leaders of the Republican party as Simon Cameron, Alexander K. McClure, Thaddeus Stevens, Hannibal Hamlin, and John W. Forney. To offset the possible influence of McClellan stumping as a soldier Democrat, the *Gazette* emphasized that Generals Grant, Meade, Hooker, Butler and others were also Democrats, but convinced Union men, some of whom were even acquiring radical tendencies. The issue devoted to McClellan was extremely popular and was widely copied by the press..

To reach all the leading newspapers of the day, arrangements for delivering the *Gazette* were made with postmasters whose loyalty to the Union cause had been established. Sixty-five Pennsylvania postmasters, representing every county in the state but two, were recipients of copies of each edition. In Philadelphia, Forney's *Press* served as a distribution point where mail agents called to pick up their bundles. By mail, by Adams Express, or by personal delivery, Union newspapers received 200 copies of each issue of the *Gazette*. The *New York Times*, the *Washington Chronicle*, the *Baltimore American*, the *Harrisburg Telegraph* and the *Pittsburgh Courier* all reprinted items from the *Gazette*.

In New Jersey, all but two counties received 200 copies each, and the nearby city of Camden regularly received 400 copies in addition to thousands that were delivered for pickup by farmers. Certain issues of the *Gazette* were placed on the busiest railroads and distributed to passengers that went from Camden to New York. Altogether, 560,000 copies of the *Gazette* were circulated in six weeks. The value of the work of the Board of Publication was inestimable, and the officers and directors of the League regarded it as the most important of its undertakings.[39]

Lincoln's plurality of 400,000 votes out of the four million votes cast brought joy at The Union League. For the Board of Publication, it provided temporary relief from its efforts, but the work of the Military Committee and those involved in various soldiers' relief agencies only increased. Wounded troops had been returning home daily. To meet the constant call for volunteers during 1864, the Military Committee raised three more regiments, the 183rd, 196th, and 198th Pennsylvania Volunteers, known respectively as the Fourth, Fifth, and Sixth Union League Regiments. The 183rd, or Fourth Union League Regiment, fought in the battles begun at Spottyslvania Court House, where a large number of troops were killed and wounded. The Fifth was sent to Illinois to guard Confederate prisoners, and the Sixth was ordered to the front at Petersburg, taking its position with the Army of the Potomac. Almost $100,000 contributed by League members went toward the raising of the first six regiments and initiating a seventh.[40]

The large sums of money expended by the various committees for the war effort would have been more than enough to pay for the new club house that was slowly rising on Broad Street. But the subscribers to the 20-year bonds made no complaint, and were as pleased as the officers and directors with their move. The League House was designed by John Fraser and built by John Crump. Its architecture reflected the tastes of the day, and its elegant interior was intended to suit all the needs of a peacetime club.

A better site could not have been chosen than the rectangular lot located on the west side of Broad Street between Sansom and Moravian, bounded by open areas on three sides. It gave Fraser the opportunity to provide an architectural concept that might have suffered under the shadow of later styles. A contemporary account described the design as being "in the French Renaissance style, having the peculiar effect of hospitality, belonging to that class of architecture, and none of the stern forbidding aspect too common among the buildings of the present day."[41]

"The facades are of granite, brick and brownstone, the base course being of granite; the rest of the building is of brick with the exception of the steps and main entrance which are entirely of brownstone. The angles of the building have brownstone rustic quoins, and the sills, architraves and pediments of the windows are of the same material. The entrance is approached from a platform from each side of which broad flights of circular steps descend to the pavement; on the front of the platform opposite the entrance are four pedestals surmounted by columns in couplings; between the couplings there is a projection six feet in depth and twelve feet wide, which is surrounded by a balustrade; this is designed as a rostrum for public speakers." . . . "The building is covered by a French or Mansard roof, above which rises a tower twelve feet square, which stands in the center of the front on Moravian Street and forms a picturesque break in the lines of the roof. The tower is to be surmounted by a vane of wrought iron and railing of the same material." Completion of the building was delayed by numerous strikes, bad weather, and a shortage of materials.[42]

The interior of the League House was marked by a spacious hall 14 feet wide, which opened onto a balcony above a charming nineteenth century garden that faced Fifteenth Street. On either side of the hall on the Broad Street end were a parlor and a smoking room, each 24 by 40 feet. Along the Sansom Street side were a reception room, the director's office, the publication room, and a private dining room. The principal dining room overlooked the garden. Opposite the reception room, a broad staircase led from the first to the second floor. Its hand-turned wooden balusters and gaslight flickering from two French style bronze figurines at the base of the staircase were new to Philadelphians.

At the top of the staircase, Sully's painting of Washington greeted the member and visitor, as it does today. A hall, equal in width to the one of the first floor, connected the library, which looked out on Broad Street, with the banquet room at the west end. Other rooms corresponded to those on the main floor, and all were connected by sliding doors. The third floor was reserved for employes; kitchen facilities and storerooms were in the basement, where the first billiard rooms were also located.[43]

It was expected that by the end of March, 1865, the League House would be fully furnished and ready for occupancy. But further delays caused by wartime priorities deferred the official opening until May 11. On that day, the League anticipated that its guest of honor would be the president of the United States.

Work on the League House in no way distracted members from the responsibilities to which they were committed, or from closely observing the daily course of the war. Since the League's annual meeting in 1864, events had moved with startling rapidity. News was received that Charleston, S.C., had been evacuated by Confederate troops on February 19. The 213th Regiment Pennsylvania Volunteers —the Seventh Union League Regiment—broke camp and moved South two weeks later, and on April 3, Richmond fell to the Union army. On April 4, the day of Lincoln's second inaugural, Charles Gibbons, representing The Union League, conducted a solemn ceremony at Independence Hall to commemorate the fall of the Confederate capitol.[44] Four days later, the 214th Regiment Pennsylvania Volunteers—the Eighth Union League Regiment—also departed for the South. Then on April 9, General Robert E. Lee met with General Grant and surrendered. Official news of the surrender of Lee at Appomattox Court House did not reach Philadelphia until 9:30 the next night. The original telegraph message, which was hurried to Forney's *Press*, was retrieved by Mrs. Forney and Louise Claghorn and taken to the League, where it was received with unrestrained jubilation. The news spread through the city like wildfire, and outdoor celebrations were held throughout the entire weekend. The Union League ordered a special salute of 200 guns.[45]

On Friday, the 14th of April, President Abraham Lincoln was shot through the head at Ford's Theater, and died the following morning. At the Petersen house where the president had been taken in a coma, Secretary of War Stanton interrogated eyewitnesses whose statements were recorded in shorthand by the legless Corporal James Tanner. This testimony, which immediately implicated John Wilkes Booth as

Thomas Sully

GEORGE WASHINGTON AT THE BATTLE OF TRENTON

the murderer, was never introduced as evidence in the trial of the alleged conspirators. Later, in 1917, still unpublished, the original document was presented to the archives of the League by Corporal Tanner.[46]

News of the assassination reached Philadelphia on Saturday morning. Joy was turned to grief and then to indignation and rage. The city was draped in black. Clergymen delivered hastily prepared sermons and Mayor Henry proclaimed a day of mourning. City Council named The Union League as the responsible institution to receive the body of the President upon its arrival in Philadelphia.[47]

Within hours after the League received the tragic news, a special meeting was called to make arrangements for a mass memorial service on the following Monday. Addresses were made by J. Gillingham Fell, Morton McMichael, Charles Gibbons, and Horace Binney, Jr. Other officers of the League also spoke with deep emotion. The Reverend Phillips Brooks, rector of the prestigious Holy Trinity Church, conducted a moving religious service. Frederick Fraley and Judge John C. Knox introduced dramatic resolutions that contained warnings of the possibility of a new rebellion by the South of which the assassination was felt to be a harbinger.[48] It was this same fear that prompted Lieutenant Colonel T. Ellwood Zell, who had formed the Pennsylvania Chasseurs with the assistance of the League's Military Committee, to plan the association of the Military Order of the Loyal Legion. So bitter were the proceedings at the memorial service that later commentators regarded them as vindictive.[49]

There were many tributes that came from League members; some remain hidden in diaries and correspondence, others were published and widely distributed. They ranged from modest appraisals of Lincoln to furious denunciations of Democrats and Copperheads, whose hostility toward Lincoln will live forever in history. Philadelphia and the nation were overwhelmed by a mass of Lincoln literature, canonizing and hagiographic. Boker's tribute to the last victim of the war was in his poem, "Our Heroic Themes." It was read at the request of Oliver Wendell Holmes before the Phi Beta Kappa Society at Harvard. Unfortunately, it has escaped the attention of present-day Lincoln anthologies, even though some critics regard it as one of the best of many poems eulogizing Lincoln.[50]

Thomas Stewardson, Jr., an early member of the League, was on the committee to receive the body of the president when it arrived at Independence Hall on April 23. He wrote affectionately of Lincoln as he "lay lifeless, gentle and tender, honest, open and pure." "Well so it had to be," he added, "but if that stab has not struck slavery the death blow, through the body of the Great Emancipator, then

UNION LEAGUE
NOTICE!

The Members are requested to meet at

THE HALL,

COR. OF FOURTH AND FEDERAL STS.

ON SATURDAY AFTERNOON,

AT 2 O'CLOCK,

For the purpose of proceeding to Philadelphia, and participating in the obsequies of our late President

ABRAHAM LINCOLN

Members will appear in Dark Clothing, White Gloves and Crape upon their Left Arm. *Badges* and *Gloves* can be procured at the League Room.

All Loyal Citizens who sympathize with us, and desire to participate are invited to join us.

BY ORDER OF COMMITTEE.

SAMUEL HUFTY,

April 21, 1865. CHAIRMAN.

S. Chew, Printer, No. 13 Market Street, below Front, Camden, N. J.

possibly Lincoln had died in vain, which it were treason against God's Providence to believe."[51]

Henry Charles Lea, however, wrote differently. In his last pamphlet relating to the war, *The Record of the Democratic Party*, which the League published in the summer of 1865, there could be no question of his feelings. "Since the surrender of the rebels, and the assassination of Mr. Lincoln, also, the hopelessness of the cause of slavery and state rights has stilled all rising agitation; and the mourning of a nation has forced those who lately attacked our chief Magistrate with ceaseless venom to beslime his memory with yet more nauseous praise."[52]

Privately, Lea communicated his reflections on Lincoln, which were also those of The Union League, to Charles Elliot Norton. "History presents many grander figures than that of Abraham Lincoln, but none who will preserve so firm a hold upon the affections of a people. His very weaknesses sprung from the traits which serve to attach a people to its ruler, while his uprightness and homely sagacity neutralized them in action. Had he been loftier he would have been less appreciated—and possibly less successful in his administration. It is singular that in our brief career we would have furnished to the world, in Washington and Lincoln, two perfect exemplars—one of the aristocratic and the other of democratic republicanism. His tragic end was all that was wanting to put the seal upon the tender remembrance with which he will be enshrined in our annals. I had three or four interviews with him last year and was much impressed by the kindly forbearance with which he strove to discharge the complicated duties of his office, and I believe that those loved him best who were brought most in contact with him. Peace be with him for he has deserved well of his country and mankind."[53]

Although the war had ended, the League mustered its last regiment, the Ninth. With its departure for the South on April 26, all recruiting came to an end. When the records of its Military Committee were filed away, along with other precious documents of the war, the League House was ready to be opened, but the gala celebration scheduled for May 11, 1865 to mark the occasion was suspended out of respect to the martyred president. Instead, a formal reception was held the following month at which General Grant was the guest of honor. He was received with great enthusiasm, and with the stump of a cigar clamped between his teeth, he shook hands with visitors for three hours. Grant was also in town to accept the gift of a home on Chestnut Street presented by the citizens of Philadelphia.[54]

In two years and five months The Union League, which might never have come into existence but for the Civil War, had done more to uphold American institutions than any other single organization that sprang up during the war. Its founders formerly had had no thought of establishing a permanent social club, but finding themselves unable to endure the existing order of social life, they withdrew to form a social club with a patriotic commitment. From its new position, the club was better able to attract a community of men with many viewpoints for the support of the administration, and to counteract the influences of Northern secessionist sympathizers. The private outpouring of hundreds of thousands of dollars to publish and distribute a literature of propaganda, organize fighting regiments, and attend to the welfare of soldiers, veterans and their families was heretofore unknown. Nor were the League's efforts confined to the homefront; 555 League members were represented in all of the branches and fought in most of the campaigns of the Union Army and Navy.

After two major elections, the diverse political elements responsible for these undertakings were gradually drawn into the Republican orbit. In spite of the League's insistence on a nonpartisan political stand, its members had come to identify themselves with the Republican Party more as a movement in American life than as a political party. This explains why men like Daniel Dougherty and his many associates, constantly claiming their adherence to the old Democracy, acted and voted as staunch Republicans. Many members who before the war had been apathetic or indifferent to American slavery had changed their minds and become active antislavery fighters, largely because of their association with the League radicals, Charles Gibbons, Abraham Barker, James Miller McKim, and numerous others. Under the influence of Henry Charles Lea, Stephen Colwell, and the post-Civil War economists and reformers, the involvement of League members in municipal problems soon became evident until there was no further question that the focus of the League's peacetime work would be turned in this direction. Many League members remained ambivalent on these later issues, but most agreed that the great purposes for which The Union League was organized had been accomplished. The Confederacy was crushed, slavery was no more, and many Northern Democrats were writhing in defeat.

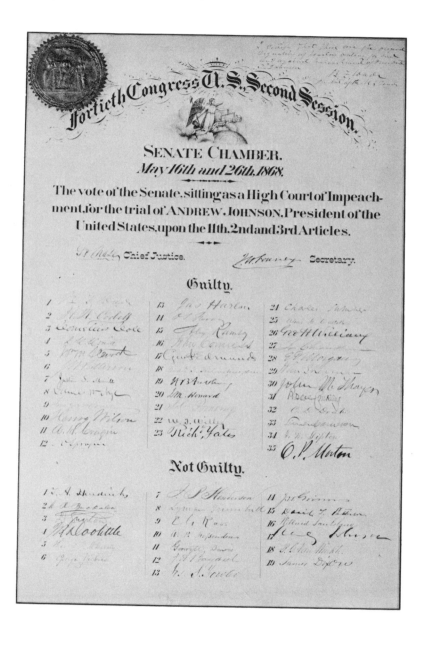

IV

❧

Patriotism and Politics

IMMEDIATELY following Lincoln's assassination, the corporate body of The Union League of Philadelphia pledged its whole-hearted support to Andrew Johnson. It expected him to take steps that would restore the Southern states to the Union. Johnson moved swiftly in this direction, adopting Lincoln's Reconstruction plan and adding a few modifications of his own. The League, in a gesture of good will, presented Johnson with its highest award, the gold medal of the League.[1]

While preparations were being made for the presentation, Johnson asked Carl Schurz to tour the South and report on social conditions and attitudes in the defeated Confederacy, an idea that met with the approval of the more radical League members.[2] More and more, the radicals were adopting the views of Thaddeus Stevens that the victor should give its terms to the vanquished, precisely as if the armies of the South were a conquered foreign nation. As it turned out, the South had taken heart from the support of its Northern sympathizers, and stubbornly refused to move from treason to reason or to accept less than equal status in the Union. The South, Boker wrote, sought "the right of equal representation in the counsels of the Nation, a power which they had forfeited by their vain appeal to arms."[3] Furthermore, as Boker summarized in his report of 1865, "The first fruit which the rebels and their Northern friends hoped for from these manoeuvres, was reorganization of their odious social system, and a practical restoration of the institution of slavery. Though the slaves had been freed by our armies from the dominion of their masters, these same masters now proposed to plunge their freedom into a more degrading slavery to the law. Nothing but the vigilance and the wise determination of the government prevented the Southern States from lapsing into a worse barbarism than that from which they just emerged."[4]

Schurz's realistic findings were reminiscent of Sidney George Fisher's insights into the unyielding prewar attitude of many Southerners. The report was distasteful to Johnson, but it so impressed the League that it issued an abridged edition of the document, originally published by the Senate, for popular distribution. Of the 56,380 copies of various pamphlets distributed by the League since the surrender at Appomattox, none excited as much attention as Schurz's report, which appeared in an edition of 20,000 copies.[5] By early 1866, the League realized that Johnson did not espouse its views on restoring the Union and on reconstruction measures. It was not long before he offended radical Republicans within and without the League. In the opinion of the League, Johnson was to become guilty of more "treachery than that which inspired the recent rebellion."[6]

Before Schurz's report was circulated, Georgia, Louisiana, and Mississippi, three of the states he had visited, enacted "Black Codes" which were intended to confine the freedmen in these states to the land, denying them mobility. Congress reacted by enlarging the powers of the Freedmen's Bureau, which had been established shortly before Lincoln's assassination to protect the rights of freed slaves. The new legislation was vetoed by Johnson. The presidential assumption that Congress had no right to legislate for unrepresented Southern states so angered the League that it accused Johnson of abrogating the pledges to restore the Union he had made in his first message to Congress, and of being unworthy of the man whom he had succeeded. There were even accusations of treason. Protesting League members demanded that their directors give immediate support to Congress.[7]

The officers of the League sought a solution to the enmity between the North and South on terms that would be dictated by the federal government, not by the ideologists of Confederacy. Such terms could have been reached, but the opportunity was lost with Johnson's veto of the Civil Rights Act of 1866, which would have extended to blacks the same civil rights granted to male whites. This setback was particularly aggravating to the 200 and more League members who had become involved in civic and legal actions to secure open public accommodations for Philadelphia Negroes, and particularly in legislation permitting their use of street cars. Fed by the new status of the Negro freedmen, the same fears that had been aroused by black troops marching through the city in a time of national crisis were again rampant.[8] Johnson's veto greatly angered the League men.

The national struggle for civil rights was focused locally in Phila-delphia. In the face of a revived postwar Negrophobia, *The Age,* once the spokesman of Copperheads, now gloated over fresh oppor-tunities to mock those efforts that favored the Negro, and to support the Democrats.

The position taken by the Philadelphia League in reconstruction measures, in helping the freedmen, and in postwar industrial de-velopment, has been distorted by partisans of the South, by Southern Democrats, and by some contemporary revisionists. These historians had accepted and spread the stereotype of the New York and Philadelphia Leagues as secret organizations formed to uphold the Republican Party. By imposing this image of the Philadelphia League, these writers started a chain of error that has continued to the present day.[9]

The first step in the process of discrediting the League was to identify it with secret proUnion societies of the middle West and far West. The second step was in associating the postbellum Loyal Leagues and the Union League of America with the Philadelphia club. According to the allegations made, the Philadelphia League maintained an alliance with the other organizations which reappeared in the South during Reconstruction. No evidence can be found to support these claims.

Both the Loyal Leagues and the Union Leagues of America sprung up again in the South after the war. Some were intended to foster interest in the Republican Party, others to sponsor a variety of activities. All continued to use the League name. In the case of the Alabama League, the name was conveniently appropriated.[10] Their leadership was not necessarily northern; a few may have been former members of Northern leagues, but this has not been sub-stantiated. The men who were active in the Philadelphia League during and after the war built their reputations with the agencies involved in social reform, and in programs to educate and elevate the former slaves as quickly as possible. To associate them with the negative activity of carpetbaggers or of the postwar leagues has no historical justification.[11] The word "carpetbaggers" unfortunately has assumed the same pejorative meaning after the war as "Copperheads" during the war.

Unlike the Philadelphia and New York clubs, other organizations that adopted the name "league" were not concerned with the dis-ruption of social life within their communities. No corporate or unofficial connection existed between the Philadelphia League and the Loyal Leagues, or the Union League of America. The latter two were founded in 1863, and neither had the financial power or held

the social position of the metropolitan clubs. They worked independently, and drew their membership from other social levels.
Their political zeal and fidelity to the Union was no less important,
but because they shared the common names of "Union," "Loyal," and
"League" they were easily confused with The Union League.[12] Like
the smaller, local leagues, they quickly declined after the war. The
smaller Leagues inspired by the Philadelphians in other sections of
the country responded to the crisis of the war, and had no need to
perpetuate their work in time of peace. They disbanded after their
purpose had been fulfilled. If they had been the offspring of the
Republican Party, it would have been to the advantage of the party
to prolong their lives.

The Leagues of Philadelphia and New York continued as corporate
institutions with patriotic and social commitments. Those of Boston
and Chicago lingered on for a few years, then suspended their
activity, and decades later were revived within a new social context.
Each club maintained an independent political viewpoint satisfactory
to a heterogeneous membership.[13]

The complexity of Reconstruction and the political and industrial
transformation of Philadelphia greatly concerned The Union League.
There was much interest in the expansion of the industries in which
Pennsylvania was preeminent—coal, iron, and steel—and in the
state's transportation system, all suggesting new potential sources of
power and political influence. So great were the peacetime changes
that a number of influential League founders recognized the need to
reevaluate the League's raison d'etre in the light of the postwar era.

Happy with the League's growth as a social club, and satisfied
with the impressive receptions offered to important military and
political figures in honor of their patriotic achievement, thoughtful
men who had carefully guided the League through a tragic war
now questioned the need for an alliance with any political party. If
the purposes for which the League was founded, the defeat of the
Confederacy, the abolition of slavery, and the quelling of Southern
sympathizers in the North, had been accomplished, could not the
League be content as a gentlemen's club with a patriotic commitment?
It is possible that the League might have rested on the glories of its
wartime accomplishments had it not been for President Johnson's
conduct in office, which was antithetical to all of the goals for which
the League had fought. Under the threat of losing its hard-won
victories, withdrawal from political activity seemed impossible.[14]

The League's new concern stretched from municipal to national
politics; it moved to aid each level of government to support legislation that in the League's judgment would reunite the Union. The
gains of the war would be hollow indeed if the nation's laws were not

revised, and if men espousing the principles of sound government were not put into office. With these goals uppermost, the fall elections of 1866 called for even greater exertions on the part of the League than did the wartime elections. The Board of Publication was reorganized, a committee of 76 was named to direct the League's election activity and J. Gillingham Fell, the second president of the League, held together a membership of radicals and moderates.[15]

Philadelphia Republicans, with the aid of the League, secured the nomination and election of Morton McMichael for mayor. Pennsylvania Republicans nominated John W. Geary, a Democrat, as their gubernatorial candidate. Hiester Clymer, chosen by the Democrats for their gubernatorial candidate, won the support of Johnson Republicans, who organized a number of Johnson-Clymer clubs. A fierce political battle was underway.[16]

In an attempt to influence the coming elections and recover congressional confidence, Andrew Johnson undertook a Northern campaign tour known as the "swing around the circle." His first stop was Philadelphia. Here he was welcomed by the Merchants Exchange, the city's insurance and brokerage center, some of whose members had had Copperhead ties, and ignored by the Corn Exchange, a leading bank that had raised a regiment under its name. When Johnson marched past the brownstone Union League House, his presence was not even acknowledged. Mayor McMichael, still editor of the *North American*, and now a vice-president of the League, absented himself from the city, possibly to avoid greeting the president. However, another League member, financier Anthony J. Drexel, thought it more appropriate to welcome the president and so joined with the Merchants Exchange.

For the third time in his career, Johnson addressed Philadelphians on the issues of peace, the Union, and the Constitution. While he carefully avoided reference to Democratic candidates and their campaign clubs, he condemned the "radical Union League," and called all who carried the name conspirators ready to "subvert the Constitution of the Union." On the following day, Forney's *Press* noted the absence of public enthusiasm for Johnson; McMichael's *North American* confined its comments to stating that excitement had been provided to amuse the city, and that the parade was enhanced by the presence of Admiral Farragut and Generals Grant and Meade. Gibson Peacock, of *The Evening Bulletin*, in a subtle twist, reprinted Johnson's Philadelphia speech of 1863 which had advocated hanging traitors. The three League newspapermen reduced the president's visit to an insignificant event.[17]

The Convention of Southern Unionists quickly overshadowed Johnson's visit a few days later. Another group of Northern Unionists met separately, and later joined in a parade through the city. Governor Curtin welcomed the convention, and Morton McMichael introduced Frederick Douglass, whose presence galled the editor of *The Age.* The League offered the hospitality of its quarters and exchanged views with the delegates on the future of the South. They were encouraged to temper antiNorthern sentiment where possible, and many of them did. Some chose to organize associations emulating The Union League. These Leagues, believed to have been founded in Virginia, are not identified, however.[18] Among the Southern delegates were the proUnion Tennessee radicals led by the rabble-rousing Parson William G. Brownlow. The Parson sought every opportunity to impress Northerners with his Unionist stand. At Independence Hall, he placed himself in the forefront of the convention. At The Union League, he managed to secure for himself a choice position on the balcony where he could see and hopefully be seen by an assemblage estimated at 100,000 people. The Parson's behavior helped to efface the visit of President Johnson, his fellow Tennesseean.[19]

The Convention received considerable notice in the Northern press, and artists from *Harper's Weekly* sketched the Parson, the delegates, and the dignitaries as they paraded before the League House. Boker recounted the event and the discussions in the League's *Annual Report* for 1866, thus allaying all suspicion of secret liaisons with the Southern Unionists.[20]

Four days after the departure of the Southern delegates, the League House was set on fire. A crowd of the Copperhead clique watching the flames soar cheered when the blaze was at its worst. The extensive physical damage was attributed to an unknown arsonist and accepted as an unpleasant fact. However, the loss of valuable war documents caused great consternation. Fortunately, insurance compensated for building repairs, and the League rewarded the firemen for their heroism in controlling the fire.[21]

In the course of the campaign of 1866, the Board of Publication issued 17 pamphlets in editions that ranged from 1,000 to 100,000 copies of each, and deluged the state with a total distribution of almost one million copies. More than 2,500 requests for campaign literature reached the desk of the Board. Although it published the platform of the National Union Party of Pennsylvania, another name for the Republican Party, the League's official resolutions presented a position which was independent of the platform. Four pamphlets explained the League's views on Reconstruction; two assailed Johnson, one was the official campaign biography of John W. Geary, and another impugned Hiester Clymer, the Democratic candidate. Six of the campaign documents appeared in German.[22]

The platform of the National Union Party cautiously approached the issues that divided Republicans over the Reconstruction policies of President Johnson. Its carefully worded tribute to the president was an expedient to avoid offending voters who still viewed Johnson with respect. However, disenchantment with Johnson almost became official when two important state Republican leaders, William D. Kelley and Alexander K. McClure, both League members, joined with Thaddeus Stevens in breaking with the president. Simon Cameron, however, wooed Johnson a while longer as he maneuvered to seize control of the state political machinery. The state party platform was clear on other issues. The former Confederate states should not be entitled to representation in Congress until their loyalty was unquestionably established. The protection of American industries was strongly favored, and recognition of Negro rights was emphasized in the belief that their "freedom shall not be a mockery."[23]

In sharp contrast to the Pennsylvania Republican platform, the League made no attempt to bid for Johnson's favor, or that of any of his supporters. The *Address,* prepared by Henry Charles Lea and delivered at the League prior to its publication, was openly hostile in its attitude toward the "unscrupulous man of narrow mind, violent passions and despotic tendencies" who "occupies the Chief Magistracy of the Nation." This severe condemnation of Johnson underlay the congressional and gubernatorial campaign of 1866.[24]

The severity with which Lea attacked Johnson was matched by Lindley Smyth, who assailed the president for his veto of the Freedmen's Bureau Bill, and attempted to convince voters that if Southern Democrats were returned to office, they would again reunite with their Northern colleagues to the detriment of the nation. The war was over, but every opportunity was seized upon to expose Democrats to the issues that once identified them with Copperheads and secessionists.[25] In publishing the views of Edwin Percy Whipple and George Sewall Boutwell, the League continued to drive at the same point. Whipple's contemptuous description of Johnson as "insincere," "stubborn," "cunning as well as unreasonable" was reinforced by the Massachusetts radical Boutwell, who charged that Johnson suffered from "fear, hatred, and ambition," and was the author of a plot to amalgamate Southern Democrats with sympathetic colleagues in the North in order to seize control of Congress and thrust the country into a new war. Repeating the charges that Johnson, or the Democrats, might renew hostilities, initiate another rebellion, or at least capture the Congress, was not an uncommon refrain in the League literature.[26]

Oddly, The Union League's antiDemocratic literature did not

affect its support of the choice of a Democrat as the Republican candidate for Pennsylvania's governor. Three months before his nomination, Major General John W. Geary still considered himself a Democrat! In assenting to Geary's nomination, the League believed it was supporting a candidate who not only possessed the attributes for winning an election, but could not be corrupted by the postwar politics of either party. Geary's Scotch-Irish ancestry was emphasized, together with his Presbyterian background and the care he gave to his widowed mother. Accounts of his life as postmaster in territorial California, as a soldier in the Mexican and Civil Wars, and as the governor of Kansas during the border warfare in 1856 presented him as the model gubernatorial candidate.[27] Hiester Clymer, lacking Geary's background, or even that of a soldier, was cast in the odious role of a Northern Copperhead of the caliber of Vallandingham of Ohio and Woodward of Pennsylvania. Clymer was an able man, but as a supporter of Johnson's Reconstruction plan he invited the derogatory political descriptions of him published in the League's campaign literature.[28]

Despite his political background, which a number of Republicans continued to question, Geary's campaign speeches placed him in the camp of the civil rights men, and marked him as an exponent of the principles outlined in the *Address* of The Union League. It was a hard-fought campaign, ending in a Republican victory. Geary won by a state-wide majority of 17,178 votes, and an overwhelming number of radical Republicans, men who hoped to influence the fate of the president, were sent to Congress. The second Republican governor of Pennsylvania warranted the support he received from the League. Not only did he fulfill campaign promises, but he upheld the interpretation of the Civil Rights Bill, challenged the power of the railroads, advocated safety legislation for mines after the Avondale mine disaster in 1869, and introduced better procedures for prisoners seeking pardons.[29]

During the campaign, League members read accounts of Northern carpetbaggers invading the South, and allegations that the Southern Leagues were engaged in conspiracy with the Leagues of the North to win Negroes over to the Republican Party. The Freedmen's Bureau was considered to be part of the conspiracy, and President Johnson looked upon the Bureau as a blemish in the Reconstruction process, and charged it with capturing the Negro vote for the Republicans. Responsibility for the conduct of the Southern Loyal Leagues was attributed to the Philadelphia League.[30] By the time Governor Geary delivered his inaugural address, the constitution of the Alabama branch of the Union League of America was being circulated throughout that state, and was imputed to have been inspired by the Leagues of Philadelphia and New York City.[31] This presumptive, unsupported charge is still viewed in many historical accounts as a Republican measure to avenge itself on the South by imposing black rule over white.[32] The source of this allegation lies in the intransigeance of the defeated plantation holders who, although forced to surrender their arms, were unwilling to surrender their hegemony.[33]

In sharp contrast to such activity, the interest of prominent League members in helping liberated slaves can be traced to the summer of 1862, even before the organization of the League. Blacks, abandoned by their masters when Union forces occupied the area of Port Royal, South Carolina, were soon faced with hunger and other privations. Their needs brought the first contingent of Northern men and women, black and white, to the South to provide immediate assistance. Known as the Pennsylvania Freedmen's Relief Association, founded in 1862, this group was a harbinger of the Freedmen's Bureau, and in time received the wholehearted support of The Union League. Stephen Colwell was president of the Association, and James Miller McKim was a prime mover in its affairs. McKim later became corresponding secretary and chief lobbyist for the Freedmen's Bureau. Other members of the League also served as officers. In addition to providing food and clothing, the Relief Association introduced a system of basic education for illiterate slaves of the Sea Islands, an effort abhorrent to Southern whites, who saw it as a nefarious Republican plot, and as a form of carpetbagging. The Association's work spread to wherever the South was liberated from Confederate hands, and as the success of Union forces mounted, more and more Philadelphians were absorbed in the undertaking and moved South to help.[34] The League continued to be involved in promoting Negro education in the South long after the end of Reconstruction, when others had abandoned their efforts.[35]

With the organization of the Freedmen's Bureau in 1865, after the persistent lobbying of McKim and many other delays, various aid societies were consolidated into it. General Oliver Otis Howard, an honorary member of the League and founder of Howard University in Washington, D.C., was named to head the Bureau. It was the work of this Bureau that Johnson found especially repugnant, and in an attempt to frustrate it, he vetoed the bill that would have made it a federal agency. League members were furious, and those who had worked so hard to pass the legislation through both houses of Congress were bitterly resentful. It is a curious fact that the public reaction of the League was ignored by Southern publicists and later by historians and apologists for the South. It is also ironic that the unwholesome aspects of Reconstruction in which the League did not participate were nonetheless attributed to it.[36]

In April, 1867, after Johnson's vetoes of Reconstruction measures were overridden, the New York League proposed that the clubs of Philadelphia, Boston, and Chicago meet with it to discuss measures to assist Reconstruction and secure prosperity. Specifically, the New York League intended to promote the Republican Party as a means to attain these ends. This idea did not originate with the New York League, however, but came in response to the request of a number of Virginians who were eager to "harmonize the discordant interests around them, and who feared that the Reconstruction policy of Congress might be retarded or even thwarted in their State . . . ." A League committee representing New York, Boston, and Philadelphia visited Richmond in June with the object of planting the Republican Party in that state. However, factionalism among the Virginians hindered their organization, and the Philadelphians, looking upon the new relationship with skepticism, withdrew whatever support they had planned to offer.[37]

The Union League equated Reconstruction and reform with patriotism and constitutional amendments, which could best be realized by support of the Republican Party. Some League members did not accept this viewpoint. Others, chiefly reform radicals, helped to strengthen the Party in the North, but hesitated to preach the cause of the Republican Party in the South. Congressman William D. Kelley however, immediately went on a speaking tour that brought him to Mobile, Alabama, where he was accused of inciting an audience of 2,000 armed Negroes against 100 "respectable" whites who also attended his address. Offensive to both blacks and whites, the accusation continued, Kelley was an example of the "kind of control that would be exercised over the blacks by alien politicians," as some Northerners were described.[38] Walter Fleming, historian of the Reconstruction and the author of these and other distortions, erroneously wrote that the New York and Philadelphia Leagues withdrew from the South after the "first year or two of Reconstruction." In fact, however, the Philadelphia League, as a corporate institution, was not at all involved in the Southern activity he attributed to it. Northerners also were charged with speculating in railroads when they were eager to develop transportation, of introducing capitalistic farming to prevent a revival of the old plantation system, and of bringing industry to the South. As for the freedmen whom they wanted to transform into literate citizens so they could benefit from the advantages of their new position, innumerable stumbling blocks had to be cleared. George Boker, reflecting the views of the League, gave a somewhat exaggerated picture when he wrote that the Negro "appears better able to do without his master than his master is able to do without him."[39]

It was folly to expect that the South would or could transform itself into a peacetime society, divested of its former economic system, as if nothing had taken place. Millions of dollars in property had been destroyed or wrested from the South, its cities were scorched, its plantations wasted, its business disrupted, and its young men decimated. The bitterness of the defeated South turned to riots and midnight assassinations that struck at the black population.[40] The Loyal Leagues of the South were held responsible for this turn of events. And the fear that Negroes would vote Republican so inflamed those imbued with the "lost cause" of Southern glory that a virulent counterforce was launched, manifesting itself in the Knights of the White Camelia and the Ku Klux Klan. They struck blow upon blow against the freedmen and their white supporters at the close of the Johnson Administration. Responsibility for the organization of the Klan and its notorious activities was laid at the door of the Northern League. Older histories, and a number originating in the revisionist schools have made no attempt to examine and clarify this charge. The Klan was not the work of the Leagues, either those in the North or those in the South; it was spawned by the stubborn refusal of the planters and landowners to recognize the rights of the free Negro. Slavery was abolished, but blacks were still deprived of economic and other rights by those who had once held them in chains.[41]

Its obsession with the course of Reconstruction solidly placed The Union League in the camp of the extreme radicals to whom it had responded. Along with Thaddeus Stevens of Lancaster, Pennsylvania, and Charles Sumner, senator from Massachusetts, it supported the Fourteenth Amendment assuring the rights of citizenship and equal protection under the law for all, a measure that Johnson vetoed. Early in 1867, the Reconstruction Acts which established military districts in the South ordered the registration of all Negro and white males previously disqualified from voting. Southern whites realized that it would now be virtually impossible for them to win over the freedmen to the Democratic Party. The Acts were vetoed by Johnson, because he considered their consequences to be too harsh for the South, but Congress overrode his veto. Even though Johnson undertook to carry out the laws, hostility from the preponderantly radical Congress was so intense that from this time on rapport between the President and the Congress became impossible. The more generous and lenient philosophy toward the South which Lincoln had advocated was lost in the vindictive struggle between the Congress and Johnson.[42]

Congress was determined to be in full command of the Reconstruc-

tion process. Some of the radicals were so zealous in their desire to
see the black man adjust himself to his new freedom that they were
insensitive to the white Southerner, who also had to accommodate
himself to a new way of life. The difficult plight of the Southerner,
whose psychological adjustment was also a very real issue, was lost
in the heat of debate. During the summer of 1867, antiRepublican
riots throughout the South contributed further to the opposition of
the Congress to Johnson. Radicals and former abolitionists sounded
their first cry for the impeachment of President Johnson.[43]

Within the Philadelphia Union League, moderates urged restraint,
in conformity with Lincoln's plan for Reconstruction. But in Washington, restraint was abandoned in a drive to control the executive
power of the president. Moving in this direction the Congress passed
the Tenure of Office Act on March 2, 1867. In flat defiance of the
constitutional rule that the power to appoint implies the power to
remove, it restricted Johnson's power to appoint or remove cabinet
and other officers for whom Senate approval was required. Violation
of the Act was a high misdemeanor. Congress had thrown down the
gauntlet, and Johnson, by attempting to remove Secretary of War
Stanton, accepted the challenge. The radicals interpreted Johnson's
defiance as grounds for impeachment. More than a year passed between the passage of the Tenure of Office Act and the preparation of
the Articles of Impeachment. While the Senate finally cast its vote,
it failed by one vote to secure a conviction against Johnson on the
charge of "high misdemeanor" in office. An original copy of the
recorded vote, following the proceedings of May 16 and 26, in which
two members of the League participated, was later forwarded to the
League archives.[44]

One of the League members who voted to convict Johnson was
Simon Cameron, Lincoln's first secretary of war. Under pressure,
Cameron had resigned this office and accepted the appointment of
minister to Russia in 1862. Within a year he returned to the United
States to run for the office of senator, but lost in the election of
1863. In 1867, after carefully bringing together diverse political forces
from opposite ends of the state, his success was assured. His son,
J. Donald Cameron, and his son-in-law, Wayne MacVeagh, joined him
in the new alignment. It was the beginning of a powerful state organization, which was frequently charged with corruption. Cameron had
tremendous insight and the ability to take advantage of the lack of
unity among his opponents and of the divisions within the Republican
Party.[45]

Republican League members, vying for state and local office, were
either drawn into the Cameron orbit, or beaten. In local elections,

Republicans were pitted against one another, and men like Morton McMichael, frustrated by the inefficiency and indifferences of city government, frowned upon Cameron's manipulations. McMichael feared that the success of the political machinery, operating under the old Pennsylvania constitution, would perpetuate the profitable control by state legislators of local street paving, sewage, and sanitation operations. McClure differed with the Republican leadership, and Forney was too disillusioned to bid for political supremacy. Both underestimated Cameron's grasp of postwar politics. Cameron successfully won some factions, but offended others. He maintained a friendly association with League Secretary Boker, but he did not win McMichael's support. His shrewdness enabled him to reward self-seeking office holders, although many men remained beyond his political influence. The Cameron strategy worked efficiently, and while he won the support of individual League members, he made no attempt to win the League as a body. The machine was so well-organized that his son, J. Donald Cameron, succeeded him in the Senate in 1877, and the ambitious Matthew S. Quay inherited the mantle of party boss. But while the younger Cameron was admitted to the League, Quay was never accepted. Simon Cameron himself was suspended from the League in 1876 for reasons that have not been determined.[46]

In the year of Cameron's success, Democrats scored victories on their own. The old party was still vigorous in Pennsylvania. Without linking Cameron to the League, Democrats, to distract attention from their own activity, charged each of them with spending huge sums of money to gain their political ends. In fact, the League did spend huge sums which, according to its accounts, were poured into political and campaign literature. The allegations concerning Cameron's expenditures have never been upheld by evidence. The Democrats owed their local successes to widespread use of illegal certificates of naturalization at the polls, and in 1867, by playing on antiblack prejudices, they frightened white voters away from the Republicans.[47]

The activities of the Democrats did not escape the attention of Henry Charles Lea. In his writings on political subjects, including municipal reform, Lea epitomized scholarship and integrity. By applying the same criteria to political corruption that he used in his medieval studies, he gathered data that attributed the 1867 Democratic victories in Pennsylvania to fraud, particularly in Clearfield and Centre counties. In a documented analysis published by the League, Lea showed that many Irish, Welsh, and German immigrants who recently had moved into the interior of the state had questionable naturalization papers. Their election taxes were paid by the Democrats and immigrant voters were moved from one polling station to another to cast illegal ballots. In Philadelphia, specific areas and wards had been notorious for the same practices since the 1840's. Machine control was so strong that illegalities went uncontested. John W. Forney later stated that it was found that 5,000 citizenship papers had been issued in a two-week period prior to one election. The questionable papers were taken to the State Supreme Court which regarded them as *nisi prius* and therefore illegal.[48] Fearing an annual repetition of Democratic success, Republicans were determined to win the newly enfranchised black voters. At the same time that election irregularities were being studied, the League sponsored an essay contest on the processes of political organization and the selection of candidates for public office. Four prize-winning essays "opened no royal roads toward a solution of the difficult subject," but in their publication the League showed its concern with a problem that disturbed many Americans.[49]

The League was convinced of the need for honest men in office as a basis for good government. Its members firmly believed that Democratic strength would be reduced in the upcoming presidential election by Republican candidates of unquestioned integrity. But the membership found itself in a peculiar quandary over election procedures that governed the choice of Republican candidates. New guidelines were imperative. Too many incompetents were being chosen; they were so "unworthy that the character of the party has suffered."[50] Republican success was endangered. To what extent these reactions could be attributed to division within Republican ranks, or perhaps to the rise of machine politics. is not indicated in the records of the League. Faced with a presidential election, and with the knowledge that fraudulent voting was widespread, the Board chose to concentrate on exposing corrupt election practices. The issue of recommending new procedures for the selection of candidates was deferred.

Five months before the Republican Convention, The Union League met to propose General Grant as the Republican nominee for president. Although fully aware of the fact that the man who led the Union army to victory had never voted the Republican ticket, the League as a corporate body also urged his nomination at the upcoming Chicago Republican Convention. Following its warm endorsement of Grant, the League called a special meeting in the Spring of 1868 to resume the plan of consideration of good men for local office. After much debate, a resolution by Edward Shippen was adopted that "a ticket composed throughout of men not only upright but beyond suspicion or reproach" should become the League's objective, and support should be given to "men whom office seeks rather than men who are seeking office." The resolution was published by McMichael

in the *North American;* there was no question about the determination of the League to upgrade city government by supporting in deed
what it projected in theory.[51]

The League faced another problem that it could not resolve.
Galusha A. Grow, Speaker of the House in Lincoln's first administration, and the author of the Homestead Act, was chairman of the
Pennsylvania State Central Committee. He revived the defunct
Pennsylvania branch of the Union League of America, which had
disappeared after the war. Grow, to further himself politically, declared himself the "Grand President." In language that was borrowed
liberally from League literature, he based the appeal of the new
organization on semisecrecy, rituals, and other superficial attractions.
It was an act of demagoguery that failed to strike a responsive chord,
and added to the confusion of groups, North and South, that assumed
the magnetic names of "Union" and "League."[52]

As soon as Grant was nominated for president, the League began
to fund some of the state party literature. It also continued to publish
its own resolutions, addresses, and views on conditions in the South.
Henry Charles Lea continued to be a spokesman of the League,
opposing the Democrats with unprecedented vigor, and flaying their
presidential candidate Governor Horatio Seymour of New York, as
if the issues of the war remained to be fought. In an address that
associated Northern Democrats with Confederate generals, he warned
against voting for Seymour, who was courting former enemies of the
Union. In the election of Grant, Lea saw the possibility of bringing
together two systems that had been in opposition before and during
the war and had continued to oppose each other long after the fury
of battle had ended. Recalling the events that led to the war, and these
two conflicting forces, Lea explained: "On the one hand were the
traditions of feudalism, of caste, of class privileges, the reaction
against modern thought and liberty, which for three generations had
moulded every institution, and had trained the people to one unvary-
ing course of thought. On the other hand were the expansion of
progress, belief in the dignity of labor, faith in the liberty of thought
—in fine, the absolute right of every man to reason for himself and
to carve out his own destiny. That systems so antagonistic should,
sooner or later, measure their strength in deadly strife was inevitable." In Lea's opinion the "expansion of progress" meant a guarantee
of liberty for all Americans and the work of Reconstruction would
remain unfinished until this concept was fully put into practice by
the South.[53]

In its five years of experience, the League Board of Publication
had accumulated such an extensive number of contacts that it was

able to reach 1,478 election districts in the state and through them obtain the names and addresses of more than 28,000 voters. The state was deluged with over one million copies of newspapers and pamphlets that heralded Grant, and urged a Republican victory.[54] On the local ticket, the League committed itself to two of its highly respected members, M. Russell Thayer and Charles Gibbons.

Grant's victory over Seymour came as no surprise—he captured 26 out of 34 states—but reactions to the president-elect and to local losses, varied among the League membership. Gross fraud invaded the city. In Philadelphia, Judge M. Russell Thayer and Charles Gibbons, who had both lost the election by a narrow margin, were the victims of political bossism and its machinery. League Republicans refused to accept the results of the election; a legal contest followed, challenging the Democratic victors. Thayer won his challenge and took office as judge of the District Court, but Gibbons' bid for district attorney was not conclusive and a court battle ensued. Subsequently, Gibbons was forced to vacate his position to a man whose victory remained in doubt. Thus, the first effort by the League to support its own "irreproachable" men was only partly successful.[55]

The reaction to Grant's victory suggested an uncertainty within the League. At the annual meeting of 1869, Boker spoke of it in the following manner: "Some feared one thing, some another; but all feared something; and burdened their predictions with their fears. The vague unfounded dread lest Gen'l Grant should in someway prove unfaithful to the principles and the policy of the party which elected him, was the underlying idea of all this distrust." Critical members declared that Grant had said nothing during the campaign that committed him to the platform of the Republican Party. Perhaps to set these members at ease, the president-elect was invited to a private reception at the League shortly after his election. The only record made of this meeting noted "that a public mention of the occasion may seem to be a step beyond rigid propriety."[56]

Lindley Smyth, who had been a feverish worker for the election of Grant and director of the Board of Publication since the end of the war, proposed a number of resolutions that opened discussion on the League's political role. In an attempt to prevent recurrence of the problems produced by the League's involvement in the current election and its outcome, Smyth firmly stated: "That hereafter the League as an organization will not take part in the political contests of the Country unless the life of the nation or the perpetuation of republican institutions should again be jeopardized, but will continue its public action to such nonpartisan efforts as will tend to secure the purity of the ballot by the prevention and punishment of frauds and the adoption of such laws as will give members of all parties a fair and equal voice in the selection of their respective candidates." Concurring with Smyth were James L. Claghorn and Edward Shippen, whose loyalties to the League and the Republican Party were beyond reproach.[57]

Only a part of Smyth's resolution was adopted. Many members were convinced that the League's wartime work was done, and with the election of Grant its peacetime mission was to continue to uphold the Union and to pursue a course of political reform. The members generally believed that the League was not a monolithic arm of the Republican Party, although it had pledged its support to the party of Lincoln. The extent of the political involvement of the League became the subject of debate for several decades.

Smyth's views had a tremendous influence in refining the attitudes expressed by the Board and at annual meetings. The national victory which carried with it the shadow of local electoral malpractice had strengthened the Republican outlook of the League. It was strongly felt that fraudulent ballots, and the forging of naturalization papers were abuses that had to be fought to be eliminated. At this juncture, influenced by Smyth and a coterie of forceful men, the League undertook to combat corruption at the polls. Rewards were offered for the detection of false naturalization papers, huge posters were printed which exposed the evils of this practice, and pamphlets informing the electorate of Democratic frauds were distributed in every city precinct. It was one of the first of many steps taken by the League to reform voting procedures.

Following this educational approach the Board of Directors undertook to do what both parties hitherto had failed to do. Immediately after the election of President Grant, the League passed a resolution introduced by Charles Gibbons which established a committee to confer with counsel and with interested members of the state legislature on revising the system of registering voters prior to an election.[58] The existing system dated back to 1834, and was antiquated. The new system would reduce, if not prevent, fraud and illegal tampering with ballots. Dead people would no longer have innumerable ballots cast in their names! In April, 1869, the law was passed by the Pennsylvania state legislature, and was signed by Governor Geary. No sooner was it enacted as the Registry Act, than it was challenged as unconstitutional. Gibbons and William Meredith appealed the decision and the Act was upheld.[59]

George Boker hailed the Act as a measure of progress, noting that "its provisions bore equally hard on either party that might attempt the commission of frauds." It struck hard at "the half frauds at which good party men are expected to wink, and the whole frauds which

bad men practice." The law contained sound provisions for registration, but it was placed in the hands of a board of aldermen who
became registrars, had no intention of enforcing the Act, and saw in
the new procedure fresh prospects for their own benefit. Those eager
to build enclaves of power quickly found loopholes within the Act that
enabled them to register votes according to partisan needs. Both
Republicans and Democrats were swept into a corrupt circle. Thus
the Registry Act which the League had promoted for the welfare of
Philadelphians became the instrument of a new political evil. Later,
the Act was completely revised, eliminating the opportunity for
abuses.[60]

In the local elections of 1869, Philadelphia Democrats were unable
to repeat their successes of the two previous years. Part of their
failure may have been due to the Registry Act, but according to
Boker, who still looked upon Pennsylvania as "the battleground of the
Union Party," the decisive factor in the election was the continuing
disagreement over wartime issues. He stated that the "same ideas which
inspired the war came again into conflict at the ballot box," and "this
state continued to be the field upon which the first fight was the
hottest." Geary was elected for a second term, with a Republican
slate that captured the City Council and other key offices, including
that of chief justice of the state. Pennsylvania was no longer the
citadel of the Democrats. Deprived of a powerful state, the Democrats
retreated in an effort to recoup their forces. The League continued
to view the Democrats as a potential hindrance to Reconstruction;
they had to be beaten on local, state, and national levels, by honest
and incorruptible men.[61]

In the League the Democrats recognized an articulate force that
had the courage and ability to stand up to the local and state political
machines. The League recognized the failure of the Registry Act
and the inadequacies of other laws that lacked statewide uniform
provisions. Furthermore, the Pennsylvania constitution was so outmoded that it required basic revisions. In the fall of 1870, the Board
of the League moved that five of its directors and five active members
be appointed to consider the propriety of state constitutional reform.
More than any other body, group of men or individuals, The Union
League of Philadelphia was responsible for clarifying the issues
and preparing the apparatus that led to the adoption of a new constitution for the Commonwealth of Pennsylvania.

On October 8, Charles Gibbons represented the committee of ten
at a special meeting of the Board that outlined the call for a new
state constitution. Speaking incisively, Gibbons described the recent
political history of the state, and "the corruptive power of corpora-

tions, seeking special favors by the temptations of bribery. The franchises of the State are bartered for money, and our Legislative halls have often been converted into market places, where important public offices have been sold to the highest bidders, by faithless and venal public servants, vested rights have been threatened and assailed for the sole purpose of extorting ransom from their lawful proprietors, and public acts which concern the common welfare are passed or registered without intelligent consideration; and thus the safety and happiness of the people are frequently impaired and imperilled by dishonest and incompetent representatives."[62]

Gibbons discussed legislative defects, the system of patronage, the lack of uniform statewide laws, the protection of political minorities, the inadequacy of public education, and other problems that had been neglected far too long. He recommended that the legislature take action to consider a special election in the spring of 1871 to vote for a convention to amend the state constitution. This and other recommendations were approved almost unanimously by the Board. Any objections that were voiced related to the procedure and not to the substance of the proposals. Frederick Fraley and Francis Jordan, two prominent League members, quickly endorsed the resolutions which were promptly submitted to the city's newspapers. Assurances were received from a number of Democrats that their party would confer with League representatives to support the undertaking. The governor and many members of the legislature welcomed the idea of the proposed convention.[63]

It was an important juncture in the early history of the League. Its membership was reminded by Gibbons and others that the institution had been founded for patriotic purposes, and that political action had been introduced out of necessity, at a time when "patriotism and politics were inseparable." The League was eager to avoid the impression that by cooperating with the Democrats it had departed from partisan politics, and stressed that it was not interested in political rancor or personal contest. It was anxious to work with all men concerned with good government and with bringing the state constitution into the context of a new era.[64]

Voters overwhelmingly approved the call for a constitutional convention. Delegates were chosen, and both parties were equally represented. Independent branches of each joined in the proceedings. The League was represented, not as an institution, but ideologically, through Edward C. Knight, one of the first Republicans in the state, William Meredith, the state's former Attorney General and the League's first president, and the economist Henry C. Carey, who dominated the social thought of the convention. The most distinguished politician from the League was Wayne MacVeagh, who in spite of his connections with Simon Cameron and the Republican political machine assumed the role of reformer.

In 1870, while the League was considering constitutional reform, a voluntary organization known as the Citizens Municipal Reform Association was founded in Philadelphia. Its purpose was to combat political corruption. Henry Charles Lea was one of its founders, and many members of The Union League were its prime supporters. Composed primarily of a spectrum of Republicans and independent Democrats, the association also worked for the new constitution.[65] In 1872 the Reform Club was founded with a similar intent to fight municipal abuses and seek appropriate constitutional remedies. Most of its founders were among the first Union League members, and comprised the city's social elite. All of them were active in the League's political affairs, but the outstanding interest in reform shown by Anthony J. Drexel, George M. Childs, Joseph Harrison, E. Dunbar Lockwood, Joshua B. Lippincott, Henry B. Tatham, John J. Ridgway, and Charles Wheeler gave special authority and status to the club. They provided an interesting contrast to other League members who had thrown their support to the political machine, and while both groups were Republican-oriented, there was a sharp division between them.[66]

The convention spent 180 working days between November 12, 1872 and December 27, 1873 studying constitutional reform. Its work coincided with the beginning of Grant's second term as president and ended in 1873 in the gloomy days of an economic depression. In its eight thick volumes of debate and discussion, recommendations and resolutions, the delegates proposed increases in the representation in the legislature in both the House and the Senate. It was recommended that senators should serve four years and members of the House two. Gibbons' sharp criticism of the manner in which bills were passed brought about the requirements that bills be clearly titled, that amendments altering the original intent of a bill be eliminated, and that each bill have three full separate readings. All amendments had to be available before the final passage of a bill.

Changes affecting municipal politics were numerous. Local elections were separated from state elections by a period of eight months. Ballots had to be numbered, and bribery was clearly defined. The Registry Act, which had been willfully corrupted and misused, was nullified, and in its place uniform registration procedures were introduced.

Another of the evils attacked by the League and by the two reform groups was the misuse of public funds collected by nonsalaried officials. By requiring all officials in communities with populations over 150,000 to be salaried, the new procedures eliminated the payment of percentage fees based on monies received for city government. This provision struck directly at the local machines.

A major change in the old constitution, which in 1838 had deprived the Pennsylvania Negro of the franchise, was the restoration of the black man's right to vote as required by federal law. The governor's term of office was extended to four years and the terms of other state officials were also extended, but none was permitted to serve for more than one term with the exception of the secretary of internal affairs. The office of lieutenant-governor was introduced for the first time.[67]

Many provisions of the new constitution were designed to divest the political machines of their power. Despite this, the men behind the machine supported its ratification. Philadelphia and Allegheny counties provided the rank and file Republican support, and a formidable amount of that endorsement came from The Union League and the reform associations. On December 16, 1873, the new constitution was voted in by a large majority of Pennsylvanians and was scheduled to take effect on the first day of 1874.[68]

A new era in Philadelphia politics was envisioned by the reform journalists. Antimachine Republicans welcomed the newly ratified constitution as a great achievement. The League expressed only a passing satisfaction with the new document whose revision it had worked so hard to secure. Henry Charles Lea, who had become the recognized leader of Philadelphia's reformers, was convinced that the convention had not gone far enough. He urged the League to act quickly to remedy what he believed to be a weakness in a number of the revisions. But the League moved slowly. Almost two months later, the League formally recognized that the new constitution, with all its improvements, had fallen short in providing sufficiently broad changes in municipal government. To secure "just and proper laws for the future government of the City," a new committee was formed to propose and promote further changes to safeguard Philadelphia voters. The League-Shippen resolution of 1868, calling for candidates "beyond suspicion or reproach" was reaffirmed. At a special meeting called to discuss new legislation, it was concluded that the professional officeholder, regardless of his party, should not receive a League endorsement unless he met League standards.[69]

A shortlived obstacle to the League's effort at state and municipal reform, the Society of Mysterious Pilgrims was founded in 1872. This counterforce drew its membership from ward politicians, from machine Democrats, and from organization Republicans. It was a political ring within a ring that hoped to bring together all of the elements that controlled city government. To give the Pilgrims an image of importance, its members entertained lavishly and extravagantly but without dignity. Their glittering exhibitions were financed by municipal funds, and by the monies obtained from collaboration with the gas trust, the men who ran the city-leased utility. The League fought the Pilgrims vigorously, all the more so because a few of its members had joined the Society. The precise number of League members within the Pilgrim organization has not been determined, but there were less than ten out of a membership of 1,900. The sharp differences between the policy of the League and that of the Pilgrims led to a public confrontation of the two groups prior to the election of 1875, when the League assigned a special committee to work in the election.[70]

At its spring meeting, the Board reviewed its political policy and pledged anew to use its influence in securing nominations for political office of men who placed the welfare of the people above party interests. Abstract discussion had failed, and published resolutions presenting the views of the League had also not been efficacious in bringing about change; the League's efforts would now go to promoting suitable nominations within the Republican Party. Candidates had to be of exceptional character, men who were eminently qualified to serve in political office. To act as a watchdog, the League Board appointed the Committee of Sixty-Two and empowered it to represent the corporate body throughout the campaign.[71]

When the Republican Party made known the state and county nominees for 1875, John F. Hartranft was chosen to run for a second term as governor, Henry Rawle was named candidate for State Treasurer, and Craig Biddle was nominated for Judge of Common Pleas Court No. I. The League, along with many voters from both parties, was pleased with the nominees. Not pleasing were the choice of General H. H. Bingham, David H. Lane, John S. Wetter, and David Martin for various local offices. Bingham was the only League member who joined after the war. These latter nominees belonged to the clique which had misruled the city and driven voters from Republican ranks. Further, the association of these four candidates with the Mysterious Pilgrims was no secret. The Committee of Sixty-Two had no intention of supporting corrupt men who were eager to hold the reins of power of the Republican Party in Philadelphia, and so it issued a strong appeal to have the names of the nominees withdrawn. The appeal was ignored, and the Committee of Sixty-Two publicly condemned "that dictatorial band of men, nominally of both parties, but without true allegiance to either, which now rules and oppresses our city, and is disgracing and destroying the Republican organization."[72]

By indulging in this attack and by making it public, some League members believed that the Committee had exceeded the responsibility invested in it. A special meeting of the League was called to consider whether the Committee had carried out its assignment properly. Almost 1,200 members attended. Numerous handbills were circulated within the League House which debated the powers of the Committee, and the press, which learned of the controversy, reported the dispute in lavish detail. It was feared that the halls of the League would be turned into a political battleground. When tensions relaxed and a vote was taken, however, it was found that a majority of members supported the conduct of the Committee of Sixty-Two. But notwithstanding the action taken by the Committee and the encouragement it received from the League membership, the doubtful candidates were not withdrawn from the slate, and they were elected along with those who were endorsed by the League. Perhaps the Committee of Sixty-Two was naive in believing that it could defeat the power of the machine.[73]

At the annual meeting of 1875, the election was assessed, and in an effort to again clarify its position on engaging in political affairs, the Board indicated the lines of conduct that were open. The League could withdraw from all political activity, rest proudly on its past accomplishments, and enjoy the comforts of club social life. Or, it could withdraw from its involvement in municipal politics, and concentrate only on national affairs. A difference of opinion existed among the membership on the League's political obligations. James L. Claghorn, for example, argued contentiously that a majority of the members did not want the League in politics. On the other hand, the socially conscious Boker insisted that the League should not remain a purely social club. Edwin N. Benson, who had not as yet emerged as a strong figure in League life, spoke vigorously in Boker's behalf, and because of his outspoken manner was defeated in his bid for the office of president at the annual League election. After some debate, the opinion was expressed that "the League as a body should not hereafter take part in municipal politics unless otherwise directed by members in General Meeting."[74] When this statement was formalized into an amendment to the By-Laws, a decision was made that influenced the League's future course in politics. Thereafter, the League's political concerns shifted to state and national elections. Murmurs of dissent continued to be heard, but the amendment was sufficiently flexible to permit local political action upon a majority vote of the members. The amendment on politics also authorized a policy of corporate League endorsement of national candidates. In fact, it now became a matter of formal procedure to do what the club actually had been doing since Lincoln's second campaign.

When Rutherford B. Hayes was nominated for president on the Republican ticket, the League called for a meeting to "consider what action, if any," should be taken. The door was opened again for debate. Claghorn registered his support of Hayes but repeated his belief that members preferred not to take part in national politics. Hayes was endorsed, and after careful consideration the principles and platform of the Republican Party were ratified by an overwhelming majority of League members. Before each national election between 1876 and 1932, the League as a corporate body, followed the same procedure of endorsing the Republican presidential nominee and ratifying the party platform at a special meeting.[75]

The emergence of The Union League as a Republican-oriented institution was the result of a number of diverse conditions that blended with the history of the Grand Old Party. The impact of the Civil War was a major factor in harmonizing the views of both; and the postwar identification of the party with Lincoln, the martyred president who could best be revered by supporting the party that brought him to office, contributed to this alignment. To the League, this was in consonance with the struggle to reunite the nation. The League was unsuccessful in its attempts to defeat some politicians, and its promotion of the Registry Act ultimately was aborted. Its influence was greater as the body that first urged state constitutional reform, but here also, the League achieved only part of what it sought.

When examined in the long range, the work of the League can be viewed in a more total perspective. It established the foundation that in time brought better government to the city. Four of its wartime members who were founders of the Citizens Municipal Reform Association, Joseph Patterson, Joshua B. Lippincott, Henry Lewis, and Charles Wheeler helped move the Bullitt bill into law in 1887. This law was intended to strengthen the power of the mayor and thereby of the city government, a condition advocated and fought for by the League president Morton McMichael. Since 1875, the League had faithfully abstained from taking part in local elections, but under the terms of the Bullitt bill, in which the League had a hand, it felt it had a right to offer the choice of a candidate for mayor. Three League members were suggested, and Edwin H. Fitler was nominated and elected. The whole recommendation was governed by corporate action. Joel J. Baily, Anthony Drexel, John Wanamaker, and William Wood were League members who also were active in the Reform Club. They were members of the nonpartisan Committee of One Hundred, which independently endorsed or disapproved candidates for local office. This was the forerunner of Philadelphia's Committee of Seventy, which became a guardian of local elections less than a century later. The secret ballot, introduced in 1891, was the culmination of two decades of work begun by the League as an institution, and carried out by its members as individuals. No other man was more active in this crusade for better government than Henry Charles Lea who as a reformer, a Republican, and a superb pamphleteer towered above the hundreds of others with whom he worked.[76]

Although the League was an ardent supporter of the protective tariff in every nineteenth-century presidential election, and guided the Republican Party on this platform plank, it did not desert its grass roots work with the Civil War veteran, or alter its determination to improve Negro life in the North and South. Its Republican orientation was interpreted to mean philanthropic service to the community. The League privately worked to upgrade the condition of the Negro. Its aid to mothers and widows of black soldiers continued without interruption; and its members committed themselves to the movement for the right of blacks to use public transportation. Without their support, the task would have been far more difficult. The well-known names of Colwell and Binney appearing on a petition for Negroes were significant and not easily challenged. While some historians have considered these efforts as a means to reach black voters, the men involved in this work had established their interest in it long before blacks were able to vote.

The League gave liberally to institutions responsible for the care of maimed white veterans, orphans' homes, and related postwar welfare. Many members participating in this work belonged to the Grand Army of the Republic, the Union veterans organization. Robert Burns Beath, its first historian, was a national commander and had lost a leg leading black troops into battle. He and his fellow commissioned officers were also active in the Military Order of the Loyal Legion.[77] The League's sponsorship of the undertakings of these veterans and others was not intended to be disclosed. However, the work was widely rumored throughout the city. The City's Irish nationalists, misunderstanding the League's community work, even appealed to the Board in 1869 for funds to distribute a newspaper that advocated striking a blow at the British Empire by invading Canada![78]

While the League was occupied with the problems of political identity and was quietly carrying out its welfare obligations, preparations were being made to celebrate the formal opening of the League House on May 11, 1870, five years after the League had moved into its new quarters. Elegant receptions had been held, but there had been no party for the families and their personal guests. The occasion was to provide an opportunity to enjoy the resources of the League House, its dining facilities, and the expertise of its staff. The affair was placed in the hands of a committee of one-hundred younger members whose arrangements surpassed in brilliance the usual Philadelphia social events. An evening free of political cares and wartime nostalgia, this first reception for the League families was immediately acclaimed an outstanding success. So pleased were the officers and directors that it was decided to hold similar entertainments at appropriate intervals. The League, without fully realizing it, was introducing a new era in the social life of Philadelphia.

An event of far greater significance and exclusiveness took place annually on December 27, when the original Union Club celebrated the anniversary of the League which it had founded. When the League embarked on its independent course, the Club had withdrawn to its own privacy. While all of its members belonged to the League, no members of the League who had not been part of the original Club could be admitted to its festivities without special invitation. Invitations and menus were elegantly engraved by Samuel Sartain; the menus repeated the courses served at their first meetings. In social arrangements of the original club, parties had been held weekly in the homes of members, who took their turns as hosts. After the war, the Union Club met annually at the League House until 1905, when there were only two survivors. Resignations were not permitted, although some were accepted because of reasons of health. Even those men who subsequently moved from the city clung to the honored body. Daniel Dougherty, who returned to the Democratic Party many years later, faithfully attended the annual meetings of the Club, even though he had resigned his League membership. Four of the original members had died prior to 1870—Benjamin Gerhard, Horace Binney, Jr., the third president of the League, and Samuel Vaughan Merrick, the noted steam engine manufacturer. At this event appropriate tributes were paid to the memory of each in brief addresses delivered by George H. Boker and Morton McMichael. At the 1870 meeting, Boker nostalgically recalled the old Club's guests of honor, who had joined in the patriotic parties, the military men and the naval heroes, the states-men, orators, poets, and playwrights. The best minds had mingled in their company. All of this was also reminiscent of the social and intellectual milieu of the disbanded Wistar Party that thrived before the war. In imitation of the Wistar Party, the Union Club issued a keepsake in the form of a book which was published in a limited edition by League member Joshua B. Lippincott. It was the intent of

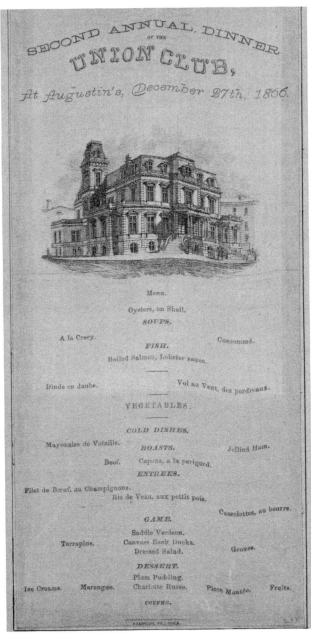

AN ENGRAVED MENU ON SILK OF THE UNION CLUB

the Club to revive the Wistar Party in the near future, in order to
heal social differences, but when the Wistar Party finally was
reorganized after the Civil War it never recaptured its antebellum
spirit.[79]

As an innerclub of the League, the Union Club became a model for
other such clubs that sprang up in the coming decades, and are still
in existence today. In accordance with the policy that it had adopted,
the Union Club met regularly until 1905. Its sole survivor, Abraham
Barker, a fighter for Negro rights, died the following year, bringing
to an end a unique organization. Club life in Philadelphia slowly
resumed a more temperate course. With the revival of the Wistar
Party as a first step, the smaller Philadelphia Club, which was
purely social, found itself dominated by Union League members. In
1869, its committee on arrangements consisted of twelve men, eight
of whom belonged to the League. Two years later, when the Saturday
Club was organized, seven of its eight officers were prominent League
members and active in the Republican Party. Henry M. Phillips, the
only nonLeague member, was an extremely influential Democrat.[80]

As 1871 drew to a close, the League honored George Henry Boker
upon his appointment to the post of minister to Turkey. For nine
years Boker worked hard as League secretary and as a major participant on many committees. He had not altogether deserted the literary
world because of these duties, but they kept him from fulfilling many
of his dreams and diverted his creativity to other fields. In his post as
the literary editor of *Lippincott's Magazine* after it was founded in
1868, he renewed contact with two South Carolinians, the novelist
William Gilmore Simms and the poet Paul H. Hayne. Boker opened
the pages of *Lippincott's* to them in a gesture of literary friendship,
providing these Southern authors impoverished by the war with access
to a Northern journal.[81]

Before Boker could return to his writing desk, he became president
of the Philadelphia Club in 1870. When President Grant offered him
the diplomatic post in Turkey, which had been vacated nine months
earlier by Wayne MacVeagh, Boker accepted the appointment
although he had never sought political patronage.

The appointment created a perfect opportunity for the League to
show its respect to a founder and faithful officer. On December 22,
1871, 263 members, as well as members of Boker's family, assembled
at the League House to share in what has been described as the
"bounteous splendor which has probably never been equalled in
Philadelphia." Two nights before, the Philadelphia Club had honored
its president with a gala party that was attended by many who were
members of both clubs. The League was not to be outdone. Its entire

second floor was turned over to the Boker reception. Its display of fine marble sculpture, bronzes and exquisite furniture, all decorated with sprays of flowers, formed a background against which the guests enjoyed a magnificent dinner and drank from a selection of choice wines. There were nine brief addresses. Two political contestants, Cameron and Forney, expressed their admiration of Boker. Wayne MacVeagh delicately touched on the political scene, and spoke of the post he had occupied that Boker now contemplated. Bayard Taylor, the West Chester poet and author, spoke as a man of letters, reading a farewell poem to his colleague, and Daniel Dougherty briefly summarized the deep respect in which Boker was held by his fellow League members. The New England authors James Russell Lowell, Oliver Wendell Holmes, Henry Wadsworth Longfellow, and William Cullen Bryant sent their personal congratulations. It was a rare evening, and established another precedent for the League receptions that honored dignitaries, statesmen, authors, and war heroes during the nineteenth and twentieth centuries.[82]

Between the League House party and the reception for Boker, the League became engrossed in projects that the war years had postponed. Among its stalwarts were the most notable Philadelphia patrons of the arts. These men were eager to see the spacious halls and rooms of the League enriched with paintings of the war and with portraits of the men who had led the Union forces to victory. Outstanding among these members was James L. Claghorn, president of the Pennsylvania Academy of Fine Arts and a founder of the Philadelphia School of Design. He was a zealous collector and was reputed to own 300 paintings from the easels of American artists. His collection of engravings, showing the historical development of this medium, was unparalleled. Henry C. Carey, Fairman Rogers, and Joseph Harrison, Jr., all of whom avidly collected American art, shared Claghorn's interest in building a League art collection that would emphasize a national concept in art without excluding works from abroad suitable to the League's taste and interest.[83]

Claghorn and Carey exhibited works from their own collections at the League House, and many artists who either taught or studied at the Pennsylvania Academy accepted the opportunity to display their paintings on the club's walls. The Academy, through Claghorn, also loaned the League American paintings from its own collections. A number of League members were professional artists. James Reid Lambdin was among them. In 1870, when the League began its acquisitions program, it acquired from Lambdin 17 portraits of distinguished Americans. Thirteen were of men who served in the army and navy during the war, two were presidents of the United

States, one was of Henry C. Carey, and one of John Marshall, the nation's third chief justice. All of the Lambdin portraits are appropriately exhibited in the League House.[84]

Two other League artist-members, Daniel Ridgway Knight, and J. Henry Haseltine, were in the art capitals of Europe when Fort Sumter was fired upon. Both immediately returned to Philadelphia to join the Union army. After the war, Knight did a full-length portrait of General Meade standing beside his horse at Gettysburg. Haseltine sculpted in marble the massive figure of Columbia, with a wreath clutched in her left hand and her head bowed in sorrow, which he called "America Honoring Her Fallen Brave." This impressive work stands at the foot of the marble staircase at the League, not far from Knight's portrait of General Meade.[85] Peter F. Rothermel, a director of the Pennsylvania Academy before the war and a signer of the League's Articles of Association, became intrigued with American historical themes after the war. His detailed painting, "Reading the Declaration of Independence," was presented to the League by Claghorn. Rothermel is best known for his mammoth painting of the Battle of Gettysburg which now hangs in the William Penn Memorial Museum in Harrisburg.[86] One of his students, Augustus George Heaton, also absorbed by early American themes, turned to the colonial scene to paint "Washington Presenting Governor Dinwiddie's Letter to Chevalier Legardeur de Saint Pierre," the French commander at Fort Le Boeuf in northwestern Pennsylvania. This, too, was added to the League collection.[87]

Edward D. Marchant, one of the portrait painters who belonged to the League, painted Lincoln from life in August, 1863. The contemplative mood of the president, sitting with a quill in his right hand and his left arm resting on a copy of the Emancipation Proclamation is given deeper meaning by the broken slave shackles painted behind him. Marchant's three-quarter portrait of Lincoln leaning slightly forward was unlike other portraits, and for two years it hung in Independence Hall before it went to its permanent home at the League. Today it is prominently displayed in Lincoln Hall. Other portraits by Marchant are of his fellow League members Henry C. Carey, and Charles Izard Maceuen; the latter was killed in battle in 1865. Marchant's half-length portrait of Thaddeus Stevens, which reveals the stern character of Pennsylvania's great radical Republican, was presented to the League at the time of Stevens' death in 1868. Horace Binney the elder, who supported the suspension of the writ of habeas corpus under Lincoln, is portrayed by Marchant as a white-haired sage.[88]

Against this background of artists, patrons, and benefactors, the

FAIRMAN ROGERS

JAMES L. CLAGHORN

JOSEPH HARRISON, JR.

HENRY C. CAREY

BENEFACTORS AND PATRONS OF THE ARTS

James Reid Lambdin

JOHN MARSHALL

J. Henry Haseltine

AMERICA HONORING HER FALLEN BRAVE

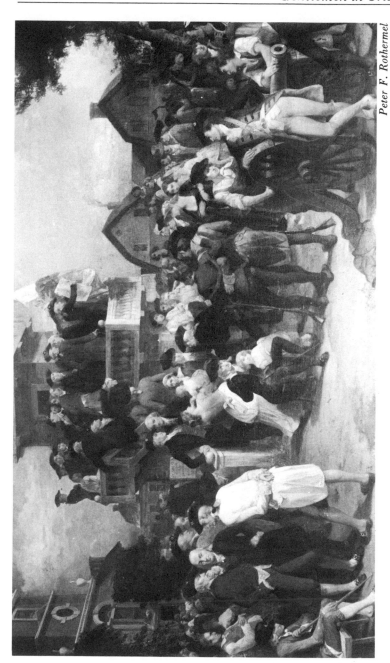

Peter F. Rothermel

Reading the Declaration of Independence

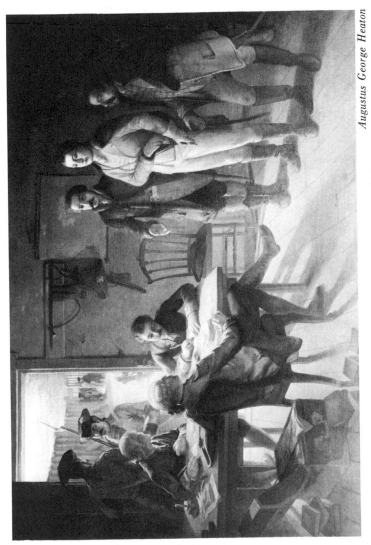

Augustus George Heaton

WASHINGTON PRESENTING GOVERNOR DINWIDDIE'S LETTER
TO CHEVALIER LEGARDEUR DE SAINT PIERRE

Edward D. Marchant
HORACE BINNEY, SR.

Artist unknown
HORACE BINNEY, JR.

cultural landscape of the League took shape. Charles Gibbons, whose family sat for Rembrandt Peale, proposed that the League consider annual art exhibitions, musical programs, and lectures on topics of interest to the membership. Immediate attention was given to all these programs, but the interest in the art exhibitions appears to have surpassed that in concerts and lectures.

Three art receptions were planned for the winter of 1870-1871 and were placed under the direction of a committee composed of Rothermel, Lambdin, Knight, and Heaton. The committee was joined by Thomas Moran, whose paintings of the Far West so impressed Congress that they helped to convince the legislature to create Yellowstone National Park. Two additional members were Samuel B. Waugh, considered one of the finest portrait painters in Philadelphia, and the sculptor Joseph A. Bailly. Working with the League's House Committee, the artists decided upon an exhibition consisting of paintings in oil and water color, and of finished drawings and statuary. The first reception was confined to works done by artists residing in Philadelphia; the second was broadened to include American artists throughout the country; and the third encouraged members to exhibit examples of American art from their own collections.[89]

Exhibitors included artists whose works have left their mark on American painting a century later. The remarkable Moran brothers, Thomas, Edward, and Peter, self-trained in Philadelphia, had moved from boyhoods in the textile mills of Kensington to recognition for high artistic merit by the League. Here they exhibited under one roof, perhaps for the first time. The paintings of Peter Rothermel, Albert Bierstadt, the Waughs, and Xanthus R. Smith, whose works are represented in the permanent League collection, were shown side by side. As members of the selection committee, they also introduced the paintings of many other artists, one of whom was Thomas Eakins. At the third exhibition Eakins showed an unidentified portrait, the property of League member Matthew H. Messchert, a member of the Board of Publication, and "The Champion Single Sculls." It is likely that after this first formal exhibition Eakins came to better know Claghorn, his early patron Fairman Rogers, and many others with whom his name is associated.[90]

All three receptions were highly successful. Beyond the interest they excited within the League, public attention was attracted as well. As a result, new League paintings were acquired, an ad hoc committee on art was formed, and in 1882 an Art Association of the League was organized.

One of the most exceptional exhibitions sponsored by the League was announced in the fall of 1873, when friends of James L. Claghorn proposed that he show his superb collection of engravings, etchings and mezzotints. The purpose of the exhibit was to illustrate the history of the development of these arts from their beginnings in the fifteenth century to their nineteenth-century refinements. Works of Martin Schongauer and Albrecht Dürer represented the early German school, while Raimondi and Da Ravenna, after Raphael, represented the Italian school. The art of Lucas van Leyden and Goltzius provided examples of two early periods of Dutch art. French and Flemish works vied with those of English artists. American engraving was represented by artists of the nineteenth century, from Asher B. Durand to John Sartain, a friend of Claghorn who was very active in Philadelphia art circles. Among the artists represented in the 221 items displayed in chronological order, there was scarcely a major figure omitted. The exhibition was a tribute to the care and knowledge with which Claghorn had chosen his collection.[91] Thereafter, exhibitions were held at the League throughout the nineteenth century, displaying works that ranged in style from Rembrandt and other world masters to the Americans, Winslow Homer and Thomas Eakins.

Toward the end of the Hayes administration, Eakins and William Garl Browne submitted portraits of the president for possible purchase by the League. The ad hoc art committee which included patrons of Eakins, preferred Browne's conventional portrait from life of President Hayes. Legend, however, persists in stating that Eakins' commissioned portrait was paid for and destroyed because he represented Hayes as red-faced and working in his shirt sleeves, an image unacceptable to The Union League, the "exalted pillar of Republicanism." But this account, created by anti-Republican critics and art historians many years later, is not supported by the records of the League or Eakins' patrons on the art committee.[92]

One of the most impressive acquisitions of the League was made in 1888 when the Association purchased a unique Tiffany clock, which not only tells the time of day, but the rising and setting of the sun, the time throughout the major cities of the world, the phases of the moon, the day of the week, the month, and the difference between solar and terrestial time. Its engraved face carries the symbols associated with the history of the United States, and its hand-carved case is in itself a work of beauty. It is the first thing that strikes the eye at the Broad Street entrance of the League.[93]

The Art Association had begun to flourish when it was established in 1882. Within 20 years it had spent over $40,000 of contributed funds to acquire works of art. The peak of its public activity was reached at the end of the century, when it sponsored two major exhibitions, one in 1898 and another in 1899. More than 70,000 visitors came to the League House to view a larger number of paintings than had ever before been displayed at one time in the city. The growth of local museums, particularly the Academy of Fine Arts, obviated the need to continue such exhibitions, and the Art Association concentrated on gradually enlarging and refining the splendid collection it had built. It continued its work as a voluntary body until the 1920's when it ceased its activity in the belief that it had accomplished its purpose of building a collection of paintings and statuary to enhance the beauty of the League House.

The art life of the League reached tens of thousands of outsiders. Somewhat more private, but gratifying to an equally receptive audience of members, was the League's program of summertime music concerts. Responsibility for the entertainment fell to the House Committee, which placed James Bellak, one of Philadelphia's outstanding music publishers, at the head of the arrangements committee. As long as the center city remained the place of residence of many League members, these concerts continued to be given throughout the summer each year. They were discontinued with the decline of the inner-city population early in the century. In an age when bands played in public parks, street musicians roamed freely, and private chamber groups performed leisurely, it was a particular pleasure for League families to attend the musical soirées at the League House. In the musical tradition of the late nineteenth century, the League commissioned Viennese waltzes and marches to commemorate special events of its own, and these were performed for the first time in the great assembly room, near the site of what later became Lincoln Hall. Music at the League was never abandoned. The concert was replaced by individual performing artists, and by musical productions with a broader repertoire. The pursuit of art and music, and the informative lecture programs received special emphasis during the Centennial of American Independence and in 1882 during the bicentennial of William Penn's founding of the Commonwealth.[94]

The proposal to celebrate the nation's one-hundredth birthday in Philadelphia originated among Union League members. William Sellers, a League founder, who became president of the Franklin Institute in 1864, urged the Institute to bring the idea of a celebration before the public. The plan caught the imagination of other Philadelphians, who sought federal support through the Congress. The observance was not intended to be a local but a national celebration, but when Congress first considered the proposition, it responded lethargically. "Pig Iron" Kelley, speaking both as a Congressman from Philadelphia and as an ardent exponent of League interests, reminded Congress that it was more than a Philadelphia holiday.

Appealing to Congress on January 10, 1871, he said: "The proposed exhibition is to celebrate events that are not merely of national but of worldwide interest. It is to commemorate not a day, but an epoch in universal history; not an event, but a series of events that occurred in rapid succession, gave birth to republican liberty, and organized a nation that stands today . . ." strong among the nations of the world.[95]

Congress however, moved slowly, and planning moved slowly. Critics of the day looked upon the idea as a hollow expression of patriotism. In 1873, the collapse of the banking house of Jay Cooke & Company, and the lean years that followed, almost brought the movement for the celebration of American independence to a halt. Difficulty in financing the Centennial was obvious. To defy the crisis and obtain the necessary funds demanded as much skill as it did enthusiasm. A Board of Finance was organized, with John Welsh as its head. Welsh, an honorary member of the League, had successfully promoted Philadelphia's Sanitary Fair during the war and brought both ability and experience to the Centennial project.

Of the 16 men who served with Welsh on the Board of Finance, eight had been members of the League since the early months of 1863; two joined the League shortly before the Centennial, and three after its conclusion. The remaining three were not members of the League. When it became clear that only limited funding would be forthcoming from Washington, John Price Wetherill, Edwin H. Fitler, Clement M. Biddle, Amos R. Little, Joseph Patterson, William Sellers, and Frederick Fraley mobilized the financial community with the same spirit that they had devoted to the League during the Civil War. Without their efforts and the support they received from the rising merchants John Wanamaker and Thomas Cochran (the latter for many years a League Treasurer), the organization of the Centennial would have faced still greater difficulties.

The concept of such a celebration had no precedent. A series of buildings was to be built on four hundred acres of Fairmount Park, west of the Schuylkill River. Three buildings were to contain exhibits on the arts, manufactures, and agriculture of the United States. The Main Building, containing the foreign exhibits, and designed by League member Henry Pettit, was to be the largest. Memorial Hall, a forerunner of the Philadelphia Museum of Art, was made possible by an appropriation of one million dollars by the Commonwealth of Pennsylvania. It was to remain as a permanent building after the Centennial. The City of Philadelphia contributed a million and a half dollars toward the erection of Memorial Hall and Agricultural Hall. It was estimated that ten million dollars would be required to build the other structures. Twenty-four states were represented by buildings of their own. The Board of Finance was authorized to raise this staggering sum through the sale of Centennial shares at not more than ten dollars each. To the thousands of unemployed and the tens of thousands who earned less than ten dollars a week, this appeared to be an impossible undertaking. But the spirit of the "Centennial," as the entire exhibition came to be known, fired the minds of rich and poor alike.

On February 24, 1874, the Board of Directors of the League appointed a committee to go to Washington to urge Congress to appropriate a special Centennial fund. Congress failed to act, and the League criticized it for its mistaken economy. The only funds provided by the government were those for its own exhibition, and a loan of one and a-half million dollars that was repaid afterward from admission receipts. Philadelphians undertook the responsibility for the celebration, and the League's supportive role greatly contributed to its success.[96]

The dramatic opening of the Centennial on May 10, 1876 was attended by approximately 150,000 visitors and guests, who strained to hear a patriotic hymn composed by John G. Whittier and "The American Centennial March" by Richard Wagner. After a series of formalities the buildings were presented to President Grant, who declared the exhibition open. It was a presidential election year, and political aspirants did their best to be seen. The Emperor Dom Pedro of Brazil was the most easily recognized and perhaps the most popular guest.

The Honorable John Bright, a member of the English Parliament whose friendship with the League stemmed from his proUnion activity during the war, was to have been a guest of the League for the celebration, but poor health prevented him from coming. However, George Boker, who had left Turkey to become Minister to Russia, returned to the United States for a brief leave of absence. He was welcomed with a splendid reception in his honor early in July. The League House had been redecorated for the Centennial through a special membership subscription, and the new and beautiful setting complemented the gracious hospitality it offered its many distinguished guests.[97]

The summer's gay mood at the League was climaxed when Governor Rutherford B. Hayes came to Philadelphia in October to celebrate Ohio Day. The Ohio house, constructed of stone from Buckeye quarries, is the only one of the state buildings erected for the Centennial that is still standing in Fairmount Park. Hayes made no mention of his candidacy for President when he delivered his address from the portico of the handsomely designed building. Later in the day he was the guest of The Union League.[98]

The planning for the Centennial had begun at a time when the economy of the nation was badly disrupted; the festivities came to a close two days after the disputed presidential election of 1876 that brought Rutherford B. Hayes to the White House. While the nation was distracted by the long wait for a congressional decision on the narrow majority of electoral votes, a number of League members had begun to focus their interest on still another historical event, Washington's encampment at Valley Forge during the winter of 1777-1778. Henry Armitt Brown, one of the younger League members who had a reputation for eloquence and devotion to American history, and Francis M. Brooke conceived the idea for commemorating the bravery of the Continental troops at Valley Forge. At the Centennial observance, Brown delivered an address paying tribute to General George Washington and his army.[99] All of this might have been ephemeral and quickly forgotten, as are so many patriotic addresses. Moreover, Brown died within the year. But Francis Brooke carried the matter further. It was he who presented the idea that Valley Forge be recognized as a historical site requiring preservation and protection. As a result of his persistent efforts, and with the support of the League, the grounds of the winter encampment of the Continental Army have been preserved to this day under the jurisdiction of the Commonwealth of Pennsylvania. When the National Memorial Arch was erected by the government of the United States, the closing dramatic lines of League member Henry Armitt Brown were inscribed on its columns.[100]

"And here, in this place of Sacrifice, in this vale of Humiliation, in this valley of the Shadow of that Death out of which the Life of America rose regenerate and free, let us believe with an abiding faith that to them Union will seem as dear, and Liberty as sweet, and Progress as glorious as they were to our fathers, and are to you and me, that the Institutions which have made us happy, preserved by the virtue of our children, shall bless the remotest generations of the time to come."

The blend of social and cultural activity within the League was made possible by the work of its corporate committees. The By-Laws of the League called for four committees—house, finance, guest, and library committee—to guide its affairs. To oversee the largest club facility in Philadelphia, and possibly the largest in the United States, was an enormous task. It required fine management, experienced staff, and constant attention to building repairs and modernization.

Requiring special care were the well-appointed chess room, a billiard room—the cost of a game was fifteen cents—and other recreational areas. The dining rooms and the services they offered were of particular importance. In each instance, the House Committee established guiding regulations necessary for the professional management of the League. Working closely with the directors during the period of the League's physical expansion before 1897, this committee was involved in the acquisition of the real estate that enabled the club to extend its building to Fifteenth Street.

A matter of considerable importance that seldom came to the attention of the House Committee was the proper conduct of members. Only two instances are recorded before 1900 where extraordinary action was taken to remove members from the roll of the League. The first was the case of James Scovel, a member of the New Jersey legislature who was expelled for supporting Andrew Johnson,[101] and the second was that of Arthur Burt, expelled in 1882 because of a personal insult to another member. The latter incident resulted in spectacular litigation against the League.[102]

Essential to the functions of the League was the Finance Committee. It met regularly to review the financial condition and requirements of the club, and introduced the procedure of publishing an annual audit before such a practice became customary. Since the House Committee was involved in the direct expenditure of funds, it was necessary for the two committees to work closely with the Board of Directors in approving recommended expenditures.

The planning activities of the Guest Committee sustained the cultural and intellectual life of the League. Guest speakers, the province of Charles Gibbons, were an established part of League activity, as were frequent receptions held by the directors. Dignitaries from home and abroad were sought not merely to entertain or to meet socially, but to expound upon subjects of importance in civic, political, and legislative fields. Washington's birthday, and later Grant's birthday became annual events at the League, and there was no lack of speakers on these occasions. In 1893, at one such celebration, Robert Todd Lincoln addressed an overflow audience on the subject of his martyred father. Founders' Day addresses offered an opportunity to League veterans to recount the events of the war and regale a younger generation with the story of the founding of the League. In planning major receptions the Guest Committee worked directly with the House Committee and the League president, inviting wartime statesmen, generals, naval heroes, and especially the presidents of the United States and their cabinet members to attend.[103]

From time to time, balls were given and the League House was elegantly decorated. Social evenings, known as Club Nights and Ladies' Nights were introduced. Gilt-edged menus presented the many courses in multi-colored typography; elaborate programs describing the occasion, often printed on vellum-style paper or bound in fine calfskin, testified to the grand manner in which the League could indulge its members. Engraved place cards and lithographed programs, models of printing, were not unusual. The embellishments were dignified rather than lavish, select rather than extravagant. The League entered into the spirit of a new age in American social life.

The need for a library was recognized the day the League began its formal work. With a membership composed of the city's most seminal thinkers and writers, men involved with the American Philosophical Society, the Historical Society of Pennsylvania, the Philadelphia Athenaeum, and The Library Company of Philadelphia, it would have been inconceivable not to have an excellent library in a club dominated by Northern intellectuals. Even though its first quarters on Chestnut Street were too limited to accommodate a library, books that came from the shelves of the city's institutional leaders and patrons quickly filled the available space. Books were presented by Carey, Colwell, and the anthologist Charles Dexter Cleveland, Boker and the Binneys, the Stillé brothers, Horace Howard Furness, the Shakespearean scholar, and Ferdinand J. Dreer, a well-known manuscript collector. Today these gifts comprise the nucleus of the League authors' collection. They were supplemented by gifts from J. B. Lippincott, a publisher whose books had a tremendous impact on American social and political thought. The Board of Publication deposited its files of contemporary journals and newspapers, while the directors presented the records of the military work of the League and numerous documents and trophies of the war. In order to manage a burgeoning collection properly, a Library Committee was budgeted during the war years and took its place with the other committees. A full-time librarian was engaged, and was given the responsibility of collecting books relating both to the war, particularly regimental histories, and to the political history of the city and state. Architect Fraser's plans for the new League House included a spacious library area on the second floor overlooking Broad Street, easily reached by the broad carpeted staircase near the main entrance to the League. Dutch-style fireplaces at either end of the room and the natural light that poured through the windows gave the room an attractive and comfortable atmosphere. In 1910, when the library was provided with even larger quarters, the old library was turned into a magnificent chess and game room.

The first committee of the League, the Board of Publication, underwent changes following the election of Grant to a second term of office.[104] It continued its work but on a smaller scale, for there was no longer the same pressing need to disseminate political information. Except for those documents that kept the membership informed of corporate activity, election literature gradually disappeared. The party that the League supported took over the publication of its own campaign material. But the Board of Publication was still responsible for printing documents on subjects of national interest and for the addresses delivered at the League. One of its outstanding undertakings was the publication in 1884 of the first history of The Union League, written by the son-in-law of Nathaniel Hawthorne, George Parsons Lathrop, which embraced the first two decades of the League. Considering the proximity of the writing, to the occurrence of the actual events, the work was surprisingly objective, and contained material not to be found elsewhere. Although there are minor errors of fact, Lathrop's book was a worthy pioneer followed by the *Chronicle of The Union League*, a history that covered the first 40 years of the institution. In 1893, the work of the Board of Publication passed into the hands of the Library Committee, whose responsibility it remains today.[105]

The only committee not called for in the first By-Laws was the committee on membership. Basic requirements for membership in the League were citizenship, and loyalty to the United States.[106] Social qualifications or political allegiance were not indicated either in the Charter of the League or its Constitution, even though the League sought men of a similar social status, but did not confine its members to that elite which has been associated with "Old Philadelphia," or "Proper Philadelphians" in some recent sociological descriptions. These terms were created to classify certain families carrying the same name, generation after generation, who were intimately identified with the history of the city. All those who fitted this description were not necessarily admitted to the League, even though "elite" families were a dominant segment of it. Hereditary and patriotic societies were still so few in number that they offered no social guidelines for membership; social registers were non-existent; and inherited wealth, a useful asset, did not necessarily guarantee easy admission. Members who had come from less affluent backgrounds and had risen to positions of success in the mercantile or professional world had as much opportunity to be admitted as those whose families had achieved the same status generations earlier. A number of men of humbler background attained the highest offices of the League. Men in banking, insurance, and the professions were attracted to the League; so were booksellers, photographers, editors

and publishers, and the intellectual fibre of the city. The machine
politician, whose reputation was often clouded, had less chance to
be admitted, if he was proposed, than almost anyone else. Matthew
Quay, and later the Vare brothers, dominant figures in the Republican
machinery, were never members.[107] National origin presented no
obstacle, as the names of nineteenth century members reveal. Members were of Anglo-Saxon, French, Portuguese, and Italian backgrounds. Nor was religion considered as a factor hindering admission.
A larger number of Roman Catholics were members than is generally
believed, some with close ties to the archdiocese, like the Horstmann
family. Jews were prominent in proportion to their relatively small
population in Philadelphia during and after the Civil War. One
Jewish member, Henry Cohen, was the president of an orthodox
synagogue, and another, Judge Mayer Sulzberger, was the city's
leading Jewish layman. Many had been officers in the war, and one
Dr. Jacob Solis-Cohen, considered the father of American laryn-
gology, held the distinction of having been commissioned by the
navy and army of the United States. Sabato Morais, minister of
Congregation Mikveh Israel, was on the clerical roll.[108]

What, then, were the grounds on which a candidate was considered
unacceptable for membership in a club that emerged as a major
social, patriotic, and political force? Lack of a Republican orientation,
an absence of the quality of amenity identified with a private club
member, and financial instability were general criteria for refusal
of a proposed candidate formulated within the Membership Committee.
These guidelines were followed closely, with minor changes, until the
last decade of the nineteenth century, when a new generation sharp-
ened the criteria for admission. The responsibility for evaluating
candidates rested solely with the Membership Committee, although the
Board of Directors could override the committee's recommendation
for acceptance of a new candidate. This, however, had seldom
happened. The Board of Directors held the power to limit the
number of members admitted, and membership rose in accordance
with the growth of the League's facilities and the limitation set
by the Board. During the war years, there was no limitation on the
number of members. By 1866, membership had soared to 1,970,
but it dropped sharply in the following decade. After the election
of President Hayes, the membership fell to 874.[109]

Three rolls were established that supplemented regular active
members: the clerical roll, instituted in February, 1863; the army,
navy, and consular roll, begun toward the end of 1887; and a correspondents' roll, actually a provision for nonresident members, introduced in 1870 which subsequently underwent a number of revisions,

including a change of name. One of the notable members on this
latter roll was Albion Tourgee, the peripatetic novelist of the Reconstruction who attracted much attention with his Reconstruction novels,
The Fool's Errand and *Bricks Without Straw.*[110]

The four vice-presidents of the League presided over the four
standing committees to which they were appointed by presidential
prerogative; the members of these committees comprised the Board
of Directors, who in turn were responsible to the membership for the
general policy of the League. These men were elected annually, and
gave unstinting, voluntary service toward maintaining the quality of
club life established by The Union League. The same arrangement
prevails to the present day. Policies formulated by the Board that
involved changes in the By-Laws, or in the operation and improvement of the League, generally required a corporate decision and
were referred to the annual meeting of the membership for approval.
In some matters, however, the Board was empowered to act independently.

The independent strength of the Board of Directors was exempli-
fied in its continuing policy of support of local Negro leadership.
When plans were made to celebrate the Fifteenth Amendment, on
April 26, 1870, the Board approved a suggestion by J. Gillingham
Fell to present an emblematic banner to Negro leaders in honor of
the occasion.[111] After a parade through the downtown area, the
leaders of the black community assembled at the League House,
where Charles Gibbons made the presentation to Professor Octavius
V. Catto, an outstanding Negro educator. This token of friendship,
which underlined the League's endorsement of political rights for all
citizens, elicited harsh criticism from some Philadelphians.[112] As the
months wore on, Philadelphia became even more unfavorably disposed to the Negro cause and outbreaks of violence erupted in the
Negro areas of the city, disturbances which were attributed to white
reaction to the recent enfranchisement of blacks and their preparations to vote in the fall election of 1871. In the two days that preceded the election, a score of Negroes were wounded, and four were
killed in cold blood. One of the dead was Octavius V. Catto. Catto,
so recently honored by the League, had worked with its members to
better the image of blacks in the army, to remove the restrictions that
limited their use of public accommodations in Philadelphia, and to
improve their educational opportunities.[113] The directors of the
League were outraged by the violence. Before Catto's funeral, a mass
meeting was organized and presided over by Henry C. Carey, who
denounced the murderers. Present were William M. Meredith, George

H. Boker, Morton McMichael, James L. Claghorn, Alexander K.
McClure, John W. Forney, Congressman William D. Kelley, and
hundreds of other League members, who sat side by side with the
most articulate Negroes of the city. William C. Bolivar, a Negro
journalist who described the tragic event, attributed the decline of
the radical disorders in the city to the determination of this group
of men to prevent any similar occurrence. Catto's funeral, the largest
since the cortège of Lincoln had passed through the city, was held
at the Armory of the First Regiment Infantry at Broad and Wood
Streets, with the military, under the command of General Louis
Wagner, present in full regalia.[114]

The bitterness that followed this outrage was not easily allayed.
The old antislavery societies had all but ceased to exist, and what
members they had were more concerned with bettering the conditions
of former slaves than with the plight of Northern blacks. No other
group came forth to fill the vacuum, and concerned Negroes drew
upon their own resources and ingenuity in an effort to develop a
strong local leadership. The Union League was an exception to the
prevalent lack of interest in Negro affairs, for it was sensitive to
the changing problems in the North. There was no need for the
League, or its members, to maintain this commitment, but the social
consciousness and belief in moral justice that had arisen among its
membership during the war persisted into the first decade of the
twentieth century. During those forty years, the annual reports of
the League reflected its awareness of the rise of a new and different
black community. Not only was the League critical of the South, a
safe and comfortable practice for many white Northerners who
usually preferred not to look into their own backyards, it was also
able to cast an objective eye on Northern treatment of blacks and to
recognize the growing black urban slum. The League attempted to
face the herculean task of assistance to the black community which
should have been undertaken by city government and not by a
private institution.

George H. Boker, who had returned to the United States from his
diplomatic assignments to become president of the League, brought
a new perspective to these issues that were not recognized by the
nation at-large until decades later. Speaking to the membership at a
reception given to Governor Henry M. Hoyt after the election of
1879, Boker reminded them that although the nation was no longer
divided militarily, sharp differences existed on the subject of its
black citizenry. "After we committed the awful national iniquity of
leaving four million of poor, ignorant, powerless Negroes, without
the provisions of land or of any kind of property to support them, to

the tender mercies of their former owners, with no defense in their empty hands except the ballot, which they scarcely understood, and which, as time went by, they hardly dared to use, we could not hope for any great spread of our political principles amongst the Southern Commonwealths."[115] Boker recognized the weaknesses of Reconstruction, the problems created by the black exodus to the North, and saw in both a possible confrontation that was later articulated by his colleagues.

The seriousness with which the new conditions were viewed became apparent in similar addresses intended to keep the membership informed. Typical of these was the lecture given by John E. Bryant of Georgia in 1881. Bryant, a founder of the Southern Advance Association, was brought to Philadelphia by Charles J. Stillé, who had become provost of the University of Pennsylvania, and by Edward M. Davis, the son-in-law of Lucretia Mott. Life in the South, Bryant stated, was opposite in every way to that in the North. Its sectional view was entrenched, its religious outlook was different, and in national sentiment, it stood apart from northern thinking. His Southern Advance Association was interested in an educational program that would reduce, and possibly eliminate, the hostility toward the North that was being inculcated into a new generation of Southerners. It was not illiteracy alone that he feared, but the substance of what was being taught. As a result of Bryant's lecture, Stillé and Davis asked the League to urge Congress to appropriate funds to revise and improve the educational system of the South.[116] Meanwhile, the League raised a fund of its own for this purpose. A more explicit examination of the state of general American education was presented to the League by John Eaton, United States Commissioner of Education. He was concerned with the widespread illiteracy uncovered by the census of 1880. More than two-million native whites and almost one-million foreign born were illiterate. The territories of the Southwest held a high percentage of Spanish speaking people, for whom no educational facilities existed. But the worst problem concerned Southern blacks, three and one quarter million of whom could neither read nor write. Eaton recognized that only federal funding of existing agencies could overcome the widespread ignorance and illiteracy. The League, which had already reached the same conclusion, acted as a catalyst for action by publishing and distributing Eaton's address in 1882, with a statistical appendix on American illiteracy. The corporate body of the League resolved that the granting of financial aid by the Treasury Department on the basis of illiteracy within given areas was an imperative supplement to public school funds in the states and territories.[117]

Without the ability of the Negro to read and write, it was clear that universal suffrage could not easily be implemented. The white South would abide in its present patterns, and blacks in Northern cities would continue to live in ignorance. New concern was generated when the Supreme Court declared the Force Acts unconstitutional. The Force Acts, passed in 1870-71, were intended to guarantee the constitutional amendments, so that registration and voting by Negroes would not be obstructed. A supplementary Civil Rights Act was passed in 1875 to give Negroes equality in the use of all public accommodations, including theaters, hotels, and places of amusement. After the Republicans lost control of Congress in 1882, the Supreme Court had declared all these measures unconstitutional. Federal law, it was maintained, offered protection against discrimination by states, not by individuals. The shaky status of Negro voters was further imperiled and prospects for better education in the North and South were reduced, and the initial safeguards against race discrimination were removed. Negroes were once again at the mercy of the states. In evaluating the situation, the annual League report for 1887 stated: "We commend to our colored fellow citizens the thought that, as the Republican Party was the one which placed the ballot in their hands and so far as it was possible by legal enactment has protected them in the use of those ballots, it is but self-protection for them to remain in the ranks of the organization to which they must appeal for help in political need. Meanwhile the duty and responsibility of accomplishing the purposes of the Civil Rights Bill by resort to other and more effective plans are worthy of our earnest consideration."[118]

A year later, the League lamented the fact that due to Jim Crow laws and other state obstructions, the mass of black voters in the South was practically disenfranchised. The Southern press, freely quoted in the League's reports, made no secret of its antiNegro stand. The Lynchburg *Virginian* stated that the "African has been vanquished and it is settled forever that the white men, whose estate this is, must rule for all time to come."[119]

The League took a strong stand against those who preached the brotherhood of man because they failed to condemn the Southern devices that interfered with the civil and political rights of black people. The League emphatically held that *"the citizen shall vote*, be he black or white, and of whatever faith." In spite of its outspoken statements and its efforts to prod the federal government to improve the educational system, both in the North and the South, the League, because of its allegiance to the Republican or dominant Party of the time, was forced to share in the blame for the default of Reconstruction, for which it was not responsible. It looked upon its work, and the program of Republicanism, as a "sacred mission," and as all the more difficult since the Southern states had returned to political power without an effective black vote to offset its influence.

In December, 1887, The Union League commemorated the twenty-fifth anniversary of its founding in gala fashion. The League House was filled to capacity, and the popular Germania Orchestra played for a grand banquet. In the addresses which followed, President Edwin N. Benson, a veteran of the war and a benefactor of the League, struck a serious note in an otherwise festive meeting. Benson gave a concise account of the League's war work and its political activities. He pointed to the indifference shown to the American flag by Northerners and Southerners alike. Discussion of the war, he noted, had come to be considered in bad taste, and respect for the flag was regarded as outmoded patriotism. A generation after the firing on Fort Sumter, the opening of the Civil War, American hearts were no longer fired with the loyalty to their nation which the event had evoked. The flag had ceased to be a symbol for which men had fought and died. Benson spoke in deep regret of these changing attitudes among Northerners.[120]

Benson then called upon George H. Boker to address the League. The retired president had not lost any of his gentlemanly demeanor, but his sharp comments and political thrusts turned the evening into a stirring occasion. At the age of sixty-three, Boker was still as fiery as he had been during the critical days of the war. Appealing to the younger members who had been children when the guns blazed at Gettysburg and who now saw in the League mainly the luxuries of a social club, he urged them not to forget the harsh struggle that gave birth to the League whose anniversary they were celebrating. To the 44 surviving original members of the League, his remarks were nostalgic, and his tone somber. He regretted that the prime mover in the founding of the League, Judge John I. C. Hare, had resigned in 1881 because of personal occupations. Boker's tribute to Abraham Lincoln was spoken as poignantly as if the president had just been assassinated. His sharpest words were reserved for the Democrats. He saw little difference between "War Democrats" and "Protection Democrats," and virtually denied the existence of any good Democrats. He deplored the divisions within the Republican Party which he believed were weakening the League, and criticized members' interest in local elections. Both were condemned as areas which the founders never thought' of entering, except as private citizens. He called upon members young and old to concern themselves with the needs of labor, the rights of capitalists, the recognition of national issues, and the importance of upholding the principles upon which The Union League was founded. A moment of silence followed his speech, and then, a burst of applause resounded through the assembly hall. It was Boker's last public address before he went into retirement.[121]

One other speaker followed, James Milliken, who was among the first men to sign the League Articles of Association on December 22, 1862. Milliken repeated many of the well-known anecdotes on the founding of the League, and added a few new ones. Like Boker, he addressed himself to the younger members, commenting on "the impending conflict between labor and capital." He closed his brief talk with a prophetic question. "We have secured the Negro freedom from slavery and have endowed him with political rights; in both he must be protected, and so protected that we do no harm to the rights of our own race. To bring the situation vividly to your understanding suppose a community where the black race are in the majority, determining local laws, assessing taxes, and in control of public schools. What would then be your action? What should the statutes provide to insure peace and harmony and to tender each race considerate of the other's welfare? I leave these subjects for your thoughtful consideration."[122]

V

⟨⁓⟩

Transition and A New Crisis

PARTICIPATION in national politics, which men like Claghorn opposed and men like Boker advocated, was a vital part of the life of The Union League. As private citizens, their allegiance to the Republican Party was unquestioned; as League members, this allegiance became stronger with each national election. Corporate participation in municipal political affairs vanished as the League advanced into the twentieth century, but not until a vigorous debate again clarified the position of the League on local politics. The desire to declare the League officially a Republican club, and to require its members to reveal their political orientation, grew among many from year to year. League members upheld and supported the platform of the Republican Party at each national convention, but no corporate step was taken to influence their choice at the polls. Behind the scenes, the League became a power; publicly, it made known its endorsement of Republican presidential, and sometimes state, candidates. A formal declaration of its affiliation seemed unnecessary.

Nothing enlisted League support more than the Republican Party plank, which concerned itself with the protection of American industry, labor, and sound money. The tariff, monetary and immigration problems, and its own political identity also continued to absorb the attention of the League. A new generation of members undertook to accommodate the outlook of the League to the great social changes and industrial advancements of the late nineteenth century.

The older generation had lost none of its influence. Prior to the Civil War, Henry C. Carey had enunciated the protectionist views which were later adopted by the League. His doctrines had moved away from those of the classical English economists. With some modifications, Carey's concepts became the core of the tariff and financial policies adopted through the administrations of McKinley, Roosevelt and Taft. Carey argued that a protective tariff would benefit farmers and working men as well as American manufacturers. His monetary theories held that the scarcity of money was responsible for high interest rates. Prosperity could better be assured by increasing the money supply, thereby contributing to the expansion of industry, and the improvement of a growing transportation system.[1]

Among Carey's followers were recognized economists identified with the League's Board of Publication. Stephen Colwell, the former ironmaster and author of *The Ways and Means of Payment,* had made his mark as a humanitarian, an expositor of Presbyterian thought, and an economist; William Elder, an antebellum essayist, emerged as a postwar political scientist; Henry Carey Baird, a publisher and author who entered the League in 1865, was Carey's nephew and his intellectual heir; Henry C. Lea, another nephew, had thoroughly absorbed the Carey philosophy. As the spokesman of American heavy industry, Carey influenced League members engaged in iron manufacture and other basic industries.[2] Foremost among these industrialists who favored Carey's theories was William Sellers, president of the Midvale Steel Company and a prime mover in the affairs of the Franklin Institute. Sellers supplied all of the ironwork for the Brooklyn Bridge and for the Centennial buildings in Philadelphia. Joseph Wharton and Robert Patterson, Philadelphia ironmasters and manufacturers, also welcomed the Carey-Colwell philosophy. Colwell died in 1871, but Carey, who lived until the age of 86 and died in 1879, was responsible for a mass of literature on the tariff and on currency. Carey and Elder contributed to the *National American,* a publication of the American Industrial League, and to *The Iron Age,* the semiofficial organ of the Iron and Steel Association, edited by John Williams, a Careyite and a League member. From the presses of Baird, and Lippincott came much of the original literature of American economic thought. The Carey school of economic thinkers supported Lincoln's monetary measures, the national banking system, and the circulation of wartime paper currency. After the war, they opposed the return to specie payments. Their views, and their interpretation of American finance, dominated the thinking of League industrialists and manufacturers and became the alarm bell of The Union League. Their contributions to the economic literature of the period exerted an influence on national thought. To a considerable extent, their ideas on tariff and currency were incorporated into the platforms of the Republican Party. One of the lesser known Careyites, "Pig-Iron" Kelley, preached the gospel of the protective tariff to hundreds of audiences, including the Congress of the United States.

Authors, industrialists, and economic thinkers mingled at the "Carey Vespers," an informal salon-type gathering where political ideas were exchanged weekly, and the conversation was animated by the excellent hock their host provided. In Carey's words, "We discuss everything and decide nothing." League guests outside Carey's immediate orbit included William D. Lewis, a prewar friend; Joseph Chandler, minister to Naples before the unification of Italy; Morton McMichael, one of Carey's publishers; President Grant; Bayard Taylor, the poet; Salmon P. Chase, Secretary of the Treasury under Lincoln; and David Wilmot, author of the Wilmot Proviso. In a sense, it was another inner "club" that met away from the League House. But here lay some of the seminal power of the League.[3]

Protection, or the practice of regulating imports and exports in order to shield American industry from foreign competition, was a major political campaign issue at the end of the nineteenth century. Its effectiveness was attacked with regularity by the Democrats in their attempt to weaken it through revision of the existing laws. The economic stagnation which prevailed in the country from 1873 to 1878 opened the door to serious challenge of protectionism, and when Democrats obtained a majority in the House in 1876, and again in 1878 they undertook either to dilute the tariff or repeal the laws supporting it. For the League protection became a vital national issue. With the rise of Democratic hopes for a presidential victory in 1880, it no longer restrained its alarm. Arguments against the national banking system, for the resumption of specie payment, and about the future of the tariff were livelier and more frequent than ever before. Once again, The Union League stepped forward to assume leadership in a political campaign it considered crucial in "thought, sentiment, and action."[4]

In an unprecedented move, the League promoted Grant for a third-term president. Senator James G. Blaine of Maine, however, was a Republican favorite. At the League, Henry C. Lea opposed the move to support Grant, and in protest resigned from the League.[5] At the Party Convention in 1880, a violent fight erupted, and the Convention peacemaker, James A. Garfield, was nominated on the Republican ticket. As soon as the convention was over, League committees were appointed, and funds contributed liberally. The League stated with pride that "not one dollar of the fund was used for corrupt and improper purposes." Time, effort, and well directed influence were expended to win the election for James A. Garfield in Pennsylvania and nearby states. Speakers accompanied by brass bands and parades were organized to campaign throughout Philadelphia. League

Union League House,

SEPTEMBER 21, 1880.

TO THE MEMBERS OF THE UNION LEAGUE.

The importance of the coming Presidential election must be apparent to every member of the League, and in order to give aid and encouragement to the Republican cause, and to make a demonstration on the side of

GARFIELD and ARTHUR,

the Campaign Committee of the Union League hereby invites every member of our time-honored organization to assemble at the League House, on SATURDAY EVENING, *September 25th*, 1880, *at seven thirty o'clock, promptly, in dark clothes, to make a short parade in the grand Republican Demonstration.*

Gilmore's Band of New York will be secured, if possible.

The Union League will leave the Right of the South Wing of the Column, and will parade in sections of eight.

COLONEL R. DALE BENSON

will act as Chief Marshal, with the following assistants :—

ASSISTANT MARSHALS.

EDWIN N. BENSON,	EDWIN H. FITLER,
HENRY C. HOWELL,	EDWARD C. KNIGHT.

AIDS.

(To be selected from the following, or all, if they will serve.)

W. H. HURLEY,	CHAS. J. FIELD,	C. H. CRAMP,
JOHN H. MICHENER,	J. B. AGNEW,	LINCOLN GODFREY,
WM. E. LITTLETON,	THOS. S. HARRISON,	JNO. PRICE WETHERILL,
THEO. E. WIEDERSHEIM,	WM. McMICHAEL,	WM. L. ELKINS,
ALBERT D. FELL,	CHAS. E. SMITH (Press),	HENRY S. FIELD,
CHARLES K. IDE,	E. DUNBAR LOCKWOOD,	L. F. BARRY,
JNO. L. LAWSON,	WINTHROP SMITH,	CLEMENT A. GRISCOM,
HENRY C. BUTCHER,	SILAS W. PETTIT,	FRED'K LOVEJOY,
J. E. SOULÉ,	JOSEPH MOORE, JR.,	WM. B. WARNE,
AMOS R. LITTLE,	SAML. B. HUEY,	LEWIS WALN SMITH,
B. G. GODFREY,	CHAS. THACKARA,	SAMUEL BELL,
JAY COOKE, JR.,	GEORGE S. FOX,	E. Z. KIENZLE.
WALTER G. WILSON,	ALEX. P. COLESBERRY,	

Union League Badges will be furnished the members, on the evening of the parade, at the League House.

In order to facilitate the arrangements, will you be kind enough to notify EDWIN N. BENSON, No. 34 South Third Street (2d floor), if you are willing to parade?

GEORGE H. BOKER, *President.*

WM. E. LITTLETON, *Secretary.*

COMMITTEE ON PARADE.

EDWIN N. BENSON,	WINTHROP SMITH,	JOSEPH MOORE, JR.,
T. E. WIEDERSHEIM,	R. DALE BENSON,	W. H. HURLEY.

A LEAGUE PRESIDENTIAL CAMPAIGN CIRCULAR OF 1880

members campaigned on the city's sidewalks. Their tactics became a model that was emulated throughout Pennsylvania, Ohio, and Indiana. It was the popular mode of the late nineteenth century, and hundreds of League members joined in the activity. League literature supporting the Republican Party flooded the state.[6] To counteract this tremendous show of strength, Democratic spokesmen presented themselves as tariff men, but voters were not heavily swayed by this guise. Fear of a defeat spread among the Democrats when Ohio and Indiana came through for Garfield. The news was blazed through gas-illuminated transparencies at the top of the League House to onlookers eager to learn the election results. Garfield was elected president by a meager majority of 10,000 votes out of almost nine million cast. Without the efforts of the League, disaster might well have struck the Republicans.

In its analysis of the election, the League depicted it as a battle between justice and oppression, between "honest ballots and systematic fraud," and between the "nation and a section" of the nation. The League maintained its strong belief that the Republican Party was successful, even though its margin of victory was narrow, because its program was one of substance. The key to prosperity, they insisted, was a high tariff; the misleading protectionist pose of the Democrats, who wanted only so much tariff as could be used as revenue, hindered the expansion of American industry.[7]

The League's great expectations for President Garfield were short-lived. Early in May, 1881 he was entertained at the League House. Two months later he was critically wounded in Washington by Charles J. Guiteau, a disenchanted office-seeker, and died on September 19. Vice-President Chester A. Arthur succeeded him in office, but his administration was subjected to criticism from many sources, including gentle censure from the League. The people, the League said, "do not feel that he has redeemed his pledge; they differed in his judgment as to the proper use of patronage." Yet the League believed that Arthur was upholding the doctrines of the Republican Party. He stood against a majority of both houses of Congress in vetoing the River and Harbor Bill because of its extravagant appropriations, and in his veto of the Chinese Exclusion Act in 1882 because the legislation was contrary to the treaty of 1880 on the subject. However, reflecting antiChinese agitation in California in opposition to the contract labor schemes which brought the Chinese to the West, Congress enacted that law placing severe restrictions on Chinese immigration to the United States. Thus, Arthur began his presidency amid bitter criticism from an uncooperative Congress; however, he maintained his independence of thought throughout his tenure of office.[8]

The tariff was a favorite topic of discussion at the League luncheon tables. Constant demands were made upon the library for theoretical and statistical literature for references, and for the innumerable tracts which favored or opposed the tariff. In spite of all this interest, no basic changes in the tariff laws were introduced in the quarter-century that followed the Civil War. League proponents of a high tariff were naturally disappointed when James G. Blaine was defeated in 1884 by Grover Cleveland, the first president to be elected on the Democratic ticket since James Buchanan. The factionalism of Pennsylvania Republicans had contributed to the national loss. Independent Republicans had supported Cleveland for his advocacy of political reform, but after his election, they denounced him as one who "has proved false to all pledges made to secure the Independent vote which elected him."[9] Far more gratifying to the League was the election to Congress of a number of Southern Republicans in 1884. This was looked upon by League members as another step toward the defeat of free trade, and it left northern Democrats too divided to be effective. In fact, it helped to reduce some of the factional disputes among the Republicans. But the South had become solidly Democratic and its Republican voice was muted.

League Republicans opposed Cleveland's conciliatory attitude to the South, and were unhappy over his repeated vetoes of veterans' pension bills. In its annual report, the League also accused Cleveland of bartering away valuable fishing rights because of his lack of knowledge of the history of American fisheries. The industry had been carefully guarded, but now the League saw it imperiled by foreign intrusion. Samuel B. Huey, writing in the name of the League in a clear historical exposition, presented the case for the North Atlantic fisheries, a matter that still remains in contention.[10]

Above all, the tariff became uppermost in the minds of both parties, so much so that the League compared it to the critical issues that it had confronted during the Civil War. Cleveland's annual message to the Congress in 1887 dealt exclusively with the tariff, and it is felt that his proposals to reduce the tariff contributed to his defeat by Benjamin Harrison the following year. Despite some sharp criticism of Cleveland, League Republicans respected his ability to maintain an independent course and to rise above his party.

Pennsylvania Republicans, including League members and their associates, hoped to soften party factionalism in order to insure a Republican victory in 1888. The election of General James A. Beaver in 1887 as governor of Pennsylvania had been one step in maintaining Republican unity. After the convention which nominated Harrison, the League as a body and its individual members threw their weight behind the campaign. Thomas Nolan, a wool manufacturer and president of the Manufacturers Club of Philadelphia, and Joseph Wharton pressed the tariff issue to satisfy Pennsylvania interests. Both were influential in the Pennsylvania Republican Party and saw the tariff as the main economic problem of the country. Joining them were John Wanamaker, the department store retailer, and Charles E. Smith, organizer of the iron and steel industry, president of the Reading Railroad, and a lifelong Republican. Wanamaker openly opposed Matthew Quay, who sought control of the Republican organization, and was not won over by Quay's promises of a cabinet post. He assailed Quay for his irregularities and corrupt practices in office, and he conducted the Republican fundraising campaign in Pennsylvania independent of any involvement with Quay's machine politics. The Pennsylvania fund is believed to have been the largest raised for Harrison. With Harrison's close victory Wanamaker was named postmaster-general, and another League member, Charles Emory Smith, was appointed minister to Russia.[11]

With a Republican president returned to office, the League once more anticipated the return of a higher tariff. They were not to be disappointed. William McKinley, the Ohio congressman responsible for the tariff of 1890, introduced major changes in the protective laws, and duties were raised appreciably. These changes came at a time when American prosperity was unsurpassed. American harvests were generous, industries thrived, trade was brisk, and wages were higher than they had been for some years. The flow of Eastern and Southern European immigration had steadily increased the population, supplying a fresh source of labor. The West was expanding, and American capital had begun to exploit its vast natural resources, attracting both native and foreign-born settlers to the new areas. Within three years, the Columbian Exposition in Chicago would capture the spirit of an enterprising United States. Meanwhile it appeared as if the conditions for another Republican victory were present. But in the congressional elections of 1890, the Republicans lost 78 seats in the House. The success of Harrison's program was jeopardized, and Republican confidence was dampened.

Contrary to the judgment of most Republicans, the conditions were ripe for a national Democratic success. Hostility to the high tariff became a major election issue, and the rise of Populism, which was a response to the decline in prices of agricultural products, worked to the advantage of the Democrats. But both parties were surprised by the extent of the Democratic victory. When the election returns of 1892 came in, Republicans were staggered by the magnitude of their loss. The League was already attuned to the swift turn in the political tide. It was even rumored throughout the League House that disenchanted members had openly supported the reelection of Democrat Grover Cleveland. These League members, dissidents in support of Cleveland's moderate stand on the tariff, favored his strong position in upholding the gold standard. This precipitated a crisis within the League which will be discussed later on.[12]

With Cleveland returned to office, the tariff debate was vigorously resumed. In 1893, an economic depression of considerable severity swept the nation. Labor unions were alienated from the administration during the Pullman strike, which was suppressed by presidential order. Early in 1894, Congressman William L. Wilson introduced a bill embodying Cleveland's tariff ideas which Arthur P. Gorman had revised by hundreds of amendments reducing the tariff by ten percent, and providing the Democrats with a victory. So distressed was the League, that its major tariff proponents asked for a special League meeting to fight the measure. Throughout September, 1894, many hours of discussion and speechmaking were spent on the tariff proposals of Wilson and Gorman. Statistical details on the conditions of foreign industry were entered on the minutes showing how American labor would be reduced to penury unless the bill was defeated. The public opposition of the League was in vain; the Senate had its way and enacted the weakened Wilson-Gorman Bill.[13]

Although the apprehension expressed by the League over the tariff reached its peak in 1894, its interest diminished only slightly thereafter. Uncertainties persisted; arguments over the complexities and legalities of the tariff echoed from the League House and were heard from the floor of the Congress, until they were muffled by the guns of a world war which the United States entered in 1917. The tariff debate had been silenced.

A dramatic development in the affairs of the League came as a result of Cleveland's second election. At the annual meeting of 1892, Charles Eugene Claghorn confirmed the fact that a clique of members had publicly worked against the principles of the League by supporting Cleveland. One of the men, George Gluyas Mercer, unhesitatingly identified himself. The exposé precipitated a controversy that spanned two annual meetings. The published reports of the meetings reveal in full the debate over the Republican identity of the League, and an overwhelming desire on the part of the majority to place the League officially in the camp of the Republican Party.[14]

The 1892 meeting, one of the best attended annual meetings in years, focused on a resolution introduced by Claghorn which protested the conduct of dissident members. While the League had no provisions for expelling such members—although it had expelled James Scovel for supporting Andrew Johnson in 1866—the resolution called for the Membership Committee to insist upon the following pledge from candidates: "I am a Republican. My political sentiments and principles are in harmony with the national policy as advanced by The Union League. I voted the Republican ticket at the preceding national election. If I change my politics I will at once resign my membership; and in the event of my not doing so, and sufficient proof is adduced that I have broken this pledge, The Union League is hereby authorized to expunge my name from the roll."

The controversial resolution was well-received. Claghorn was fully aware that his resolution could not be enacted without 30 days notice prior to an annual meeting. He also was aware that even if it was adopted, it would have to be consonant with the Charter and By-Laws of the League. By asking that this resolution be adopted by the Membership Committee at the time candidates were interviewed, he hoped that the committee might introduce this procedure; at the same time, he hoped to avoid a conflict with the corporate laws of the League. Once he made clear his intentions, however, he saw no purpose in deferring the resolution for a full year, and he withdrew it.

Carefully observing the proceedings was General Louis Wagner, who had fearlessly paraded the United States Colored Troops in review before The Union League. Glancing about him, he reintroduced the resolution that Claghorn had withdrawn, adding the provision that it be posted for 30 days in accordance with the requirements of the By-Laws.

An effort was then made to amend the resolution by adding a demand for an expression of Republican fidelity during the state and municipal elections. Wagner rejected it on the grounds that it would hamper the consideration of the original idea. The new resolution was adopted almost unanimously, although the vote would not take place until the following year.

In the ensuing discussion, one of the reasons for the Claghorn-Wagner resolution was divulged. Rudolph Blankenburg, of the new generation of League members and a future mayor of Philadelphia, called attention to the nomination by the Republican Party of a Democrat in Pennsylvania's third congressional district. While the League could not control such a nomination, he asked that League members who directly and indirectly supported it be censured, along with all Pennsylvania Republicans who had been responsible for it. In Blankenburg's opinion, such conduct was outrageous. He considered it a national issue, particularly at a time when one or two congressional votes could swing the balance in important legislation. Blankenburg presented a resolution condemning League members' support of Democrats. The response was so overwhelming that the chairman saw no need to announce the vote.

Amid the clamor and excitement, Alexander K. McClure obtained the floor to introduce a completely different matter. He proposed that President Harrison be tendered a banquet by the League upon his retirement from office. The tension relaxed momentarily. McClure added that every member would approve the invitation, whatever his political affiliation. Again, voices of protest could be heard. Many recalled that in 1874 McClure had sought the support of Democrats in a local election. General Wagner demanded the floor. He charged McClure with introducing a motion, no matter how pleasant, that invited opposition. Facing McClure and calmly stroking his white closecut beard, Wagner declared that he looked with suspicion on Greeks who bear gifts. Despite his challenge to McClure, however, Wagner was also eager to have Harrison present at the League. McClure responded with equal calm, urging that his motion be carried and reminding the members that some had celebrated Cleveland's election on the League premises. The motion was carried, and the meeting ended in the early hours of the morning.[15]

Throughout 1893, the League was preoccupied with improving its property, acquiring the houses along Sansom Street west of its building, and projecting plans that would lead to a major expansion of the club house.[16] Its facilities and service were already renowned, and the rapidly growing League library was becoming outstanding. In addition to its collection of American political literature, Civil War regimental histories, and state and local history, the Library Committee had strengthened its section on European and American literature. Balzac and Hugo, Carlyle and Dickens, Heine and Goethe were read avidly, according to League records. Books written by members, covering a broad range of subjects, were noted with pride. The library shelves were filled with the handsome volumes of Shakespeare's works, edited by Horace Howard Furness, the medieval writings of Henry C. Lea, and the writings on American history by Charles J. Stillé, Charlemagne Tower, Jr., and Joseph P. Rosengarten. Hundreds of minor authors presented personal memoirs and studies on such diverse topics as women's rights and Italian literature. Also to be found there was the essay on librarianship by Lloyd P. Smith, librarian of The Library Company of Philadelphia, and treatises on biblical law by Judge Mayer Sulzberger, the eminent bibliophile. By the end of 1893, the Library Committee indicated its need for additional space.[17]

On the eve of the following year, in November 1893, 30 days before the annual meeting, the resolution concerning a Republican pledge for new members was duly posted and mailed to all members. At the meeting, the League House was unusually crowded, and murmurs and speculations of what might transpire could be heard throughout its spacious halls. By eight o'clock, when the meeting was convened, the halls leading to the assembly room were thronged with members. President John Russell Young quickly reached the main point of the evening's business, and General Wagner, chairman of the committee read his report. In essence, it said:

"Candidates for membership must be of good character and repute, and politically affiliated with the Republican Party, and in harmony with its principles as recognized and supported by The Union League. Failure at any time after the admission to membership, to maintain these qualifications shall subject the members to suspension, as here-inafter provided, for acts or conduct hostile to the League."[18]

Wagner was asked to provide the reasons that influenced the committee in arriving at its recommendation. Before he could do so, an amendment was introduced to review the whole matter in order to determine if the recommendation was in violation of the Charter and By-Laws, thereby deferring action for another year. Rufus E. Shapley presented a lengthy, well reasoned legal analysis of the resolution. Essentially, he stated that any effort to incorporate such a qualification for membership into the By-Laws would be discounte-nanced by every legal interpretation. Judging from the applause and cheering, Shapley's opinion had many supporters who agreed that any change in the By-Laws had to be made in a manner that the courts would uphold. Wagner rose to the challenge with a touch of sarcasm. Although he was a banker, not a member of the bar, he shredded the arguments of the lawyers, insisting that a vote be taken for or against the resolution. If the resolution was carried, he insisted, it would then be a case for the courts to decide. He drew upon the wartime history of the League to show the need to uphold Republican policy, but this was quickly countered by statements that the League had been composed of men of varying political back-grounds. Reminiscing for a minute, Wagner, like Charles Gibbons had done earlier, charged his challengers with bias toward Democrats and referred to those now dead, "Daniel Dougherty amongst others," who had claimed special political rights within the club.

Wagner continued his argument by quoting the local *Press*, which had stated recently that "The League is regarded as the leading Republican organization in the country, and, as it is located in the strongest Republican city. in the United States, its views upon national questions always attract attention." He argued further that it was the League that decided the qualifications of the men who sought membership, not the Republican National Convention, nor any

other political group. Just as the Membership Committee was concerned with the reputation and character of a candidate, so it also had
the right to approve his political affiliation. If in fact the League had
become known to the nation as a Republican institution, why then,
could it not incorporate this identity into its legal structure? "The
Union League should resume her proper place in the front rank of
Republican leadership, and make and direct Republican policy as in
days gone by."

When Wagner yielded the floor, he was followed by Silas W.
Pettit, a veteran of the Civil War and an outstanding constitutional
lawyer who succeeded Young to the presidency of The Union League.
Pettit called attention to those members present who had expressed
satisfaction over the election of Cleveland and the defeat of League
interests. It was this episode that had brought the League to the
present debate. If the supporters of Cleveland had shown the good
judgment of restraint, instead of displaying their feelings, the present
amendment might not have been introduced. Pettit called for unanimity, "and if there is a man here who wants to vote the Democratic
ticket, he ought to keep it to himself, as far as the League is concerned." Pettit reviewed the principles to which the League was committed and called for a vote.

Unable to contain himself, George G. Mercer, an outspoken Democrat, addressed the chair to declare his legal and moral right to vote
as he saw fit, and to say that no act of the League could suspend him
from membership. Before he was shouted down, he requested that
an outside legal opinion which he had obtained be read by another
member. The fact that an independent opinion had been sought
showed the extent to which some members had been concerned and
aroused. The opinion was prepared by John G. Johnson, the lawyer
who in 1882 had represented Arthur Burt in his suit against expulsion
by the League. Johnson found the proposed By-Law illegal. Mercer
was unable to regain the floor, although both General Wagner and
John Russell Young wanted to hear what he had to say. Finally,
Wagner called for a vote on the resolution defining membership qualifications. When the ballots were counted, the amendment failed to
obtain the necessary two-thirds vote.

After more than two hours of intense and at times heated argument,
the following compromise resolution was introduced and accepted
with applause: "That it is the sense of this League that it is a
distinctively Republican organization, and that the Directors ought
not to admit to membership any applicant not politically affiliated
with the Republican Party and in harmony with its principles as
recognized and supported by the League." Rufus E. Shapley, who had

opposed Wagner's By-Law on legal grounds, seconded the resolution. It was a curious meeting, dominated by the legal profession, who argued as if they were in a court of law; but it was also a major policy-making meeting, which determined the course of the League in accepting future candidates. The compromise principle concerning the admission of new members was adopted on December 11, 1893, and has been adhered to ever since.[19] But it was never made part of the By-Laws.

The prolonged discussions of the 1870's over participation in municipal elections, the dismay over the failure of Reconstruction measures, and concern over its political identity in the 1890's did not interfere with the League's pursuit of its other interests. Continuing its policy of supporting veterans, the League backed their claims for an increased pension and increased employment by federal agencies. Especially active in this effort were League members who had fought in the war. They, too, belonged to the Grand Army of the Republic, the veterans organization that was active in presenting the claims of its membership, and the Military Order of the Loyal Legion, whose members were all commissioned officers of the Union Army. The two organizations had proved effective in securing veterans claims.

Corporal James Tanner, who had recorded the first testimony in connection with the assassination of Lincoln, had become an articulate spokesman and officer of the GAR. His frequent appearances at The Union League to speak on the pension needs of veterans were usually in conjunction with national political campaigns. An appearance by Tanner, especially when it coincided with a GAR encampment, meant open house at the League to the common soldier of the Union Army, whose military uniform was a ticket of admission. An ardent Republican, Tanner addressed audiences eager to hear the events of the war, in which he lost both legs. As a result of his popularity, and the support he received from the League and from military societies, Tanner was able to bring about the employment of 817 additional veterans by government agencies in 1882. Six years later, he was appointed to head the federal Pension Bureau. Thereafter, monthly pension allowances for veterans were raised dramatically. Some considered his zealous efforts on behalf of veterans an extravagant abuse of federal funds. Tanner was dismissed in the Harrison administration amid intraparty disputes. But the League continued to support his work with the GAR.[20]

Throughout the late nineteenth century, veterans also obtained support from such individual League members as Robert Burns

Beath, the official historian of the GAR, Oliver C. Bosbyshell, one of
the first defenders of the national capitol and subsequently superintendent of the United States Mint, William H. Lambert, the pioneer
American collector of Lincolniana, and Edwin N. Benson, who
became a member of the League while still in uniform. Benson
developed strong military interests, and after the war, in 1875, he
organized the Veteran Corps First Regiment Infantry, National
Guard of Pennsylvania. Benson's name is associated with numerous
gifts to the club. Among them is the stained glass memorial window
commemorating the life and work of Meredith, Fell, Binney and
McMichael, the first four presidents of the League. The Benson Annex
was named in his memory. He also initiated annual celebrations held
at the League by the First Regiment Infantry and the Pennsylvania
Commandery of the Military Order of the Loyal Legion.[21]

The reverence with which the veteran was regarded continued so
long as there were men who remembered the war. The local veterans
orphans' home was supported by the League until there was no longer
a need for the institution; when its official history was written, the
League helped with its publication. Decoration Day, honoring those
who had fallen in battle, was observed by the League with solemn
dignity. The great bronze memorial statue of Abraham Lincoln, which
the League helped erect in Fairmount Park not far from the Philadelphia Museum of Art, was decorated annually in an appropriate
ceremony by League members.[22] This custom is continued to the
present day.

Another bronze sculpture of significance commemorates the
Union League Civil War regiments. Following the Spanish American
War, the League raised a fund to honor the men who had served
in it, but it was decided that the fund would be better used to mark
the greater military activity of the League in the Civil War. The
tablet, with the figures in high relief, was done in Philadelphia by
the eminent sculptor Henry K. Bush-Brown. Measuring twelve feet
in height by eight feet in width, its central figure is the Goddess of
War, who is distributing munitions to soldiers. To her right is a
soldier grasping for weapons; and to her left is a drummer boy and
standard-bearer, leading a group of soldiers. Other figures are
symbolic of the period. Flanking the group are two columns surmounted by a sweeping arch. On each column the names of the regiments and their officers are inscribed, and on their cornices are cupids
bearing shields dated 1861 and 1865. The elaborate bronze relief is
at the Broad Street entrance of the League, on the north wall opposite
the grand staircase, where it was placed in 1902.[23]

Inspired by the Bush-Brown bronze, a group of nine League

H. K. Bush-Brown

MEMORIAL TO THE REGIMENTS RECRUITED BY
THE UNION LEAGUE OF PHILADELPHIA

veterans instituted an annual visit to the battlefields where they had fought and only narrowly survived. Early in 1903 they organized an associate group of twenty-five others whom they took on an annual tour to Gettysburg and through the Virginia valley. George P. Morgan and Richard T. McCarter guided their group to Chancellorsville, Spottsylvania, The Wilderness, Harper's Ferry, Winchester, Antietam, and numerous other battle sites. Mementos of the war, which they recovered, twisted swords and battered muskets, and photographs of themselves reliving daring episodes, today are in the collections of the League. Morgan, one of the last survivors of the group which called itself the Pilgrims to the Battlefields of the Rebellion, published a volume for its members that recounted personal experiences and reflections of the battlefields. Among the League Pilgrims were men who visited the public schools of the city and state, fascinating children with stories of war and heroism, of despair and death, and shocking both teachers and pupils by quoting General Sherman's three-word statement, "War is Hell."[24]

One of the great movements that affected the future of the United States after the Civil War was the vast immigration from Eastern and Southern Europe. The character of immigration underwent a vast transformation during the administration of Chester A. Arthur. League men, who opposed free trade in the belief that American labor would be undermined, compared the conditions in the textile mills of England, Scotland, and Germany with the more favorable conditions of American workers. Even the conditions of the American "sweatshop" system that clothed the nation were looked upon as superior to those existing in Western Europe. As the tariff debate continued, special meetings were held to discuss its effect on immigration. British emigration was attributed to the poor economic conditions of late Victorian England.[25] However, only a few were aware of the upheavals in the Czar's Empire, the economic despair in the Balkans, and a downtrodden peasantry on the shores of the Mediterranean. New faces looked to America's cities of promise, as a vast emigration was set into motion. Between the administration of President Arthur and the outbreak of World War I, millions of immigrants swelled the American population.

Unlike the Chinese, Eastern European and Mediterranean peoples came through open doors. Boston, New York, Philadelphia and Baltimore were inundated by Italians, Greeks, Poles, Ukrainians, and Jews of many countries. In Philadelphia, the nativist attitudes that had reached a peak before the Civil War were no longer as apparent. To the contrary, the first wave of immigrants was welcomed. Daily

THE PILGRIMS OF THE BATTLEFIELDS OF THE REBELLION

press reports condemned the barbaric outrages perpetrated by the Czarist government against Jews. Tens of thousands were on their way to the United States. Most of those who came to the port of Philadelphia traveled on ships of the American Steamship line, built by William Cramp & Sons, prominent League members and nationally known shipbuilders.[26]

A great deal of League sympathy for the plight of the immigrant groups, to cite one example, was the pogroms of 1881 against the Jews in Russia. The wanton destruction of lives and property, and the hundreds of thousands that were left homeless, attracted both League and city-wide attention. Older League members joined with younger ones in supporting a fundraising effort to assist Russian Jewish refugees seeking asylum in Philadelphia. A town meeting at the Academy of Music was arranged in the spring of 1882 by Mayor Samuel King, who elicited the support of the League. John Wanamaker, the outstanding Presbyterian layman in Philadelphia, drew up a resolution of protest to the Russian government which was endorsed by his League colleagues. It condemned "the cruel torture and murder alike of the aged and infirm, and the infant at the mother's breast; of a drunken and wanton soldiery, brutally assaulting their wives and their daughters . . . And such stories . . . as should be remanded from the chronicles of a civilized and Christian nation in the nineteenth century back to the records of the darkest ages. These narratives of woe have inspired the American people with horror."[27]

The resolution recognized the American policy of noninterference with the internal affairs of other governments, but stressed the necessity of rising above "polite and conventional forms of diplomacy" in order to present wrongs and seek their redress. Wanamaker appealed to the God-fearing people of Philadelphia to contribute liberally to aid the unfortunate exiles.

The resolution was forwarded to President Arthur with the request that it be presented to the Russian government at St. Petersburg. Copies were sent to the secretary of state, to the senators and members of the Congress, and to the Russian ambassador at Washington. The protest was unique. No other organized voice made itself heard, for no other major city or port could muster so powerful and influential a group of men to speak out against such atrocities.[28]

The attitude of the League toward the new immigrants was not unlike the reaction of a greater part of the nation, except that League members had taken a positive action. Despite its generally supportive stand, however, the League condemned the Haymarket bombings in Chicago in 1886, which were attributed to German anarchists. It was also shocked by an immigrant anarchist's attempt to assassinate Henry C. Frick in Pittsburgh during the Homestead Strike of 1892. But the

League did not view these violent eruptions as typical of the millions of immigrants who were being forced into a stereotype that blamed innocent strangers for the acts of an isolated few anarchists. The League was eager to see this new mass of people turned into "a body of citizens with intelligent views and devoted to a free government."[29]

For a long time, Republicans felt it was an imperative obligation to spread the knowledge of American institutions, if for no other reason than for their own benefit. J. Levering Jones, writing in the name of the League, emphasized that it did not align itself with one class against another, and that it was not seduced by false political theories. In referring to the dilemma of the immigrants, he contrasted the abundant harvests of America with the failure of the grain crops of Europe and of India, and the tremendous exportations of grains to both lands by the United States. But even with aid from the United States, late nineteenth- and early twentieth-century Europe continued on its path of economic decline. A disoriented European population looked across the Atlantic for a brighter future.[30]

In 1890, the population of Philadelphia passed the one million mark. Of this number, 269,480 were foreign born. A city census, carried out two years later, showed an increase of one-hundred thousand, most of whom were either of foreign birth or Southern black migrants. The rise in population was paralleled by an increase of public buildings and private housing. A new post office was completed in 1884, the Reading Railroad depot on Market Street was finished in 1893, and the new buildings of Drexel Institute were opened in 1891. The impressive Broad Street Station of the Pennsylvania Railroad was considered a model for an inner-city station. A series of office buildings sprung up within walking distance of the League House, and many of the offices were occupied by League members. Although tens of thousands of new homes were being erected throughout the city, their numbers failed to keep pace with the demands of population growth.[31]

The League began to consider plans for its own expansion. Since 1881, at the urging of Edwin N. Benson, many changes and a number of extensions had been made to enlarge the House. Benson became chairman of the Building Committee, raised a subscription, contributed liberally himself, and thus made possible building the annex that carried his name. It provided a recreational area, additional dining space, and a fine assembly room. South of the Benson Annex, a new garden was planted adjoining the restaurant. Today, the rebuilt Benson Annex is located on the original site, adjacent to the South Marble dining room. Other than this addition, no long term building plan was envisioned.

In the process of enlarging the property, it became necessary to purchase adjoining properties, mostly two story-houses, on Moravian and Sansom Streets. Between 1869 and 1881, four properties were bought. Thereafter, efforts were made to purchase the entire block between the rear of the League and Fifteenth Street. The acquisition of these properties was viewed as necessary to protect League interests.[32] Three of the dwellings were described as houses of prostitution, and their elimination would be to the benefit of the League, the nearby Baptist Publication Society, and the residents whose homes fronted Fifteenth Street.[33] Also behind the movement to acquire property was the drive of the natural growth of the League, and the demand to increase the membership roll. Whether such an increase could be approved was dependent upon the enlargement of the physical facilities. Membership during this period was not stabilized. Deaths, resignations, removals from the city, and the effects of an economic depression had taken their toll. In an attempt to offset their losses and stabilize the financial condition of the League, the annual dues were increased. The dues had to be readjusted regularly to meet changing economic conditions and the changing needs of the League. There was a steady rise in membership after 1882, and by 1890 it was restricted to 1,400, a figure much lower than the 1,970 members reached in 1866. Two years later, the active membership roll was increased to 1,500. During the 1890's the entrance fee was raised from $50 to $100, and then to $200. The League had become such an attractive and desirable club that the waiting list of candidates had risen to 900 in 1895. But no more than 15 new members were admitted monthly, and these admissions were governed by deaths and resignations. When it was proposed that the membership roll be set at 1,600 in 1895, discussion on the expansion of the League House took on a serious turn. With an enlarged membership and active use of its facilities, the League House would have to be enlarged.[34]

Toward the end of 1896, it was decided to plan for an extension of the League House to Fifteenth Street. An Advisory Real Estate Board was created at the annual meeting of 1897. Meanwhile, properties on Sansom and Moravian Streets were acquired one by one, including the former residence of Sir William Osler, the world-famous physician who had taught at the University of Pennsylvania Medical College. One residence, later occupied by the League steward, could not be purchased, and it was leased until 1908. Sansom and Moravian Streets were cleared of brothels, dilapidated buildings were razed, and those in good condition were retained, improved, and rented. The responsibility of the Advisory Real Estate Board was to report on the feasibility of extending the building and to make recommendations on the choice of an architect, to determine the kind of building most suited to club needs, and to evaluate whether the handsome brown-stone exterior of the original League House should be retained, altered, or built over. The instruction from the directors was that "The distinctive aim of The Union League should be to create the model club building in the country." It was urged that every oppor-tunity for the expression of architectural beauty be utilized. When these preliminary considerations were decided, League financing could better be determined and new figures could be established for the membership roll. Before the numerous plans and studies were sub-mitted, the total membership in 1900, including life members, the clerical roll, and the army, navy, and consular roll, exceeded 2,000.[35]

Plans for the extension of the League quarters and a concomitant increase in membership coincided with the National Republican Convention at St. Louis in 1896. Preliminary to the Convention, the League again defined its position on the nation's currency, stating that "every dollar of which, whether in gold, silver or notes, shall be of stable value and of equal purchasing power." A committee was appointed to prepare a declaration to be inserted in the Republican platform opposing the free coinage of silver and insisting on the maintenance of the gold standard. The League's unequivocal policy on protectionism was also urged for inclusion in the national platform. Any other approach to currency and protection was looked upon as a potential economic disaster. The declaration was presented at St. Louis by Boies Penrose. After the convention, and the nomination of William McKinley of Ohio, the League met to unanimously approve the platform and the McKinley-Hobart ticket. A campaign committee of 50 was named that included many of the more recent members of the League. Among them was German-born Rudolph Blankenburg; Clayton McMichael, the son of the newspaper publisher Morton McMichael; James Elverson, Jr., also a newspaper publisher; Isaac N. Solis, scion of a colonial Jewish family; Edward T. Stotesbury, better remembered as a financier than as a president of the League; and Craige and Robert Lippincott of the publishing firm. Experienced members of the League campaign committee were Charles Emory Smith, John Russell Young and Joseph G. Darlington, the fourteenth president of the League. One member of the committee who was spiralling his way into the political scene was Boies Penrose.[36]

Penrose came from a background of culture and wealth. He was graduated from Harvard College in 1881, and returned to Philadel-phia to read law with Wayne MacVeagh and George T. Bispham. Three years later they proposed him for League membership and he was duly elected. Penrose was the coauthor of *A History of Municipal*

Development, published in 1887, which contained one of the first analyses of the Bullitt reform charter. Penrose appeared bent on becoming a political reformer. His intense interest in politics lured him from the practice of law and the study of political science to the mainstream of the Republican Party. In 1884, after becoming a League member, he was elected to the state legislature and the following year to the state senate. His reputation grew rapidly. A man with a towering frame and a desire for political conquest, in 1895 Penrose challenged fellow League member Charles F. Warwick for the mayoralty. Penrose was defeated. In less than two years, however, his defeat was turned to advantage when J. Donald Cameron retired from the Senate of the United States. Competing with another League member for the Senate seat, Penrose was elected by the General Assembly of the State to the office of United States Senator. His opponent, John Wanamaker, received only one vote. It was against this background that Penrose was launched into the first McKinley campaign and a long career in politics.[37]

Other political forces also surfaced for the first time in Philadelphia. The three Vare brothers of South Philadelphia, George A., Edwin H., and William S., linked themselves to Matthew S. Quay. Quay who succeeded in getting the vote for Penrose, was in turn bound to Penrose, until the Senator cast him aside. Regardless of the fact that they were held in contempt by some Republicans, denied membership at the League, and scorned by the Democrats, it was the Vares who obtained funds for the support of the area hospitals, extended the school system to lower South Philadelphia, improved a sadly neglected sanitation system, and brought the immigrant population of South Philadelphia into the Republican fold. Between 1895 and 1897, George and Edwin Vare became members of the state legislature, tightening their grip on South Philadelphia, formerly the most neglected quarter of the city, a section they were to win for McKinley.

VI

❧

From High Tide to World War I

THE determination of the League to do everything within its power to obtain a national Republican victory in the election of 1896 was reminiscent of its Civil War zeal. Once more a series of committees was formed that worked independently of the Republican organization. Committees on finance, public meetings, and publications moved into action. The Publication Committee prepared, edited, and distributed 845,000 copies of 12 pamphlets. Their distribution was not confined to Pennsylvania, but reached out to the Southern and Western states and into areas that otherwise might have been neglected. The pamphlets concentrated on two themes, sound money and protection. One contained the speech of General Daniel H. Hastings, governor of Pennsylvania and a League member, who opened the Ohio campaign in Canton, William McKinley's home. He expounded on the issues emphasized by the League, stressing a protective tariff as the major issue of his party, and attacked William Jennings Bryan, the Democratic candidate, for his advocacy of the free coinage of silver. He placed Bryan in the camp of the Populists and Socialists. Hastings' speech received wide attention in Ohio.[1]

The intensive campaign work of the League was of tremendous importance, and mainly offset the powerful influence of the Hearst press. Without question William Randolph Hearst was a vicious opponent of McKinley. There was no limit to the abuse which was directed at the Republican candidate. Hearst's chain of newspapers, which campaigned for Bryan, used every opportunity to injure McKinley politically; but it was of no avail.[2]

Using its many years of rapport with veterans to advantage, the League worked closely with the Veterans Committee of the Republican

Party. Colonel Robert Burns Beath of the GAR, Chairman of the War Veterans' Club, arranged a series of meetings under the auspices of the League at which Generals Oliver O. Howard, Daniel E. Sickles, and the articulate Corporal James Tanner hailed the Republican Party. The most notable of these political meetings was at the Academy of Music on the evening of October 24, 1896.

So certain was the League of a Republican victory at the polls that preparations were made for League men to parade along Chestnut Street as soon as the returns indicated a majority of electoral votes for McKinley. Of the 57 men who were chosen as marshals and aides, 24 had been commissioned officers in the Union Army, two held important posts in the National Guard of Pennsylvania, one was a former governor, and one later became a governor of the Commonwealth; two had been in the diplomatic service, one was a mayor of Philadelphia, and one was later to become a mayor. When McKinley's triumph became known, this elite group of League members led an impressive parade from the League House to Independence Hall and back.

The League arranged for a victory reception to McKinley and his cabinet within two months after the president's inauguration. Of the hundreds of receptions that had been held at the League House since its opening, this was the grandest. For the first time in the history of the nation, the president and his cabinet had returned to the city where the first president of the United States and his cabinet had met in 1790. The elegant arrangements, the programming, the thoughtful security, and the respect that the president showed the League in accepting the invitation, turned the event into a city highlight.

On May 14, 1897, President McKinley was escorted from his hotel to the League by the Veterans Corps, First Regiment Infantry, National Guard of Pennsylvania. Colonel Theodore W. Wiedersheim, among the first defenders of the Union and a prominent figure in the National Guard and in the League, preceded the president and his cabinet. Company D of the regiment brought up the rear, and in the evening acted as a special guard to the dignitaries.

Upon entering the League, the Veteran Corps and Company D were divided into two files, to make a path for President McKinley. Members and their guests were assigned to various dining rooms; the arrangements were extremely precise. Provisions were made for almost 2,500 people, and the League House was filled to capacity. Members who had had doubts about the need to expand the club facilities were converted before the reception was over.

The old dining room was fitted up with the finest furniture in the house. Its center tables offered an assortment of sherry, brandy, whiskey, and bitters, and were dressed with lobster, chicken salad, and small sandwiches. Champagne flowed in abundance. Fresh flowers and a variety of plants provided an appropriate background against which League directors stood while guests moved along the marble hallway to greet President McKinley. Behind the flower arrangements, standing in a semicircle, were members of Company D.

Following the reception, dinner was served. A multicolored program and a menu from the press of Bailey, Banks and Biddle, listing seven courses accompanied by ample Amontillado, an 1889 Brut, and Mumm's Extra, gratified the tastes of the most discerning guest. The addresses were brief, the president personally expressed his appreciation for the compliment paid him by the League, and autograph seekers and members retired well satisfied with the evening.[3]

On the following day, the League had arranged for a parade on Broad Street, and a special viewing stand to accommodate League members was erected on the east side of the street facing the League House. Throngs of Philadelphians crowded into the area to celebrate McKinley's visit. In the fall of 1897, the League elected McKinley to honorary membership.

It was a year enriched by other receptions and celebrations. Founders' Day honored 12 of the surviving members of the original Union Club; Lincoln's Birthday was quietly observed, and on Washington's Birthday, the historian Charlemagne Tower, Jr., chose for his address, "The Earl Cornwallis and the Siege of Yorktown." Two months later Tower, the secretary of the League, was honored by being appointed as Envoy Extraordinary and Minister Plenipotentiary to Austria-Hungary. Hampton L. Carson, a prominent member of the bar and legal historian, read a paper on "The Curiosities of the Law." Also during 1897, the League mourned the loss of the eminent collector of Washingtoniana, William S. Baker, and two of its outstanding physicians, Dr. Peter P. Keyser, an ophthalmologist, and Dr. William H. Pancoast, professor of surgical anatomy at Jefferson Medical College.[4]

League President C. Stuart Patterson, who had been responsible for bringing President McKinley to the League, was not only interested in the nation's finances, but was directly involved in the finances of banks and railroads. He was named by McKinley to represent the League at the Monetary Commission meeting at Indianapolis in 1898. The Commission was a nonpartisan body composed of men from all sections of the nation. After lengthy discussion, they concluded that the gold standard should be maintained and that United States bank notes below ten dollars ought to be gradually withdrawn "so as to avoid injurious contraction of the currency." They advocated a

The President of the United States
Honors
The Union League of Philadelphia,
May 14th 1897.

His Excellency The Honorable William McKinley,
                                        President of the United States.
The Honorable Garret A. Hobart,
                                        Vice-President of the United States.
The Honorable Lyman J. Gage,
                                        Secretary of the Treasury.
The Honorable Russell A. Alger,
                                        Secretary of War.
The Honorable Cornelius N. Bliss,
                                        Secretary of the Interior.
The Honorable James A. Gary,
                                        Postmaster General.
The Honorable Joseph McKenna,
                                        Attorney General.
The Honorable James Wilson,
                                        Secretary of Agriculture.
Guests of the Union League, Philadelphia,
        Friday evening, May 14th 1897.

A PAGE OF THE PROGRAM ISSUED UPON THE OCCASION OF THE
SPECIAL RECEPTION TO PRESIDENT MCKINLEY AND HIS CABINET

banking system to furnish credit to every part of the country with the object of equalizing rates of interest. The plan was recommended for adoption by Congress.

All the details of these proposals, especially the value of paper money and its relation to silver and gold, were disclosed at two special meetings at the League, one on January 8 and the other on January 29, 1898. Essentially they were in line with Republican views. In spite of the strong advocacy by the League in support of the recommendations of the Monetary Commission to stabilize the country's currency, they attracted little attention.[5]

Clouding the horizon was the Spanish oppression of Cubans, and the destruction of American sugar plantations on the island by natives as a means of involving American owners in the problems of the island. Widely exploited by the press, these events presaged the war with Spain. Offers by the United States to secure the independence of Cuba were rejected, and while Spanish concessions were made, they had little effect in curbing the insurrectionary movement or in relaxing Spain's determination to retain power over the Caribbean island. McKinley's antiwar attitude and his desire to move slowly in securing an arrangement that would not injure American interests were both shattered when the battleship *Maine* was destroyed in an explosion in Havana harbor on February 15, 1898. The president still attempted to adjudicate differences peacefully. By the time the Spanish yielded and agreed to McKinley's proposals, voices in and out of Congress were heatedly demanding war and intervention in Cuba. The Spanish concessions arrived too late. On April 20, Congress adopted a joint resolution empowering the president to employ the armed forces of the United States against the Spanish fleet, to assure Cuban independence, and to bring peace to the island. Diplomatic relations were broken and a blockade of Cuban ports was ordered.

Assistant Secretary of the Navy Theodore Roosevelt alerted the forces at sea to be in position to reach any island under Spanish control in the Atlantic and Pacific Oceans. The Spanish fleets were successfully engaged and destroyed at Manila Bay and Santiago harbor. Hawaii was taken for strategic reasons over the protests of Japan, having proved itself of value as a naval installation. Puerto Rico was occupied with ease, and compared to other wars, land battles had minor military significance. With the termination of hostilities and the drafting of a treaty of peace, Spain relinquished Cuba and ceded Puerto Rico and Guam to the United States. The Philippines awaited a disposition that was prolonged by a three-year uprising against American occupation.

From the time war was declared on Spain, the League threw its weight behind the president. Although the American navy was at the peak of its strength, the army was comparatively weak, poorly organized, and medically unequipped to wage a semi-tropical war. But the League saw no need to join in raising regiments, nor had it supported the yellow journalism that cried hysterically for war. John Wanamaker, however, felt otherwise, and was personally responsible for raising, at his own expense, "eight full companies, fully equipped and armed with Springfield rifles, for service in the First Brigade, N.G.P."[6]

Although Lincoln's Birthday that year was celebrated by an appropriate banquet, celebration of Grant's Birthday was omitted because of the war. When news reached the League on July 4, 1898 of the victory at Santiago, an enthusiastic demonstration was held among the members, and Charles Emory Smith, McKinley's post-master general, gave an impromptu address.

To commemorate the close of the Spanish-American War, a dinner was given for President McKinley. It coincided with Philadelphia's Peace Jubilee arranged for the last week of October. This time officers of the army and navy were present at the League House and the number of guests was limited. Splendidly decorated with plants and flowers, and with the Veteran Corps, First Regiment Infantry again acting as the president's escort, the hospitality of the League was in its best form. Joseph G. Darlington welcomed McKinley and spoke on behalf of the League. He noted that by uniting Southerners and Northerners in a common cause, the hostilities with Spain had been a step toward healing the wounds of the Civil War. The dinner for the president was as fine in every way as the one following his inauguration.[7]

Summarizing the events of 1898, in the annual report of the League, secretary J. Levering Jones gave a sweeping overview of American naval growth for the century. He wrote that at the beginning of the nineteenth century American arms had been compelled to sweep the pirates of Tripoli from the sea and beat them in their own ports; and as the century drew to a close, Admiral George Dewey had destroyed the naval might of Spain in one morning.

As to the expansion of the nation, he expressed a popular view on the potential world dominance of the United States. "The footsteps of the Anglo-Saxon race reveal the march of a conquering people. It has been its province by means of commerce, of religion, and of the sword, to distribute ideas of liberty, of justice, of equality. It is the leader of mankind in the diffusion of moral principles and of those conceptions of government which tend to advance the individual, secure his rights, and form a refined and domestic social life. It seems impossible for this race to escape from its obligation to humanize and improve the semi-barbaric nations of the East. The instinct of colonization is ever active in its blood, whether as exhibited in England by the creation of organized colonies, or by America pushing forward into new territory, subsequently formed into great states. England has traversed the seas to found new empires; the Union has moved overland to found them in the distant West. The innate spirit of colonization has in each instance been the same."[8] Jones' likening of the westward American expansion on contiguous territory to the expansionism of the British Empire was not really an accurate comparison; however, it represented the Anglo-Saxonism of the period.

However, Jones also spoke of the tendency toward national cohesion in America. Few could challenge his statement on the growing monolingualism among the diverse, nonEnglish-speaking nationalities settling in the United States. In looking forward to a complete fusion of all peoples in the country, he anticipated the melting pot theory of a fusion of nationalities, soon to be articulated by historians. A common language, a common land, and the adaptation to a national culture springing from American soil did become characteristics of American life, despite certain latter-day ethnocentric tendencies.

There was no need, Jones added, for Americans to seek outlets for their population in Africa and the Orient. "The United States, with its boundless unoccupied territory, its unsurpassed resources, its ocean and internal sea coast, which exceeds that of all Europe, needs to proceed with caution in securing new acquisitions, inhabited by a people practically without religion, letters, or law. We must not allow too vivid dreams of imperialism to disturb or endanger our present security and our steady majestic progress."[9]

By the time these words were in print, the Treaty of Peace had been signed in Paris. The Peace Commissioners, upon their return to the United States, were the guests of The Union League on February 4, 1899. McKinley regretted his inability to be present, but was officially represented by Charles Emory Smith. The president took note of the League's interest in the national tendency toward imperialism.[10]

Jones was the first League spokesman to introduce the subject of American nationality, a matter that was absorbing the attention of those who associated Americanism with colonial heritage. He was also among the first to weigh the impact of war with a European nation. Each subject was reviewed in detail as the League studied the involvements of the United States in the Caribbean and in the far-flung islands of the Pacific. Following the reception of the Peace Commissioners, arrangements were made for a series of speakers on the new international role of the United States and its evolving foreign policy. The speakers predicted that national policy would soon create a Pacific empire.

Among the first on the roster of speakers for 1899 was Albert J. Beveridge, the 36 year old senator elect from Indiana. The occasion was a banquet in honor of Lincoln's Birthday. The one-time slave, Booker T. Washington, had been invited to give the Lincoln address. Washington already had earned a national reputation for the educational program he had introduced at Tuskeegee Institute in Alabama. The Lincoln banquet offered an unusual opportunity to present the views of a black leader and of a young conservative Republican. On the eve of the banquet, a violent snowstorm disrupted the plans of the League and its speakers. Washington was detained halfway between New York and Philadelphia, and Beveridge was stranded for the night at Coatesville, Pennsylvania. The speakers arrived the following day. New arrangements were made, but the continued inclement weather discouraged the likelihood of a large audience. Washington's address was given to a small group at the home of Henry C. Davis, one of the men who had been involved in raising black regiments in the Civil War. They listened attentively to his theme of "working with the hands" as an essential step toward educating southern blacks. He elaborated on the programs of Tuskeegee Institute and paid tribute to Lincoln, the great emancipator of whites and blacks. There was nothing new or startling in Washington's brief remarks, but his talk helped banish a growing feeling that the League had cut itself off from its interests in the affairs of the Negro.[11]

Foreign policy was of little concern to Washingon, but to the boyish-looking Beveridge it surmounted all other national interests. He had already established himself as an apostle of imperialism and as an advocate of the superiority of the United States, which in the near future would control world destiny. He firmly believed that the islands of Cuba and the Philippines had been rightly seized by the American government, and should forever remain under its control. It was only natural for the United States to move in this direction. Mere occupation, administration, or even temporary domination was not enough; it was an obligation of people of Anglo-Saxon descent to civilize a still "barbaric" territory like the Philippines. Any other interpretation would border on treason. Beveridge's brief luncheon address, given at the League, and attended by approximately one-hundred members, was received with mixed feelings. It was essentially the same speech that he was to give again as his maiden address before the Senate of the United States. Washington's and Beveridge's addresses were published for distribution among the members.[12]

Less dogmatic in his approach than Beveridge was Senator John M. Thurston. Thurston lauded the annexation of Hawaii, which he had originally voted against. Although he was uncritical of the occupation of Cuba and the Philippines, he offered no program for the future status of the islands. He stressed the new destiny of the United States as a world power, but did not define this destiny. American emphasis was shifting from its internal growth, from the development of a vast land between the oceans, to international power that would greatly depend on the increase of its naval strength.

On this subject, Secretary of the Navy John D. Long also linked foreign policy with the navy. Recalling that the American maritime fleet had been swept from the high seas during the Civil War and never fully replaced, he argued for the expansion of a maritime fleet that would no longer depend on foreign ships. Expanding upon this view was Jacob Gould Schurman. His prediction, that the theater of history in the twentieth century would be the Pacific Ocean, revealed greater insight. Schurman, president of the Philippine Commission, did not indulge in the passionate expansionism of Beveridge, and in his moderate analysis he came close to the reality of the events that shaped the twentieth century.[13]

Four months later, Senator William P. Frye of Maine, president *pro tem* of the Senate, gave an address before the League which enunciated the official position of the Republican administration. The acquisition of island territory was vital to the expansion of trade, he said, and demanded the development of a large merchant navy. He emphasized that the natural resources of the Pacific islands under American control, when exploited, would prove extremely beneficial to the future welfare and economy of the islanders and a boon to enterprising Americans. The United States should shine as a naval power, and reflect its strength across the seas to all ports of the world.[14]

Frye was followed by Secretary of the Treasury Lyman J. Gage. Gage took a backward glance at the economic vicissitudes of the nation. He presented a statistical history of money, banking, and the fluctuation of the dollar between 1870 and 1893. Looking forward to the twentieth century in a year when the revenues of the government were sufficient and the credit of the commercial community sound, he cautioned that financial problems never cease. Old errors are repeated, new problems arise from changing conditions, but all have to be met. The basic institutions of the United States, he stated, made it possible to confront and overcome these changes. American financial conditions were a backdrop for its foreign policy.[15]

One of the problems that loomed in the minds of many Americans was the nation's future relationship with Puerto Rico. The island of one-million people, with an illiteracy rate of more than 85 per cent, had been ceded by Spain to the United States. One-third of its population was unemployed. In August, 1899, a devastating hurricane destroyed its coffee plantations and leveled thousands of homes. Immediate relief from the United States was imperative. In less than four months, legislation that would govern the island was in preparation, and long exhausting debates followed that were concerned more with a free trade policy for Puerto Rico than with improving her unfortunate internal conditions. Senator Joseph B. Foraker of Ohio was the author of the act that provided for the establishment of civil rule, territorial status, and ultimate citizenship for Puerto Rico. Ten days after the Foraker Act was passed, the senator addressed The Union League on the merits of the bill, the opposition to it, and more important, stressed the fact that the United States was attempting not to place any additional burdens on an already harassed and mistreated island community.[16]

In its own assessment of the situation, the League concluded that under the protection of the United States, Puerto Rico gradually would be raised to an economic and educational level higher than it had ever attained under Spanish rule. The Philippines, too, would improve once the insurgent Aquinaldo and his guerilla movement were suppressed. The most important question raised in the League discussions was whether or not the islands should become permanent colonies of the United States. The League decided that it could not judge the status of the islands until the Supreme Court had decided on the constitutionality of such questions.[17]

It was an exciting year for the League, which had focused a great deal of attention on the disposition of the newly acquired island possessions. When word reached its directors that the Republican National Convention was to be held in Philadelphia in June, 1900, it prepared to open its doors to the party leaders. The privileges of the League House were extended to cabinet members and congressmen. Banquets and receptions were frequent; informal addresses were made by Marcus A. Hanna, chairman of the Republican National Committee, Henry Cabot Lodge, senator from Massachusetts, and many other active participants. Vice-President Garret A. Hobart, ailing and with only a few months to live, was unable to appear. None of the delegates questioned the renomination of McKinley, but there was no consensus expressed as yet on whether Theodore Roosevelt, the former assistant secretary of the navy, organizer of the volunteer cavalry in the Spanish-American War, and governor of New York, would become McKinley's running mate. Once the convention machinery got moving, Roosevelt's nomination, strongly pushed by

Hanna, was unchallenged. On June 21 the nominations were announced, and four days later, before all of the convention delegates had left the city, the League met to ratify the proceedings and the Republican platform of 1900, and endorsed the McKinley-Roosevelt ticket according to its accepted custom. The corporate body of the League confidently announced "that the Republican party's restoration of adequate protection to American industry, its resistance to the free coinage of silver, its successful establishment of a stable currency and its triumphant conduct of a foreign war, all alike vindicate its claim to the approval of the considerate judgment of the American people, and its unflinching devotion to its patriotic principles entitles it to a renewed mandate from the people."[18]

McKinley thanked the League for its warm support, and, to assure the Republican victory it was so eager to see, the League again marshalled all of its financial resources and publication skills for the upcoming campaign. William Jennings Bryan, the Democratic candidate, advocated the cause of free silver, as he had in 1896. After the candidates argued through the maze of the issues of bimetalism, the tariff, and constitutional rights for the island acquisitions, McKinley defeated Bryan a second time. The League was gratified by the victory. But League Secretary Dimner Beeber wrote questioningly of the new American role as a world power, and of the wise and informed statesmanship needed to fulfill this obligation. Not all League members believed that the government should be launched upon an era of expansionism similar to the imperialism and militarism of European countries. This was a direction that many Americans feared, and Beeber's comments indicated that the League was far from monolithic in its views, and not subservient to a foreign policy that emanated from outside its walls.[19]

Discussion of the many problems that had dangled in mid-air during the campaign was resumed. Foremost were the status of the navy, and the expansion of the merchant marine. Since the end of the Civil War, it had been clear that the technology of shipbuilding was of major importance. Iron and steel had replaced the coppered wooden hulls; steam had eliminated the use of sails on vessels; and merchant ships had gradually increased their tonnage. For a rapidly growing nation, the United States had not taken full advantage of the new technology. Except for its marvelous coastwise trade, American vessels were not carrying the product of its mills and factories across the seas, but these exports were reaching foreign ports in foreign carriers. For the fiscal year of 1900, it was reported that less than eight per cent of American imports and exports was carried on American ships.

The condition of the navy and the merchant fleet was considered to be of such importance that it was made the subject of the League Founders' Day address in 1901. A new program, that later led to the organization of the Merchant Marine Congress and the upgrading of the navy, was loudly enunciated in the halls of the League House. "The enlargement and improvement of our merchant marine, the development of a sufficient body of trained American seamen, the promotion of rapid and regular mail communication between the ports of other countries and our own, and the adaptation of large and swift American merchant steamships to naval use in time of war are public purposes of the highest concern."[20] It was a convincing rationale for the increase of the navy, expressed almost a decade and a half before the United States' need to rely heavily upon a resourceful navy in World War I.

In the eyes of the Republican Party, the introduction of programs such as these lifted the nation onto a higher plane. Party policy had been carefully scrutinized in the aftermath of the Spanish-American War. Island possessions were a novelty in American history. The League could state with confidence in 1901 that a Republican Congress had moved correctly in improving the status of Puerto Rico, that it had made equal progress in the Philippines, and that peace would bring to the intelligent people of the Pacific islands developments never envisioned under Spanish rule. The great question that remained unsolved was the future of these territories. Should these islands remain permanent possessions? Would the benign influences of peace bring education, security, and prosperity to them? In both instances the League stressed that the absence of tyrannical rule and the presence of the United States were important attributes, until such time as the future of Cuba, Puerto Rico, and the Philippines could be determined.

McKinley planned to tour the country as one of his first public acts after the inauguration. A high point in the trip would be the launching of a new battleship, the *Ohio*, in San Francisco harbor. On his return to the East, his trip would conclude with the celebration at the Pan-American Exposition at Buffalo. On his tour, the president intended to elaborate on two subjects that had been obscured by campaign issues: the extension of reciprocal trade agreements, and the control of trusts.

At the Pan-American Exposition, McKinley delivered an address that clearly emphasized the two themes uppermost in his mind. At the close of his speech, his exuberant and admiring listeners responded with uproarious applause. On the following day, the occasion was held in the Temple of Music, and McKinley, well-guarded by various branches of the police, detectives, and the secret service,

ROBERT LEE MacCAMERON STANDING BEFORE HIS
FINISHED PORTRAIT OF PRESIDENT McKINLEY

flanked on the left and right by his aides, shook the hands of numerous well-wishers in the baking heat of the day. Handkerchiefs were in abundance for those who frequently made themselves more comfortable by mopping their faces. And a handkerchief was the disguise used by the assassin Leon Czolgosz to cover the short-barreled revolver with which he fired two shots at less than an arm's length at President McKinley. One of the shots was to prove fatal.

Pandemonium spread through the unsuspecting crowd while McKinley, still conscious, begged that his assailant not be harmed. The news was telegraphed across the nation. The wires of the Associated Press told the tale of horror, and the bluish characters that were fed out on the crisp yellowish tapes brought the information to a shocked and startled League membership. On the League bulletin board was the terse statement that "The President of the United States was shot by an assassin in the Temple of Music, at the Pan-American Exposition, Buffalo, on the afternoon of Friday, September 6, 1901." Day after day, the telegraph streaked its bluish letters telling of the president's condition to the nation. As soon as they reached the League, they were posted on the bulletin board. They reported improvement, a possible recovery, and gave hope to the country. But eight days later, McKinley died.[21]

A bereaved nation paused to lament his death. Sorrow was expressed universally, and the League was profoundly affected by the blow because of its great affection for McKinley as a human being and one who so often had shared the hospitality of the League. In addition to its official representatives who attended the funeral services in Washington, the League held its own memorial service on September 20, 1901. The addresses by League president Joseph G. Darlington, Dimner Beeber, Joel Cook, A. Louden Snowden, and Senator Boies Penrose all emphasized the strong personality of McKinley, his absolute integrity in his personal and public life, and a fine character that could withstand the closest scrutiny. A number of McKinley's presidential policies had been announced from the halls of the League, where he had been able to relax and join in the celebration of League anniversaries. The most important resolution that emerged at the memorial meeting was the condemnation of anarchist and criminal immigrants, and a statement of the compelling need to curb the admission of such elements to the United States.[22] Although Leon Czolgosz, a proclaimed anarchist, was of Polish background, he, like the assassins of Lincoln and Garfield, had been born in the United States. The condemnation of anarchists, and the association of immigrants with American anarchism, stigmatized immigrants who knew nothing of the philosophy of violence and were ignorant of the extreme radicalism that had burst upon the nation. Nonetheless, as a result of the McKinley assassination, it was advocated that immigrants, particularly those of Slavic and Italian backgrounds, should be deported if they were not naturalized. This anti-immigrant mood was new to the League, and the passionate exclamations at the memorial meeting eventually stirred action toward the proscription of many innocent foreigners. The proceedings closed solemnly, and a final resolution pledged the support of The Union League of Philadelphia to Theodore Roosevelt, the new President of the United States.[23]

Opponents of William McKinley had accused him of being an imperialist and a political puppet of the Republican Party, charges that still remain open to question. When the League appraised the events of the year 1901, after the day of eulogy had faded, McKinley's service to the nation was freshly examined. He was recalled by his contemporaries not just as a martyred president, but as a man of dignity who had upheld the principles of a high tariff, the gold standard, and the traditions of the Republican Party. Above all, his human qualities endeared him to The Union League. A portrait of McKinley, painted by Robert Lee MacCameron, was added to the collection of League presidential portraits, and placed in the old banquet room where McKinley had shared the hospitality of the League and introduced a number of the ideas which later became national policy.[24]

The death of McKinley found the League at high tide. It was looked upon as a major force in the Republican Party, its membership represented the most influential men of the city's professional and mercantile life, and admission to membership had become increasingly difficult as a new generation of Philadelphians sought identity with one of the best clubs in the nation. In the face of its recent growth, its social position, and its political influence, fears were frequently expressed by some members that the patriotic role of the League would be submerged by its club life. Boker's admonition that the League should not lose sight of its patriotic commitment, and should not concern itself with minor or local politics, was frequently recalled. "In such affairs we have not sought to impose an obligation upon our associates, either by the voice of a majority of our body or by that of the officers of the League." In those matters that concerned the state or nation, the League was urged never to idly stand by. As a further reminder, portions of Boker's address were reprinted and circulated as part of an informal policy of the League, intended as a constant reminder to the membership that the League had been chartered as an institution to uphold the government of the United

States. A new generation had to be informed of this fundamental principle. The party with which the League had associated itself had represented the patriotic spirit of its membership during the Civil War.[25] With peace restored, and a generation or more of men imbued with the events of the war, the League had held steadfast to the Republican Party. Over a period of three-and-a-half decades, it had learned that it could not eliminate the ills of the local political machinery, and hence it had withdrawn from municipal politics. The new generation, indoctrinated by Republican views, recognized the national influence of the League and its role in Philadelphia society. Members who enjoyed the attributes of club life also had to be reminded that its patriotic commitment transcended personal ambition, social life, and the pursuit of politics for its own sake.

This attitude dominated the League at the opening of the twentieth century, when Theodore Roosevelt, only forty-two years old, was sworn in, under somber circumstances, at Buffalo, New York, as President of the United States. A socialite turned cowboy, a writer and historian with a penchant for politics, he had an obsession for physical fitness. He had been a federal Civil Service commissioner before he became assistant secretary of the Navy. His work in the Navy department had ended abruptly during the Spanish-American War when Roosevelt resigned to help organize the "Rough-Riders," a spectacular regiment which fought in Cuba. His popularity had helped him in the gubernatorial race in New York in 1898. His interest in reform frightened the New York political machine, which saw an opportunity to curb Roosevelt and remove him from New York politics by urging his nomination to the vice-presidency in 1900. Roosevelt was of the same generation that had begun to pick up the reins at the League, and he approached them as a robust epitome of a still young America. In the opinion of the League, Roosevelt was a fortunate successor to McKinley, whose new potential waited to be appraised.[26]

Roosevelt's first appearance as the presidential guest of the League was at the Founders' Day meeting in the winter of 1902. Roosevelt had recently invited the Negro leader, Booker T. Washington, for a luncheon at the White House, an action for which he was severely criticized as offensive to the South. But no word of criticism came from the League. League president Joseph G. Darlington welcomed Roosevelt and members of his cabinet, among them Secretary of War Elihu Root, and Senator Henry Cabot Lodge of Massachusetts, and various local dignitaries representing the academic and cultural institutions of Philadelphia. It was another of the splendid occasions for which the League had become known. The personality of Roosevelt pervaded the League House in the same way that it had impressed itself upon the nation. Following the customary toast, and a thunderous round of applause, the president addressed the League. He was not a wordy man who had too much to say, as some later-day critics have maintained, but one who on this occasion addressed himself thoughtfully to a review of the McKinley administration and to his own first year in office. In the twenty-minute address he gave, no great issues were explored, but he alluded to the trusts and the burgeoning industrial combinations as institutions whose roles had to be reconsidered. Roosevelt offered no solution to the problems arising from mercantile expansion, but added that a means must be found to reduce the power of the trusts, a subject to which he referred again at a later meeting at the League.[27]

Founders' Day that year brought to the League speakers who told the story of how a nation of four million soared to 80 million in a century. The amazing saga of the development of American industry —the United States had become the greatest producer of steel in the world—or the fabulous growth of the nation as a granary producing "more wheat than France and Russia combined, three times as much as India, eight times as much as Germany and twelve times as much as the United Kingdom," was told by Congressman John Dalzell with pride and with appreciation for the farmer and his problems. All Europe was being fed with American meat products; and three-quarters of the world's cotton supply was grown on American soil! American exports equalled those of France, Germany and England. Other lands endowed with the same natural resources hungered for American products. No wonder the descendants of the Pilgrims who gathered at the League expressed pride in the swelling growth of the nation, in the organization which they had recently founded. The speakers expressed the sentiments that America long ago had ceased to be composed of descendants of the first white pioneers, but was becoming a composite of many nationalities, which added muscle and intellect to the land as it expanded from generation to generation. These views were in direct opposition to the passionate anti-immigrant exclamations that had followed McKinley's assassination, and were applauded with considerable appreciation.[28]

The long-awaited *Chronicle of The Union League* was distributed at the Founders' Day meeting of 1902. Intended originally as a history of the League, the idea was proposed in 1893 by John Russell Young. Work on it was postponed when McKinley appointed Young as the Librarian of Congress. Upon Young's death in 1899, it was again resumed by a committee of League members chaired by J.

Levering Jones. Basically the book chronicled those events which suited the tastes of its compilers, who extracted sections from the annual reports. No attempt was made to interpret the social life, the political activity, or the behind the scenes details of the League's broad civic and patriotic achievements. But it faithfully adhered to the record of the annual printed reports. In addition, a series of reminiscences on the founding of the League by surviving members enhanced the *Chronicle*, as did the valuable membership data it included. Publication of the *Chronicle* was delayed further when it was decided to include the details of the McKinley assassination, and the reaction of the League. The *Chronicle* was perhaps the largest American club history to be published up to that time, and it was the first League publication to carry the motto officially adopted by the League in 1899, *Amor Patriae Ducit,* "Love of Country Leads." Lathrop's history which had been published in 1884 was no longer available, and the new book aimed to introduce the history of the League to the twentieth-century membership.[29]

The appearance of Roosevelt at the League, and the publication of the *Chronicle,* coincided with a new era in American journalism and fiction, the rise of muckraking. This journalistic and literary movement undertook to expose political corruption and the power of the trusts, and is closely identified with the Roosevelt administrations. Muckraking literature was actually established before Roosevelt gave it the name by which it is now known. Its journalism was significant both for Philadelphia and for The Union League. After the appearance of Lincoln Steffens' article in *McClure's Magazine* in 1903, entitled "Philadelphia: Corrupt and Contented," this description attached itself to the city for decades to come. What the League had fought as early as the 1870's was told only in part three decades later. The impact of Steffens' article on the writing of social historians has been a lasting one, but so far as the role of the League is concerned, its confrontation with political corruption has been overlooked. Between 1899 and 1903, Mayor Samuel H. Ashbridge pursued a career of open, undisguised pilfering of franchise grants. Large profits fell into his pockets. Yet he resented the League because of its refusal to entertain him socially as the Republican mayor of Philadelphia! And his ring-controlled newspapers attacked the League for its failure to do so.[30] Bossism, political rings, and the machinery which made them possible, reached a high level unprecedented in urban politics. The Bullitt Charter of 1887, which at first had been looked upon as a great reform of political excesses, was completely obviated by the mayor's activities. Trickery, bribery, graft, and fraudulent voting, in which both political parties unscrupulously participated, were rampant in the city. Why did the reform spirit of the League fail to tackle such a serious problem? Was the League among the contented? In fact, a dilemma did exist, for in this area the League was restrained by a decision not to become involved in local politics. Its reformers were compelled to act independently, and its proponents of clean politics failed to muster sufficient strength to crush the corrupt machinery that governed the city. The few voices raised in protest were influential, but inadequate. Typical of the reaction of this small number of men was the investigation undertaken by League member Rudolph Blankenburg and reported by Lincoln Steffens in his article.[31] Blankenburg started a mail investigation of political fraud within one city division by sending a registered letter to each voter. According to Steffens, 63 per cent of these inquiries were returned by the postal authorities because the addressees were deceased, removed, or no longer present at their assigned residences. Another ardent League reformer was John Wanamaker. Still seething over what he considered an irregularity by Quay in the 1896 election of Boies Penrose to the Senate of the United States, he carried on a one-man campaign in exposing Quay's bossism and domination of Pennsylvania politics. Wanamaker exposed Quay and his operation in a series of addresses between 1897 and 1905.[32] McMichael's *North American*, which was purchased by Wanamaker's son Thomas, waged a campaign against the state and local machines that was so effective that the editor's life was threatened, and an unsuccessful attempt was made to blackmail Wanamaker. The turn of the century Municipal Reform League, an outgrowth of the earlier reform movements, continued Blankenburg's investigation in an attempt to clean up old voting lists, but was unable to prevent them from being used again after they were invalidated. This opposition came from League members who acted individually.

After the administration of Mayor Samuel H. Ashbridge and the publication of Steffens' exposé in 1903, other dissatisfied League members formed a Committee of Twenty-one to counteract fraud and bribery. Several unidentified committees, composed of League members, also were organized for the same purpose. The Philadelphia newspapers implied that the League was behind this movement. If the committees used the name of the League without first obtaining permission to do so, they would have violated an unwritten agreement prohibiting involvement in local politics. A special meeting was called in the fall of 1905 to restrain members from involving or using the name of the League in private activities. The various committee representatives repudiated the charge that they spoke for the League. They had abided by the policy which they believed to be in the best interest of the League, but they added: "The movement in which we are interested is a sincere effort upon the part of men who have always been consistent Republicans, who will not tolerate the continuance in power of men who have permitted the present intolerable condition of affairs, which has justly roused the indignation of all good citizens—but who insist that the wrongs and evils, committed under a Republican administration, shall be corrected, by Republicans within the Party."[33]

It was not to be the last political crisis that was brought to the floor of the League, but it was the last that sprang from dissension over local political corruption. Discontent simmered, but to the contemporary observer, and to future social and political historians, Philadelphia remained politically corrupt and apathetic. The conflict within the League, and its frustration, and discontent, had escaped the attention of Lincoln Steffens.

Nationally, The Union League was certain of its focus. The presidential campaign of 1904 did not involve sharply defined issues; it was devoid of excitement, and the absence of concern about its outcome was proved when Roosevelt was returned to office by the largest popular vote cast up to that time. It was a personal victory for the president, and exceeded by far the cautious expectations of the League.[34]

The nation was still celebrating the one-hundredth anniversary of the Louisiana Purchase when the Republican Party prepared to celebrate its jubilee year. It was a unique occasion for the League House, which was dressed in colorful bunting and political banners, against a blaze of electric lights. It was also a splendid opportunity to relate the League history to the party that rose to power for the same reasons that the League was organized. It was this sense of identity that continued to bind a local, independent club to a major political party. The Founders' Day banquet for 1904, arranged for the convenience of President Roosevelt, emphasized this historic relationship. The reception for the president was confined exclusively to members. It was now a familiar occasion, that blended social associations with political interests. Over carefully selected courses and choice wines, numerous toasts lauded the history of the League and praised the greatness of the nation.

Edward T. Stotesbury, a dean of American bankers, a partner of Drexel & Company, and an associate of J. P. Morgan, rose as the president of The Union League to commemorate the occasion and to introduce Roosevelt. The president's address was somewhat shorter than the brief talk given the previous year. In the presence of men who were involved in some of the nation's great corporations, including Stotesbury, Roosevelt spoke about curtailing their power; to the directors of the Pennsylvania Railroad, who also sat in the audience, he spoke of rates and rebates, but within a comfortable context that would neither impede their growth, hinder their expansion, nor injure the aims of labor. He proposed government supervision of interstate commerce and greater control of the railroads engaged in it. This could be done equitably, he said, without disadvantage to capital, or to the nation.[35]

McKinley, in his last address to the League, had expressed concern about restraining the growth of the young but powerful trusts, but his short-lived second administration had made it impossible for action to be taken against the trusts. Roosevelt took this task upon himself and brought suits against 44 trusts. One of the most notable of these was against the gigantic Morgan-controlled Northern Securities Company.

The League's Founders' Day became a forum at which ideas of national importance were either first introduced or expanded upon. Year after year, the annual banquet was held, and when a Republican president was in office, his attendance at the event was assured. Cabinet members, senators of different states, economists, and historians added to the prestige of the occasion and were also provided with the opportunity to expound upon public issues and problems. After the appearance of William Howard Taft at the League in 1913, the Founders' Day celebration declined in prominence; during World War I it was revived, only to diminish again in the 1920's.

Founders' Day also became an occasion on which to recognize the survivors of The Union Club and early League members. Each year their number dwindled. Clarence H. Clark, an outstanding financier, a bibliophile, and a former president of the Academy of the Fine Arts, died in 1906. Abraham Barker's death the same year brought the membership of The Union Club to a close. The announcement of Barker's death summoned forth that lesser known aspect of the League's involvement in the war in which Barker was particularly active. More than any other member, he had been responsible for the Supervisory Committee for the Enlistment of Colored Troops and for recruiting five of the black regiments for service. In a memorial tribute to the man who had been the last survivor of the Club, the League noted that it was not this alone that was of value to his memory, "but as well in the elevating of these men in their own self-respect and in the esteem of the loyal public; and this service involved more than labor, because, confronting deep-seated prejudice, it encountered no little opposition, entailed hazard, and risked social

For the Union League of Philadelphia
in the grateful appreciation of its support.
April 27th 1912   yours Wm H Taft
90th Anniversary of the
birth of General W. S. Grant.

A TYPICAL FOUNDERS' DAY PROGRAM

ostracism." At the Founders' Day meeting in 1902, Barker had spoken of the League continuing as a "power for justice, truth and integrity," and urged that the members of the new century maintain the high standards of the early founders.[36]

Year after year, now, the League was called upon to mourn the loss of its first members, who were dying in quick succession. Among those who left a permanent mark upon the history of the League was Edwin N. Benson, who died in 1909, and who was one of the men responsible for the physical expansion of the League.

Although Benson died at the time that the cornerstone was laid for the Fifteenth Street Building, plans for its development had been under study for twelve years.

A competition had been in progress to meet the problem of a new or an enlarged building. Fifteen architects submitted a variety of designs, rich in sharply contrasting ideas. Philadelphia's changing architectural concepts emerged in these plans. One considered building over and around the original brownstone building; another contemplated a Greek revival front that could be extended in unbroken rhythm for a city block; a third conceived of a seven-story structure of vertical walls; while others preferred not to touch the old League House but to extend it in two sections. Tempers flared at the suggestion that the original Fraser building, full of historic memories, would even be touched. Most members agreed that the interior should provide all club necessities, although a handful of men grumbled that the inclusion of sleeping rooms would turn the League into a hotel, or that additional card and chess rooms, pool and billiard rooms, and a bowling alley would convert the League into a recreational center or an athletic club. No one argued against private dining rooms and larger restaurant facilities, but opposition to sharing a family and ladies' dining room on the same floor with members defeated the proposal for such a plan. It was considered more convenient, so the argument went, to assign the family and ladies' dining room to a choice entrance on the ground level at Broad Street. Three times its present space was allotted to the library and a separate area was designed for a museum facility whose plan remained to be interpreted. These suggestions were enthusiastically approved, along with the addition of an assembly room that could comfortably seat more than 800 people. When the competing plans were reviewed, architect Joseph M. Huston's design was chosen.[37]

For more than a year the plans were studied, revised, and modified. Huston's plan was found to be too costly and, inasmuch as all of the architects were League members, it was decided to select one by closed ballot. Horace Trumbauer was the final choice. Obstacles and opposition, although minor, still had to be overcome. No construction was possible until the last remaining site at 1418 Sansom Street was purchased. The owner finally yielded and sold the house, leasing the land to the League for 99 years. There were still a few members who thought that the idea should be scrapped in favor of erecting commercial properties, on top of which the League could erect the extension to the clubhouse.

Trumbauer's design was for a five-story building with two levels below ground. A granite base was proposed, with walls to be built of Indiana limestone, which at that time was very popular in Philadelphia. Provisions for a roof garden were accepted. The building was to be so constructed that if at any time in the future it was decided to remove or alter the exterior of the original structure, the same architectural theme could be extended. Discussions on financing the new building were no less arduous and lengthy than developing the architectural design, and by the time that both were concluded the presidential campaign of 1908 was well on its way.

In keeping with its traditional custom, the corporate body of the League ratified the nomination of William Howard Taft of Ohio for president and of James Schoolcraft Sherman of New York for vice-president of the United States. Taft was strongly supported by Roosevelt, who refused to be a third-term candidate. With a record of having been the first governor of the Philippine Islands, Roosevelt's secretary of war, and his personal choice for the presidency, there was no question of Taft's obtaining the full support of the League. Taft's Democratic opponent, William Jennings Bryan, had lost twice in a bid for the presidency and his apathetic campaign doomed him to defeat a third time. In urging support of Taft by the League, Judge William W. Porter described Taft as a man with "the courage of a Roosevelt, with a wiser discretion of method. This man has the prudence of a McKinley, with more momentum. This man has the persistence of a Grant, with a broader knowledge of statecraft. This man has the conscience of a Lincoln, with perhaps a sunnier disposition."[38] Most of the qualities of this portrait were accurate.

While the virtues of Taft were being enumerated, news reached the League on June 24, 1908, that former President Grover Cleveland had died. Judge Porter unhesitatingly stated that the former Democratic president had risen above his party when he believed it to be wrong, that even if he had been a political enemy, he had been respected by the League, and that in his term as president he had demonstrated that patriotism did not belong to one man or to one party. Porter asked that a message of sympathy be sent to the family of the ex-president. An appropriate condolence was forwarded.

In the last days of the campaign, under the auspices of the National Campaign Committee of The Union League, a mass meeting was held at the Academy of Music. Senator Philander C. Knox of Pennsylvania, the incoming secretary of state, James S. Sherman, the vice presidential candidate, and Generals Oliver O. Howard and Horatio C. King spoke to an overflow audience. The meeting was chaired by Dimner Beeber, president of the League. A few days later, in a nonpolitical vein, the guest committee of the League entertained Major General Grenville M. Dodge who gave his personal recollection of General William T. Sherman. It was a grand opportunity for the old soldiers of the League to meet again, sit in the large cafe, and reminisce about politics and the presidential elections of former years, and a war that had been fought two generations ago.[39]

Almost six months after the inauguration of President Taft, on October 9, 1909, the cornerstone for the Fifteenth Street building was laid in an auspicious ceremony. The incumbent governor of Pennsylvania, Edwin S. Stuart, who had been president of the League during 1906, and Dimner Beeber, his successor, had nurtured the building project and brought it to fruition. Beeber officiated at the ceremony and Stuart gave an account of the tremendous social and political strides made by the League since its founding. All of the objects deposited in the cornerstone were enumerated as follows: a copy of the United States Constitution and one of the Commonwealth, the city's charter, a history of the League, its officers and members up to 1909, and an example of one each of the gold and silver coins of the nation. Then the stone was set in place, and a silver trowel, designed for the occasion, was used by James F. Hope— League president from 1909 through 1911—in a grand flourish to spread the first batch of cement and to complete the ceremony. Miniature replicas of the trowel were distributed to the audience as a remembrance of the occasion. The building was now on its way, as Stuart stated, by the grace of the Architect of the Universe. The ceremony closed with a benediction invoking a prosperous future for The Union League of Philadelphia.[40]

More than a year was required for the construction of the Fifteenth Street section of the League House. On November 14, 1910, the last meeting was held in the old assembly hall, in the middle section of the property, to pay tribute to its past. For the remaining survivors of the war who had watched the great strides made by the League with pride and for those who intimately recalled the memorable occasions held in the old assembly hall, it was a nostalgic, sentimental celebration.

The history of the League was eloquently captured by the speeches presented at this meeting. Even before its location on Broad Street,

THE UNION LEAGUE HOUSE 1913. A BLENDING OF THE OLD AND THE NEW

Presidents Lincoln and Grant had visited the League. And within its present walls, President Grant, Hayes, Harrison, McKinley, Roosevelt, and Taft had been received and entertained. It was in this hall that president-elect Grant had assured League members that he would uphold the principles of the Republican Party in 1868; and it was in this hall that President McKinley, Vice-President Hobart, and all the members of the cabinet had been entertained in an unprecedented visit from Washington in 1897 to celebrate McKinley's victory. It was here that the generals of the Union Army, the captains of the Navy, and those who fought at Santiago and at Manila Bay had received gold medals of the League, and honorary memberships for their heroic contributions in war and for their civic contributions in peace. Here the grand receptions had been held, national policies announced, state government upheld, and the many crises in politics debated. In this hall Meredith, Fell, Binney, McMichael, and Boker had addressed the League and its many friends on subjects of national importance, and here the membership had been continuously reminded that The Union League was more than a social club, more than a politically oriented club—rather an institution devoted to upholding the ideals of the United States, and its principles of freedom and liberty.

Judge Dimner Beeber was warmly congratulated for his efforts as League president to accelerate the plan to improve the League's quarters. His response was poignant, and not limited to the record of the past. He spoke of eminent men, and of important events and ideas. He was proud of the League's Republican association, but he added, "Let us not forget that among the founders of this club and their associates were men who were *not* members of the Republican Party. While we cling to the Republican banner and are faithful to Republican doctrines, let us not forget that in the greatest crisis of this nation the Great Leader did not hesitate to call for, to plead for and to gratefully accept the assistance and cooperation of every American citizen. Therefore I say to you we must not narrow the spirit and the influence of this Club; and I say to you we must not be recreant to the memory of those patriotic men who, though they did not train with the party to which we belong, are entitled to their share of the credit that is given to this organization and all other organizations that assisted in the maintenance of the Union."[41] Beeber pointed dramatically to the portraits surrounding them of Democrats who had unselfishly performed patriotic services for the national government. But he was not satisfied to glory in the past, he said, not content to rest upon the laurels won by others. What is the League?, he asked. It is not limited to recreation, not just a

Thomas Pollock Anschutz

Dimner Beeber

luncheon club, not an institution to promote art, but first and foremost bound by the test of patriotism in peace and war. While he lauded the Republican Party, he also admonished it, and The Union League, for failing to "strike hands as a [united] Republican body. Then there would not be . . . any excuse for reform outside the lines of Party." With Beeber's words still ringing in the air above an enthusiastic response, the members marched along the marble halls, past the glittering, white circular marble staircase that rose five floors, to the new wing of the League House.[42]

Within ten days the transfer of major facilities was begun. The old home of the library underwent a vast change. All of the books which had been carefully gathered for more than 45 years were transferred to the new library under the supervision of librarian Alfred Lee. It was a formidable but well-organized undertaking that was completed in one night. The main reading room of the new library was larger than the total space allotted to the former library. Abundant light, arched ceilings, and ample shelving providing space for 25,000 volumes were the outstanding features. The valuable collection of books was housed in a richly furnished "noble suite of rooms." On the south wall, above the fireplace, was hung a portrait of George S. Pepper, a benefactor of many Philadelphia libraries, including that of the League, which received a financial bequest in 1899 that was carefully invested and is still active in the League's centennial year. Albert Uhle's portrait of Pepper was an appropriate recognition. On the north wall was placed the delicate seascape painted by William T. Richards, a gift of the League's Art Association. Later, it was replaced by Albert Bierstadt's nationally known *Bombardment of Fort Sumter*. Between the north and south walls, facing the entrance to the reading room, were placed the matching figures of the elegant white marble sculptures of *Washington and His Hatchet*, and *Franklin and His Whistle*.[43] The arched ceiling of the reading room, divided symmetrically by mahogany beams, was reminiscent of the woodwork of French and English clubs of the nineteenth century, but less austere in appearance. On the Moravian Street side, the room known as the Library Lounge connected with the reading room, and was intended for the American history collection. The Sansom Street side, with a room of equal size, was projected to house Lincolniana and the Civil War collection, and was to be consecrated as a memorial to Abraham Lincoln.

The former library was turned into a chess and card room, and decorated in soft tones. Later, chess exhibitions were held there which drew many renowned United States champions, from Harry N. Pillsbury to Samuel Rashevsky. There were as many interesting associations with the old library as there were with the banquet room. In spite of a widely felt need for a larger and more commodious reading room, nostalgia for the old quarter persisted. Men of letters, social historians, and advocates of women's suffrage had met here in quiet discussion. Here the works of the poet who sang of America, Walt Whitman, could be read and reflected upon above the tumult of the city, and here the neglected novelist, Herman Melville, could be remembered by members who had worn out his novels by frequent reading. Men came here not just to seek out literary preferences, or to reinterpret the military and political history of the Civil War, but to examine the works of Karl Marx, whose ideas had not as yet penetrated the mind of America. Here, John Russell Young worked on the *Memorial History of Philadelphia;* Albion Tourgee, prepared copy for his short-lived journal, *Our Continent;* and Herman L. Collins, under the pseudonym of "Girard," wrote his columns for *The Press,* and later for *The Philadelphia Inquirer.* To this spot came Major William H. Lambert, a veteran of the war, an ardent admirer of Lincoln (he owned an original manuscript of Whitman's "O Captain, My Captain"), and the possessor of the most superb collection of Lincoln books and memorabilia, a portion of which was exhibited in the library in 1909.[44] In addition, his collection of Thackerayana was unrivaled in the United States and even excelled the magnificent collection of William M. Thackeray's daughter. Others who frequented the library and whose interests flowed in various directions, were such well-known bibliophiles as Governor Samuel W. Pennypacker, Judge Mayer Sulzberger, and the nationally known bookseller, Edwin S. Stuart, whose bookshop, Leary-Stuart & Company, was the oldest in the United States. Here a generation of members on the clerical roll quietly prepared their weekly sermons, and here a generation of League secretaries prepared their annual reports. It was no wonder that the passing of the original library room was a matter for deep regret to those who had used it.

Within its quiet arcades had arisen one of the great state controversies over muzzling the freedom of the press. Two prominent League members had been involved, Governor Pennypacker and Charles Emory Smith. Pennypacker had signed the Grady-Salus Libel Act of 1903, perhaps out of a personal pique, and in justifying the measure he wrote against calling an unnamed mayor a "traitor," and an unidentified United States senator a "yokel with sodden brain," and himself for being caricatured as an "ugly little dwarf." Although Pennypacker was responsible for numerous state-wide reforms, he was unable to withstand the criticism of the press on the Libel Act. Smith, who wrote editorials for *The Press,* a newspaper once asso-

MAYER SULZBERGER

ciated with the name of John W. Forney, undertook the unpleasant task of drafting the blistering editorial attacking the governor, a fellow League member, and an otherwise respected colleague. Smith used the League library to prepare his protest. In 1907, when Edwin S. Stuart succeeded Pennypacker in office, the Libel Act was repealed on the basis that adequate legislation existed to provide for libelous writing without harsh discrimination against newspapers.[45]

In spite of this unpleasant altercation, which was whispered about in the comings and goings of the antagonists, Pennypacker was looked upon as an honest and well-meaning man. He was a recognized bibliophile, a prolific writer on state and local history, and he shared his interests in particular with Mayer Sulzberger, the foremost collector of Hebraica and books on early English law at that time. Both had met on the bench, and a bookish friendship had grown out of their judicial association. Senator Boies Penrose, whose political involvements often countered those of Pennypacker and Sulzberger, found their company exciting, although he generally did not form associations with men of literary tastes.

Under these circumstances this diverse trio met in a corner of the Library with the Speaker of the House "Uncle Joe" Cannon, on his visit to the League in 1906.[46] The goateed Pennypacker was peering at Cannon through his pince-nez, and Sulzberger's leonine head was raised upward to Penrose, whose huge frame, even while sitting towered above them, while they discussed the illiteracy clause of the Dillingham Bill. Pennypacker disliked it. Sulzberger, as president of the newly formed American Jewish Committee, found it unwarranted.[47] If the Dillingham Bill became law, it would mean that the United States would close its doors to the worldwide flow of immigrants. The exclusionary provision of the Bill hinged on a literacy test, and with a high percentage of illiteracy among the new immigrants, the literacy restrictions could easily accomplish their purpose. But no one expected the adroit, manipulative Cannon, who had the support of Penrose and a whole circle of congressmen willing to act at his command, to frustrate the passage of the Bill by eliminating the literacy clause.[48] Some of the groundwork for Cannon's opposition was laid quietly in the library of the Philadelphia Union League. Neither he nor Penrose had adverse feelings toward immigration which, at the time of this discussion in 1906, was reaching a new height. This episode in the internal history of the League was to hurt Cannon, who drew fire from such opposing forces as the anti-immigration American Federation of Labor and nationalistic purists such as the Massachusetts senator, Henry Cabot Lodge. But Cannon's motives were not only political nor was he merely exercising congressional power; he believed that "America was a hell of a success" because its immigrants had built the nation.[49]

With the passing of the old library and its interesting, behind-the-scenes associations, the new library undertook a new role in its effort to become the best of its kind among private American clubs. While it was not remarkable in its number of annual accessions, its selections catered to a quality of interests that reflected the intellectual stature of the League membership.

On Tuesday, January 3, 1911, construction and revision of the middle section of the League House was begun. It was expected that the work would be completed within the year. Weather conditions, a series of labor disputes between bricklayers and stone cutters, and a strike by marble workers delayed the completion of the building. Notwithstanding these inconveniences, the work of the League was carried on. Its social functions were observed without interruption, namely, the traditional New Year's Day reception, Washington's Birthday, and a reception for the retiring governor, Edwin S. Stuart. In spite of the various delays, a major portion of the building was completed, and it was possible to hold the annual meeting that year in the new assembly room which later was named Lincoln Hall.[50] Among the numerous acquisitions received in 1911 was the life-size

H. K. Bush-Brown
A Soldier of the Gray Reserves Known as "The Spirit of '61"

bronze by H. K. Bush-Brown of a soldier of the Gray Reserves, a Civil War unit, which was incorporated into the First Regiment Infantry, and later into the National Guard of Pennsylvania. It was the occasion of the fiftieth anniversary of the war and the donor, the Veteran Corps, had been unable to find an appropriate city site for the statue. It was placed just south of the Broad Street entrance of the League, and the heroic marching figure, with pack, accoutrements, and broad brimmed hat, standing on a polished granite pedestal, is an impressive reminder of the war.[51] Early in 1912, the middle section of the League House was completed and fully furnished.

After accomplishments that came from many years of hard work, careful planning and a great expenditure, League members enjoyed their enlarged house and attempted to bring more beauty and style to the interior of the building. The additional decor included newly panelled walls, fine sconces, and a magnificent centennial chandelier with thousands of shimmering crystals which illuminated Lincoln Hall, the largest room in the League House. Eventually it became a gallery for the portraits of League presidents. To the east and west of Lincoln Hall were three spacious private meeting rooms named after Generals Grant, Meade, and Admiral David G. Farragut. All were decorated in a manner illustrative of their careers. The wall circling about the broad marble staircase leading to all of the floors of the new section was an appropriate area for the many portraits of eminent Americans and military figures of the Union forces.

Before the middle section was inaugurated by a social event, pressing political matters required its use. A special meeting was requested on May 12, 1912 by 504 active members to determine "What The Union League should do to assist in securing the renomination of President Taft." The excitement engendered by the special meeting was so great that the new appointments in the assembly room seemed to go unnoticed; they would have to await another occasion to be fully appreciated.

More than a thousand members crowded into the new room to hear C. Stuart Patterson officially explain the purpose of the meeting. A rift within the Republican Party was feared, as dissident Republican voices had made themselves heard. Lured by the newly organized Progressive Party, Theodore Roosevelt, who had been the key supporter of Taft in 1908, was making another bid for the nation's highest office. The Republican machinery, however, favored Taft. Fourteen influential League members circulated their own petition pleading for caution and restraint, and opposing any premature action that might endorse Taft as a nominee prior to the convention. As soon as Patterson, president of the League in 1897 and 1898, called the

HENRY CLAY

John Neagle

HENRY CLAY

meeting to order, he reminded the members that the circular was entitled to the same respectful attention as the call for the special meeting. Its authors, he said had no "desire to discredit the candidacy of Mr. Taft, nor to advocate anyone else."[52] Their objection was made in the belief that the special meeting was contrary to traditional League policy in that it was advocating a presidential nominee in advance of the Party convention.

Then, reviewing the record of the League's past support of presidential nominees, Patterson enumerated the steps taken by the League in being the first association in the United States to propose the renomination of Lincoln in 1864, six months before the Republican convention chose him for a second term. In 1868, five months before the Republican convention met in Chicago, the League went on record for the nomination of General Ulysses S. Grant, who "had never voted a Republican ticket." The Party had rallied to this first public debut of the political Grant, and had nominated him for the presidency although some League members doubted the choice. Again, before the Republican convention met in 1872, keeping in mind the criticism which had been leveled against irregularities in Grant's administration, the League proposed Grant for a second term, and the party followed in the path of the League. Patterson also added that the League consistently had been the forerunner on the issues of the tariff, sound money, and other national matters incorporated in the Party plank. Were not these precedents to be emulated? Was the League "to adopt the servile policy of following and not leading?"[53]

Edward T. Stotesbury rose to second the resolution introduced by Patterson, endorsing Taft for a second term. He was followed by historian Charlemagne Tower who spoke at great length of Taft's record, stressing his service in various official offices and the importance of returning him to the presidency. William Jay Turner immediately challenged the previous speakers. He refreshed the memories of those who had forgotten that these historical precedents had received the unanimous vote of the membership because the peculiar conditions of the time had called for such action. Similar circumstances did not exist now, in 1912. The resolution, Turner insisted, was contrary to the traditions of the League. Furthermore, if adopted, it would reduce the League to a mere political club and political activity alone, he stressed, should never be permitted to dominate the League. He was neither a "Roosevelt Boomer" nor a Progressive, nor were the men responsible for the circular supporters of a Roosevelt movement. This was the point of the debate. If a secession took place within the Republican camp at the coming convention, whom would the League support? The men who signed the circular were

not opposed to Taft, but feared that the League might become partisan
and factional and hurt rather than help the Republican Party. And
to Charlemagne Tower who spoke of crisis in the midst of plenty,
Turner replied, "There is no crisis today except the crisis in The
Union League."[54] Turner offered a substitute motion which asked
the League to wait until a nominee was chosen at the convention and
then have the League as a corporate institution pledge its full support
to the men chosen.

The secretary of the League, John W. Hamer, presented another
view. The League, he stated, is an association conforming to a
patriotic purpose and that purpose must be equated with unquestioned
support of the Republican Party. A further quandary arose when it
was noted that the two possible contenders at the convention, Taft
and Roosevelt, were both honorary members of the Philadelphia
League. It would be unwise to endorse either one and if the wrong
choice was made, embarrass the League. It was also contended that
the crisis was not confined to the League but was spread throughout
every state in the Union, and that hostile differences would weaken
the Republican Party as well as the League. Another speaker, moving
away from the main discussion, insisted that "the platform of the
Republican Party may not be written in Wall Street . . . nor in the
office of a railway company, nor in the office of any banking house at
this time, but the men who work in the mills, and in the mines, and
on the railroads, and on the farms may have something to say through
their delegates in Chicago."[55]

The tension was broken by General Wagner, who informed the
members that it was the birthday of League president William J.
Tilden; the time had come to vote. All but 138 members present
stood for the Patterson resolution to renominate William Howard
Taft. The meeting ended abruptly.

The interparty division spread to the Republican convention. Pennsylvania Republicans seized control of the State convention and
pledged themselves to Roosevelt. Taft, however, was the successful
nominee, but the Roosevelt men split from the Party to nominate him
as the candidate of the Progressive, or Bull Moose Party. The League
called its second special meeting a few months later to ratify the
nomination of Taft and the Party platform. The split between Pennsylvania Republicans who opposed Taft and the Penrose machine
which upheld him weakened Republican strength in the State. Although many of Roosevelt's League followers threw their support
to Taft in order to conform with League policy, an undetermined
number remained faithful to "TR," as he was popularly called. League
spokesmen for Taft envisioned a close three-way fight, perhaps one of

the most difficult political battles faced, because of the fragmentation of Republican strength. Governor Woodrow Wilson of New Jersey, the Democratic opponent, a historian and the former president of Princeton University, had the backing of a united party.

Public opposition to the split was voiced at League sponsored campaign meetings. Republican electioneers underestimated the strength of the Bull Moose leader, while they focused their attacks upon Wilson and the omnipresent antiprotectionist philosophy of the Democrats. A begrudging recognition of the Socialist Party whose strength had grown was also evident, but neither the Socialists or the more extreme radical movements were looked upon as a serious threat. A narrow approach to the power of the new political parties and deep differences within Republican ranks resulted in a defeat that brought Wilson to the White House for a stay in office that was crucial to American and European history.

Other presidential campaigns had not distracted the League from its customary activity as much as the election of 1912. So great was the inner dissension that the Roosevelt portrait had to be removed; most of the manuscript records of the controversy disappeared, and old-time friends ignored one another. That year the League published the largest annual report in its history, revealing to the public eye the contentious election debates and providing a record not present in the archives.[56] Yet League members were not unmindful of other commitments and events. The League hosted the commission to arrange for the Fiftieth Anniversary Celebration of the Battle of Gettysburg, of which General Louis Wagner was chairman. The guest committee entertained Congressman John W. Weeks of Massachusetts, who spoke on the national currency question. Then the League mourned the loss of George and Harry Widener, victims of the *Titanic* tragedy. Both men had been active in the League's Art Association. Twelve days after the sinking of the *Titanic*, on April 27, 1912, Grant's birthday was celebrated with President Taft as the guest of honor. Later in the year Governor John K. Tener of Pennsylvania, who won his election by a narrow margin, and Mayor Rudolph Blankenburg, known as "Old Dutch Cleanser" because of his unremitting reform activity, were also entertained by the guest committee. One of the major plans projected for the following year was the celebration of the fiftieth anniversary of The Union League.[57]

The semicentennial celebration of the League's founding was scheduled appropriately on the 104th anniversary of Lincoln's birthday in 1913. It was intended to blend the patriotic, political, and social history of the League into one event. A different perspective on the Civil War had emerged, partly because of new historical writings on the subject and partly because League members attracted to the history of the war were evaluating it as one of the many events that had reshaped the political structure of the nation. Lincoln too, was under historical reevaluation. Recognition of the men, diverse and contending, professional politicians and office seekers, wealthy and of modest means, who supported Lincoln came in the numerous biographies that appeared in the twentieth century. The 50th anniversary was significant in that it demonstrated the maturity of the League following the defeat of a presidential candidate it had favored. Its resilience in the face of this loss, and its desire to mend differences with Roosevelt and his followers, were expressed by the retiring President. As the guest of honor at a celebration which was the most elaborate up to that time, Taft directly addressed this issue. He underscored the popular tendency to canonize Lincoln, a tendency in which Taft differed "with those who claim Lincoln as a trade mark for every nostrum that is offered to change the government." His appeal to League Republicans for the necessity to uphold "civil and religious liberty which cost so many lives, so much agony of effort" was an ideal not too high for the Republican Party to reach. With these objectives in mind, Taft said, more people should be invited into the Republican Party: "make your propositions of reform, if we approve them . . . we will go ahead and carry them out with the government we have, because we believe that this government as it is can be adapted to any reform that is useful to the people. And with that proposition cannot we go to those who have left us and invite them to return?" Taft's bid to restore dissident Republicans to the Party, and to attract new cadres, helped heal the rift of 1912.[58]

As a memento of the celebration the banquet committee published a beautiful lithographed program, one of the last in a notable series. A historical memoir of the war years containing Lincoln's Gettysburg Address, with the address of President Taft, handsomely bound, was sent to every high school boy in the city of Philadelphia.[59]

VII

❦

War, Peace and Depression

ON August 14, 1914, war broke out on the continent of Europe. A series of diplomatic blunders that thinly disguised German military aggression were still not obvious when Archduke Francis Ferdinand was assassinated at Sarajevo, signaling the rapid mobilization of the more advanced armies. Great Britain, France, and Russia allied themselves against Germany and the Austro-Hungarian Empire. A long, hard war, lasting four years, brought an end to the imperial government of Germany and to the empires of Austro-Hungary and of the Czar.

The impact upon the United States was gradual. Feelings for the contestants ran high. With the exception of the French, millions of Europeans had emigrated to the United States in the previous three decades. Most Americans quickly sided with Britain and her allies. The American Neutrality League, made up of a strong proGerman element, was very active in Philadelphia and carried on a wave of antiBritish propaganda in the hope of winning American sentiment to the side of the Germans. The Wilson administration was eager to maintain Britain's balance of strength and most Americans shared his view.

At first the "foreign war" was viewed with indifference at the League. With the exception of the increased cost of French vintage wines, the League was undisturbed by battles in unfamiliar French towns. Moving picture entertainment was introduced by several showings of "The Story of David Copperfield" in 1914, and the Art Association boasted a number of additions to the League collection. Chess tournaments and billiard championships were held as usual. In 1915, the League celebrated the golden anniversary of the opening of the Broad Street building and published a special booklet for the occasion.[1]

In time, the paralysis of European shipping brought home to the League the enormous opportunities that existed for the American shipping trade. American industries lacked sufficient merchant vessels to carry their goods across the seas and to fill the commercial needs caused by the reduction of European manufactures. The volume of American shipping soon rose considerably as American shipyards increased their production of merchant vessels. And, as they did, German submarines preyed on neutral American ships bound for European ports. By 1915, the cry of "preparedness" resounded throughout the nation; it was especially strong at The Union League.[2]

Passions were aroused by the sinking of the *Lusitania* by a German submarine on May 7, 1915. They were not subdued by the grand receptions held for George P. Morgan, for many years the chairman of the Membership Committee, and New York's Senator Elihu Root, or the fiftieth anniversary of the opening of the League House.[3] But soon thereafter the subordination of personal and party interests was urged, and in 1916, when another presidential campaign rolled around, election issues were focused upon the war. The Republican policy of protectionism had moved into second place; Wilson's advocacy of protection for revenue only was no longer as crucial at the League. While Democrats spoke of prosperity, peace, and preparedness, the Republicans assailed this as an unacceptable policy; preparedness was inadequate, peace was imperiled at home by Mexico and by provocation on the high seas, and prosperity was an artificial result of the war. The League endorsed Supreme Court Justice Charles E. Hughes for president and Charles W. Fairbanks for vice-president. Roosevelt defected from the Progressive Party and gave his support to Hughes, but the fetching slogans of the Democrats on neutrality and preparedness, and the popularity of Wilson, who "kept us out of the war," were effective in re-electing Wilson for a second term, the first Democrat to succeed himself since the Civil War.[4]

Germany's refusal to abandon submarine warfare and to stop harassment of American vessels led to the severance of diplomatic relations by the United States. Wilson made this announcement on February 3, 1917. No time was lost before a petition of League members was drawn up calling for a special meeting to consider the League's attitude toward President Wilson's response to the crisis. American neutrality was no longer possible. The Union League of Philadelphia, after careful debate, placed country above party and resolved to support the President "in whatever action may be necessary to defend the United States."[5] The resolution was forwarded promptly to Wilson who just as promptly acknowledged it, although coming from an institution which six months earlier had fought him on a partisan issue. On April 6, 1917, the United States declared war upon Germany. A new technology that utilized airplanes, underwater craft, iron-sheathed tanks, and the advances in chemistry and biology for warfare were drawn upon to wage what was then considered the greatest war in history.

At the annual meeting of 1917, the League explored its position as it related to the war. How could it best serve the nation? Judge William W. Porter, reading from the Charter of the League, recited its purposes: that fostering and promoting the love of republican government meant, in the language of the twentieth century, upholding democracy; that the preservation of the Union meant the support of the national government, and that extending aid to the soldiers and sailors of the country meant active aid to the armed forces of the nation. He expounded further on the historical philosophy of the League in noting that not one syllable in the Charter suggested a provision for a social club. But, he continued, the club aspect of the League was for the purpose of maintaining the organization in order to serve the nation both in time of peace and in time of war. All other functions of the League—its fine restaurant, its ornate interior, its physical comforts—were subordinate to national interests. As for himself, he was prepared to scorn all comforts, to reject increases in dues for members who went into the service, and, if other increases were made, he recommended that they should go to support the war.[6]

In less than eight months, 110 League members had joined the armed services; more were on their way, and League employees were enlisting as rapidly.

Porter insisted that the dues of members in the armed forces be suspended for the duration of the war, and that allowances be made for employees who had enlisted. Both measures were approved. It was the beginning of a more comprehensive plan of involvement for the League. Funds were raised quickly for two field ambulances and sent to France, where the name of the League could be seen not far from the field of battle. A greater undertaking was the provision of some facilities for men in uniform who had no place to go while on leave, or while waiting to embark. A first thought was to make available a section of the League House. But it was decided as more practical to secure a separate building for the exclusive use of soldiers, sailors, and marines. A search was made of the center city for a suitable site, and League member William Bryant, the owner of an unoccupied church building at Broad and Spruce streets, made the property available for a recreation center without cost to the League. John

AMBULANCE OF THE AMERICAN HOSPITAL - Lycée Pasteur Neuilly-Paris
Arrival of wounded - Arrivée des blessés.

A UNION LEAGUE AMBULANCE AT THE AMERICAN HOSPITAL IN PARIS

Gribbel, the incumbent president of the League, immediately opened a members' subscription for funds to renovate the church interior and adapt it to the needs of the servicemen. Fifty thousand dollars poured in at once, with assurances that additional funding to support the center would continue as long as necessary. Much of the renovation was done at cost, and a variety of gifts useful for a recreation center were presented by League members. Player pianos, victrolas and records, a library with abundant material, billiard tables, chess and checkers, luncheon tableware and a huge quantity of stationery were among the gifts. Stage and screen entertainment was a regular feature of the center. The League was responsible for all arrangements, and it named the center The Soldiers' and Sailors' Annex of The Union League. It was constantly in use. More than 700 men in uniform took advantage of the Annex each day of the week. It was so successful that League members and their wives, who were responsible for the work at the Annex, shared both food and entertainment. No military supervision was necessary and no untoward incidents occurred to make it necessary. Only an unforeseen epidemic of influenza, striking the city in October and November, 1918 slowed down its work.[7]

While the center was not a far-flung undertaking, it was significant in that no other facilities existed which offered relaxation for the enlisted men in the Philadelphia area. In its brief history, which lasted until demobilization, it used over a million sheets of paper and a variety of stationery for letters. So great was the outgoing correspondence that a special post office box was installed in the Annex. The Annex was the real forerunner of the United Service Organization that came into being during World War II. It offered comfort and conveniences to a broad mass of men, and filled needs of the military that could not be met by the various YMCA's and similar organizations that aided in wartime service.

As soon as the first United States government Liberty Loan was announced in June 1917, the corporate body of the League organized a subscription among its members that raised $1,751,000 for the loan; the subscription for the second Liberty Loan doubled the first, reaching the sum of $3,560,000, and though the third drive dropped slightly below the second, the fourth and last Liberty Loan under League sponsorship soared to $9,191,200. The 17 million dollar total was one of the largest raised by any institution of its kind in the United States. To stimulate the purchase of wartime loans, League members issued their own literature and distributed it by parading through the center city to the Liberty Statue located on the south plaza of City Hall. Over 75 per cent of its membership were active participants in the loans, and they oversubscribed their quota by 25 per cent.[8]

PARADE SPONSORED BY THE UNION LEAGUE ON BEHALF
OF THE LIBERTY LOAN DRIVE

With the energies of the League diverted by the war, its internal affairs and social life were diminished. A strict wartime economy was introduced in compliance with a national order that was emphasized by Secretary of the Treasury William G. McAdoo, a major speaker at the League in 1917. A scarcity of labor, and changes in employee status and wages, all affected the customarily smooth operation of the League. There were meatless Mondays and drastic changes in the menu. For a period of six weeks, the League was almost deserted because of the influenza epidemic. Both members and employees were saddened by the news of the first battlefield casualty when the League learned that Patrick J. Egan of the 315th Infantry, 79th Division, was killed at Montfaucon, France. In his memory, a large bronze plaque was mounted prominently on the wall of the president's office by the members of the Open Table, whom he had served as a waiter. It remains there to the present day.

Before the war was over more than 200 League members were in the armed forces and many others were performing civilian duties. One of the men who left behind a notable military record was Major-General William G. Price, Jr., of the 53rd Artillery Brigade who participated in Marne, Argonne, and other American operations in France. Price was active in the National Guard of Pennsylvania throughout his lifetime. During his service abroad he made many friends, among them C. Brewster Rhoads; both men were later to become presidents of the League.[9]

For the duration of the war, the subject of politics was dismissed. There was no criticism of President Wilson, and he "unceasingly received in his defense of American rights the earnest and united support" of the League. Corporate action was confined to matters which involved internal affairs of the League. The long debated problem of increasing the membership was partly resolved when the number of active members was raised from 2,600 to 3,000, even though 2,800 still remained on the candidates list.[10]

An event that could not be deferred because of the war was the completion and dedication of the Lincoln Memorial Room. This impressive room, originally intended as an extension of the library, called for a permanent tribute to Lincoln and a series of memorials commemorating the League's participation in the Civil War.[11] The Art Association volunteered to raise funds for a life-size bronze statue of Lincoln, which John Otto Schweizer was commissioned to execute. It stands in a concave niche of pale marble against the west wall. Schweizer recaptured Lincoln's resolute attitude, the attitude which prevades the Gettysburg Address. The figure of Lincoln, his left arm bent, his fist raised, and his determined face, dominates the Memorial

WEST WALL OF THE LINCOLN MEMORIAL ROOM

Room. The motto of the League, *Amor Patriae Ducit,* is engraved in the marble behind the statue.[12] Spread across the top of the west wall, carved in gilt letters, is the Gettysburg Address in its entirety. Beneath it is a series of bronze medallions, also by Schweizer, of eight of the generals who led the Union armies to victory. Under the medallions are eight bronze tablets listing the names of more than 550 League members and the branches of service to which they were enlisted. The list was compiled with precision by a committee of nine League veterans, four of whom wrote the official histories of their regiments. One such veteran, Captain S. Emlen Meigs, had stood alongside of Lincoln at Independence Hall in 1861, and had been a League member since May, 1863. He was a constant advocate of the preservation of Civil War historic sites and artifacts. A year before the United States entered the war, he had convinced the League to pass a resolution to aid in the conservation of Grant's Cabin, which the General had occupied immediately before the surrender at Appomattox. It was later removed to Fairmount Park in Philadelphia. Unfortunately, Meigs died two months before the Memorial Room which he had helped plan was dedicated.[13]

Hand-carved vertical panels depicting artifacts symbolic of the war divide the marble niche from the bronze tablets. Above the fireplace on the east wall is a rectangular bronze plaque listing the regiments raised and equipped by the League. On either side are two large exhibition cases containing Lincolniana and artifacts of the war. Although League members Boker and Leland were responsible for the broadside printing of the 48 copies of the Emancipation Proclamation which were autographed by Lincoln, the League's own copy was presumably lost in the fire in 1866. President John Gribbel presented a copy to the League from his own collection for display in the Lincoln Memorial Room. Encircling the convex perimeter of these exhibition cases are bronze guidons of Pennsylvania's Civil War regiments.

Before the adjacent high-rise buildings blocked the sun's entry into the Memorial Room, a blaze of light streamed through the three sections of stained glass windows displaying the insignia and accoutrements of the United States army, navy, and marine corps. On the north and south walls are built-in book cases that shelve rare books on Lincoln and the Civil War. The unique historical interpretation of the Lincoln Memorial Room has no counterpart in any other American club.

At the dedication, William Renwick Riddell, Justice of the Supreme Court of Ontario, was the main speaker. Corporal James Tanner, still sprightly and energetic, was to be a guest of honor, but could not

TRIUMVIRI AMERICANI
ONE OF A NUMBER OF PATRIOTIC PLAQUES IN THE LINCOLN MEMORIAL ROOM

attend. Tanner used this opportunity to send to the League the almost forgotten testimony of the eyewitnesses to the assassination of Lincoln, and a rare legal holograph document prepared by Lincoln while he was a circuit lawyer in Vandalia, Illinois, in 1842.[14]

The dedication of the Lincoln Memorial Room and the appearance of Secretary of the Treasury McAdoo were the only formal ceremonies held at the League for the remainder of the war. The addresses delivered in the final months of the war discussed the tide of misfortune that was sweeping Europe, the toppled kingdoms and monarchies, the collapse of the Czarist empire, and its ultimate overthrow by the Bolsheviki. When the Imperial Army of Germany was crushed, and an armistice signed on November 11, 1918, the excitement at the League was immeasurable. Starting at 7 A.M., two hours after the news of the impending armistice reached the city, members crowded into the commodious League House for a day-long celebration. The sophisticated among them were not unconcerned by the revolutionary upsurge that was spreading across war-torn Europe. New governments were rising from the ashes of the old, and the rights of a multitude of nationalities were being asserted and awaited recognition. The Wilsonian slogan, "The world must be made safe for Democracy," was earnestly believed. The devastated low countries recovered slowly, and Herbert Hoover, an American engineer of unusual administrative capability, was sent by the United States to organize food relief programs for Belgium.

Before these events could be appraised, and before the beginning of peace negotiations, the League rejected Wilson's appeal to return a Democratic majority to the Congress in 1918. Its self-imposed ban restricting criticism of the administration was immediately abandoned.[15] Wilson's move signaled the end of the wartime truce on politics between the League and the Democratic administration. In the same year, Edwin S. Stuart, a former governor of the state, was reelected to the presidency of the League for a second term after an absence from office of 12 years. He was instrumental in securing members' approval in 1919 for the framework of the Committee on National Activities. The purpose of this new League committee was to enlist friends for the Republican Party, and its formation was in anticipation of Wilson's political announcement.[16] Decades later, it was succeeded by the Committee for Patriotic Action and the Political Affairs Committee. League member William C. Sproul of Delaware County won the gubernatorial election in 1918, keeping the Republicans at the helm of the state. In the same election, Republicans won a majority in the United States Senate, frustrating Wilson's appeal. The time was ripe for Republican forces in Pennsylvania to fling themselves into the mainstream of another presidential election.[17]

A WAR-TIME PARADE IN FRONT OF THE LEAGUE HOUSE
APRIL 6, 1918

The year 1919 brought the death of Theodore Roosevelt, and a special memorial meeting was held. Old political differences had vanished and the League paid tribute to one of its honorary members. In the same year, the Volstead Act, designed to ban the sale of intoxicating liquors, which became the 18th Amendment, required the League to dispose of its fine stock of vintage wines and whiskeys. The League reluctantly obeyed the new law. On Founders' Day of 1919, the George G. Meade Post, No. 1 of the GAR, officially presented to the League its library of Civil War books. Even more significant was the Post's presentation of Pennsylvania battleflags. Two of these painted on silk by a neglected Negro artist, David B. Bowser, were of the 2nd and 6th United States Colored Troops. The presentation marked the closing of an era for the Meade Post, and marked the rapid passing of the old soldiers of the GAR as well.[18]

A year and a half later, the 19th Amendment providing for woman's suffrage brought about a revision of the League's By-Laws. Up to that time there was no stipulation in the Constitution and By-Laws that prevented women from becoming members. With the ratification of the 19th Amendment, the word "male" was added to the By-Laws as a condition for League membership.[19] The 1920's saw a return of Republican power, unprecedented prosperity, and a revolution in morals and manners. The automobile boom, the popularity of the radio, and the extravagant style of life enjoyed by many cloaked much of the nation's poverty. At The Union League significant changes, not readily obvious, had also taken place. Its Republican stance was greater than ever before, and its roll of prospective candidates had grown far beyond the number that could be admitted in three, five, or even eight years. While the League showed no evidence of being affected by the mood of the rising "Jazz Age," or of the "Roaring Twenties," its social strength and political power went uncontested in the city and was acknowledged throughout the nation. Before the decade ended, however, an economic depression of great severity gripped the state and the nation.

The presidental election of 1920 deeply involved the League and the activities of its individual members. Boies Penrose convinced the Republican old guard to choose Senator Warren G. Harding of Ohio for the presidency. Governor Sproul, a friend of Harding's, received strong Pennsylvania backing for the presidency, but "it was the vote cast by Governor Sproul," former President of The Union League, on behalf of the Pennsylvania delegation, that made the Harding nomination secure.[20] The nominations of both Harding and his running mate, Calvin Coolidge, were ratified at the League. It was an unusual meeting. Former president C. Stuart Patterson introduced the reso-

lution ratifying the nominees and the party platform. A striking figure, with his white beard just touching a flaming red necktie, he spoke
dramatically of "a crisis not second in importance to either of those
we have passed." Patterson set the tone for a meeting that was critical
of the manner in which the war had been conducted, the rapid demobilization that had followed, and Wilson's Fourteen-Point program for
peace. He stressed that millions of men had perished in the greatest
war in history. Europe had been laid to waste, and the United States
was duty-bound to rehabilitate her. But America would not do so
through a League of Nations that would deny it its independent sovereignty. Wilson's ideal was the work of an autocrat to whom neither
the League nor the Republican Party would bow. According to Patterson, the Democratic administration had shown itself to be without
an understanding of world needs. Patterson was followed by Sproul,
the junior former president of the League. Sproul attended the Republican convention and naturally spoke with affection of his friend,
Senator Harding. Then, Congressman George S. Graham of Pennsylvania spoke, and he was followed by Mayor J. Hampton Moore of
Philadelphia, William Jay Turner, a former Roosevelt Progressive,
Owen J. Roberts, who became an associate Justice of the United States
Supreme Court in 1930, and General William G. Price, Jr., commander of the 53rd Artillery Brigade of the 28th Division. The speeches
echoed the words of the Chicago Convention. Arrangements were
made by the League for a mass meeting at the Academy of Music,
where addresses were given by Governor Sproul, Kansas Governor
Henry J. Allen, and the vice-presidential candidate Governor Calvin
Coolidge of Massachusetts. They all predicted a Republican landslide, and, in fact, it was an overwhelming defeat of their Democratic
opponents, James M. Cox and 38-year-old Franklin Delano Roosevelt.[21]

Boies Penrose, a moving force behind the choice of Harding, died
on the last day of 1921. An extraordinary career that was built on the
political foundation established by Simon Cameron had come to an
end. A brief struggle to control the Pennsylvania party ensued. Diverse
Republican factions fought for the mantle of Penrose. On the one side
were League members of considerable influence—W. W. Atterbury,
president of the Pennsylvania Railroad, Harding's Secretary of the
Treasury Andrew W. Mellon of Pittsburgh, and Joseph R. Grundy of
Bristol, president of the Pennsylvania Manufacturers' Association.
Each one vied to control the choice of a new senator. All three had
been League members for several decades.[22] NonLeague Republicans,
like the Vare brothers of South Philadelphia, and the environmentalist-
Progressive Gifford Pinchot, whose sights were set on the upcoming
gubernatorial nomination, were on the other side, also grappling for

the seat of power, But none of the contenders for the control of Penrose's senatorial seat were successful. They finally compromised on George Wharton Pepper, who later became a member of The Union League, as Penrose's successor in the Senate.[23]

State government under William C. Sproul raised the level of education in Pennsylvania as a result of the Edmunds Act of 1921. A system of modern roads to meet the increased automobile traffic was introduced by the highway bureau, and the National Guard, the banking, and the insurance departments were reorganized. The administration of state government was modernized. Nonetheless, Progressive Gifford Pinchot challenged these accomplishments by emphasizing failures of the administration, and by appealing to women voters and to prohibitionists of the middle counties of the state.[24]

Before Sproul completed his term of office, President Harding, who was scheduled to be the League's guest of honor for the fall of 1923, collapsed and died. Calvin Coolidge quickly accommodated himself to the office of the presidency, and pushed for the unqualified approval of the Mellon Plan to readjust and reduce federal taxes. Strong support for the Mellon Plan was voiced by the League, which made a special point of emphasizing that Mellon had been a member since 1888.[25] Muffled rumblings of an economic recession were heard in 1923. But whispers about a scandal uncovered by the Public Lands Committee grew louder each day. The secret lease of reserve naval oil lands at Teapot Dome, Wyoming, during the short-lived Harding administration was particularly resented by President Coolidge and he was eager to punish any wrongdoers. Harding's poor judgment of his appointees had been largely responsible for this episode, although his choices of Charles Evans Hughes as Secretary of State and Herbert Hoover as Secretary of Commerce were above criticism. At the recommendation of Senator Pepper, League member Owen J. Roberts was chosen by Coolidge to make a full inquiry into the facts involving Teapot Dome. The oil reserves were finally repossessed by the government, but to the dismay of the League the record of the Harding administration was smirched because of corruption by his subordinates. As a result of his capable work, Coolidge submitted Roberts' name for appointment as associate justice of the Supreme Court. Roberts' nomination was confirmed by a vote of 68 to 8. Accusations of Republican maladministration had no effect on the renomination of Calvin Coolidge in 1924. Attempts to discredit Coolidge with the Teapot Dome scandal failed, and the dry and taciturn incumbent president was elected in 1924.[26]

Prosperity was a key word of the Coolidge administration. In the many addresses delivered at the League during his term of office, members were reminded constantly of American economic progress and of the financial health of the nation. The continued industrial advance seemed to be without parallel, the tariff had proved its effectiveness, and immigration restriction was referred to by a number of speakers as an additional boon to American labor. On one hand, the contributions of immigrants to the growth of the nation were praised; on the other, little opposition was voiced when the policy of an open door to immigrants came to an end with the Johnson-Reed Act of 1924.[27] The addresses, covering a wide variety of subjects, were given by congressmen and governors, military men and civic leaders. Their topics ranged from Major Vivian Gilbert's description of the British Army's historic march into Jerusalem, in which the speaker had been a participant, to a talk on the nature of the judicial process by the state's Chief Justice, Robert Von Moschzisker.[28]

New approaches to the role of the Republican Party were revealed by the political speakers, who feared that in 1924 an attempt would be made to form a third party. But these fears were unfounded. A reunification of the Party had taken place and it was stronger than ever before. It was solid and uncompromising in its adherence to its platform. For the first time at the League, a significant degree of attention was given to the ominous appearance of the still infant Communist Party, to the vote-getting LaFollette Progressives, and to the Socialists. Their presence was acknowledged, but little thought was given to the American Communist Party's connections with a far-flung international movement under the leadership of the Soviet Union, whose single purpose was to overthrow the governments of capitalist society and to seize power wherever possible.[29]

Both Founders' Day and Lincoln's Birthday celebrations had regained their prewar popularity. The wide range of speakers chosen for these occasions presented diverse interpretations of the events that had led to the Civil War, and the circumstances that had led to the founding of the League. Abraham Lincoln also was recast in a new image. Albert J. Beveridge, the Indiana Senator whose first speech after he was elected was delivered at The Union League in 1899, came to give the Founders' Day address 25 years later. Meanwhile, he had written a biography of John Marshall, the third chief justice of the United States, and was hard at work on a book on Lincoln. He chose to speak on the evolution of constitutional law as it affected current treaties with the nations of Europe, the League of Nations, and the Supreme Court. The League audience listened spellbound. No longer the brash young senator who had advocated the United States as an imperialist power of the future, Beveridge was now a man whose ideas were carefully reasoned and well-presented.[30]

Reverend Joseph Fort Newton who had been "proclaimed one of the most brilliant and intellectual occupants of the American pulpit," and who was the author of a standard work on Lincoln, gave the Lincoln Day address in 1926, probing the spiritual life of the Civil War president. Unlike some of the speakers who fell into the trap of overglorifying the president by making comparisons of his second inaugural address of 1864 with the Sermon on the Mount, or by finding in the extensive Lincoln literature a nostrum for all of America's problems, Newton's evaluation was more prudent in its comparisons.[31]

The Sesquicentennial of American independence was celebrated in Philadelphia that year with considerable fanfare, but it lacked the glamor of an exposition such as the one that celebrated the growth of the United States in 1876. Charges of corruption regarding the choice of the South Philadelphia site clouded a memorable occasion. However, The Union League made independent arrangements to receive the governors of the 13 original colonies and their representatives. League president William C. Sproul, a former governor of Pennsylvania, chaired the reception. He extended the greetings of the League and quipped that so many unrepentant Democrats had not been seen before at the League at one time. New York Governor Alfred E. Smith, the Democratic presidential candidate for 1928, ignored the comment, and responded warmly. The Southern governors lamented, with humor in their remarks, that the Democrats envisioned a return to office in 1928. The New England governors addressed themselves to the historical aspects of the celebration, and spoke of their states at the time of the American Revolution. It was a brief and friendly reception.[32]

On Founders' Day, 1927, President Calvin Coolidge received the gold medal of the League and an honorary membership to the club. As a token of the occasion the League had a medal struck commemorating the event for its members. Although brief, Coolidge's response managed to cover many of the subjects that aroused contemporary interest: the war, patterns of peace, the League of Nations, a healthy economy, and the vigorous, enterprising nature of recent immigrants. Somewhat ironically, he noted that the great development of national resources, the growth of industry, and a rapidly increasing population necessitated the recent restrictions upon immigration. To an allusion that Coolidge might run for another term, the president did not flicker an eyelid. Instead, he cautioned his League audience of impending economic disaster if the wealthier segment of the nation did not forego its luxurious mode of living.[33]

The same honor that was conferred on Coolidge was extended to John J. Pershing on Lincoln's Birthday in February, 1928. The presentation was made to the commander of the American Expeditionary

Forces by General William G. Price, Jr., who had served under Pershing. The recipient of the gold medal spoke in terse, sharp sentences on Lincoln, and though he was attired in formal clothing his erect military bearing was unmistakable.[34]

Club Nights and Ladies' Nights had risen in popularity. These were attractive events at which members, their families, and guests enjoyed recitals given by different choral, chamber groups, and symphony orchestras. On one occasion, a delegation of Pueblo Indians gave a performance of songs and dances illustrative of the life and culture of their tribe. Saturday afternoon concerts were revived after a long absence, and more and more, motion pictures helped to diversify League entertainment.[35]

To encourage a greater use of the library, Colonel Louis J. Kolb, a bibliophile and member of the Library Committee instituted an attractive program in 1928, commonly known as "Library Nights." These nights began with musical recitations which were followed by a speaker on some aspect of the library and its collections. Herman L. Collins, a popular newspaper columnist writing under the name of "Girard," introduced the series by discussing the resources of the League library, and Noah H. Swayne, 2nd, recited the "Battle Hymn of the Republic" from Julia Ward Howe's original manuscript in the collection of Colonel Kolb. Other library functions that followed included as speakers the world-renowned bibliophile, A. Edward Newton, who spoke on his collections, and Cheesman A. Herrick, president of Girard College, who spoke on Lincoln books in the League Library. It was the opening of a notable series that has continued far beyond the League centennial.[36]

The success of League functions depended upon the abilities of a well-trained staff. Most club histories have not examined the contribution of their employees to the smooth, daily operation of their clubs. The manager and his associates, an outstanding chef and his colleagues in the restaurant department, dishwashers and doormen, waiters and waitresses, the controller's department and other categories were the backbone of the successful social occasions. In 1928, the number of League employees reached 362. In the first decades of the League almost all of the male employees had been veterans of the Civil War. These men were given preference by the League long before federal legislation enacted provisions for veterans. Their women employees were often those who lacked male support as a result of being widowed, or who had been otherwise affected by the war. Within this 19th century milieu, both approaches were unique and significant because they were independent of outside forces, such as the clamor of the suffragette movement.

An outstanding example of the League's attitude toward its employees was shown following the death of Alexander Gilchrist. Gilchrist's employment with the League began in 1869, when he worked as a porter. Subsequently, he became a hallman and then held the position of head doorman until he died in 1897. After 28 years of faithful service, the Board of Directors expressed its appreciation by paying his funeral expenses and relieving his widow of a $1,700 mortgage on the house in which he resided. At a time when death benefits for employees and similar compensations were virtually non-existent, this gesture was far advanced. But it was not atypical for the League.[37]

Many new faces among the employees made their appearance at the League toward the end of the 19th century, and young men who came to work for the League then are still remembered for their many years of service. Alfred Lee spent almost 40 years working in the library; controller Tom Jones, who came in 1898, and his colleague Clayton Morris, who came in 1899, did not retire until more than a half-century later. James Rawlings managed the pool and billiard room from 1872 to 1924, and an associate, Leroy Holmes, who arrived in 1918, recounted many of the championship games played up to 1972. Norris Comegys, who also worked in the game rooms, equaled these life-long records of service. All three men oversaw the billiard tournaments, pocket billiards, cowboy pool, and bowling. Restaurant manager William A. Cloak completed 50 years, and Kurt Lautenbach, headwaiter in the ladies' dining room, gave 40 years of service. William F. Homiller, the League manager, completed a quarter-century and was rewarded with a gold watch in 1931, the year before young Daniel M. Layman came to work at the League.

In 1926 all employees who had been with the League for more than one year were covered by group insurance that ranged from $500 to $1,200. The use of visiting nurses, and compensation for disability which went beyond the requirements of state law, were incorporated as part of this insurance plan. A physician drawn from the League membership was assigned to the staff. With this as a basis, the League extended its responsibility to its staff from decade to decade, prior to the institution of mass medical and government insurance programs. As a special recognition of employee service, starting in 1899, every year at Christmas cash gifts were presented to all members of the staff.

One of the unique social characteristics of the League that evolved in the early and middle twenties was the growth of inner clubs and club-tables. Their origin is not entirely clear, although the original Union Club itself was a club within the League. In 1884, the Kettle

Club was founded by Thomas K. Ober, more as a members' association for nature outings than as a table or inner club. But it established the principle of sharing a common interest among a small group. Seven years after the Kettle Club was begun, the Lincoln Club was founded. Its purpose was to further Lincoln and Civil War studies, and in 1893 the Lincoln Association was started by John Russell Young for collectors of Lincolniana. About 1896, the Kindergarten Club was founded by a group of men who had been chided for childish conduct in the billiard room. Out of this humorous reproach, an association was formed that once a year held a celebration that took on the character of a kindergarten ring. Dressed in infants clothing, and supplied with bibs, toys, cribs, and other items of the nursery, new members were introduced at the annual Christmas season party. Throughout the year, their regular meetings are devoted to the discussion of more serious matters. A fourth club, of which there is only scant evidence is the Oyster Bar Table. Eight known club tables which are still in existence, met regularly for luncheon purposes. They were founded before World War I: the Hearth, and the Wishbone were founded in 1904; the Inglenook in 1905; the Canteen, made up of members of the National Guard of Pennsylvania, was founded in 1910; the Ground Hog and the Wilderness were founded in 1912; the Pirates' Crew Table and the Open Table were founded in 1913; and the Horstmann Table was founded in 1917. With the enlargement of the League House, and in the years following the war, a number of other tables were founded, whose members were involved in various public and private social and cultural affairs. The Right Angle Table and the Grafters were founded in 1922; and the Open Table evolved into the Benson Table, one of the largest in the League and named after benefactor Edwin N. Benson. Not all of the inner clubs occupied a luncheon table or met on a daily basis. Each governed its own affairs and held such social arrangements as suited its tastes. By the time of the League centennial, the number of active tables had grown to 34, and represented a multitude of interests of more than one third of the League members who belonged.[38]

The social and political aspects of League life had become even more attractive in the twenties than it had been at the turn of the century. Membership was prized and highly sought, confronting the League with a swelling roll of candidates. Candidates could not be admitted quickly enough. However, despite deaths and resignations admission was a lengthy process. The candidates register had reached 3,869 in 1924 and approximately 125 were admitted annually. Maximum membership had been fixed at 3,000. Since the controversy of 1893 over the political identity of members and candidates, the membership committee had

AN EARLY PROGRAM OF THE KINDERGARTEN CLUB

defined the phrase "in harmony" with Republican principles to mean that a candidate had voted for Republican presidential and congressional candidates. After the division within the League over Taft and Roosevelt in 1912, all candidates were asked how they had voted in national elections. From that time on, what appeared to be a passing qualification became institutionalized. By 1924, a new generation of members took it upon themselves to describe the League basically as a Republican club, equating its political orientation with its patriotic purpose and history. The description was acceptable to the thousands who were eager for membership, and were prepared to wait from eight to twelve years to be admitted.[39]

To circumvent this long waiting period, members had begun to enter the names of their teenage sons, nephews, and even grandsons on the candidate's register. Thus, mere boys or children, to whom long years of waiting would make no difference, were competing for membership with men like Senator George Wharton Pepper, who was admitted in 1931 after a long wait. Young men were thereby enabled to become members at the age of twenty-one. Some proposers of candidates losing sight of the purpose for which the League was founded, fancied it a hereditary institution and viewed it as a step closer to Philadelphia upper-class society; others had begun to look at the League as a canopy for business and professional organizations, while a lesser number were pushing hard to establish an exclusionary policy without regard for political identity.

When youthful candidates came to be interviewed at the age of twenty-one, since many had never voted, they could assert a political preference, but not a political record. This became irksome to the Membership Committee, which voiced its objections to the practice of submitting such young members at the annual meeting in 1924, based on the belief that a younger generation possibly would change its political affiliation after admission. When these facts became known and were fully debated, it was resolved that no one could be proposed for membership who was under the age of 18 thereby deferring admission at least to the age of 25 under the current waiting period. Those whose names were on the candidates' roll prior to the resolution were unaffected by the new ruling.[40]

Against this competitive background, exclusionist policies developed. The old guard, which identified itself with the admission criteria of the late 19th century, continued to adhere to the basic principles of the Charter, demanding loyalty to the United States. The generation that assumed position and strength after the Bull Moose debacle, however, ignored the imprecations of President Taft, who stressed civil and religious opportunity and equality as Republican ideals. They also ignored the earlier experience of the New York Union

League in barring members of different religious background from admission to the club. In 1892, an applicant who was favorably reported on by the Membership Committee, was rejected by a minority of the membership and the episode was made public. Other Republicans repudiated this action; members of the clerical roll denounced it; and the press across the nation carried the embarrassing story on its front pages.[41] The Philadelphia League, as a corporate body, was reluctant to introduce a religious restriction, and members like Judge Norris S. Barratt and Robert von Moschzisker, who had witnessed the change from earlier attitudes, made known their opposition to exclusion from membership on account of religion. Yet the Membership Committee had some members who were so adamant in their views that a policy was introduced that made difficult the acceptance of people of Italian, Jewish, and of Slavic background. Throughout the history of the League there had always been Italian and Jewish members, but their number had declined sharply in the decades following World War I. Although exclusionary practices based on ethnic or minority origin were eventually overturned, this represented another of the many crises that the League was compelled to face. By the time Calvin Coolidge declared that "I do not choose to run for president in 1928," there were 4,780 candidates on the membership roll, the highest in the history of The Union League of Philadelphia.[42]

On June 15, 1928, a special League meeting was called to ratify the nominations of Herbert Clark Hoover, then secretary of Commerce, and Senator Charles Curtis of Kansas for the highest offices in the United States. The loyal support of the League was pledged to the platform adopted at the Kansas City, Missouri, convention of the Republican Party. Hoover, a man who had risen from humble circumstances, had great appeal to the voters, and the League prepared itself to help assure the success of the Republican ticket.

The League Campaign Committee developed new techniques for its political work, both locally and nationally. A series of four campaign luncheons was planned for the month of October at which the speakers would be the former governor of Kansas, Henry J. Allen, Congressman George S. Graham from Pennsylvania, Congressman Carroll L. Beedy from Maine, and Connecticut Senator Hiram Bingham. For Governor John S. Fisher of Pennsylvania, a League member, a nationwide radio broadcast was arranged on which he would discuss presidential issues. This kind of political exposure was unique to the League and new to the state. Also innovative was a special reception for Mrs. Hoover held in Lincoln Hall, under the auspices of the Republican State Committee. Ten thousand women from all sections of the state came to Philadelphia to greet Mrs. Hoover at the League.[43]

Democrat Al Smith, the "Happy Warrior" from the streets of New

York, also seemed to be a strong popular candidate who possessed the necessary political support. The Republican platform still clung to the tariff, and it upheld prohibition and the foreign policy of Coolidge. Further, it advocated a federal farm board for the distribution of agricultural products through cooperatives. Farm relief was an important plank in both party platforms. The Democrats also supported prohibition, but Smith urged a repeal of the 18th Amendment. The Democrats condemned the much-debated labor injunction of the twenties, as well as Coolidge's foreign policy, and emphasized collective bargaining for the first time in a major election. Smith's showing was poor. He lost five Southern states because of his stand on prohibition, and lost in other areas because he was a Roman Catholic. Hoover received a popular vote of more than 21 million, and Smith more than 15 million, but the Republican candidate received 444 electoral votes over the 87 received by his opponent.

Seven months after Hoover's inauguration, the American stock market, fed by years of speculation, began to decline. Between October 19 and November 13, 1929, it plunged rapidly downward. An age that was marked by high living, prohibition, and a new morality had come to an end. The roaring twenties had been silenced, and the tide of prosperity reversed.

The economic catastrophe settled in slowly. Industries declined. Businesses closed their doors. Breadlines and soup kitchens were amazing sights in the large cities where officials did what they could to stave off starvation among those who were immediately affected. In the ensuing three years, 75 billion dollars was lost in the stock market, and the wealth of the nation appeared to be wiped out.

The League held its annual meeting five weeks after the collapse of the stock market. If there was uncertainty about the future, it was not expressed at the annual meeting at which a president, officers and directors were elected. Members were more concerned with the choice of a president of the League than with the economic scene. It was too soon to comprehend the impending crisis. Weeks before the election was scheduled, a high level of excitement, such as had not been seen at the League for nearly three decades, pervaded the League House. Five candidates had been nominated for the presidency. William G. Price, Jr., a former League president, and George Stuart Patterson, the son of a former League president, had declined to run. The field was left open for Melville G. Baker, a prominent banker, Miers Busch, who had been a vice-president for nine years, and Colonel Louis J. Kolb, the only incumbent officer. Patterson preferred to run for the office of vice-president and declined the higher office. Although there were no restrictions as to the number of candidates, three nominees was an unusually high number, and aroused attention. The uncommon competition at once attracted the attention of the press, which considered everything pertaining to the League a matter of public interest.[44]

When 32 members were nominated for the posts of 15 directors, the excitement was compounded. However, before the meeting on December 9, 15 of these members, including the powerful Pennsylvania political figure, Joseph R. Grundy, withdrew their names. Among the contenders for directors' offices were J. Howard Pew, an oil industrialist, Ira Jewell Williams, a lawyer and Pinchot Progressive, and E. Lawrence Fell and Judge Otto Robert Heiligman, two future League presidents. Colonel Kolb was favored for the office of the presidency, but Melville G. Baker received 757 of the 1,591 votes cast and won the election. Miers Busch received insignificant support. Williams, despite his previous aid to Governor Gifford Pinchot, and Pew, a committed Republican, were elected by a large vote, along with Fell and Heiligman. Three months after the election, fate robbed Baker of his victory. The 54-year-old League president died suddenly at a church meeting, and George Stuart Patterson, a lawyer and cotton broker, was unanimously elected as president according to the provisions of the By-Laws. Patterson and his father were the only father and son presidents in the history of the League.[45]

By the end of 1930, the swift changes in the economy and the hardships that dealt severely with the nation had affected The Union League in common with numerous other institutions. Its candidates' roll dropped by 200, and in 1931 it was reduced by another 400. Resignations, hitherto small in number, totaled 124 in 1931 and 246 in 1932. Almost 250 candidates did not qualify or withdrew their names in 1931, while only 8 failed to qualify in 1932. In two years the active membership roll fell from 3,000 to 2,679, although the register of candidates was still above the 4,100 mark. The sting of the depression was still too minor to be painful, however. Every effort was made by the League to maintain its traditional program of speakers. The fortieth anniversary of the Lincoln Club was celebrated quietly, and the Reverend S. Parkes Cadman, who had delivered the Lincoln address in 1930, described in florid rhetoric "the raw rustic of 1834" as "the giant of 1864".[46] During the first two years of the depression none of the League speakers fully grasped the enormity of the economic disaster that had descended upon the nation. The roster of speakers was drawn up by the Committee on Public Affairs, which presented the political observer and editor David Lawrence, a supporter of the Hoover program. The Guest Committee arranged for Pennsylvania Senator David A. Reed to discuss the financial and economic problems facing the Congress. At this meeting League president E. Lawrence Fell contributed his own views on the efforts of Republicans in the crisis. To find relief from the focus on politics and economics, the Library Committee invited Arthur Hobson Quinn, the distinguished historian of American drama, to speak on his favorite subject.[47] And when in 1931, President Hoover briefly stepped away from the burdens and pressures of his office to come to the League and accept a portrait of himself which they had commissioned, it was not to discuss public questions of the state of the nation. He spoke for less than ten minutes, referring only briefly to the fever and tumult that had swept Washington since he had taken office.[48]

Even though the annual reports of the League were subdued on the subject of the depression, the League did not remain a silent observer. It was the first private body in Philadelphia, and perhaps in the entire state, to attempt to grapple in a realistic manner with the crises of unemployment, poverty, and disease. Before the Christmas season of 1930, 12 of its members were charged by the directors to form a committee on unemployment in the name of the League. Its purpose was to raise a substantial fund to furnish work for unemployed heads of families, and to provide breakfasts for schoolchildren who might otherwise go hungry. The fund was to be administered by the newly organized Philadelphia Committee for Unemployment Relief. Edward T. Stotesbury solicited the cooperation of League members, and he was joined by J. Howard Pew, John Gribbel, General William C. Price, Jr., and Judge Robert von Moschzisker and other League notables. E. Lawrence Fell, treasurer of the League committee, worked zealously to organize the campaign. In less than two months, $40,000 had been raised in the League House. Although League membership continued to plummet, and its register of candidates was cut in half by withdrawals from the waiting roll, its philanthropic program was maintained.[49]

The depression, which by now had become worldwide, jolted the Republican Party. In the congressional election of 1930, Republican strength was reduced to a minority in the Senate, and in the House of Representatives, it was chopped down to a majority of two. Hoover was now confronted by an uncooperative Congress dominated by Democrats and opposition Republicans. To combat the depression, Hoover determined that the government should intervene, but not without the support of business and labor. A series of well-publicized meetings was held involving key leadership in order to rally the country in a program in which business pledged not to halt production or cut wages, and labor was asked not to urge an increase in wages. The government would tackle deflation and institute a major tax cut. Liberal credit would be provided by the Federal Reserve and

TO THE MEMBERS OF THE UNION LEAGUE OF PHILADELPHIA

February 23, 1931.

DEAR SIRS:

We again take the liberty of calling to your attention the present serious situation with respect to unemployment in Philadelphia.

The Committee for Unemployment Relief, of which Mr. Horatio G. Lloyd is Chairman, is at the present time rendering aid to over 115,000 individuals in the following form:

> 7,500 men receiving employment and pay at made work.
> 17,000 families receiving relief.
> 2,600 homeless men at the shelter.
> 12,000 school children receiving breakfast.

A careful investigation discloses the fact that there are 17,000 individuals who are urgently in need of work, and if 12,000 men are to be provided with such work and pay, a total sum of $3,000,000 would be required for the period up to April 30th, and if the total 17,000 men are employed during March and April, an additional $500,000 would be required. The fund is far short of this minimum of $3,500,000.

THE UNION LEAGUE OF PHILADELPHIA has received from its members, to February 16th, cash and pledges aggregating $39,187.

Your Board of Directors recognizes that appeals such as this to the members of THE UNION LEAGUE are unusual, and that many demands for contributions for charitable purposes have been made upon you during the last few months; but, on the other hand, it is unusual to have thousands of people in our midst literally facing starvation simply because they cannot find employment. Under the circumstances we feel the immediate importance of the present situation justifies us in asking you to consider further contributions to the work of Mr. Lloyd's Committee.

Each of us has a vital interest that Unemployment Relief shall not cease by reason of inadequacy of funds, and it is quite clear that such result will follow unless the Committee can secure further contributions.

If you have already contributed, we ask you to give again; if you have not contributed, we urge you to do so at once and as generously as you can afford. Those who are in a position to know, say the situation is critical.

Contributions will be received by Mr. E. Lawrence Fell, Treasurer.

Yours truly,

GEORGE STUART PATTERSON,
President.

Approved by the Board of Directors.

UNEMPLOYMENT RELIEF SPONSORED BY THE UNION LEAGUE

the Farm Board would bolster prices. Congress was asked to approve the astounding sum of $423 million for public works. All of this was new to government. Hitherto no economic crisis had made such demands. On other issues, Hoover was firm in insisting upon a balanced budget and sound money, two strong Republican principles that were echoed at The Union League. He was equally determined in his view that direct relief was a local and state responsibility.

Democrats launched an attack on Hoover, insisting that he abandon the voluntary aspects of his program and shift to direct massive federal spending. Hoover remained adamant in his policies. Meanwhile, economic conditions in Western Europe had worsened. European securities were dumped on the American market, foreign gold was withdrawn from American banks, and American trade suffered a severe decline. Foreign goods, especially the products of Japanese industry, undermined the sale of American manufactures. The American tariff had become a sham.[50]

In enacting legislation that might stem or reverse the depression, the Democratic Congress and a few dissident Republicans moved so slowly that deliberate sabotage was feared. Finally in January, 1932, Congress created the Reconstruction Finance Corporation, which during that year loaned one-and-a-half-billion dollars to banks, businesses, and railroads in the belief that by helping business, employment would be increased. Assistant Secretary of the Navy Ernest Lee Jahncke speaking at the League, summarized Hoover's work in a manner that has generally been accepted by later commentators. He hailed Hoover for the Unemployment Relief Organization that coordinated relief activities with local organizations; for strengthening the Federal Land Bank System in the interests of the farmer; for assistance to home-owners through the Home Loan Discount Bank; and for relief to depositors of closed banks.[51]

Even these measures were not adequate to meet the needs of the nation. Economic conditions worsened. So great were the problems that gnawed at the heart of the economy, that no power seemed capable of restoring stability. Meanwhile, the number of unemployed and dispossessed grew, and Republicans were held responsible for the enormous economic debacle.

In an effort to determine the cause of the depression and a solution to its problems, both capital and labor failed to offer an accurate diagnosis, or to find a remedy. The federal government groped to find a system of relief and to find sources of employment that might uphold the concept of "rugged individualism." Hoover could not provide an answer, and neither could the Democrats who controlled the legislative reins, labor leaders, reformers, or the most astute economists. Theories were offered on overproduction, the hoarding of money, and the decline of purchasing power. Panaceas were proferred from all quarters. But the men who offered these remedial theories were far from the breadlines, the soup-kitchens, and starvation. Theory had no ties with reality.

Radicalism was on the march. The Communist Party gathered strength from areas it least expected. While it failed to have a strong impact on the masses of Americans, it continued to point to Soviet Russia as a model of society. Russia, the Party said, was the land of social planning and of full employment. That a vast system of inequality existed there, and that Communist oppression equalled, or was worse than Czarist oppression, was of little importance to American Communists, who willingly repeated the words of Joseph Stalin. In their eyes, Hoover represented the epitome of capitalist decay. By the summer of 1932, when the major political parties were preparing for their national conventions, Hoover had become the target of malicious and unwarranted abuse from other sources as well.

The Democrats supported Hoover's measures for recovery with reluctance, and counted on the depression to bring them success at the polls long before the presidential election of 1932. Popular support for the Republican Party had faded considerably since 1928, and the election of 1932 was fought against a background of decline in faith of Republican ability. On June 27, the Democratic Party Convention met at Chicago and nominated the governor of New York, Franklin Delano Roosevelt, for president, and John Nance Garner of Texas for vice-president. At a League campaign meeting Roosevelt was described as a gentleman of a cultured background, "a graduate of Groton and Harvard, with a professional career who lived among conservative associates, and men of affairs."[52] He was known for his attractive, magnetic personality. His nomination, however, was made possible by diverse groups of his party, to whom he would be in debt if elected. The Republicans renominated Herbert Hoover (whom Roosevelt had wanted as a Democratic candidate in the presidential election of 1920) and Charles Curtis of Kansas.

The platform of the Democrats contained many similarities to that of the Republicans: a sharp cut in government spending, a balanced budget, sound currency, and appropriate farm relief. It offered guarantees against unemployment, proposed a system of old age insurance, and promised the repeal of the Prohibition Amendment. On the controversial subject of veterans' pensions, the Democratic platform made certain to state that these were for service-connected disabilities, essentially what the Republicans had been advocating since the end of World War I. A variety of economic regulations, for which Roosevelt later campaigned, were to be introduced "only as a last resort." Hoover contended, justifiably, that Roosevelt's concept of governmental control was a sharp break with traditional American beliefs. The League's efforts on behalf of the Republican nominee included financial support and a series of campaign luncheons at the League. The first of the luncheons was addressed by Charles Evans Hughes, the tenth chief justice of the United States, and a second by Major General J. G. Harbord. The major address of the campaign was made by Secretary of State Henry L. Stimson. Stimson spoke on the foreign policies of the Hoover administration directly from the League's Lincoln Hall, over a nationwide radio broadcast, a medium that was becoming significant in election campaigns. An issue of great importance, in Stimson's view, was the threat of war in the Far East and its consequences for the United States. The Civil War in China delayed that nation's progress, and the American "Open Door" policy offered an enlightened principle of trade with a nation undergoing vast political changes, and a step toward the territorial integrity of China. But Japan's recent invasion of Manchuria threatened peace and American commercial ties, and was a deadly omen of the future. This harbinger of an even greater war within the decade went unrecognized.[53]

As an added internal campaign item, the League had earlier prepared a handbook of its historical events up to 1931. Its use was recommended prior to the election, particularly for new members.[54] On the eve of the election, E. Lawrence Fell, while addressing the membership, was unable to restrain an ironic partisan, though humorous, comment, based on the fact that a member of the League had been chairman of the Democratic National Committee since 1928: "We appreciate the compliment," Fell stated in an address, adding that the Democrats owed more to the League than to their own party. The chairman, whose name went unmentioned that night, was John J. Raskob, one of the leading industrialists of the nation.[55] The election results reported that Roosevelt had swept through 42 states; Hoover had carried four New England states, Delaware, and Pennsylvania. The Keystone State still commanded Republican strength.

The first days of the Roosevelt era, as recounted in the annual report of The Union League, were not, as many have implied, filled with wrath and recrimination. There was considerable disagreement over the new presidential policies. Roosevelt was charged with repudiating the platform on which he was elected and opposed for his federal price controls—a practice that was anathema to most Republicans then as well as now—and for appropriating credit for measures that Hoover had attempted to introduce. While the League carefully studied Roosevelt's introduction of a series of new programs, its good faith toward the president's efforts was expressed at a meeting of the Board on March 14, 1933, in the following words:

"The officers and Board of Directors of The Union League of Philadelphia are heartily in sympathy with the passage of the act known as the 'Roosevelt Economy Bill.' They feel that it is the duty of every citizen to support the President of the United States at this time and to encourage him in every way in the necessary legislation he is now proposing."[56] The Board also extended its thanks to the Republican Congressmen of Pennsylvania for supporting the bill. Furthermore, President Fell noted, Roosevelt, unlike Hoover, did not have to face the harrassment of a Congress that opposed his programs, but had obtained the comfortable support of both houses of the legislature.

It was a bleak year for the nation, and the dismal mood extended to the League House. There were no receptions, or were any guests entertained; the membership roll continued to decline, and while 220 new candidates were admitted, the active roll was 500 below the maximum of 3,000. Repairs to the League House were reduced to a minimum. A decrease in the League's gross annual income was matched by a considerable reduction in its operating costs. Never before had the League Finance Committee worked so arduously to manage the budget.[57]

The Committee on Public Affairs, in a continuing effort to provide speakers on current problems, sponsored a lecture by Merle Thorpe, soon after the inauguration of Roosevelt. Thorpe, editor of *Nation's Business,* reviewed the history of American business cycles and economic depressions. He spoke of men like Matthias W. Baldwin, the locomotive builder, Hamilton Disston, the tool manufacturer, John Wanamaker, the department store merchant, and John B. Stetson, the prominent hat manufacturer, all of whom had been League members, and men who had risen from obscurity in the dark days of other depressions, to develop businesses and industries. He believed that the same opportunities were open to many in the current depression, and he sounded a positive note in one of the most discouraging years of the thirties. Thorpe's address had some effect on improving the mood of the League.[58]

To stave off the declining membership and hurry the admission of candidates, the Board invited members who had resigned in good standing because of financial reverses to return to the League without paying the initiation fee. The plan was effective to a small extent. However, it was not sufficient to offset other resignations. This condition continued until the eve of World War II, when the candidates roll was reduced to a figure that was uncomfortably low.

With the appearance at the League of Virgil Jordan, president of the National Industrial Conference Board and economist for *Business Week,* some thoughtful views on the depression were expressed. Jordan was one of the few American economists who, before the stock market collapse, had believed that the prosperity of the twenties would be of short duration. He recognized that the nonbusiness world was becoming aware of a period in American life that would be witness to fundamental changes in the social, economic, and political organization of the nation. His most important criticism was that overproduction alone was not responsible for the depression, but that "overproduction resulting from maldistribution of income" among wage earners had contributed to the nation's instability. This fundamental fact, Jordan explained, also had affected the agricultural and rural population. Prices of farm products were not comparable to prices of manufactured goods, nor did the earnings of farm workers compare to the earnings of city workers, a condition which added to the maldistribution of income. Further, according to Jordan, the philosophy of Roosevelt's New Deal, whatever its ultimate outcome, had one basic weakness: the social legislation it proposed which was intended to relieve the misery of the depression was making millions of people dependent on government aid. People thereby were denied the responsibility of guiding their own lives. It was not a matter of maintaining "rugged individualism," a term that had been used by Democrats to mock the Hoover administration, but of maintaining personal independence. Temporary relief carried with it the possibility of becoming permanent. To Jordan, this state of affairs was a catastrophe. The "genial and ingratiating president" had said (and written a book) *On Our Way;* but where, and in what direction, was the country going, Jordan asked?[59]

As Republican criticism of the New Deal grew louder, its disagreements with the Roosevelt administration became clearer. The Democratic promise of reducing federal expenditures by 25 percent turned into an increase of 100 percent. The cause of sound money was undermined by the failure to pay government debts in gold, and by a reduction of the gold content of the dollar. At the same time, to increase the supply of money, it was proposed, but never acted upon, that three billion dollars in greenbacks be printed. The long list of criticisms included agricultural policies as well. Cotton crops had been ordered destroyed when the nation was improperly clothed, six million hogs had been eliminated from the market when millions were in need of food and wheat and corn crops had been ploughed under.

The New Deal, as Roosevelt's program for relief and recovery came to be known, was initially hailed by business. It did not come under direct attack by the League until the creation of the National Recovery Act (NRA) in 1933, which called for industrial self-regulation. Such regulation was to be under government administration, a concept that had been put to use during World War I. However, it brought about as many problems as it attempted to resolve. The corporate body of the League looked upon it as an act that violated the Constitution, and in 1935, the Supreme Court ruled it unconstitutional because of its price fixing, its injuries to small business and its tendency to encourage monopolization.

Senator Daniel O. Hastings, speaking at the League in 1935, summarized it this way: "Under the NRA we saw all of our business people regimented and controlled, annoyed, abused, prosecuted and persecuted, for a period of about two years before the strong arm of the Supreme Court could be raised to protect them. We see the Utility Holding Companies and the coal operators going through the same process today, not yet knowing definitely whether there be any protection under the Constitution."[60]

A series of social reform programs coming under the Second New Deal were launched in 1935. Virgil Jordan had pointed to these programs even before they were instituted: unemployment security, old age pensions, and nationwide slum clearance. The most important aspect of this new phase was the Works Progress Administration (WPA). It marked the removal of the federal government from direct relief, which was turned over to local and state administration. It was precisely this kind of plan that Herbert Hoover had advocated, and Roosevelt had adopted. In other areas, League speakers referred to Roosevelt scornfully, charging him with repudiating his promises and besmirching the party he represented. The Democrats, said Hiram Bingham, a former senator and a one-time professor at Yale and Princeton, now were advancing the same kind of public works program that they had charged as wasteful when it was advocated by Hoover.[61]

Many of these addresses delivered at the League were in preparation for the presidential election of 1936. Following the Republican Convention, the League ratified Kansas Governor Alfred M. Landon and Colonel Frank Knox as candidates for the nation's highest offices. The Committee on Public Affairs arranged for a series of campaign meetings, whose theme would consist of economic and educational topics. Senator George Wharton Pepper, Clinton L. Bardo, president of the National Manufacturers Association, and James P. Warburg, a prominent Jewish banker and author, spoke on similar topics. They impressed the League with the need to keep government out of business and to confine it to the role of arbiter, to lower taxes and to expand business and industry.[62]

The election of 1936 brought an astounding victory to Roosevelt. His overwhelming electoral majority came from 46 of the states, including Pennsylvania, formerly the strongest Republican state in the Union. Maine and Vermont went to Landon, and the Democrats won a striking majority in both houses of Congress. It was the first election in which the Communist Party had received an impressive vote, and the Socialists also had indicated their growing strength.

When the realization of a second Roosevelt landslide became known in Philadelphia, thousands of Democratic voters crowded into the center city. They were making their way to The Union League, where they had been lured by a pre-election promise of John B. Kelly, chairman of the Democratic City Committee. By midnight, crowds surrounded the Broad Street entrance, awaiting Kelly's arrival to make a victory speech on behalf of Roosevelt. Kelly and a colleague, Matthew H. McCloskey, Jr., were rushed up to the brownstone portico. Many onlookers were positive that they saw Kelly climb up the flag pole to remove the League flag. Whatever Kelly said has not been accurately recorded because of the intense shouting and booming noise, and whatever his athletic prowess, he could not have reached the flag. Kelly was escorted from the portico by a police guard and the club doorman. The event was significant because the League was looked upon as a Republican stronghold, and therefore a contributor to the ills of the nation. Kelly, it was later said, regretted the incident. What Kelly's supporters did not know was that their hero was a regular frequenter of the League, as a guest and enjoyed its hospitality, as did other prominent Democrats.[63]

Roosevelt's power now seemed unlimited, but it was not long before his political leadership was severely contested. His obvious disagreements with the Supreme Court because of its antiNew Deal decisions led him to propose an increase in the number of justices in the high court from 9 to 15. Other recommendations for changes in the judicial structure aroused wide opposition. Although the bill was never implemented, the court was changed because of a number of deaths and resignations of the justices. As a result of Roosevelt's advocacy of this policy, there were defections from the Democratic ranks that were later evident in the congressional elections of 1938. In Pennsylvania, a Republican governor, Arthur H. James, was returned to office.

Minor divisions also disturbed the seemingly monolithic political position within the League. A small number of influential League members had worked openly for Roosevelt's second election. The

League, faithful to its principle of not asking politically dissident members to resign, remained silent though it found the situation distasteful. However, Judge Otto Robert Heiligman, after he became president of the League, acted otherwise. Not until the defeat of Alfred M. Landon in 1936, however, did he make the statement attributed to him a few years later that "Common decency demands that such men should no longer be members of a club which stands first for the principles of Republicanism and the ideals of Abraham Lincoln whose political belief inspired its foundation. . . . I know of some who come into the category who are not true Republicans, and I will serve notice on them to get out. If any members know others who are not heart and soul Republicans, let them send their names to me, and I will serve notice on them too."[64]

Though it caused a stir, Heiligman's pronouncement did not produce the response that was reported in the press. The old *Philadelphia Record*, the voice of Philadelphia's Democrats, which inaccurately described a number of resignations as having taken place the day after Heiligman's statements, cried out gleefully, "Horrors. Democrats in The Union League." Indeed, there were resignations, but among the hundreds of men who resigned in those years, very few have been identified as Democrats. The exceptions were Horace M. Barba, a Roosevelt supporter in 1932, who resigned on June 30, 1933, prior to Heiligman's demand; H. Edgar Barnes, a Democratic Supreme Court Justice, who never resigned but remained a member until his death in 1940; and Luther A. Harr, the Bituminous Coal Consumers' counsel, possibly the only member reacting to Heiligman when he resigned on March 10, 1936. Joseph M. Gallagher, the local postmaster, resigned on October 31, 1937, and John J. Raskob, who had been chairman of the Democratic National Committee since 1928, resigned quietly on October 31, 1938.[65]

For the remainder of the second Roosevelt administration, the League's Board of Directors took no open political stand. There were three addresses given, and the custom of celebrating Lincoln's birthday was revived. The 150th anniversary of the adoption of the Constitution of the United States was celebrated quietly. An essay contest was conducted for young men between the ages of 18 and 25 on the subject of "The American Idea of Government." Prizes were awarded to nine contestants on Constitution Day, when Bainbridge Colby spoke on "Some Aspects of Constitutional Government in the United States." He introduced himself saying, "I come to you tonight as a Democrat." The limited programs were well-balanced by addresses by Reverend Joseph Fort Newton on the memories of a Lincoln student in search of unpublished data, and by Ohio Governor John Bricker, who also spoke

on Lincoln. Bricker recalled the influences of the Civil War on two
distinguished men of African descent, Dr. George Washington Carver,
the scientist, and the talented Ohio poet, Paul Lawrence Dunbar. The
most entertaining event of the late thirties at the League was a performance of sketches and monologues by Cornelia Otis Skinner to a
Ladies' Night audience that overwhelmed the facilities of the League.
No other social activities were undertaken, in order to conserve
League funds following the economic recession of 1938.[66]

Under these conditions of financial hardship it seemed like an act
of courage when the League decided to publish a complete catalog of
its art works. Arthur Edwin Bye, art historian and compiler of the
catalog described and interpreted the paintings within the context of
the day. His brief biographical notices of the artists and evaluations
of the subjects were both useful and informative, even though art history and criticism has undergone vast changes. The catalog did not
appear until 1940, and quickly went out of print. Its publication was a
credit to the former Art Committee of the League.[67]

The official records of The Union League make no mention of the
rapid political deterioration of the countries of Western Europe at this
time. Hitler's "New Order" was enveloping the European mind. The
philosophy of a German "master race" had effectively taken root.
With it came the grandiose plan to seize and dominate all Europe and,
if possible, all of Western civilization. Nazism, which embodied the
new German thinking, found ready converts in depression-ridden
Europe. But only a few realized the implications of Hitler's words.
Far too many believed that he offered a sound solution to the economic
problems of Europe, of America, and of the world. Political indoctri-
nation paved the way to Germany's seizure of surrounding European
states, and a policy of diplomatic appeasement by other European
nations gave encouragement to the "New Order."

The pattern of German conquest was begun with the occupation of
the Rhineland in November, 1936, and by the spring of 1938, Austria
was annexed. In the fall, attention was drawn to the Sudetenland and
to Czechoslovakia. It created a flurry of action that led to the Munich
conference, in which Prime Minister Neville Chamberlain agreed that
the Czechs should yield to German demands for the sake of peace.
This costly arrangement, imposed upon Czechoslovakia, eased the way
for Germany to make further demands elsewhere. Although France
and Britain gave guarantees to preserve the Czech borders, these
guarantees proved meaningless. The threat of war became clear. These
events filled the American press, but Americans were not touched in
depth by the European crisis. To the contrary, a strong isolationist
trend had set in, revealing an inability to comprehend European con-

cerns and the danger from Hitler's plans for world conquest. President Roosevelt urged a quarantine of all aggressors, primarily directed at the Japanese, whose movements in the Pacific had become alarming to the United States. However, huge quantities of scrap metal that could be used for war materials continued to be shipped to Japan. The ensuing boycott of Japanese goods resulted from Roosevelt's quarantine speech. A similar attempt to boycott German goods had little effect, because of greater sympathy among Americans for Germany than for Japan.

Few people heeded the warning of the *Panay* incident, when Japanese planes bombed a United States gunboat, and few recognized the degradation resulting from the grand appeasement at Munich. The League was no exception to this pervasive lack of awareness. Diplomatic charges followed the incident; the Japanese presented a formal apology, and continued their aggressive tactics. Slowly, the dangers inherent in Hitler's propaganda of Nazism, and the Japanese master plan for the Far East, became unveiled. To complicate this state of affairs, Soviet Russia and Nazi Germany, ideological enemies to their deepest roots concluded a nonaggression pact on August 23, 1939, stating that either would abstain from attacking the other, or would remain neutral in the event that one was attacked by a third party.

On September 1, 1939, this inexplicable pact was partially unmasked. Germany invaded Poland and demanded the surrender of Warsaw. Sixteen days later, the Red Army also invaded Poland, and declared war on Germany. It was too late to contain the might of the German military machine. She soon violated Belgium's neutrality, as she had in World War I, using the lowlands for a military pathway to France. She then invaded Norway and placed the puppet Vidkun Quisling in power. French and British troops coming to the aid of Belgium were quickly forced into a humiliating retreat from Dunkirk. Within months, German panzer divisions forced their way across the Somme, while her ally, Italy, invaded southern France. On June 14, 1940, German divisions could be seen marching on the boulevards of Paris. As part of her clever scheme, Germany agreed to an armistice with Marshall Henri-Phillippe Pétain, and permitted him to establish his own puppet government at Vichy.

The American reaction was still undecided, unless one assumes that neutrality on the eve of a global war was a decision. By this time, however, League members and much of public opinion had begun to react to Prime Minister Winston Churchill's appeal for arms. When Roosevelt asked Congress to repeal the embargo, the Senate and the House acted favorably on this request.

The war in Europe had an unforeseen impact on the American

economy, which was moving upward but still in a state of depression. Production of war materials and of the shipping so vital to their delivery assured a return of mass employment. Under these conditions, the depression of the thirties vanished.

Nineteen-hundred and forty was an exciting year, as the nation was gradually absorbed by the war abroad, and by arguments over the virtues and evils of Hitler and the injustices committed by the Russian Communist government. It was also a presidential election year. Earlier, the League had broken with an important tradition concerning its involvement in local politics. It was directly responsible for the choice of Judge Robert E. Lamberton as the Republican candidate for mayor of Philadelphia. Although the selection was not made by corporate action, it received corporate sanction. Unlike similar attempts in the past this one went unchallenged, received wide support, and helped in the election of Lamberton.[68]

In local elections Republican strength was maintained; statewide strength fluctuated. George H. Earle, a successful independent Republican who emulated Roosevelt, was governor from 1935 to 1939. Earle was not a League favorite, even though his grandfather had been a founder of the Republican Party in Philadelphia, and had joined The Union League in November 1863.[69] But Earle divested himself of this family association. His successor, Arthur H. James, and the victorious Lamberton, gave signs that Pennsylvania would recapture its full Republican strength. These views were debated at League meetings. New factors had to be taken into consideration. E. Lawrence Fell stated that the old image of the League, as an institution respected for its political integrity, was undergoing transformation. It was difficult to obtain prominent Republican political figures to speak at the League. Such an appearance, it was rumored, "would be unfortunate politically and detrimental to the future" of a candidate. Fell commented further that the men of the League were looked upon as "reactionaries," conservatives who had not changed since the decade of McKinley. In fact, the League was charged with living in a "political wilderness."[70]

Men like Fell considered these characterizations to be more vindictive than true, more within the context of the era of Rooseveltian liberalism, whose advocates were eager to downgrade the historical role of Republicans in a dominant two-party system. A factor that was not yet fully appreciated at the League, however was the changing voting patterns of Philadelphians, and of urban Americans in general. Black voters were moving along Democratic Party lines; Italo-Americans had more than doubled their support of the Democrats between Roosevelt's first election and his second, and Jews, who formerly had clung strongly to the Republican Party were committed to Democratic ranks by 1940. The Irish, traditionally Democratic, were proud to follow the leadership of men like Kelly and McCloskey. And many descendants of older American families had become the base on which Democratic support was built.[71]

The transformation of voting habits, combined with a decade of depression, demagoguery, European war, and local civic problems that had been unmet for many years, were gradually recognized at the League. If, temporarily, the League was unable to attract national political figures, it was still a platform for the discussion of urban problems.

It is interesting to note that before an improved mass transportation system was advocated, its concept was made public at a meeting of The Union League. Moreover it was at the League that a unique program "to establish a health center run by colored people for colored people in a colored neighborhood" was first proposed by Mayor Lamberton. The object of the latter program was to decentralize city hospitals, and by involving Negroes in meeting community problems, to raise their level of self-esteem. Both of these programs failed to be implemented due to events that were beyond the power of the League. Unfortunately, the voting public was unaware of these voluntary civic interests or commitments of the League, because the public shied away from League-endorsed candidates and clung to the stereotyped image of the League that had developed in the previous two decades.[72]

Against the changing background, the League participated in the Republican Convention that met in Philadelphia in 1940 to nominate Wendell L. Willkie for president, and Oregon Senator Charles L. McNary for vice-president. Roosevelt informed the Democratic National Committee meeting at Chicago that he did not desire to be a third-term candidate, but allowed himself to be "drafted," breaking tradition in that he was the first president to run for a third term. Secretary of Agriculture Henry A. Wallace was nominated for vice-president. In spite of its confidence and belief that Willkie had a splendid chance to win and in spite of a hard-fought battle, the League was disappointed again. Willkie captured only 10 of the 48 states. Once again, when the election returns showed a Roosevelt triumph, tens of thousands of Philadelphians concentrated in the city's center. The Union League was the focus of jeering throngs, for no other reason than its identification with Republicanism.[73]

While the American election campaign was being carried on, Japan had met with Germany and Italy to create a common axis, pledging mutual assistance to one another. In his annual message, Roosevelt proposed the Lend-Lease program for the nations allied against

Hitler. Secret military negotiations with England gave assurance that the United States would support the beleaguered country if necessary. The road to war had been defined. In June of 1941, the might of the German army was turned against Russia. Their nonaggression pact proved worthless when German forces opened a 2,000 mile eastern front.

The grim proportions of war, the frightening successes of the German army in Europe, and the favorable reception given to corrosive Nazi propaganda in the United States were understood more fully in the early months of 1941 than they had been in the entire decade of the thirties. The ambivalence at that time over who was the worst enemy, Russian Communists or German Nazis, had been as popular as the trend toward isolationism. After the German invasion of Russia, the need for aid to Russia was recognized because at that time, the Nazi Germans were a greater threat to humanity. However, Germany's ideological supporters in the United States, as well as the many Nazi associations, persuaded an untold number of Americans that the German cause was a worthy one. American intelligence agencies were placed on a new alert.

With an eye to obtaining further intelligence, the Military Affairs Committee of the Senate had asked Colonel William J. (Wild Bill) Donovan to visit the continent of Europe, England, and the Mediterranean area to learn more of the propaganda operations of the Germans. Donovan, a colorful figure who had led the famous Irish 69th Regiment of New York City in World War I, willingly accepted. Donovan went to North Africa and visited the Balkan states before they capitulated to the German army. Upon his return to the United States, League President E. Lawrence Fell invited him to address the League on what he had seen and experienced. Donovan's incisive comments were of considerable importance. He revealed the process and methods of infiltration used by the Germans before each invasion of the southeastern European countries. He exposed the common belief that Germany would entrench herself for a thousand years in Europe, and establish the "master race" over lesser peoples. The people in top leadership positions to whom he had spoken were convinced that if German fascism failed to conquer, Russian communism would. All Europe was being divided and conquered. England's valiant stand could only continue with the military aid supplied by the United States. And what if England failed? What would be the role of the United States if Germany succeeded?[74]

Significant in Donovan's address was his stress on the need for the total support of England, the elimination of American isolationist policies, and an awareness of foreign infiltration as part of the process of undermining peaceful countries. Donovan's active interest in the subject of intelligence operations abroad and in the study of strategic information made him an appropriate choice as director of the Office of Strategic Services, a position to which he was appointed in June, 1942, almost a year after he had hinted at its necessity in his League address. The OSS, as it was known, was the forerunner of the now highly criticized Central Intelligence Agency.

With each German strike, whether it was the night-long devastation of the civilian population of Coventry, or an isolated island in the Aegean Sea, tension grew in the United States. In giving a full overall picture of a spreading global war, two other League speakers attacked the continuing isolationism among certain Americans. Following Donovan, Colonel Franklin D'Olier spoke on the tremendous need to supply England with war materials. A month later, on October 23, 1941, the former Ambassador to France and Russia, William C. Bullitt, gave a major address at the League based on his intimate knowledge of these two countries. Bullitt, a well-known Democrat, berated both Democrats and Republicans who placed the interests of their party over those of their nation. His presence belied the myth that Union League members were reactionary or unwilling to listen to Democrats. He impressed his audience with the worldwide danger of Hitlerism, and argued strongly against those in the United States who said, "What difference does it make to us? Let the Germans have Europe and Africa. Let the Japanese have Asia. We can sit here and be all right." He envisioned certain men in the United States as the leaders of an American Nazi State, and others as part of a Soviet America. Bullitt paid tribute to Wendell Willkie, the unsuccessful Republican candidate, who in defeat continued to mount an enthusiastic campaign among Republicans to thwart the aims of fascist Germany.[75]

THE LIBRARY IN 1887

THE LIBRARY IN 1941

VIII

Turmoil and Reappraisal

PHILADELPHIA'S Broad Street was sullen and misty on Sunday, December 7, 1941. Members standing on the Broad Street portico of the League House watched a parade of Communists mourning one of their local members. At 1:20 P.M., before the marchers had disappeared, all American radio programs were suddenly interrupted by an announcement that American installations at Pearl Harbor were under devastating attack by Japanese air forces. On the same day, the Japanese destroyed other American installations across the Pacific Ocean. Nine American ships were sunk or disabled. More than 120 aircraft were reduced to scrap, 2,335 American soldiers and sailors were killed, and about 2,000 were wounded during the day. With all the advance warnings of Japanese military presence, the Americans had failed to provide adequate defense measures. Precautions that Donovan had implied were necessary for Europe had not been considered for the Pacific area.

On December 8, the day of the scheduled annual meeting of the League, the United States Congress declared war on Japan. As soon as the minutes and reports of the preceding meeting were dispensed with, Thomas K. Ober, Jr., rose to address the League in one of the crucial hours in American history. In a joint resolution prepared by Ober, and former Senator George Wharton Pepper, the total support of the corporate body, and of the membership as individuals, was asked for and pledged to the president of the United States in whatever steps he might deem necessary to protect the national interest. Approval for the resolution was unanimous.[1]

This important decision was only the first step in a broader program of the League. A War Emergency Committee was established

and made responsible for introducing and carrying out the assignments of the Board of Directors. One of the first of these was to raise
a fund to aid in a recruiting drive for three regiments of the National
Guard of Pennsylvania. An additional 1,150 men were required
to fill up these regiments. The League helped to accomplish this objective. For a short time, this work was reminiscent of the League's
recruitment activity during the Civil War. But it was no longer necessary for a private institution to do what the government was now
able to accomplish through a selective service system. Many of its own
members were of military age, and its employees responded to the
enlistment call as well. Members' dues were remitted, and employees
entering the armed services were given a free month's pay and the
guarantee of their job after the war was over.[2]

In 1942, when the United War Chest announced its drive for funds,
and the Red Cross launched a financial drive of its own, the League
acted immediately with a unanimous decision allocating $25,000 for
the two agencies. By 1944, the amount raised by the League for these
agencies had almost doubled. These funds were appropriated from
the League treasury, and charged to operating expenses. As soon as
United States War Savings Bonds were introduced to help finance the
war, hundreds of thousands of dollars in bonds were purchased by
League members and by the corporate body, on an annual basis.[3]

The League acted promptly in its compliance with the wartime
economy. It conserved fuel, observed blackouts, limited itself to certain foods, and reduced most luxuries. The third floor of its Broad
Street building was made available for use by the United States Coast
Guard Reserve; women employees were introduced into departments
where formerly only men had worked, for, one by one, key men of the
League staff were departing for training and the battlefield.

Throughout 1942 and 1943, addresses at the League were confined
to the issues of the war. John W. Hanes, a Democrat and a former
assistant secretary of the treasury, speaking at the League in the
spring of 1942, urged the total defeat of Germany, Italy, and Japan.
Looking ahead to the conclusion of a war that was still young, his
deepest concern was how the United States would survive in a postwar
period. Pennsylvania's governor, Edward Martin, stressed the imperative need for the United States to rapidly build a military machine
that would equal the nine years of careful planning that Germany
had the benefit of, the 20 years that Russia had the advantage of, and
the 25 years of Japan's meticulous military preparations. Governor
John W. Bricker of Ohio spoke similarly.[4]

The election to office of two Republican governors was an indication of the growing Republican strength throughout the states. Martin

noted that 1936 had been the darkest year in the history of the party. At that time, there had been only 17 Republican senators and 89 representatives in the Congress; the states could only claim eight Republican governors and control of nine legislatures. But after the election of 1942, there were 38 Republican governors, and 27 Republican-controlled legislatures. The upward Republican trend in the midst of war was unmistakable, and the hard-won victories of the Republicans promised a major success in the upcoming presidential election of 1944.[5]

When Thomas E. Dewey and John W. Bricker were endorsed by the League as the Republican candidates, although no longer through the traditional process of having numerous League members articulate their political support, a Campaign Committee of 100 was formed. It used all of its resources to oppose Roosevelt in his unprecedented bid for a fourth term. At The Union League, the fourth term was assailed as "malignant," and as a conspiracy headed by certain trade union leaders working closely with the Democratic Party. A careful distinction was made between union leadership, and the millions of trade unionists who, according to G. Mason Owlett, president of the Pennsylvania Manufacturers Association, were being deliberately misled.[6] Furthermore, the official support of Communist leadership for Roosevelt gave League speakers their best argument against Roosevelt. Communist adherents, whose main interest was American aid to the beleaguered Russian army, supported Roosevelt's bid for reelection. Most Americans, including those who had doubts, or were even opposed to a fourth term, believed that the incumbent president was most familiar with the world military situation and was best able to coordinate worldwide battlefronts. Dewey and Bricker went down in an unforeseen defeat by Roosevelt, but Roosevelt did not win the sweeping successes of his first two terms.

Other than political or wartime addresses, only a few League social occasions were held during this election year, among them the celebration of the tricentennial of the birthday of William Penn, the founder of the state. William Wistar Comfort, emeritus president of Haverford College, addressed the membership on Penn. Clare Boothe Luce, at the pinnacle of her career, spoke to 1,800 members and their ladies on Ladies' Night, taxing the League facilities. One of the most unusual dinners held at the League in many years was the governor's conference, which had reconvened at the League from Hershey, Pennsylvania.[7]

At about the same time that the League launched its presidential election campaign, news was received that assistant doorman Edward L. Piatkowski had fallen in battle following the invasion of Normandy.

Then came news of the death of George Bedell, another employee. Three members—Robert Cresswell, Donald R. Ferguson, M.D., and Warwick Potter Scott—also gave their lives for their country. Colonel Jay Cooke lost an eye leading his unit of the 28th Division in the Normandy invasion. Veteran war correspondent Ivan H. Peterman, whose faithful reports from the battlefront attracted wide attention, was a witness to the events that led to the fierce counterattack by the Germans against inadequately held American lines in the Ardennes, popularly known as the Battle of the Bulge.[8]

Of the 187 members and the 27 employees of the League who weathered the rigid campaigns that drove the Axis to defeat, many were still with the League at its centennial celebration in 1962. Daniel M. Layman, the future League manager, fought in the invasion of North Africa, across Sicily, then in Normandy, in the campaigns in France and Belgium, and was with the first units to cross the Remagen Bridge to secure a bridgehead on the east bank of the Rhine River. The present League steward, Edward A. Kalinowski, who received his basic training with Layman at Camp Wheeler, Georgia, saw considerable duty in North Africa and Italy. Cornelius McKinney, later assistant manager, was with the army of occupation in Italy. The late Arthur T. Fields, head of the coatroom staff, served in a similar wartime capacity, and Jimmy Lewis, who began as a League busboy and became restaurant captain, spent three and one-half years with the Air Force. Ralph Collins served with the army of occupation in Japan before he was placed in charge of food services in the Oak Room.[9]

Before Hitler was driven to his last bunker, or Mussolini was torn to shreds by antifascist Italians in the town of Dongo, Franklin Delano Roosevelt died suddenly on April 12, 1945, less than three months after his inauguration. Vice-President Harry S. Truman succeeded him in office. The League appropriately mourned the loss of a president of the United States. In the closing weeks of April 1945, Germany was crushed, and her battered government capitulated on May 7. On August 6, the United States dropped an atom bomb on the military base of Hiroshima, destroying a greater part of the city, and on August 9, the naval base of Nagasaki also was struck by an atom bomb. The unconditional surrender, rejected by the Japanese in July, was accepted immediately after the new, still secret weapon had wreaked its devastating havoc.

In accordance with the commitments of its Charter, the League instituted a program to find employment for homecoming veterans. An office was set up in the League's billiard and pool room to interview veteran jobseekers, and to utilize employer contacts from within the League membership. In the course of approximately 18 months,

3,990 applicants were interviewed, and, with League help, 1,215 obtained jobs. The others were benefited by the numerous connections of League members in this voluntary operation, which was conducted by ex-servicemen at League expense. The work of this War Veterans Committee was reminiscent of the League's Civil War program.[10]

Inspired perhaps by the League's military work, and a long tradition of cooperation with the Military Order of the Loyal Legion, this relationship was commemorated in 1946. A plain bronze tablet was placed at the foot of the marble stairway on the main floor, telling briefly of the loyalty and friendship between the two organizations since 1865. Of the original companions of the Pennsylvania Commandery, as members of the Loyal Legion are known, 220 were members of the League. At the time of the dedication of the tablet, descendants of many of the original companions were still in the League membership.[11]

Another expression of appreciation was represented by the erection of a much larger bronze plaque listing the names of the League members who had served in the armed forces during World War II. Three hard-working League members, Joseph M. Baldi, 2nd, John A. Lafore, Jr., and Herbert L. Phillips, compiled the military data. The plaque was placed in the main hall of the Broad Street building, not far from a similar plaque memorializing League members of World War I.[12]

In 1945, in the aftermath of war, the League hoped for universal peace with the establishment of the United Nations. One of the fundamental purposes of the world organization was to prevent another global disaster. From its very beginning, the United Nations was confronted with an inner dispute over voting procedures. The United States faced its first deadlock with Russia on this point. Offensive accusations by Russia, describing American aid to Europe as an "imperialist" act, set the tone for the "cold war" that described the postwar relationship between the two powers. General George C. Marshall, Truman's secretary of state, initiated the program that carried his name, the Marshall Plan, to provide massive relief and reconstruction for both the defeated and liberated countries of Europe. Billions of dollars were spent to restore the economy of Europe, to aid persons displaced by the war, and the surviving victims of the incomprehensible Nazi holocaust. The plan was carried out in the belief that free institutions had to be re-established.

To counter American influence in Europe, the Soviet Union, with its own program of aid, established a plan of assistance for five European nations contiguous to its borders. The friendship that had existed between Russia and the United States faded quickly under the changing circumstances. Competition in the development of atomic weapons deepened the distrust, and created worldwide fear.

AntiAmericanism sprang up among the European nations who were recipients of American aid, and, in the United States, anticommunist hostility became a dominating political factor. Japanese and German war criminals were brought to trial for their crimes against humanity, and those found guilty were imprisoned or executed. One League member, Judge Robert L. Kunzig, was a coprosecutor in the notorious Buchenwald extermination camp trial. Many Nazis fled and disappeared permanently.[13] Russia's internal crimes were not yet known. In the aftermath of war, Russia adroitly accomplished her plan of undermining the new Democratic countries, such as Czechoslovakia, seizing power not by fomenting revolution, but by bringing about internal erosion, paving the way for political upheavals that accomplished the same end. Russian designs upon Europe, the Mediterranean countries, and other countries in the Western Hemisphere were already in preparation. To disguise her own master plan of world conquest, her well-ordered propaganda was directed against the United States, charging this country with being a perpetual warmonger. The division of Germany into east and west zones of occupation, and the differences in opinion over the control of the former German capital, led ultimately to the Russian blockade of Berlin, which closed all routes to the city. The United States organized a successful counterblockade in order to prevent Berlin from coming into the Russian orbit. When these issues came before the United Nations Security Council, the Soviet Union utilized the disputed veto power to thwart both the philosophy and the program of the UN, establishing a pattern of voting at the world organization that was repeated to suit Russian political needs.

In the midst of these rising tensions, another presidential election was fought. Successive political victories had restored a majority of Republicans to the Congress for the first time in 14 years. Leading Republicans appeared before the League membership at a major reception prior to the Republican National Convention. A number of governors and a number of senators listened carefully to two of the aspirants for office, Senator Robert A. Taft of Ohio, and Governor Earl Warren of California. The peacetime economy of the nation had come under careful scrutiny, and both speakers advocated a choice of candidates who could better restore the economy with a Republican administration. With fresh confidence, the Republican National Convention, meeting in Philadelphia in June, 1948, nominated New York Governor Thomas E. Dewey and Governor Earl Warren.[14] Harry S. Truman and Alben W. Barkley were nominated by the Democrats. For the first time, a States' Rights ticket emerged in the South to challenge the civil rights plank of the Democratic Party. Truman won by a majority popular vote, three million more than his opponent, and the Democrats regained control of both houses of Congress. For Republicans, who had felt certain of victory, it was a shattering defeat; for League members, their sense of loss was compounded by a fear of Democratic entrenchment. Further, it was believed that Senator Taft, whom the League had favored for the nomination, might have achieved victory.

The retention of power by the Democrats, although in actuality their strength had declined when compared to the Roosevelt successes, had a sharp impact upon the League. Its Political Activities Committee was reactivated, and its support of state Republicans was assured by lively fundraising campaigns within the membership.

A depression and a devastating war had reduced many of the League activities. Republican losses had dampened the spirits of many members, but the League leadership showed its resiliency in the late forties and fifties. These years were devoted to a restoration of Republican strength, and to a revitalization of its traditional civic and social interests. Broad opportunities, in which the League could use its influence for the benefit of the general community, waited to be explored. One idea that excited the imagination of League President Millard D. Brown, was jointly proposed by Wesley M. Heilman and Edward L. Davis. Davis, a grandson of League founder Charles Gibbons, suggested to his friend Heilman a program of work with young boys. After the suggestion was introduced to the Board, a poll of the membership disclosed that over 60 members were involved in a variety of Philadelphia's youth organizations. Their work brought them to neighborhoods, churches, and institutions that focused attention on the affairs of boys. It seemed natural to sponsor such a program, in which the League would cooperate with such agencies. The first committee to plan the cooperative venture was made up of Heilman, who was named chairman, Davis, Robert L. Johnson, president of Temple University, John R. Stewart, and H. Birchard Taylor.[15] Contacts were made with the agencies, and when the League's thinking on the matter had crystallized, in October 1946, a plan was adopted to present award medals and certificates for good citizenship to all boys recommended by the various agencies. This modest recognition of the city's boys later grew into a major undertaking. It was launched officially in the spring of 1947 by an annual dinner. Recommendations for awards were based on merit and character. Race, color, or religious background were not factors considered in determining good citizenship. Thirty-four agencies selected 232 boys between the ages of 12 and 17 for the first presentation. Funds for its sponsorship were provided voluntarily. The response to the League request was splendid, and League members participated as hosts to their young guests. To add interest to the annual award dinners, outstanding personalities drawn from the world of sports and entertainment contributed to the success of the Boys' Work evenings. They included such notables as band leader Paul Whiteman, fighter "Jersey" Joe Walcott, and baseball's leading figure, Connie Mack of the Athletics.[16]

The first Committee on Boys' Work, its official name, was enlarged by the inclusion of outstanding men in the contemporary history of the League, George M. Brodhead and Samuel E. Fulton, both future League presidents, and Earl R. Yeomans, vice-president of Temple University and director of its Athletic Association. L. Alan Passmore, David B. James, and J. Permar Richards, Jr., were also among the later League presidents involved with the newly founded Committee.[17]

The Committee on Boys' Work was diverse in its talents, and had a zealous approach to the new program. Aware that the new activity was unique to a metropolitan community, it brought the interest of boys' agencies under one canopy, and gave stimulus to these agencies, with whom it cooperated to filter its program through to all of the city's youth. To prevent the annual dinners from becoming lofty, formal affairs, Yeomans was named an early toastmaster; later Samuel E. Fulton, a delightful raconteur, was made toastmaster for evenings that were attended by an array of nationally prominent football players, who mingled with their youthful audience. Autographed baseballs, footballs, and basketballs were prized by their fortunate winners, who drew lucky numbers to win them. Connie Mack's baseball team was required by contract to appear at the Boys' Work dinner. The occasion was later broadened to include a tour of Philadelphia's Navy Yard and short cruises down the Delaware River under Navy auspices. For many years, the Fourth Naval District and the admirals and their staff responsible for this branch of naval affairs went beyond formalities to make these occasions memorable.[18]

The most significant aspect of the Boys' Work program was not in the daytime tour, or the evening of entertainment, but in the development of a program that was in advance of other similar undertakings in Philadelphia. More than one-third of the League membership responded annually with voluntary contributions. At the end of each year, a surplus of funds remained. To expand this work and put excess funds to use, a scholarship plan was suggested and approved in 1955. During the term of office of League president Joseph W. Henderson, it was decided that recipients of the good citizenship award should be made eligible for League scholarships. In the first years of the scholarship program, presided over by Henry B. Bryans,

CONNIE MACK (CORNELIUS McGILLICUDDY) AUTOGRAPHING PROGRAMS
AT A BOYS' WORK DINNER, MAY 8, 1952

the number of scholarship grants were few; they grew yearly as funds increased, and as colleges and universities became aware of the League's program. From among the first group of these scholarship recipients, many entered diverse careers in science, the arts, vocational activity, and the military, achieving recognition in their chosen fields. The scholarship fund is a major tax-free program and its many supporters have grown yearly.[19]

To president Millard D. Brown, who gave impetus to the organization of the Committee on Boys' Work, belongs further credit for sanctioning the employees' Twenty-Five Year Club. He obtained approval for a suggestion made by League barber Joseph A. Connell that recognition be given to employees for their many years of service, and their loyalty to the League. In 1948, employees with 25 years or more of service established their own club. Appropriate insignia designating the term of service—from bronze to gold emblems—were awarded at annual dinners by the officers and directors who were the sponsors. At the first dinner, on January 28, 46 employees qualified. Two had worked more than 50 years, and 17, more than 35 years. It was an admirable record. Many who had come to work at the League in the mid-twenties or earlier were already identified with the history of the League.[20] Assistant manager Eli C. Schmidt, a thoughtful, soft-spoken man, had been with the League since 1910; Tom Jones, who was completing his 50th year when the club was organized, and Michael Lerner, who had been an ice cream maker for 35 years, received special awards for their lengthy service.[21] Although rapport between League officers and directors and employees had never been lacking, the annual dinners, with entertainment chosen by the employees, cemented the warm working relationship between them and at the same time created a relaxed atmosphere.

The Twenty-Five Year Club reflected a great deal of staff stability. Yet, numerous changes among employees occurred over the years. In 1950, William H. Stauffer resigned as manager and was succeeded by Daniel M. Layman. Layman's 18 years of experience in various departments of the League, and his knowledge of the potential social use of the physical facilities made him a fine choice. Layman rapidly adapted himself to the responsibility, and became active in the Club Managers Association, of which he was the Philadelphia president in 1953. He also was elected president of the Club Managers Association of America in 1959.[22]

Each year, new candidates were admitted to the Twenty-Five Club: Marie DeGange, captain of the South Marble dining room, Peter Grassi, the League's highly respected chef, and a long list of others that included Fred Wittman, a League doorman since 1926. At the same time the demands of war in Korea had called away David J. Redmond, who was later to become Grassi's successor as chef to The Union League. Many were eager to retire after periods of long service.[23] In the mid-1950's, League president Joseph W. Henderson appointed a committee to review the organization's pension and retirement fund, which time and changing economic conditions had made inadequate. A new retirement plan was introduced by drawing upon funds from current annual income as a reserve for the employees' retirement fund. But this, too, was modernized within a few years under the administration of Samuel E. Fulton, when a formal group insurance plan and pension fund were adopted.[24]

With the retirement of Tom Jones and Clayton Morris, the old-timers of the comptroller's office, Howard Welch assumed the responsibilities of his predecessors. A policy of furthering employees' education in special areas was introduced in 1956. The League paid for those who went to accredited business schools or to nationally recognized cooking schools. Whenever possible, this continuing education was encouraged. Many employees had improved their status by gradually working their way from lesser jobs to key positions. There were no barriers to advancement because of color, or national origin, and promotions were based upon competence and an understanding of social amenities.[25]

Among the numerous changes that affected The Union League, as well as other city clubs in the postwar period, was the relocation of businesses in suburban areas. A continuous movement away from the city to nearby residential New Jersey towns and to the northern and western suburbs of Philadelphia, the gradual decentralization of industry, and the removal of offices to industrial parks, were major factors contributing to this change, A five day work week, and an increase in the number of holidays, also contributed to the decline in the use of League facilities. Country clubs increased in popularity, luring away inner city club membership. Although the League lost none of its attractiveness, many of its members joined area country clubs. A major program of renovating the League interior was undertaken to help the club retain its urban strength.[26]

The use of the south billiard room, fronting 15th Street, once the site of national championships and exhibitions, had been reduced considerably. In order to convert this space into a more useful area, a modern panelled oak restaurant facility was installed called the Oak Room, and affable Ralph Collins was placed in charge of it. Here lunches could be served more promptly than in the large north and south marble dining rooms. In these "marble" rooms most of the club tables met daily. A few years later, another room was remodeled and

Cornelius Krieghoff

BREAKING UP THE SLEIGHING PARTY

named the Meredith Room, after the League's first president. Its luncheon specialty, roast beef, was new and its quiet atmosphere was enhanced by a background of genre paintings. Cornelius Krieghoff's Canadian scene, "Breaking Up the Sleighing Party," Henry S. Hubbell's "Coachman," and a view of Broad Street showing The Union League under the shadow of City Hall, added to the attractiveness of the League's smallest dining room, which was attended by Jimmy Lewis, its first captain. One of the most imaginative restorations was the Old Cafe, completed in 1961. Located on the north side of the Broad Street building, its late Victorian splendor was recaptured, and its period furniture helped revive the old atmosphere. Members and their guests were able to sip their drinks leisurely, while enjoying Jacques Joseph Tissot's brilliant "Café Royal," and Edward Grützner's "The Wine Tasters."[27]

Essential to all these modernized dining rooms and to the new styles in food was a well-functioning kitchen facility. Located on the ground floor, with its bright and shiny equipment spaciously arranged, the League kitchen is one of the largest in the city. Its staff includes a baker who has refined his art, a sauce cook who adds superb flavor to each dish, skilled and swift oystermen, fish butchers who filet fish and bone shad with finesse and discipline, and meat butchers who handle their chores magnificently, all extremely well-trained. With approximately 35 kitchen people under Chef Redmond's supervision, all culinary needs are met exactly and promptly.

The League membership for whom these and other improvements were made had come once more under serious discussion. On the eve of the war, 2,435 active members were on the roll, showing a decrease of 130 since 1936. The old 1930 waiting list of 4,000 had been reduced to 100 by 1940. There were only 19 members under the age of 30. Members reviewing these conditions decried the fact that not enough was done to attract younger men to the League to "offset the idea that The Union League is old-fashioned and going to seed like the Republican Party." Those who insisted that new younger members ought to be descendants of older members supported their position by statements that the League was "a father and son club, and it should remain that way." The issue of hereditary descent had been argued without real effect in the 1920's, but it made even less of an impression in the postwar era. Although no one protested that such a practice was not consonant with the patriotic aims and purposes of the League, more members were of the belief that a broad age spectrum was essential, and objected to a confining approach to admissions. Annual dues and admission fees were also scrutinized as rising costs required more income. Both gradually were raised, although in the

Jacques Joseph Tissot

CAFÉ ROYAL

face of strong opposition.[28] Slowly, the candidates register began to climb. This increase coincided with the presidential election campaign of General Dwight D. Eisenhower. It was an exciting year for the League. Membership issues had been set aside in order to devote full time to campaign for the popular Republican candidate. Ohio Senator Robert A. Taft, and Eisenhower's running mate Richard M. Nixon, along with Pennsylvania Governor James H. Duff and New Jersey Governor Alfred E. Driscoll, were entertained at the League. The League was overjoyed at the Eisenhower victory, which returned a Republican president to the White House, the first in 20 years.[29]

In the years between Eisenhower's first and second elections, an upward trend in the economy boosted the steady growth in membership. At the end of 1953, there were 1,435 applicants waiting to be admitted. A long-term improvement of the League House, including the introduction of air conditioning, was projected. The new proposals, and rising costs, had made it imperative that entrance fees as well as dues be increased to aid in carrying out the improvement plans. On the occasion of the centennial of the Republican Party in 1954, Vice-President Richard M. Nixon and Mrs. Nixon were the guests of honor at an informal reception at the League before the Party proceeded to Convention Hall for a public dinner. In the presence of Republican celebrities, the history of the Party was reviewed, and the first suggestion for the presidential campaign of 1956 was made. Confidence in Eisenhower was not misplaced, and once again Republican power was retained. For the next four years, League presidents James M. Anderson and Russell P. Heuer concentrated their efforts on the work of the Political Action Committee to insure a Republican retention of power, insofar as the ability of the League could do so. Membership problems were not resolved, however, and interest in the establishment of a junior roll continued. It was debated at three annual meetings. Finally, it was moved and accepted in 1959. The nonresident roll was revised, establishing a membership without voting privileges for those who lived outside a 125-mile limit. The clerical roll was carefully reviewed, reduced in number, and more clearly defined on the basis of a proposal made by Arthur Littleton, one of the city's outstanding lawyers.[30]

Changes in the membership composition allowed for a more rapid increase in the various rolls. During the discussion of the establishment of the junior roll, and the improvements to the League House, the social functions of the League came under study by a special committee on entertainment appointed by League President James M. Anderson. J. Permar Richards, Jr., and M. Roos Wallis, two of the younger members, worked closely with Samuel E. Fulton in revising old programs and introducing new ones. Thanksgiving dinner, one of the first holidays celebrated at the League, was revived on an annual basis as a League function. Two consecutive evenings of family Christmas parties, with concerts of classical choral music and traditional carols, became seasonal features. A father and son night, providing popular entertainment for all young males of a member's family, was quickly followed by a similar annual program for daughters of members. Dinner at the League on Mother's Day and on Easter Sunday also was institutionalized. Dinner dances and Club Nights were raised to a high level of entertainment. These arrangements soon became a permanent part of the social calendar of the League.[31]

Between 1958 and 1959, when these features were introduced or improved, the Library Committee, looking forward to the centennial of the Civil War, reviewed its own series of programs which had been in existence since 1928. This series complemented the programs centered around Lincoln's birthday, and provided diversity and intellectual stimulation that appealed to and satisfied other interests of the membership. To set the scene for the Civil War Centennial, the Library Committee invited the distinguished historian Professor Roy F. Nichols of the University of Pennsylvania. Nichols spoke on the Civil War era, a field in which he had made original contributions. It was, however, the divergent interpretations of the life of Lincoln by the various speakers that warrant comment. William Mather Lewis, president of Lafayette College, mingled his father's recollections of the aftermath of Lincoln's assassination with his own boyhood impressions of the fate of those involved. Other speakers expressed a reverence for Lincoln that continues to grow to this day. Lincoln was recast as a deeply religious man. In doing so, the object was to identify Lincoln with formal religion by exploiting his spiritual qualities. Benjamin Franklin and George Washington had undergone a similar metamorphosis to make two great American figures even more acceptable. The look on Lincoln's face, a remark in one of his speeches, a phrase in a letter that evoked deep emotion—any one of these was enough to serve as a point for an exegetical interpretation of the religious life and character of Lincoln. But the facts of Lincoln's life indicate that he was not a regular churchgoer; regardless of how religious he was, he showed no preference, nor was he tied to a formal religious life.[32]

The Union League Library, and the successive committees that oversaw its work, were made responsible for the *Bulletin of The Union League of Philadelphia*. Started in March, 1944, it had the benefit of a tireless editor, Thomas K. Ober, Jr., and Adelaide T. Gilmore, the first woman secretary to work in the manager's office. Its content varied considerably from committee to committee. In addition to club news and a calendar of events supplied by the manager, it contained brief pithy editorials on civic matters, political interests, and occasional comments on the history of the League. During 1956 and 1957 it published a series of viewpoints by Ivan H. Peterman on the history of the League. At the suggestion of David B. James, Jr., and the members of the Library Committee which he chaired, these were later collected and published in pamphlet form in 1958 under the title, *Milestones of Union League History.*

Exhibitions of books, displays of historical materials pertaining to the League's activities, and members' collections, placed the work of the library on an important level. Outstanding exhibitions illustrated the work of Shakespeare and the inventions of Leonardo DaVinci. Of course, its own permanent collection of rare books, and books by League members added to the inner quality of a club library.

The services of the library attracted large numbers of members, more than one-third of whom made use of its facilities. Of its holdings of approximately 25,000 books concentrated in American history and literature, and a modern collection of basic reference works in many fields, its collection of Civil War books is outstanding. Its current periodical literature is extensive, and covers many areas of interest. Four of its library patrons, Joseph H. Taulane, W. Kirkland Dwier, Walter T. Bradley, and John Louis Haney, were benefactors as well.[33] In the first century of its history, the League had four librarians. Before the death of Alfred Lee in 1929, the library had been modernized according to the methods of that day, and John J. Moraski had come to work for the League. He remained there for 41 years.

On the eve of the League's centennial, novelists, biographers, historians, and sociologists found the Philadelphia institution a subject for writing in their various fields. Boston club life found a careful observer in novelist John P. Marquand, who successfully penetrated the inner life of Brahmin society. Some found his insights revealing and delightful, others viewed them with scorn, but readers of his novels found them provocative, enjoyable, and informative.[34] Philadelphians have not found an observer of social life and its mores to equal him. Other than the two biographies of Henry Charles Lea and George Henry Boker, both by E. Sculley Bradley and written in a previous generation, partisanship has been a common characteristic of some of the writing under consideration.

In John O'Hara's novels, his characters move unnoticed across the League stage using it as a token of prestige which they carried home to O'Hara's fictional Pennsylvania town, Gibbsville. Nothing of the club's intimate life, its politics, its food, or its social nuances in language or manners is reported.[35] Arthur Lewis' biography of Chippy

Patterson, whose father and brother were League presidents, is an interesting book—if its fictionalized characterizations are not accepted for fact—but a lack of knowledge about the League is evident in the references to it. Lewis makes clear that Chippy Patterson was a renegade from upper-class society, but the measured technique, so valuable to biography, does not reveal to the reader the nature of his revolt, only his bizarre conduct.[36]

In a serious attempt to study the sociology of upper-class Philadelphians, E. Digby Baltzell brought new methods of interpretation in his book, *Philadelphia Gentlemen*. In a semiquantitative approach that examines those who have found admission into the *Social Register*, *Who's Who*, and similar directories used as criteria of achievement, Baltzell provides a fascinating study of social elevation. However, his conclusions are not fully sustained by League records. The problem faced in such a sociological approach is that the examination of the social anatomy of club life is an external one. The view is from a remote vantage point, not one that is seen from within. Nonetheless, Baltzell's work approaches the nature of the League more closely than other popular works on American social and political life.[37]

Nathaniel Burt's *Perennial Philadelphians*, a pleasant book, is the work of a man who had an antecedent of the same name among the League founders, and whose father wrote nostalgically of the Philadelphia of preceding generations. Burt disliked the architecture of the League, and viewed its members as nineteenth-century perennials, writing about them with a grand display of light anecdotes. However, his brief portrait of George Henry Boker is vivid. Again, the core of the League is untouched.[38]

It is in the area of the political and patriotic history of the League that its significant contributions have suffered most. Many writers, among them the revisionist school of American historians, have failed to grasp its motives and its role in American life. Even the *Encyclopaedia Britannica*, a work frequently questioned as to its accuracy on American history, still describes the Philadelphia League as an organization founded as a secret society by Republicans during the Civil War.[39] It is to the credit of many younger contemporary historians, who have chosen to study the war years, reconstruction, and urban politics for doctoral themes, that new light has been focused on the Philadelphia League.[40]

In 1960, a presidential election year, Vice-President Richard M. Nixon and Henry Cabot Lodge were nominated as the Republican candidates. Their Democratic contenders were Senators John F. Kennedy of Massachusetts and Lyndon B. Johnson of Texas. Nixon, a two term vice-president, strongly indicated his chances of winning and readily attracted the support of the League. After his nomination, he attended a special reception at the League and shortly thereafter, the League immersed itself in a Republican fundraising campaign chaired by two prominent business leaders, Thomas B. McCabe and Joseph A. Fisher. The League membership worked feverishly and received contributions from 4,182 members and their ladies.[41] When the election returns came in, it became clear that the popular vote was almost equally divided. The difference was so slim that of 68,335,642 votes cast, Kennedy won by only a thin margin of 118,550.

League members naturally were dismayed by a loss which many were eager to challenge, particularly in the state of Illinois, where the division was the closest. But a corporate reaction to the Republican defeat was not recorded, and the League turned to its plans for its hundredth anniversary.

As a national factor in upholding the Union during the Civil War, as an important participant in the political life of the state, and as a contributor to the civic and cultural life of the city, the League had much to celebrate. If the men who formed the League had done nothing else other than recognize the crisis of their time, and carry on its work to strengthen the slender political position of Lincoln in 1862, this in itself would have been cause for a celebration. Its first members had brought about a division with the Wistar Party, fragmenting the social and cultural life not only of an eminent club, but of prominent Philadelphians. Thereafter, the League excluded anti-Union elements from its social life and was held together by patriotic fervor. Its commitment to clean government established the League as a counterforce that fought machine politics.

To commemorate this spirit, the Board of Directors resolved to hold a series of centennial celebrations. At its 98th annual meeting on December 20, 1960, a centennial fund was approved for which members agreed to a modest assessment. Former League President C. Brewster Rhoads was named chairman of the Centennial Committee, whose members included George M. Brodhead, J. Grey Emmons, Jr., Samuel E. Fulton, J. Permar Richards, Jr., and Robert L. Trescher. At the ninety-ninth annual meeting, Thomas B. McCabe hesitantly permitted himself to be nominated for the League presidency. He publicly admitted to a heavy schedule, but his attachment to the League was too great for him to bypass the honor. He later confessed, in a tone of affection, that the "rascal Sam" Fulton had assured him that all details pertaining to his office would be managed efficiently by the House Committee of which Fulton was then chairman. McCabe persuaded former president Dwight D. Eisenhower to appear at one of the series of four centennial celebrations. However, he was not successful in his efforts to induce General Douglas MacArthur to address the Lincoln Day celebration.[42]

The centennial program was ushered in on Lincoln's birthday, 1962, with the music of Harl McDonald and the production of Aaron Copeland's, "A Lincoln Portrait," at the Academy of Music. Basil Rathbone was the narrator. Morton Gould's stirring "American Salute" based on "When Johnny Comes Marching Home," was followed by Rathbone's magnificent recitation of the Gettysburg Address and Carmen Dragon's "Memories of America." Temple University's Chorus sang and performed admirably in its part of the program. Admiral Felix B. Stump delivered the main address.

On May 14, Philadelphia's Broad Street had the opportunity of viewing an unusual peacetime military pageant. Its purpose was to recall the Civil War military work of the League, whose members were the first to undertake and sponsor the recruitment of troops, filling a serious gap that the government could not cope with. It also was a reminder of the first black troops under federal colors who had paraded in 1863 over the same street, defying a hostile population. Nine branches of the United States Army participated. In the parade were infantry, artillery, and engineers, all in uniform.

More than 7,000 spectators watched the procession. Standing on the League portico was General Eisenhower, flanked by President McCabe, Vice-President Samuel E. Fulton, C. Brewster Rhoads, chairman of the Centennial Committee, Pennsylvania's Senator Hugh Scott, and Lt. General Milton G. Baker of the Valley Forge Military Academy. The color guard was comprised of the Military Order of the Loyal Legion, the Sons of the Revolution, the Washington Grays, and the Veteran Corps, First Regiment Infantry, National Guard of Pennsylvania. The guard of honor was provided by the United States Marine Corps.

In the evening, a dinner was tendered General Eisenhower at the League House. Two thousand members and their guests joined in the dinner festivity prior to the larger ceremony at the Academy of Music. The former president of the United States was the recipient of honorary membership, and was presented with the gold medal of The Union League. Eisenhower responded with a stirring address which was telecast directly from the Academy. The Bethlehem Bach Choir under the direction of Ifor Jones, sang excerpts from Bach's "Mass in B Minor," bringing the memorable evening to a close.[43]

Eisenhower was an overnight guest of the League in quarters that were specially prepared for him and are still referred to as the "presidential suite." While breakfasting at the League the following

AT THE LEAGUE CENTENNIAL CELEBRATION
SAMUEL E. FULTON, GENERAL DWIGHT D. EISENHOWER, HENRY B. BRYANS,
MRS. FULTON, THOMAS B. MCCABE (HIDDEN), GEORGE W. ELKINS, JR.,
AND BISHOP FRED P. CORSON

morning, he recalled for manager Daniel M. Layman the precise time and location of an event that had taken place outside of London in the days prior to the Normandy invasion. His sharp memory was as retentive as ever. After breakfast, he was taken on a tour of the League House, visiting the library and the Lincoln Memorial Room, where an exhibition of 39 examples of bronze sculpture by Agnes Yarnall covering a variety of Civil War themes was on display. The former president then departed for his Gettysburg farm.

It was an appropriate time to honor those League Members whose association had exceeded 50 years or more. A special centennial luncheon was held for the occasion, and each member received a silver tray with his name and date of admission inscribed. In the fall of that year, the officers and directors hosted a special dinner for all employees as a token of appreciation for their cooperation during the exciting centennial engagements.[44]

On the lighter side, the League sponsored two evenings of entertainment provided by outstanding orchestras at the Academy of Music, and in the League House. All of the normally scheduled social events for 1962, the dinner dances, and the annual festivities held for the children of members, were in some way associated with the centennial celebration. Towards the end of the year, another exhibition was held showing Winslow Homer's original battlefield drawings, most of which had not been exhibited previously. They were in the collection of League member Edmund L. Zalinski, to whose father they had been presented by the artist in 1904.[45]

The League's Civil War paintings had become better-known as a result of the publication of a catalog describing its holdings. When the Corcoran Gallery of Art borrowed Albert Bierstadt's "Bombardment of Fort Sumter" and Joseph John's "Harvest Home: When the War Was Over" for its Civil War exhibition, these choice paintings attracted considerable attention. Since then, the "Bombardment of Fort Sumter," one of the great American marine paintings, has been exhibited in the major galleries of the United States.[46]

The League also made available to the Philadelphia Civil War Centennial Committee materials from its extensive Civil War collection, to be placed on public exhibition. For the first time in its history, Philadelphians had a picture of the Civil War activity of the League. During the centennial year, the League became the official owner of H. K. Bush-Brown's bronze statue, which had become a center city landmark. For fifty years, its owners, the Veteran Corps, First Regiment Infantry, National Guard of Pennsylvania, had searched for a suitable location in Fairmount Park. On the occasion of the centennial, title to the statue of the soldier of the Gray Reserves Regiment was presented to the League, some of whose first members wore its uniform during the years from 1861 to 1865.[47]

The one hundredth annual meeting of The Union League of Philadelphia was one of the most unusual in its history. It was free of the trials of war, free of the debates over meeting internal problems of the League, and free of any immediate crisis. A Republican was returned to Harrisburg in the gubernatorial election, and it was the official close of the anniversary of the League. In an unexpected gesture, the customary order of business was waived, and a number of nonmembers, most of whom were the successful Republican candidates in the Pennsylvania election of 1962, were invited to be present. The annual meeting was turned into a Founders' Day celebration. Another unprecedented step was the delivery of an invocation at the annual meeting. Appropriately, Brigadier General John A. Borneman, a League member, and the Presbyterian chaplain, who had survived the cruel trials by the Japanese captors at Corregidor, prayed for the remembrance of those who had devoted their lives to the preservation of the Union.

Governor-elect William W. Scranton, Lt. Governor Raymond P. Shafer, the new Attorney General Walter E. Alessandroni, and State Supreme Court Justice Samuel J. Roberts were all welcomed at the League. Each spoke briefly. The newly elected congressman-at-large from Ohio, Robert A. Taft, Jr., was also among the League guests, thus becoming the third generation of Tafts to address the League. Before the proceedings of the evening were concluded, the new president, Samuel E. Fulton, a man always eager to bring unnoticed talent to the forefront, invited Kathlean A. Dennis, one of the black housemaids, to sing two spirituals of her choice. Kathlean sang "His Eye is on the Sparrow," and "How Great Thou Art" to an audience that responded to her soprano voice with overwhelming applause.[48]

Fulton envisioned in the centennial celebration more than just the presence of celebrities who shared the festivities. He saw the possibility of a program to make available the archives, the artifacts, and the art work of the League for scholarly study, and for exhibition purposes. As a result, the League introduced a formal archival program after the centennial that has been honored faithfully by his successors. As an ongoing part of the Civil War commemoration, the League undertook a major exhibition based on its own materials, covering the Civil War years and beyond. It was opened to the public, enabling thousands to see precisely what the League's political, civic, and patriotic role has been. Its aims in education, its cultural heritage, and its devotion to American history were carefully documented. In the presence of such a detailed array of materials, it would have been difficult to underplay the central theme of the League's existence, "Love of Country Leads." The exhibition was later transferred to the William Penn Memorial Museum in Harrisburg, under the title, "Civil War and Civil Rights." It has been estimated that over one-half million people have visited this exhibition, exposing them to the broad role of The Union League of Philadelphia.

The past had been commemorated. The vagaries of the American political system, which had changed considerably since the founding of the League, had shut out a Republican president from office in the years between 1932 and 1952. This was only a fleeting episode in the history of a young nation. But whatever the political trend, the League was governed by the unchanging patriotic motivation ordained in its charter. This century-old commitment gave the League new strength and fresh courage to face the issues that might arise after its centennial.

The words of C. Brewster Rhoads spoken at the centennial meeting in the Academy of Music exemplify this philosophy: "Any commemoration ceremony which looks backward without a glance to the future is an empty and hollow observance."

And so The Union League of Philadelphia turned its face to the future and embarked on its second century.

Appendix

The Founders
of
The Union Club of Philadelphia

ANTHONY J. ANTELO   (1815-1903), banker, maritime broker and railroad director, he also was an early Republican and a well-known patron of the arts.

JOHN ASHHURST   (1809-1892), banker and shipping merchant who was active in the movement to secure civil rights for Negroes.

WILLIAM H. ASHHURST   (1815-1885), merchant, brother of John Ashhurst, was a major figure in the formative years of The Union League.

ABRAHAM BARKER   (1821-1906), banker and financial publisher, was a collateral descendant of Benjamin Franklin, and an early Republican. He is credited with raising five regiments of black troops.

THOMAS A. BIDDLE   (1814-1888), broker, politically active in The Union League, he was a descendant of a revolutionary war family.

HORACE BINNEY, JR.   (1809-1870), lawyer and abolitionist, he was the son of the distinguished federalist judge, Horace Binney, Sr.

GEORGE H. BOKER   (1824-1890), poet, dramatist and cofounder of The Union Club and The Union League. He was the first secretary of the League, and its president from 1879 to 1884 inclusive.

ADOLPH E. BORIE   (1809-1880), merchant and financier, was an early vice president of The Union League. He was Grant's first secretary of the navy.

CHARLES L. BORIE   (1819-1886), brother of Adolph and member of his father's shipping firm.

ALEXANDER BROWN   (1815-1893), banker and philanthropist, who was involved in the antislavery movement. His firm was the forerunner of Brown Brothers Harriman and Company.

273

ROBERT B. CABEEN   (1812-1876), iron merchant, active in the wartime affairs of The Union League.

GEN. GEORGE CADWALADER   (1806-1879), lawyer and soldier, was a member of one of Philadelphia's oldest families.

HENRY CHARLES CAREY   (1793-1879), publisher, economist, and author, was a major advocate of tariff in the nineteenth century.

JAMES LAWRENCE CLAGHORN   (1816-1884), merchant and patron of the arts, he was the first treasurer of The Union League and had retired from business to devote his time to its undertakings. For many years he was president of the Pennsylvania Academy of The Fine Arts.

CLARENCE H. CLARK   (1833-1906), financier, bibliophile and patron of the arts, he was one of the last two surviving members of the original Union Club.

STEPHEN COLWELL   (1800-1871), ironmaster, economist and anti-slavery worker.

DANIEL DOUGHERTY   (1826-1892), lawyer, orator, and the city's most prominent Democrat.

FERDINAND J. DREER   (1812-1902), antiquarian, widely known for his collection of autographs and manuscripts which were presented to The Historical Society of Pennsylvania. He was a founder of the Academy of Music, a member of the American Philosophical Society and a lively advocate of the fine arts.

J. GILLINGHAM FELL   (1817-1878), shipping merchant and mine operator, he was a participant in obtaining rights of Negroes in the use of public accommodations. He was the second president of The Union League.

SAMUEL MORSE FELTON   (1809-1889), civil engineer, railroad president and an influential figure in Civil War military transportation.

FREDERICK FRALEY   (1804-1901), merchant and banker occupied in the civic, public and cultural life of Philadelphia. He was a member of the American Philosophical Society, and a leader in the founding of the Franklin Institute.

THEODORE FROTHINGHAM   (1816-1873), wholesale commission merchant who was active during the early years of The Union League.

BENJAMIN GERHARD   (1810-1864), lawyer and legal author, was a prominent Episcopal layman and Provost Marshal for superintending the draft in Philadelphia. He was a director of the League in 1863 and 1864.

CHARLES GIBBONS   (1814-1884), lawyer, orator, state senator and abolitionist who devoted all his time to the activities of the League. He was a vice-president of the League from 1870 to 1874 inclusive.

JOHN INNES CLARK HARE   (1816-1905), jurist and legal author. He was a cofounder of The Union Club and The Union League, and a member of the American Philosophical Society. His father, Robert Hare, was a noted chemist.

JOSEPH HARRISON, JR.   (1810-1874), engineer and locomotive designer who was the author of books on the history and technology of the steam locomotive. He was a member of the American Philosophical Society and a patron of the arts.

WARD B. HASELTINE   (1811-1886), participated in the political work of the League.

ALFRED D. JESSUP   (1826-1881), paper manufacturer, insurance executive and publisher.

ABRAHAM J. LEWIS   (1791-1877), importer and banker, he was active in raising funds for recruiting Negro soldiers.

EDWIN M. LEWIS   (1812-1884), shipping merchant, banker, he was involved in the Civil War endeavors of The Union League.

WILLIAM DAVID LEWIS   (1792-1881), merchant and banker who spent many years in Russia before the Civil War. The first American translator of the Russian poet Alexander Pushkin. It was he who proposed that The Union League support the movement to organize Negro troops.

JOSHUA BALLINGER LIPPINCOTT   (1813-1886), publisher, founder of the School of Veterinary Medicine at the University of Pennsylvania.

MORTON McMICHAEL   (1807-1879), editor and publisher, a leading proponent of the Whig party, he was a mayor of Philadelphia and the president of The Union League from 1870 to 1874 inclusive.

SINGLETON A. MERCER   (1810-1867), banker, active in the political affairs of The Union League. He resigned from the League shortly before his death.

SAMUEL VAUGHAN MERRICK   (1801-1870), manufacturer of heavy machinery and the promoter of the Pennsylvania Railroad. Builder of lighthouses and steam vessels. He was a member of the American Philosophical Society and a founder of the Franklin Institute.

E. SPENCER MILLER   (1815-1879), lawyer and poet, descended from a colonial and revolutionary war family.

JAMES MILLIKEN   (1824-1902), iron manufacturer, prominent in the wartime work of the League and an exponent of Negro rights.

BLOOMFIELD H. MOORE   (1818-1878), paper manufacturer and partner of Alfred D. Jessup in the largest company of its kind in his lifetime.

JOHN B. MYERS   (1804-1864), one of the incorporators of The Union League and a vice-president for 1863-1864.

JAMES W. PAUL   (1816-1897), lawyer, prominent in professional and social circles, and active in all the affairs of The Union Club and The Union League.

CHARLES JACOBS PETERSON   (1819-1887), editor, publisher and author associated with Philadelphia's outstanding journals.

WILLIAM HENRY RAWLE   (1823-1889), lawyer, legal author and veteran of the Civil War. He was a member of a distinguished colonial family.

JOHN MEREDITH READ   (1797-1874), Justice of the Supreme Court of Pennsylvania in 1872 and grandson of George Reed, a signer of the Declaration of Independence, he was a prolific writer on legal subjects. He was a member of the American Philosophical Society.

SAMUEL J. REEVES   (1816-1878), iron manufacturer, president of the American Iron and Steel Association, who supplied the materials for major bridges and railways throughout the United States.

FAIRMAN ROGERS   (1835-1900), civil engineer and a prominent socialite who fought in the Union cavalry. He was active in the Franklin Institute, a benefactor of the Pennsylvania Academy of The Fine Arts and a founder of the Academy of the Natural Sciences, but is best remembered as a sporting coachman.

WILLIAM SELLERS   (1824-1905), iron manufacturer and inventor, he was president of the Franklin Institute, a member of the American Philosophical Society and an influential figure at the Academy of the Natural Sciences. Much of the success of the 1876 Centennial was owing to his efforts.

DANIEL SMITH, JR.   (1790-1884), maritime broker and fire insurance executive, he was a conspicuous worker for sick and wounded soldiers. For many years he was a Union League director.

WILSON CARY SWANN, M.D.   (1806-1876), philanthropist, active in the organization of The Union Club, was the first president of the Pennsylvania Society for the Prevention of Cruelty to Animals and founder of the Fountain Society to provide public fountains for animals and people.

WILLIAM M. TILGHMAN   (1805-1900), inventor and lawyer and an active worker for The Union Club and The Union League.

JOHN HENRY TOWNE   (1818-1875), iron manufacturer, engineer, and partner of Samuel Vaughan Merrick under the firm name of Merrick and Towne. Active in many public and civic undertakings.

JOSEPH B. TOWNSEND   (1821-1896), lawyer and communal leader who devoted most of his time to The Union League of which he was a director from 1863 to 1867 inclusive, and a vice-president in 1892. He was one of the men responsible for funding the loan to build The Union League House.

GEORGE TROTT   (1809-1899), merchant, was one of the six organizers of The Union Club and an incorporator of The Union League.

JOHN P. VERREE   (1817-1889), iron manufacturer and a congressman who had been a Whig prior to becoming a prominent Republican. He served The Union League as president in 1875 and 1876

HENRY MILLER WATTS   (1805-1890), lawyer, diplomat, iron and coal merchant, descended from a colonial and revolutionary war family. Made large contributions to the support of League projects; he was United States minister to Austria in 1868.

GEORGE WHITNEY   (1819-1885), car wheel manufacturer and partner in the Baldwin Locomotive Works, he was a patron of the arts and active in civil service reform as well as reform politics.

Officers and Directors of
The Union League of Philadelphia
1863-1975

The first election for officers previous to the incorporation of The Union League was held on Thursday, January 22, 1863, and resulted in the unanimous choice of the following:

President

WILLIAM M. MEREDITH

Vice-Presidents

WILLIAM H. ASHHURST
HORACE BINNEY, JR.
JOHN B. MYERS
ADOLPH E. BORIE

Directors

MORTON McMICHAEL	BENJAMIN GERHARD
J. I. CLARK HARE	JOSEPH B. TOWNSEND
CHARLES GIBBONS	GEORGE H. BOKER
JAMES L. CLAGHORN	GEORGE WHITNEY
JOHN B. KENNEY	

Subsequent elections were held on the second Monday of each December, and the dates given are for the years following.

Presidents

*WILLIAM M. MEREDITH .... 1863, '64
*J. GILLINGHAM FELL .... 1865, '66, '67, '68
*HORACE BINNEY, JR. .... 1869 to Feb. 3, '70
*MORTON McMICHAEL .... Feb. 19, 1870, '71, '72, '73, '74
*JOHN P. VERREE .... 1875, '76
*CHARLES E. SMITH .... 1877, '78
*GEORGE H. BOKER .... 1879, '80, '81, '82, '83, '84
*EDWIN N. BENSON .... 1885, '86, '87, '88
*WILLIAM C. HOUSTON .... 1889, '90
*EDWIN H. FITLER .... 1891, '92
*JOHN RUSSELL YOUNG .... 1893, '94
*SILAS W. PETTIT .... 1895, '96
*C. STUART PATTERSON .... 1897, '98
*JOSEPH G. DARLINGTON .... 1899, 1900, '01, '02
*EDWARD T. STOTESBURY .... 1903, '04, '05, '22, '23
*EDWIN S. STUART ....1906, '19, '20, '21
*DIMNER BEEBER .... 1907, '08
*JAMES F. HOPE .... 1909, '10, '11
*WILLIAM T. TILDEN .... 1912, '13, '14
*JOHN GRIBBEL .... 1915, '16, '17
*WILLIAM C. SPROUL .... 1918, '26, '27
*E. PUSEY PASSMORE .... 1924, '25
*WILLIAM G. PRICE, JR. .... 1928, '29
*MELVILLE G. BAKER .... Dec. 9, 1929 to May 13, '30
*GEORGE STUART PATTERSON .... May 20, 1930, '31
*E. LAWRENCE FELL .... 1932, '33, '40, '41
*FRANK M. HARDT .... 1934, '35
*OTTO ROBERT HEILIGMAN .... 1936, '37
*ALLEN M. STEARNE .... 1938, '39
*ARCHIE D. SWIFT .... 1942, '43
*WILLIAM I. SCHAFFER .... 1944, '45
*MILLARD D. BROWN .... 1946, '47
*HENRY B. BRYANS .... 1948, '49
*J. WILLIAM HARDT .... 1950, '51
*C. BREWSTER RHOADS .... 1952, '53
*L. ALAN PASSMORE .... 1954, '55
*JOSEPH W. HENDERSON .... 1956 to July 25, '57
*DAVID B. JAMES, JR. .... July 30, to Dec. 9, 1957
JAMES M. ANDERSON .... 1958, '59

*Deceased

RUSSELL P. HEUER .... 1960, '61
THOMAS B. McCABE 1962
SAMUEL E. FULTON .... 1963, '64
THOMAS E. WYNNE .... 1965, '66
J. PERMAR RICHARDS, JR. .... 1967, '68
GEORGE M. BRODHEAD .... 1969, '70
E. JOHN HESKETH .... 1971, '72
EDWARD J. DWYER .... 1973, '74
BURTON H. ETHERINGTON, JR. 1975

Vice-Presidents

*WILLIAM H. ASHHURST .... 1863, '64, '65, '66, '67, '68
*HORACE BINNEY, JR. .... 1863, '64, '65, '66, '67, '68
*JOHN B. MYERS .... 1863, '64
*ADOLPH E. BORIE ..... 1863, '64, '65, '66, '67, '68, '69, '70, '71, '72
                     '73, '74, '75, '76, '77, '79 to Feb. 5, '80
*MORTON McMICHAEL .... 1865, '66, '67, '68, '69, '70
*J. GILLINGHAM FELL .. 1869, '70, '71, '72, '73, '74, '75, '76, '77, '78
*DANIEL SMITH, JR. 1869
*CHARLES GIBBONS .... 1870, '71, '72, '73, '74
*WILLIAM SELLERS .... Feb. 19, 1870, '71, '72, '73, '74
*EDWARD C. KNIGHT .... 1875, '85, '86, '87, '88
*CHARLES E. SMITH .... 1875, '76
*JAMES V. WATSON .... 1876, '77, '78
*JOHN P. VERREE 1877
*EDWIN R. COPE 1878
*B. H. BARTOL 1878
*EDWIN N. BENSON .... 1879, '80, '81, '82, '83, '84
*J. FRAILEY SMITH .... 1879 to June 26, '80
*WILLIAM C. HOUSTON . 1879, '80, '81, '82, '83, '84, '85, '86, '87, '88
*SAMUEL C. PERKINS .... Feb. 10, 1880, '81, '82, '83, '91, '92
*EDWIN H. FITLER .... July 13, 1880, '81, '82, '83, '84
                                   '85, '86, '87, '88, '89, '90
*THOMAS DOLAN .... 1884, '85, '86, '87, '88, '89, '90
*SAMUEL B. HUEY .... 1889, '90, '92
*THEODORE E. WIEDERSHEIM .... 1889, '90, '91
*SILAS W. PETTIT .... 1891, '92, '93, '94
*JOSEPH B. TOWNSEND 1891
*JOHN H. MICHENER 1892
*ELISHA A. HANCOCK 1893
*JAMES DOBSON .... 1893, '94
*WILLIAM H. HURLEY .... 1893, '94

*H. Earnest Goodman, M.D. .... 1894, '95 to Feb. 3, '96
*Joseph G. Darlington .... 1895, '96, '97, '98
*Fayette R. Plumb .... 1895, '96
*George Campbell .... 1895, '96, '97
*R. Dale Benson .... Mar. 10, 1896, '97, '98
*Joseph S. Neff, M.D. .... 1897, '98, 1907
*Harry F. West .... 1898, '99, 1900, '01
*James Butterworth 1899
*Lincoln K. Passmore 1899
*Charles E. Pugh .... 1899, 1900, '01
*Charles S. Forsyth .... 1900, '01
*Edward I. Smith 1900
*Alfred F. Moore 1901
*William B. Van Lennep, M.D. .... 1902, '03, '04
*James F. Hope .... 1902, '03, '04
*Edward T. Stotesbury 1902
*William M. Coates .... 1902, '03, '04, '05
*Charles K. Barns 1903
*Edwin S. Stuart .... 1904, '05
*William T. Tilden .... 1905, '06, '08, '09, '10, '11
*Dimner Beeber .... 1905, '06
*John Sailer .... 1906, '07, '08
*William W. Porter .... 1906, '07, '09, '10
*Charles D. Barney .... 1907, '08, '09
*Morris L. Clothier .... 1908, '09, '10, '11
*William Henry Brooks .... 1910, '11
*Thomas J. Jeffries .... 1911, '12, '13, '14
*Howard B. French 1912
*E. Eldridge Pennock 1912
*William C. Sproul .... 1912, '13, '14, '16, '17
*Joseph B. McCall 1913
*George B. Evans .... 1913, '14, '15, '16
*John Gribbel 1914
*Harrison Townsend 1915
*Miers Busch .... 1915, '16, '17, '18, '19, '20, '26
*Charlemagne Tower .... 1915, '16, '17
*William T. Elliott 1917
*Alexander W. Wister, Jr. 1918
*Charles R. Miller .... 1918, '19, '20, '21, '22
*Charles A. Porter, Jr. 1918
*Charles M. Schwab 1919
*E. Pusey Passmore .... 1919, '20, '21, '22, '23
*William R. Lyman .... 1920, '21, '22, '23, '24, '25

*George A. Walker .... 1921, '22, '23
*Charles J. Webb 1923
*J. Warner Hutchins .... 1924 to Feb. 4, '25
*William G. Price, Jr. .... 1924, '26, '27
*John T. Riley .... 1924 to Feb. 10, '25
*Bayard Henry .... 1925, '26
*Melville G. Baker .... 1925, '26, '27
*Charles E. Roberts .... 1927, '28
*W. Kirkland Dwier .... 1927, '28
*George Stuart Patterson .... 1928, '29 to May 20, '30
*Charles P. Vaughan .... 1928, '29
*Louis J. Kolb 1929
*Frank A. Bedford 1929
*Lewis H. Van Dusen .... 1930, '31, '32, '33, '34
*Frank M. Hardt .... 1930, '31, '32, '33
*Charles H. Ewing .... 1930, '31
*Ernest T. Trigg 1931
*Otto Robert Heiligman .... 1932, '33, '34, '35
*Frank H. Caven .... 1932, '33
*J. Willison Smith 1934
David Burpee .... 1933, '34, '35
*Ira Jewell Williams .... 1935, '36
*Harry S. McDevitt 1935
*Frank van Roden ...... 1936, '37, '38, '39, '40, '41 to July 13, '42
*Wilmer Krusen, M.D. 1936
*Herbert J. Tily .... 1936, '37
*George Wharton Pepper .... 1937, '38, '39, '40
                                        '41, '42, '43, '44, '45
*Allen M. Stearne 1937
*Spencer L. Jones 1938
J. Wesley McWilliams 1938
*Maurice W. Sloan .... 1939, '40
*Franklin S. Edmonds 1939
*Joseph F. Stockwell .... 1940, '41, '42 to Jan. 28, '43
*John C. Taylor 1941
*Benjamin S. Mechling .... 1942, '43, '44
*William M. Davison, Jr. .... Aug. 11, 1942, '43
*Robert T. McCracken .... Feb. 9, 1943, '44, '45
*Thomas K. Ober, Jr. .... 1944, '45
*J. William Hardt .... 1945, '46, '47, '48, '49
Gordon A. Hardwick .... 1946, '47, '48, '49, '50
*William Steele, 3rd .... 1946, '47, '48, '49
*Henry B. Bryans .... 1946, '47

*RAYMOND M. REMICK .... Dec. 8, 1947 to Oct. 12, '48
*C. BREWSTER RHOADS .... Oct. 20, 1948, '49, '50, '51
RICHARD P. BROWN .... 1950, '51
*ARTHUR LITTLETON .... 1950, '51, '52, '53
*JOSEPH W. HENDERSON .... 1951, '52, '53, '54
*L. ALAN PASSMORE .... 1952, '53
REVELLE W. BROWN 1952
JOHN ARTHUR BROWN .... 1953, '54, '55, '56
*DAVID B. JAMES, JR. .... 1954, '55, '56 to July 30, '57
*GEORGE W. ELKINS, JR. .... 1954, '55, '56, '57
JAMES M. ANDERSON .... 1955, '56, '57
THOMAS B. MCCABE .... 1957, '58, '59, '60
JOSEPH A. FISHER .... Sept. 10, 1957, '58, '59, '60
RUSSELL P. HEUER .... 1958, '59
*FRANK P. WILL .... 1958, '59 to Aug. 10, '60
*MARK E. LEFEVER .... 1960, '61, '65, '66, '67, '68
SAMUEL E. FULTON .... Sept. 13, 1960, '61, '62
JOHN F. E. HIPPEL .... 1961, '62, '63, '64
STANLEY L. THORNTON .... 1961, '62, '63, '64
*HENRY L. SCHIMPF, JR. .... 1962, '63, '64, '65
GEORGE A. BAILEY 1963
J. PERMAR RICHARDS, JR. .... 1963, '64, '65, '66
IVAN H. PETERMAN .... 1965, '66, '67, '68
GEORGE M. EWING, JR. .... 1966, '67, '68
E. JOHN HESKETH .... 1967, '68, '69, '70
DAVID F. MAXWELL .... 1969, '70
EDWARD J. DWYER .... 1969, '70, '71, '72
*JOHN S. PEAKE .... 1969, '70, '71
BURTON H. ETHERINGTON, JR. .... 1971, '72, '73, '74
*WILLIAM V. GRIER .... 1971, '72, '73, '74
J. VICTOR O'BRIEN .... 1972, '73, '74, '75
HAL L. BEMIS .... 1973, '74, '75
WILLIAM J. MCCARTER 1975
NELSON G. HARRIS 1975

Secretaries

*GEORGE H. BOKER .... 1863, '64, '65, '66, '67, '68, '69, '70, '71
*STEPHEN A. CALDWELL .... 1872, '73, '74
*WILLIAM CAMAC, M.D. 1875
*SILAS W. PETTIT .... 1876, '77, '78, '89, '90
*WILLIAM E. LITTLETON .... 1879 to Sept. 22, '80
*SAMUEL B. HUEY .. Sept. 22, 1880, '81, '82, '83, '84, '85, '86, '87, '88

*WILLIAM POTTER .... 1891 to Nov. 22 '92
*JOSEPH G. DARLINGTON .... Nov. 22, 1892, '93
*JOSEPH S. NEFF, M.D. .... 1894, '95
*C. STUART PATTERSON 1896
*CHARLEMAGNE TOWER .... Dec. 15, 1896 to Apr. 13, '97
*J. LEVERING JONES .... Apr. 13, 1897, '98, '99
*DIMNER BEEBER .... 1900, '01, '02, '03
*WILLIAM H. LAMBERT .... 1904, '05, '06, '07
*GEORGE P. MORGAN .... 1908, '09, '10 to Oct. 10, '11
*JOHN W. HAMER .... Oct. 10, 1911, '12, '13, '14, '15, '16
                    '17, '18, '19, '20, '21, '22, '23, '24 to Sept. 1, '25
*HAROLD B. BEITLER .... Sept. 8, 1925, '26, '27, '28, '29
                                                        to Jan. 15, '30
*THOMAS SHALLCROSS, JR. .. Jan. 15, 1930, '31, '32, '33, '34, '35, '36
*J. CLARK MOORE, JR. .... 1937, '38, '39
*JOHN BLAKELEY .... 1940, '41, '42, '43, '44, '45, '46
*L. ALAN PASSMORE .... 1947, '48, '49, '50, '51
*FRANK G. SAYRE ...... 1952, '53, '54, '55, '56, '57, '58, '59, '60, '61
                                                       to Sept. 11, '62
GEORGE M. BRODHEAD .... Sept. 11, 1962, '63, '64, '65, '66, '67
                                                         to Oct. 8, '68
STANLEY L. THORNTON .... Oct. 8, 1968, '69, '70, '71
                                                   '72, '73 to Oct. 8, '74
JOHN J. HERD .... Oct. 8, 1974, '75

Treasurers

*JAMES L. CLAGHORN ...... 1863 to Oct. 1, '65, 1868 to Aug. 25, '84
*EDWARD S. CLARKE .... Oct. 1, 1865, '66, '67
*THOMAS COCHRAN .... Aug. 27, 1884, '85, '86, '87, '88, '89, '90
*WINTHROP SMITH 1891
*HARRY F. WEST .... 1892, '93, '94, '95, '96, '97
*EDWARD I. SMITH .... 1898, '99
*EDWARD T. STOTESBURY .... 1900, '01
*M. RIEBENACK .. 1902, '03, '04, '05, '06, '07, '08, '09 to May 10, '10
*JAMES E. MITCHELL .... May 10, 1910, '11, '12, '13, '14, '15
                    '16, '17, '18, '19, '20, '21, '22, '23 '24 to Apr. 19, '25
*E. LAWRENCE FELL .... May 12, 1925, '26, '27, '28, '29, '30, '31
*JAY GATES .... 1932, '33, '34 to May 14, '35
*ARCHIE D. SWIFT .... May 14, 1935, '36, '37, '38, '39, '40, '41
*JAY V. HARE .... 1942, '43, '44, '45
*HARRY F. RICHARDS .... 1946, '47, '48, '49, '50, '51, '52,
                    '53, '54, '55, '56, '57, '58, '59, to Mar. 20, '60

*George W. Elkins, Jr.   Apr. 12, 1960, '61, '62, '63, '64 to June 5, '65
Earl K. Mueller .... July 13, 1965, '66, '67, '68, '69, '70
William B. Carr .... 1971, '72
Maurice A. Webster, Jr. .... 1973, '74, '75

Directors

*Morton McMichael .... 1863, '64
*J. I. Clark Hare .... 1863, '64, '65, '66
*Charles Gibbons .... 1863, '64, '65, '66, '67, '68, '69
*James L. Claghorn .... 1863, '64, '65, '68, '69, '70, '71
'72, '73, '74, '75, '76, '77, '78, '79,
'80, '81, '82, '83 to Aug. 25, '84
*Benjamin Gerhard .... 1863, '64
*Joseph B. Towsend .... 1863, '64, '65, '66, '67
*George H. Boker .... 1863, '64, '65, '66, '67, '68, '69
'70, '71, '72, '73, '74, '78
*George Whitney .... 1863, '64, '65, '66
*John B. Kenney .... 1863, '64, '65
*Lindley Smyth .... 1865, '66, '67, '68
*Daniel Smith, Jr. .... 1865, '66, '67, '68
*N. B. Browne .... 1865, '66
*James H. Orne .... 1865, '66, '67, '68, '69, '70
*H. C. Lea .... 1865, '68
*William Sellers .... 1865, '66, '67, '68
*Ellerslie Wallace, M.D. .... 1865, '66
*Cadwalader Biddle 1865
*Edward S. Clarke .... 1865, '66, '67, '68, '69, '70
'71, '72, '73, '74, '75
*Stephen A. Caldwell .... 1866, '67, '68, '69, '70, '71, '72, '73, '74
*Edward Browning .... 1866, '67, '68
*A. H. Franciscus .... 1866, '67, '68
*George J. Gross .... 1867, '68
*Andrew Wheeler .... 1867, '76
*John P. Verree .... 1867, '68, '69, '70, '71, '72, '73
*Evan Randolph 1867
*Saunders Lewis 1868
*E. C. Knight .... 1869, '70, '71, '72, '73, '74
July 13, '80, '81, '82, '83, '84
*Henry Lewis .... 1869, '70, '80, '81, '82, '83 to Jan. 8, '84
*Samuel C. Perkins .... 1869, '70, '71, '72, '73, '74, '75, '79
to Feb. 10, '80, Sept. 9, '84, '85, '86, '87, '88, '89, '90
*Richard Wright .... 1869, '70, '71, '72, '73, '74, '75

*Henry Winsor 1869
*Joseph Trimble .... 1869, '70, '71
*John Rice .... 1869, '70, '71
*Edwin R. Cope .... 1869, '70, '76, '77
*Alfred D. Jessup .... 1870, '71
*J. Frailey Smith .... 1870, '71, '72, '73, '74, '75, '76
*Charles K. Ide .... 1871, '72, '73, '84, to Apr. 15, '85
*William E. Littleton ..... 1871, '72, '73, '74, '79 to Sept. 22, '80
*Charles Gilpin .... 1871, '72, '73, '74
*Lewis Waln Smith .... 1872, '73, '74
*Henry H. Bingham .... 1872, '73, '74
*Edwin N. Benson .... 1872, '73, '74, '76
*Edwin H. Fitler .... 1874, '79 to July 13, '80
*William D. Gemmill 1874
*James V. Watson 1875
*F. A. Comly 1875
*William C. Houston .... 1875, '76
*George Philler 1875
*William Camac, M.D. 1875
*John J. Hartmann .... 1875, '76, '77
*Robert Gray 1875
*Thomas Hart, Jr. 1875
*John Hockley, Jr. .... 1875, '76
*Silas W. Pettit .... 1875, '76, '77, '78, '79, '80, '81, '82
'83, '84, '85, '86, '87, '88, '89, '90
*Edward S. Buckley .... 1876, '77, '78
*B. H. Bartol .... 1876, '77
*Aubrey H. Smith .... 1876, '77, '78
*Frederic Collins .... 1876, '77, '78
*William Brockie .... 1876, '77
*Alexander Biddle .... 1876, '77
*Thomas A. Boyd .... 1877, '78
*James E. Caldwell .... 1877, '78
*Isaac Hinckley .... 1877, '78
*Henry Pettit .... 1877, '78
*Joseph Lapsley Wilson .... 1877, '78
*Amos R. Little 1878
*Henry Armitt Brown 1878
*John Wright 1878
*Charles H. Cramp .... 1878, '79, '80, '81, '82, '83
*Strickland Kneass .... 1879, '80, '81, '82, '83
*John L. Lawson .... 1879, '80, '81, '82, '83, '84, '85
'86, '87, '88, '89, '90

*Samuel B. Huey ..... 1879, '80, '81, '82, '83, '84, '85, '86, '87, '88
*H. P. Smith .... 1879 to Sept. 14, '80
*Francis P. Steel 1879
*L. F. Barry .... 1879, '80, '81, '82, '83, '84
*J. E. Soule .... 1879, '80, '81, '87 to Feb. 14, '88
*Winthrop Smith .... 1879, '80, '81, '82, '83, '84, '85 to
Apr. 13, '86, '87, '88, '89, '90, '91
*William H. Hurley . 1879, '80, '81, '82, '83 to Jan. 8, '84, '85, '86
*Thomas Dolan .... Feb. 10, 1880, '81, '82, '83
*Wayne MacVeagh .... Sept. 22, 1880, '81
*Theodore E. Wiedersheim .... Sept. 22, 1880, '81, '82
'83, '84, '85, '86, '87, '88
*Robert S. Davis .... 1882, '83
*Joel J. Baily .... 1882, '83, '84, '85, '86, '87, '88, '89
*Thomas Cochran .... 1884, '85, '86, '87, '88, '89, '90
*Samuel B. Thomas .... Dec. 11, 1883 to Nov. 30, '84
*Hamilton Disston .... 1884, '85, '86, '87, '88
*James B. Agnew .... 1884, '85, '86, '87
*S. Emlen Meigs .... 1885, '86
*Joseph Bernard Wilson .... 1885, to Mar. 25, '86
*Thomas McKean .... 1885, '86, '87, '88, '89
*John R. Fell .... May 12, 1885, '86, '87, '88, '89
*Richard A. Lewis .... 1886, '87
*Merle Middleton 1887
*Samuel S. Sharp .... 1888, '89, '94
*John F. Stoer .... 1888, '89, '90, '91
*Joseph S. Neff, M.D. .... 1888, '89, '90, '91, '92, '93, '94, '95, '96
*John H. Michener .... Feb. 14, 1888, '89, '90
*Francis W. Murphy .... 1889, '90
*George H. Colket .... 1889, '90, '91, '92
*William B. Warne .... 1889, '90, '91
*Charles E. Pugh .... 1890, '91, '92, '93, '94, '95, '96
*Elisha A. Hancock .... 1890, '91, '92
*Jacob Naylor .... 1890, '91, '92
*William Potter .... 1890, '91, '92
*Joseph G. Darlington .... 1891, '92, '93
*George H. North .... 1891, '92, '93, '94
*H. Earnest Goodman, M.D. .... 1891, '92, '93
*Fayette R. Plumb .... 1891, '92, '93, '94
*Harry F. West .... 1891, '92, '93, '94, '95, '96, '97
*Charles Thackara .... 1891, '92, '93
*John Russell Young 1892
*N. Chapman Mitchell 1892

*EFFINGHAM B. MORRIS .... 1892, '93, '94
*THOMAS D. STINSON 1893
*JAMES POLLOCK .... 1893, '94, '95
*GEORGE CAMPBELL .... 1893, '94
*JAMES BUTTERWORTH .... 1893, '94, '95, '96
*EDWARD I. SMITH .... 1893, '95, '97, '98, '99
*LOUIS A. FLANAGAN .... 1893, '94, '95
*R. DALE BENSON .... 1894, '95 to Mar. 10, '96, 1916, '17
*GEORGE C. THOMAS .... 1894, '95, '96, '97
*LINCOLN GODFREY .... 1894, '95, '96
*C. STUART PATTERSON .... 1894, '95, '96, 1916
*ALFRED F. MOORE .... 1895, '96, '98, '99, 1900
*COLLINS W. WALTON .... 1895, '96
*THOMAS POTTER, JR. .... 1895, 1901, '02, '03
*JOHN T. BAILEY 1895
*SAMUEL B. STINSON .... 1896, 1902, '03
*CHARLEMAGNE TOWER .... 1896 to Apr. 13, '97, 1922 to Feb. 24, '23
*JAMES F. HOPE 1896
*EDWARD F. KINGSLEY .... 1896, '97
*LINCOLN K. PASSMORE .... 1896, '97, '98
*ROBERT C. LIPPINCOTT .... Mar. 10, 1896, '97, '98, 1900, 01, '02
*GEORGE R. HOWELL .... 1897, '98, '99
*ALFRED C. HARRISON .... 1897, '98, '99
*J. ALBERT CALDWELL .... 1897, '98, '99
*J. LEVERING JONES .... 1897, '98, '99, 1904
*CHARLES S. FORSYTH .... 1897, '98, '99
*ALAN WOOD, JR. 1897
*HENRY S. GROVE .... 1897, '98, '99
*JAMES C. BROOKS 1897
*HENRY E. GARSED .... Apr. 13, 1897, '98, '99, 1902, '03
*EDWARD T. STOTESBURY .... 1898, '99, 1900, '01, '16
*M. RIEBENACK .... 1898, '99, 1900, '02, '03, '04, '05
                                  '06, '07, '08, '09, to May 10, '10
*SAMUEL GOODMAN 1898
*HENRY C. DAVIS .... 1898, '99, 1900
*JOEL COOK .... 1899, 1900, '01, '04, '05, '06
*THEODORE C. SEARCH .... 1899, 1900, '01
*JOHN C. LOWRY .... 1899, 1900, '01, '11, '12, '13
*WILLIAM B. VAN LENNEP, M.D. .... 1900, '01
*WILLIAM M. COATES .... 1900, '01
*DIMNER BEEBER .... 1900, '01, '02, '03, '16
*CHARLES K. BARNS .... 1900, '01, '02
*E. BURGESS WARREN .... 1900, '01

*Jacob E. Heyl .... 1900, '01
*Frederick S. Hovey 1900
*Edwin S. Stuart .... 1901, '02, '03, '16
*George W. Elkins .... 1901, '02
*William T. Tilden .... 1901, '02, '03
*J. S. W. Holton .... 1902, '04, '05
*James B. Walker, M.D. .... 1902, '03, '04
*Herman P. Kremer .... 1902, '03, '04
*William H. Lambert .... 1902, '03, '04, '05, '06, '07
*John D. Thomas, D.D.S. .... 1902, '03, '04
*Alba B. Johnson .... 1903, '04, '05
*Christian C. Febiger .... 1903, '04, '05
*John Sailer .... 1903, '04, '05
*William Disston 1903
*Samuel P. Rotan .... 1904, '05, '06
*John B. Parsons .... 1904, '05
*Charles D. Barney .... 1904, '05, '06
*William H. Jenks .... 1904, '05
*Morris L. Clothier .... 1905, '06, '07
*George V. Massey .... 1905, '06
*Francis L. Potts 1905
*J. Bertram Lippincott .... 1905, '06, '07
*Rudolph Blankenburg .... 1906, '07, '08
*Wendell P. Bowman .... 1906, '07, '08, '09
*Richard L. Austin .... 1906, '07
*William Henry Brooks .... 1906, '07, '08, '09
*Charles Gibbons Davis .... 1906, '07, '08
*George H. Hill .... 1906, '07, '08, '09
*John B. Lober .... 1906, '07, '08
*George P. Morgan .... 1907, '08, '09, '10, '11
*Thomas J. Jeffries .... 1907, '08, '09, '10
*Howard B. French .... 1907, '08, '09, '10
*James E. Mitchell .... 1907, '08, '09, '10, '11, '12, '13, '14
                '15, '16, '17, '18, '19, '20, '21, '22, '23, '24 to Apr. 19, '25
*William C. Sproul .... 1908, '09, '10, '11
*John Kisterbock .... 1908, '09, '10, '11
*John W. Hamer .... 1908, '09, '10, '11, '12, '13, '14, '15
                '16, '17, '18, '19, '20, '21, '22, '23, '24 to Sept. 1, '25
*E. Eldridge Pennock .... 1908, '09, '10
*George B. Evans .... 1909, '10, '11, '12
*Thomas K. Ober .... 1909, '10
*Joseph B. McCall .... 1909, '10, '11, '12
*Frank C. Gillingham .... 1910, '11, '12, '13

*Louis Wagner .... 1910, '11, '12
*William M. Scott 1910
*Louis P. Posey, M.D. .... 1910, '12, '13, '14, '15
*Clarence Bispham Collier .... 1911, '12, '13, '14
*John Gribbel .... 1911, '12, '13
*Harrison Townsend .... 1911, '12, '13
*John Bancroft .... 1911, '12, '13, '14
*William K. Haupt .... 1911, '12, '13, '14
*William J. McClary 1912
*T. Ellis Barnes .... 1912, '13, '14, '17, '18
*Miers Busch .... 1913, '14
*William R. Lyman .... 1913, '14, '17, '18, '19
*Robert P. Hooper .... 1913, '14
*George S. Graham .... 1913, '14, '15, '17
*William T. Elliott .... 1914, '15, '16
*Charles M. Gudknecht .... 1914, '15, '16
*Charles R. Miller .... 1914, '15, '16, '17, '24, '25
*W. Atlee Burpee .... 1914, '15
*Charles A. Porter, Jr. .... 1915, '16, '17, '21, '22, '23, '28, '29, '30
*John D. Johnson 1915
*Alexander W. Wister Jr. .... 1915, '16, '17
*Charles E. Cattell .... 1915, '16, '17, '18
*Horace C. Jones .. 1915, '16, '17, '18, '20, '21, '22, '23, '25, '26, '27
*John T. Riley .... 1917, '18, '19, '21, '22, '23
*Harry T. Stoddart .... 1917, '19, '20, '21, '22
*John L. Clawson .... 1917, '18
*Herman Haupt .... 1917, '18, '19
*Charles S. Calwell 1918
*E. Pusey Passmore 1918
*J. Howell Cummings .... 1918, '19, '20, '21
*George A. Walker .... 1918, '19, '20
*Edwin F. Keen .... 1918, '19, '20
*Samuel M. Clement, Jr. .... 1918, '19, '20
*Joseph W. Cooper .... 1919, '20, '21
*Joseph M. Steele .... 1919, '20, '21, '22
*Francis Murphy Brooks .... 1919, '20
*J. E. Cope Morton .... 1919, '20
*D. L. Anderson .... 1919, '20, '21, '24, '25
*Charles J. Webb .... 1920, '21, '22, '26
*Harry S. Sharp .... 1920, '21, '22, '23
*William G. Price, Jr. .... 1921, '22, '23, May 12, '25
*Melville G. Baker .... 1921, '22, '23, '24
*J. Warner Hutchins .... 1921, '22, '23

*Jonathan Jenks .... 1922, '23, '24
*Edward A. Stockton .... 1922, '23, '24
*Harold B. Beitler .... 1922, '23, '24, '25, '26, '27, '28, '29, '30
*Wm. Henry Smedley .... 1923, '24, '25, '27
*Bayard Henry .... 1923, '24, '25 to Sept. 17, '26
*Edgar G. Cross .... Mar. 13, 1923, '24, '25
*Charles E. Roberts .... 1924, '25, '26
*J. Harry Mull .... 1924, '25, '26
*W. Kirkland Dwier .... 1924, '25, '26
*Robert M. Green, Jr. 1924
*E. Lawrence Fell .... 1925, '26, '27, '28, '29, '30, '31
*Charles P. Vaughan .... 1925, '26, '27
*Walter P. Sharp .... 1925 to Mar. 13, '26
*William J. Montgomery .... 1925, '26
*George Stuart Patterson .... 1925, '26, '27
*William L. Supplee .... 1926, '27
*William H. Folwell .... 1926, '27
*William C. L. Eglin .... 1926, '27 to Feb. 7, '28
*Louis J. Kolb .... 1926, '27, '28
*William H. Kingsley .... Apr. 13, 1926, '27, '28, '29
*Frank M. Hardt .... 1927, '28, '29
*Frank A. Bedford .... 1927, '28
*Charles H. Ewing .... 1927, '28, '29
*Irving L. Wilson .... 1927, '28, '30, '31
*Owen J. Roberts 1928
*Lewis H. Van Dusen .... 1928, '29
*Otto Robert Heiligman .... 1928, '29, '30, '31
*Edward C. Deardon .... 1928, '29, '30
*Ernest T. Trigg .... 1928, '29, '30
*Robert J. Nash .... Mar. 13, 1928, '29
*Frank H. Caven .... 1929, '30, '31
*J. Willison Smith .... 1929, '30, '31, '32, '33
*Jay Gates .... 1929, '30, '31, '32, '33, '34, '35
 David Burpee .... 1929, '30, '31, '32
                 '40, '41, '42, '46, '47, '48, '49, '60, '61, '62
*Thomas Shallcross, Jr. ..... 1929, '30, '31, '32, '33, '34, '35, '36
*J. Howard Pew .... 1930, '31, '32
*Ira Jewell Williams .... 1930, '31, '32, '33, '34
*Charles J. Hepburn .... 1930, '31, '32, '33
*Charles S. Wesley .... 1931, '32
*Albert P. Gerhard .... 1931, '32, '33, '34
*Burton C. Simon 1931
*William P. Beeber 1931

*Herbert J. Tily .... 1932, '33, '34, '35
*Harry S. McDevitt .... 1932, '33, '34
*Franklin R. Maxwell 1932
*Wilmer Krusen, M.D. .... 1932, '33, '34, '35
*Archie D. Swift ..... 1932, '33, '34, '35, '36, '37, '38, '39, '40, '41
*John R. Sproul .... 1932, '33, '34
*Allen M. Stearne .... 1933, '34, '35, '36
John Arthur Brown .... 1933, '34, '35, '36, '38, '39, '40
                    '44, '45, '46, '47, '49, '50, '51, '52, '59, '60, '61, '62
*J. Henry Radey Acker 1933
*George Wharton Pepper .... 1934, '35, '36
*Spencer L. Jones .... 1934, '35, '36, '37
J. Wesley McWilliams .... 1934, '35, '36, '37
*Charles C. Norris, Jr. .... 1934, '35, '36
*Frank van Roden 1935
*John A. Lafore .... 1935, '36
*Charles J. Maxwell .... 1935, '36, '37
*J. Clark Moore, Jr. .... 1935, '36, '37, '38, '39
*Maurice W. Sloan .... 1936, '37, '38
*Franklin S. Edmonds .... 1936, '37, '38
*Charles A. Tyler 1936
*Harry J. Haas .... 1936, '37, '38
*H. P. Liversidge .... 1937, '38, '39
*Theodore J. Grayson .... Dec. 14, 1936 to Dec. 23, '37
*Frank J. Fell, Jr. .... 1937, '40, '41, '44, '45, '46
*William R. Mooney .... 1937, '38, '39, '42, '43
*Joseph F. Stockwell .... 1937, '38, '39
*Arthur E. Pew, Jr. .... 1937, '38, '39
*Thomas M. Scott .... 1937 to Jan. 11, '38
*William A. Schnader .... 1938, '39, '40, '52, '53, '54, '55
*John Blakeley .... 1938, '39, '40, '41, '42, '43, '44, '45, '46
*George H. Elliott .... 1938, '39, '40, '41
*John C. Taylor .... 1938, '39, '40
*J. Grey Emmons .... 1939 to Jan. 9, '40
*Benjamin S. Mechling .... 1939, '40, '41
*Jay V. Hare .... 1939, '40, '41, '42, '43, '44, '45, '46
*Raymond M. Remick .... 1939, '40, '41, '44, '45, '46, '47
*William M. Davison, Jr. .... 1940, '41 to Aug. 11, '42
*William A. Wiedersheim, 2nd .... 1940, '41, '42
*Theodore A. Van Dyke, Jr. .... 1940, '41
*Robert T. McCracken .... Feb. 13, 1940, '41, '42
*Robert S. Gawthrop .... 1941, '42, '43
*Stuart W. Buck .... 1941, '42

*C. Harry Johnson .... 1941, '42, '43
*Thomas K. Ober, Jr. .... 1942, '43
*Thomas Wriggins .... 1942, '43, '44
*Walter D. Fuller .... 1942, '43
Richard P. Brown .... 1942, '43, '46, '47, '48, '49
*H. Birchard Taylor .... 1942, '43, '44
*J. William Hardt .... Aug. 11, 1942, '43, '44
*S. Horace Disston 1943
*Millard D. Brown .... 1943, '44, '45
*Thomas S. Strobhar .... 1943, '44, '45
Gordon A. Hardwick .... 1943, '44, '45
*Philipp E. Lueders .... 1944, '45, '46, '51
*Henry B. Bryans .... 1944, '45
*Ira W. Barnes .... 1944, '45, '46, '47
*Harry F. Richards .... 1944, '45, '46, '47, '48, '49, '50
        '51, '52, '53, '54, '55, '56, '57, '58, '59 to Mar. 20, '60
*William Steele, 3rd 1945
Frank H. Mancill .... 1945, '46, '47, '48
*David B. James, Jr. .... 1945, '46, '47, '48, '50, '51, '52, '53
*C. Brewster Rhoads .... 1946, '47, '48
*L. Alan Passmore .... 1946, '47, '48, '49, '50, '51
*Arthur Littleton .... 1946, '47, '48, '49
*Joseph W. Henderson .... 1947, '48, '49, '50
*D. Webster Bell .... 1947, '48, '49, '50
*Hudson W. Reed .... 1947, '48, '49, '50
*William J. Meinel .... 1947, '48, '49, '50, '51
*Charles E. Kenworthey .... Dec. 8, 1947 to May 11, '48
Revelle W. Brown .... 1948, '49, '50, '51
*Z. Taylor Hall, Jr. .... 1948, '49, '50, '51, '53, '54, '55
*Brenton G. Wallace .... May 11, 1948, '49, '50, '51, '52
*Russell Conwell Cooney 1949
*Frank G. Sayre .... 1949, '50, '51, '52, '53
        '54, '55, '56, '57, '58, '59, '60, '61, '62
*George W. Elkins, Jr. .. 1950, '51, '52, '53, '60, '61, '62, '63, ''64
        to June 5, '65
*O. Howard Wolfe .... 1950, '51
*Charles S. Redding .... 1950, '51, '52
*Roy A. Manwaring .... 1951, '52, '53
*William T. Galey, Jr. .... 1951, '52, '53, '54
James M. Anderson .... 1952, '53, '54
*W. Henry Gillam, Jr. .... 1952, '53, '54, '55
De Haven Develin .... 1952, '53, '54, '56, '57, '58
*G. Harlan Wells, M.D. .... 1952, '53, '54, '55

*Mark E. Lefever .. 1952, '53, '54, '56, '57, '58, '59, '63, '64, '70
'71, '72
Thomas B. McCabe .... 1953, '54, '55, '56
Albert J. Nesbitt .... 1953, '54
Joseph A. Fisher .... 1954, '55, '56 to Sept. 10, '57
*Henry L. Schimpf, Jr. .... 1954, '55, '56, '58, '59, '60
61, '67, '68, '69
Carroll A. Haines .... 1954, '55, '56
Russell P. Heuer .... 1955, '56, '57
*Byron A. Milner .... 1955, '56, '57
*John W. Lord, Jr. .... 1955, '56, '57, '58
*Frank P. Will .... 1955, '56, '57
Samuel E. Fulton .... 1955, '56, '57, '59, '60
*E. Leroy van Roden ...... 1956, '57, '58, '59, '61, '62, '63, '64, '66
'67, '68, '69
George A. Bailey .... 1956, '57, '58, '60, '61, '62
Lewis H. Van Dusen, Jr. .... 1957, '58, '59, '60, '73, '74, '75
John F. E. Hippel .... 1957, '58, '59, '60
J. Permar Richards, Jr. .. 1957, '58, '59, May 10, '60, '61, '62, '63
*Charles E. Dearnley .... 1958, '59, '60, to Aug. 19, '61
J. Grey Emmons, Jr. .... 1958, '59, '60, '61
Benjamin F. Sawin, 3rd .... 1958, '59, '60, '61
Stanley L. Thornton .... 1958, '59, '60, '67, '68, '69, '70, '71
'72, '73, '74, '75
George M. Brodhead . 1959, '60, '61, '62, '63, '64, '65, '66, '67, '68
Robert L. Trescher .... Sept. 13, 1960, '61, '62, '63
Ivan H. Peterman .... 1961, '62, '63, '64
Earl K. Mueller .... 1961, '62, '63, '65, '66, '67, '68, '69, '70
Hal L. Bemis .... 1962, '63, '64, '69, '70, '71, '72
Anthony H. Whitaker .... 1962, '63, '64, '65
George M. Ewing, Jr. .... 1962, '63, '64, '65
Ignatius J. Horstmann, 2nd .... 1962, '63, '64, '65, '68, '69
'70, '74, '75
Rolland A. Ritter .... 1963, '64, '66, '71, '72, '73
Norman J. Greene .... 1963, '64, '65, '66
Walter A. Schmidt .... 1963, '64, '65, '66
E. John Hesketh .... 1964, '65, '66
*Earl R. Yeomans .... 1964, '65, '66, '67
J. Victor O'Brien .... 1964, '65, '66, '67, '69, '70, '71
C. Brewster Rhoads, Jr. ....1965, '66, '67, '68, '70, '71, '72
Robert E. Fulton .... 1965, '66, '67, '69, '70, '71
*John S. Peake .... 1965, '66, '67, '68
*E. Paul Gangewere .... 1965, '66, '67, '68, '69

EDWARD J. DWYER .... July 13, 1965, '66, '67, '68
JOHN R. WANAMAKER .... 1966, '67, '68, '69, '71, '72, '73
DAVID F. MAXWELL .... 1967, '68
*WILLIAM V. GRIER .... 1967, '68, '69, '70
BURTON H. ETHERINGTON, JR. .... 1968, '69, '70
GEORGE S. MEINEL .... 1968, '69, '70, '71, '73, '74, '75
JOHN J. HERD .... 1969, '70, '71, '73, '74, '75
WILLIAM B. CARR .... 1969, '70, '71, '72 to Nov. 1, '73
RICHARD C. BOND .... 1970, '71, '72
MAURICE A. WEBSTER, JR. .... 1970, '71, '72, '73, '74, '75
HAROLD F. STILL, JR. .... 1971, '72, '73, '75
H. WOODWARD MCDOWELL .... 1971, '72, '73
WILLIAM J. MCCARTER .... 1972, '73, '74
ROBERT G. WILDER .... 1972, '73, '74
NELSON G. HARRIS .... 1972, '73, '74
F. BRUCE BALDWIN, JR. .... 1972 to June 12, '73
PERRIN C. HAMILTON .... 1973, '74, '75
HAROLD M. MYERS .... June 12, 1973, '74, '75
HARRY C. ZUG .... 1974, '75
SAMUEL H. BALLAM, JR. .... 1974, '75
CHARLES K. COX .... 1974, '75
LLOYD E. LONG .... 1974, '75
HOWARD S. ROBERTS, JR. 1975
LOUIS T. KLAUDER 1975

Recipients of The Gold Medal of The Union League of Philadelphia

ABRAHAM LINCOLN 1863

*WILLIAM M. MEREDITH (League member) 1864

ANDREW JOHNSON 1865

MAJOR GENERAL GEORGE G. MEADE 1866

LINDLEY SMYTH (League member) 1868

JOSEPH B. TOWNSEND (League member) 1879

EDWARD C. KNIGHT (League member) 1879

GEORGE H. BOKER (League member) 1880

JAMES L. CLAGHORN (League member) 1883

EDWIN N. BENSON (League member) 1889

SAMUEL B. HUEY (League member) 1889

EDWIN H. FITLER (League member) 1893

REAR ADMIRAL A. E. K. BENHAM 1894

GEORGE P. MORGAN (League member) 1911

ELIHU ROOT 1915

*CALVIN COOLIDGE 1927

*GENERAL JOHN J. PERSHING 1928

FRANK VAN RODEN (League member) 1939

THOMAS SOVEREIGN GATES (League member) 1948

MAJOR GENERAL WILLIAM G. PRICE, JR. (League member) ... 1954

*GENERAL DWIGHT D. EISENHOWER 1962

GENERAL WILLIAM G. WESTMORELAND 1969

BOB HOPE 1972

*EUGENE ORMANDY 1974

*Gold Medal and Honorary Membership

Abbreviations in Notes

ARULP   Annual Report, Union League of Philadelphia

DAB   Dictionary of American Biography

HSP   Historical Society of Pennsylvania

MBBD   Minute Book, Board of Directors

MBBP   Minute Book, Board of Publication

MBGM   Minute Book, General Meetings

Pa. Mag.   Pennsylvania Magazine of History and Biography

PD   Publication Distribution Records

ULA   Union League Archives

Illustrations

All of the illustrations used in this book are from the pictorial archives of The Union League of Philadelphia.

Notes

Chapter I   The First Crisis

1 The Original Constitution and List of Members of the First Republican Club, Formed in the City of Philadelphia (Philadelphia, 1856). MS., *ULA*. A copy of the first platform of the Republican Party is included in this document.

2 William Rotch Wister (1827-1911), admitted to the League in Jan., 1863, was the author of *Some Reminiscences of Cricket in Philadelphia before 1861* (Philadelphia, 1904). At the time of his death he was the senior member of the League. John W. Jordan, *Encyclopedia of Pennsylvania Biography*, II (New York, 1914), 633-634.

3 Hector Tyndale (1821-1880) did not become a member of the League until 1865, after he was discharged from service with the rank of Brevet-Major General, U.S. Volunteers. Frank H. Taylor, *Philadelphia in the Civil War, 1861-1865* (Philadelphia, 1913), 293; *DAB*, XIX (New York, 1936), 100; *Chronicle of The Union League of Philadelphia, 1862-1902* (Philadelphia, 1902), 408; 519; and [John McLaughlin], *A Memoir of Hector Tyndale* (Philadelphia, 1882), 7-8.

4 Joseph Reese Fry (1812-1865), lawyer, banker, author and librettist, became a member of the League on Jan. 16, 1863. *Chronicle*, 414, 485; and Francis S. Drake, *Dictionary of American Biography* . . . (Boston, 1872), 344. *University of Pennsylvania Biographical Catalogue of the Matriculates of the College* . . . *1749-1893* (Philadelphia, 1894), 81.

5 Charles Gibbons (1814-1884) entered the law offices of Charles Chauncey and began practice in 1838. In 1844 he received the Whig nomination for state senator, was elected, and served, for three years. *North American*, Aug. 15, 1844. He was related to Edward M. Davis, Lucretia Mott's son-in-law: see note 17, *infra*, and Appendix.

6 William D. Kelley (1814-1890) was a "radical" Democrat, judge of the Court of Common Pleas for Philadelphia and a delegate to the Republican National Convention in Chicago in 1860. He was a Republican representative in Congress from 1861 to the time of his death. Ira V. Brown, "William D. Kelley and Radical Reconstruction," *Pa. Mag.*, LXXXV (1961), 316-329.

7 See note 1, *supra*. The 51 men whose names appear in the *Original Constitution . . . Republican Club*, are published in *Officers and Members of The Union League of Philadelphia, October 1st, 1863* (Philadelphia, 1863).

8 Henry C. Carey (1793-1879) is regarded as the founder of the American school of political economy. For Carey's participation in the state convention, see J. Thomas Scharf and Thompson Westcott, *History of Philadelphia. 1609-1884*, I (Philadelphia, 1884), 722.

9 Morton McMichael (1807-1879) left the Democratic Party out of disagreement with its low tariff policy. Howard Gillette, Jr., *Corrupt and Contented: Philadelphia's Political Machine, 1865-1887* (Ann Arbor, Mich., 1971), 18, unpublished doctoral dissertation.

10 William M. Meredith (1799-1873). *DAB*, XII (New York, 1933), 548-549; *Chronicle*, 502 for his admission to the League on Jan. 26, 1863.

11 William B. Thomas (1811-1887), Philadelphia's first Republican candidate for mayor, was a flour manufacturer, an early League member, and an officer in the Union army. Scharf and Westcott, *op. cit.*, 1, 720-721; William Dusinberre, *Civil War Issues in Philadelphia, 1856-1865* (Philadelphia, 1865-) 98-99, and Taylor, *op. cit.*, 219-247, 277. Stephen N. Winslow, *Biographies of Successful Philadelphia Merchants* (Philadelphia, 1864), 75-86.

12 Scharf and Westcott, *op. cit.*, I, 722.

13 Stanton Ling Davis, *Pennsylvania Politics, 1860-1863* (Cleveland, 1935), 38, unpublished hectograph edition.

14 John Paul Verree (1817-1889) an iron manufacturer, had been a Know-Nothing member of the select council of Philadelphia from 1851-57 and a Fillmore supporter. He was elected as a Republican to the Thirty-sixth and Thirty-seventh Congresses, 1859-1863. Scharf and Westcott, *op. cit.*, I, 721: *Biographical Directory of the American Congress, 1774-1971* (Washington, D.C., 1971), 1857.

15 R. McKinley Ormsby, *A History of the Whig Party or some of its Main Features* (Boston, 1859), 355-363, and Henry R. Mueller, *The Whig Party in Pennsylvania* (New York, 1922), 229-234.

16 Raymond M. Bell and Frank R. Baird, "James Nixon and Thomas Milhous," *Pa. Genealogical Magazine* XXVIII (1974), 30, *passim. Constitution . . . Republican Club, op. cit.*, unnumbered, lists Will P. Nixon; *Young Republicans of Philadelphia, Minute Book,* (Apr. 1, 1891), 2, *passim.*

17 James Miller McKim (1810-1874) was born in Carlisle, Pa. In 1837 he was ordained in the Presbyterian Church. He succeeded John G. Whittier as editor of the *Pennsylvania Freeman* and was closely associated with Lucretia Mott. Her son-in-law, Edward M. Davis, also was related to Charles Gibbons. All were staunch abolitionists. *In Memoriam Sarah A. McKim, 1813-1891* (New York, 1891), 10-22; Anna D. Hallowell, *James and Lucretia Mott: Life and Letters* (Boston, 1884), 130; for McKim-Gibbons correspondence see James M. McPherson, *The Struggle for Equality: Abolitionists and the Negro in the Civil War and Reconstruction* (Princeton, N.J., 1964), 207, note 43.

18 *A Testimonial of Gratitude and Affection to Henry Clay* (Philadelphia, 1845), unnumbered.

19 Scharf and Westcott, *op. cit.*, I, 731.

20 *In Memoriam Sarah A. McKim*, 12.

21 *Speech of Hon. Charles Gibbons, delivered at National Hall, Philadelphia, October 5th, 1860* (Philadelphia, 1860). The speech first appeared in the *North American*, Oct. 8, 1860.

22 Davis, *op. cit.*, 58, and Alexander K. McClure, *Old Time Notes of Pennsylvania*, I (Philadelphia, 1905), 387, 390.

23 A comparative examination of the members of the cultural and scientific societies in Philadelphia prior to the Civil War shows the same family names on their lists as those that appear on the rolls of the city's clubs.

24 Anne H. Wharton, "The Philadelphia Wistar Parties." Unidentified article in the archives of the War Library of the Military Order of the Loyal Legion. In the official history, *Sketch of the Wistar Party of Philadelphia* (Philadelphia, 1898), 13, its author writes, "The suspended condition of the Wistar Party left a notable gap in the social activity of Philadelphia, and an effort was made to fill it by the organization in 1862 of the Union League."

25 *A History of the Schuylkill Fishing Company of the State in Schuylkill, 1732-1888* (Philadelphia, 1889), 212-215.

26 [Owen Wister], *The Philadelphia Club, 1834-1934* (Philadelphia, 1934).

27 Wharton, *op. cit.*, 987.

28 Kenneth M. Stampp, *And the War Came, The North and the Secession Crisis, 1860-1861* (Ann Arbor, Mich., 1950), 123-125, discusses the impact of secession on the economic relationship between North and South.

29 See Nicholas B. Wainwright (ed.), *A Philadelphia Perspective. The Diary of Sidney George Fisher Covering the Years 1834-1871* (Philadelphia, 1967), 563, for genealogical data on the Ingersoll family; see *Chronicle*, 42, for Meigs.

30 Wister, *op. cit.*, 38.

31 John Campbell (1810-1874) is described in W. Brotherhead, *Forty Years Among the Old Booksellers of Philadelphia* (Philadelphia, 1891), 36-41. A filiopietistic account is provided by his grandson *One Hundredth Anniversary Catalogue of Scarce and Interesting Books* (Philadelphia, 1950), 1-2. For his Chartist background, see Mark Hovell, *The Chartist Movement* (Manchester, 1918), 199, 261.

32 Wainwright, *op. cit.*, 391, 399, and 402.

33 Dusinberre, *op. cit.*, 35.

34 Davis, *op. cit.*, 128; Dusinberre, *op. cit.*, 98.

35 The Philadelphia returns showed that Lincoln received 39,233 votes, the combined Breckenridge and Douglas tickets 30,053 votes, and the Bell ticket received 7,131. Lincoln had a majority of 2,000. Scharf and Westcott, *op. cit.*, I, 734.

36 Wainwright, *op. cit.*, 401.

37 *Public Ledger,* Dec. 14, 1860, in which issue all three speeches are reported.

38 Joseph R. Ingersoll, *Secession as a Folly and a Crime* (Philadelphia, 1861); *Chronicle,* 400.

39 *Public Ledger,* Dec. 14, 1860.

40 Stampp, *op. cit.,* 49, 53, is the first historian to cite the evidence of Woodward's private views which he expressed to Jeremiah S. Black, Nov. 18, 1860.

41 Charles Gilpin (1809-1874) was mayor of Philadelphia before the consolidation of the city in 1854. He signed the League Articles of Association, Jan. 8, 1863. *Chronicle,* 486; Jordan, *Encyclopedia,* VI (New York, 1916), 1963.

42 Daniel Dougherty (1826-1892) was an active Democrat before the war. For a report of the meeting, see Scharf and Westcott, *op. cit.,* I, 741-742. *Appletons' Cyclopaedia of American Biography,* II (New York, 1887), 210-211. By 1880 he was again in the Democratic Party and delivered the speech nominating General W. S. Hancock for president at the Democratic convention. See tribute to him by League member J. R. Young in the Washington, D.C., *Evening Star,* Sept. 17, 1892.

43 George Parsons Lathrop, *History of The Union League of Philadelphia* (Philadelphia, 1884), 12-13; Scharf and Westcott, *op. cit.,* I, 746-747.

44 Roy P. Basler (ed.) *Collected Works of Abraham Lincoln,* IV (New Brunswick, N.J., 1953), 266. The full text reads: "In doing this there needs to be no bloodshed or violence; and there shall be none, unless it is forced upon the national authority."

45 *The Palmetto Flag* appeared on Mar. 30, Apr. 6, and Apr. 13, 1861. The first and third issues are at the Historical Society of Pennsylvania and the second issue is in the American Antiquarian Society. They are all rare.

46 *Ibid.*

47 *North American,* Apr. 16, 1861.

48 In *ex parte Merryman,* Fed. Cases No. 9487, a United States Circuit Court ruled with Chief Justice Taney filing an opinion that the Executive lacked the power to suspend the writ, stating that this power belonged to the Congress. Lincoln ignored this ruling, but later Congress authorized suspension of the writ.

49 Horace Binney (1780-1875) the elder was not a member of The Union League but an ardent supporter of its programs: See note 54, *infra.*

50 See Wainwright, *op. cit.,* 562, for Fisher.

51 *Ibid.,* 401.

52 George Henry Boker (1824-1890): see Edward Sculley Bradley, *George Henry Boker, Poet and Patriot* (Philadelphia, 1927).

53 Wainwright, *op. cit.*, 401.

54 Horace Binney, *The Privilege of the Writ of Habeas Corpus* (Philadelphia, 1862). The preface is dated Dec. 23, 1861.

55 Dusinberre, *op. cit.*, 130.

56 See note 31, *supra*. John Campbell, *Negromania* (Philadelphia, 1859). Curiously, one of the editions of Binney's pamphlet was published by Campbell.

57 Henry B. Ashmead (1834-1904) published 37 of the 102 Civil War pamphlets issued by the Board of Publication. See *Chronicle*, 468, for his admission to the League on March 28, 1863. At the time of his death Ashmead's printing establishment was the oldest in Philadelphia.

58 Joshua Ballinger Lippincott (1816-1886) was one of the most important publishers of the literature of social and political science in the nineteenth century. Lathrop, *op. cit.*, 30, states that Lippincott signed the Articles of Association while he was in the midst of a typhoid fever siege.

59 Robert P. King and Alexander Baird, under the imprint of King and Baird, published twenty-two pamphlets for the Board of Publication. King became a member of the League Mar. 3, 1863; *Chronicle*, 496.

60 See Edward Sculley Bradley, *Henry Charles Lea* (Philadelphia, 1931), 82-85, for background of Lea's involvement in publishing.

61 See note 45 *supra* for *The Palmetto Flag;* also the detailed account provided by Scharf and Westcott, *op. cit.*, I, 753. On Aug. 22, 1861, the type fonts of the *Christian Observer* were seized and all copies of the paper confiscated by a Federal marshal at the direction of President Lincoln.

62 On Jan. 27, 1863, Albert Boileau, editor of the *Evening Journal* was arrested and his paper suspended. Nicholas B. Wainwright, "The Loyal Opposition in Civil War Philadelphia," *Pa. Mag.*, LXXXVIII (1964), 300.

63 John Wien Forney (1817-1881) was a devout supporter of Buchanan until 1857, when for reasons of personal distrust he broke with the president and drifted into the Republican camp. His career as a journalist was outstanding but his political career was unstable. He returned to the Democratic fold in 1878. *DAB*, VI (New York, 1931), 526-527; Elwyn Burns Robinson, "The Press: President Lincoln's Philadelphia Organ," *Pa. Mag.*, LXV (1941), 157-170.

64 John Russell Young (1840-1899) came into the employ of Forney at the time that the senior editor separated from the Democrats and was launched on a distinguished career in journalism. May D. Russell Young, (ed.) *Men and Memories, Personal Reminiscences* I (New York, 1901), xiii, 2-6; *ARULP* (Philadelphia, 1899), 65-66.

65 Louis Antoine Godey (1804-1878). *DAB*, VII (New York, 1931), 133-134, states that he took no part in political life, but to the contrary he was an active Republican and worked closely with Morton McMichael whose friend he was.

66 Charles Jacobs Peterson (1819-1887) was a founder of the publishing house of T. B. Peterson & Brothers. *Peterson's Magazine* reached the largest national circulation of any journal in its time. *Chronicle*, 507, for his admission to the League, Jan. 8, 1863.

67 Gibson Peacock (1822-1893) became associated with the *Daily Evening Bulletin* toward the end of 1859 when Alexander Cummings was editor, and entered into partnership under the name of Cummings and Peacock. Both were members of the League. *A Checklist of Pennsylvania Newspapers* I (Harrisburg, 1944), 58; *Chronicle*, 479 and 507.

68 *Fast Day Sermons: or the Pulpit on the State of the Country* (New York, 1861). George Harmon, "The Northern Clergy and the Impending Crisis," *Pa. Mag.*, LXV (1941), 171-201. Chester F. Dunham, *The Attitude of the Northern Clergy Toward the South, 1860-1865* (Toledo, Ohio, 1942).

69 *An Authentic Exposition of the "K.G.C." "Knights of the Golden Circle"; or, A History of Secession from 1834 to 1861* (Indianapolis, Ind., 1861) is the fullest contemporary account of this society.

70 Charles Ingersoll, *Letter to a Friend in a Slave State* (Philadelphia, 1862) and *The South: A Letter from a Friend in the North. With Special Reference to the Effects of Disunion Upon Slavery* (Philadelphia, 1856). The latter pamphlet was published anonymously and is not usually noted in the Ingersoll literature.

71 Charles Janeway Stillé (1819-1899) studied law under Joseph R. Ingersoll (see note 29, *supra*), took a leading part in the U.S. Sanitary Commission, and was the author of numerous pamphlets and books on American history. His widely circulated pamphlet, *How a Free People Conduct a Long War* (Philadelphia, 1862), evoked a favorable response from Lincoln; see Joseph George, Jr., "Charles J. Stillé, 'Angel of Consolation,'" *Pa. Mag.*, LXXXV (1961), 306-308; William Quentin Maxwell, *Lincoln's Fifth Wheel: The Political History of the United States Sanitary Commission* (New York, 1956), 345, and other references to Stillé. *Chronicle*, 516, for Stillé's admission to the League, May 8, 1863.

72 M. Russell Thayer, *A Reply to Mr. Charles Ingersoll's "Letter to a Friend in a Slave State"* (Philadelphia, 1862). *Chronicle*, 517, for Thayer's admission to the League, Feb. 23, 1863.

73 Lathrop, *op. cit.*, 20.

74 Taylor, *op. cit.*, 14; Scharf and Westcott *op. cit.*, I, 763-764.

75 Wister, *op. cit.*, 41, and Wood Gray, *The Hidden Civil War, The Story of the Copperheads* (New York, 1942), 213.

76 [George H. Boker], *Proceedings of a Meeting of The Union Club of Phila-delphia* . . . (Philadelphia, 1871), 10-11.

77 Unsigned, undated document, MS., *ULA.*

78 Boker, *Proceedings,* 13-14.

79 *Ibid.,* 18, 25.

80 *Ibid.,* 19, 20.

81 Lathrop, *op. cit.,* 31.

Chapter II   A Wave of Strength

1 Chronicle, 303; Boker, *Proceedings,* 4.

2 Stephen Colwell (1800-1871). Henry C. Carey, *A Memoir of Stephen Col-well: Read before the American Philosophical Society, Friday, November 17, 1871* (Philadelphia, 1872). A useful bibliography of Colwell is at the end of the memoir.

3 *Evening Star,* Sep. 17, 1892, contains a description of the controversy on the founding of the League by John Russell Young. It was reprinted in the *Chronicle,* 45-50, and later included in Young, *Men and Memories, op. cit.,* 42-47. For Charles J. Biddle. see Nicholas B. Wainwright, "The Loyal Op-position in the Civil War," *Pa. Mag.,* LXXXVIII (1964), 306-307.

4 The draft Articles are in the *ULA.*

5 *Articles of Association and By-Laws of The Union League of Philadelphia.* Organized December 27, 1862 (Philadelphia, 1863), 3-4.

6 *Union League of Philadelphia* (Philadelphia, Dec. 27, 1862), folio circular listing names of the original members of the League. A marked copy in *ULA* lists all those who were Republicans and Democrats, and was prepared by Edward S. Mawson. For Mawson, see Henry S. Morais, *The Jews of Phila-delphia* . . . (Philadelphia, 1894), 64.

7 Boker, *Proceedings,* 39-40.

8 William H. Ashhurst (1815-1887) and James Lawrence Claghorn (1817-1884) rented the Kuhn mansion, which was opened for use on Feb. 23, 1863. It was later occupied by Matthias W. Baldwin and razed in 1901: see *North American,* July 7, 1901. The Philadelphia *Press,* Feb. 24, Mar. 12, 16, 1863, describes the activities in the League quarters. For biographical data on Ashhurst and Claghorn, refer to Appendix.

9 *MBGM*, Mar. 5, 1863 for gifts of trophies and in particular the presentation of General Philip Kearney's battle flag. On Jan. 9, 1863, Ferdinand J. Dreer obtained on loan from Thomas Sully his equestrian portrait of Washington. It was purchased toward the end of the year. See Ferdinard J. Dreer to the Board, Oct. 14, 1863, and letter of Sully, Feb. 10, 1863: *ULA*.

10 Ashhurst's relatives are listed in *Chronicle*, 463. John B. Myers (1804-1864) was an original member of the Union Club and a vice-president at the time of his death on Sep. 29. Adolph E. Borie (1809-1880), also an original Union Club member, was Grant's first secretary of the navy. See Appendix for other details. For the sons of Horace Binney, Jr., see Charles C. Binney, *Life of Horace Binney* (Philadelphia, 1903), 373.

11 George H. Boker, *The Purposes for which The Union League of Philadelphia was founded* . . . (Philadelphia, 1863), circular, three pages. Henry W. Bellows, *Historical Sketch of the Union League Club of New York: Its Origin, Organization and Work, 1863-1879* (New York, 1879), 13, 19, 30, 35. The New York Club was proposed to be an "elite of the elite."

12 Benjamin Gerhard (1810-1864), an attorney, was the first member of The Union Club to die. John Hill Martin, *Martin's Bench and Bar of Philadelphia* (Philadelphia, 1883), 271, and Daniel R. Goodwin, *Southern Slavery in its Present Aspects: Containing a Reply to a late work of the Bishop of Vermont on Slavery.* (Philadelphia, 1864), iii. See Appendix.

13 The first printed announcement of the Board of Publication appeared on a single sheet in Feb. 1863. Ninety-six members subscribed $250 each to its work, according to the manuscript list attached to a retained copy of the circular.

14 Frank Freidel, *Union Pamphlets of the Civil War* I (Boston, 1967), 4-8, *passim*, provides a similar analysis. The recent discovery of the *MBBP*, and a volume of the distribution records present new bibliographical data on this subject.

15 *PD*, a manuscript volume, possibly one of four, covers the areas of distribution and the recipients of League literature from Feb. to Aug., 1863.

16 *List of Pamphlets Distributed by the Board of Publication of The Union League of Philadelphia* (Philadelphia, 1866) lists 15 German pamphlets published between May, 1863 and Oct. 1864. This does not include circulars in German for which no record is found.

17 *The Irish Patriot. Daniel O'Connell's Legacy to Irish Americans* (Philadelphia, 1863) is typical of this literature.

18 *MBBP*, Mar. 5; Mar. 26, 1863.

19 Lindley Smyth (1816-1898). See Chapter IV, note 25, for other details.

20 A useful comparison for the study of American intellectual forces is George M. Fredrickson, *The Inner Civil War, Northern Intellectuals and the Crisis of the Union* (New York, 1965), which not only fails to mention the work of the Philadelphia Union League, but limits the Philadelphia Union League "intellectuals" to Horace Binney, Jr. and to Charles J. Stillé. His book should have been subtitled "New England and New York Intellectuals . . ."

21 Thomas Webster (1818-1895) submitted Whiting's pamphlet at the suggestion of Edward M. Davis on Feb. 26, 1863. Webster became chairman of the Philadelphia Supervisory Committee for Recruiting Colored Troops.

22 William Whiting (1813-1873), solicitor of the War Department from 1863 to 1865, first published *The War Powers of the President . . .* (Boston, 1862). It was revised and enlarged as conditions of the war and Reconstruction demanded and it grew from a work of 143 pages to a volume of 695 pages when it reached a forty-third edition in 1871.

23 Matthew Huizinga Messchert (1808-1871) was the first secretary of the Board of Publication. See *Chronicle*, 502, for his admission to The Union League, Jan. 28, 1863.

24 See note 71 chap. I.

25 *MBBP*, Mar. 5, 1863.

26 Charles Summerfield Porter (1804-1870) came to Philadelphia from Boston in the spring of 1863 and delivered this sermon, *A Fast Implies a Duty* on April 30, at the Arch Street Presbyterian Church. William Stewart Bell (1818-1903) delivered his sermon *The Nation's Sins and the Nation's Duty* in Pottstown, Pa., on the same day which was a national fast day.

27 *MBBP*, Apr. 23, 1863, for the acceptance of Stillé's second pamphlet. Several lines from pages 42-44 of the first edition were deleted to meet the Board's views on emancipation. These variant editions are unnoted.

28 *Ibid.*, May 28, 1863. The resolution was rescinded June 11.

29 *The African Slave Trade. The Secret Purpose of the Insurgents to Revive it. No treaty stipulations against the slave trade to be entered into with the European Powers. Judah P. Benjamin's intercepted instructions to L.Q.C. Lamar, styled commissioner, etc.* (Philadelphia, 1863). *MBBP*, Apr. 9, 1863.

30 *MBBP*, Mar. 26 and Apr. 9, 1863.

31 *Ibid.*, May 14, 1863.

32 Herman Bokum, *The Testimony of a Refugee from East Tennessee* (Philadelphia, 1863) and *Das Zeugniss eines Flüchtlings von Ost-Tennessee* (Philadelphia, 1863). Frederick A. P. Barnard, *Letter to the President of the United States, by a Refugee* (Philadelphia, 1863) first appeared in the N. Y. *Daily Tribune*, Jan. 21, 1863. It was approved for publication on Mar. 26, 1863. Barnard later became president of Columbia College.

33 *MBBP*, Mar. 26, 1863, where the publication responsibilities are spelled out.

34 Phillip S. Paludan, "The American Civil War Considered as a Crisis in Law and Order," *The American Historical Review*, 77, (1972), 1021.

35 *Chronicle*, 63, for Montgomery Blair.

36 *PD*, Feb. 28, 1863, records the first day of pamphlet distribution. Among others, George Templeton Strong, a prime mover in the founding of the New York Union League and of the Loyal Publication Society, was sent 600 copies; Charles Eliot Norton of Cambridge, Mass., was sent 500 copies.

37 Nathaniel Borodaille Browne (1819-1875) delivered his *Address before the Union League in the 24th Ward, Philadelphia*, at its opening celebration, May 9, 1863 . . . (Philadelphia, 1863). See *Chronicle*, 474, for his admission to the League on Jan. 22, 1863.

38 Leonard Myers (1827-1905) contributed to the assassination literature in *Abraham Lincoln. A Memorial Address Delivered . . . June 15, 1865, before The Union League of the Thirteenth Ward* (Philadelphia, 1865). See *Biographical Directory of the American Congress 1774-1971* (Washington, 1971), 1460, for his record in Congress.

39 *PD*, May 1, 1863; Davis was the agent for Cheltenham Township, Montgomery County, Pa.

40 *Ibid.*, Apr. 13, 1863 to Thomas Allibone, Pemberton, N. J.; May 7, 1863, to Joseph Leclere, Burlington, N. J.; May 18, 1863, to Jacob L. Rowand, Haddonfield, N. J.; May 29, 1863 to Charles Gibbons while on a visit to Salem, N. J., *passim*.

41 Pennsylvania Leagues also were located in York, Montrose, Doylestown, Bethlehem, West Middletown, Washington, Waterford, Erie, Hollidaysburg, Darlington, and Rochester Station in Beaver County, Pittsburgh, Holmesburg, Bellefonte, New Castle, Danville, Lebanon, Northumberland, and Lewisburg.

42 S. H. Parker to George H. Boker, San Francisco, Calif., July 9, 1863.

43 *PD*, Apr. 24, 1863, to L. A. Dembitz, Louisville, Ky. Alpheus Thomas Mason, *Brandeis, A Free Man's Life* (New York, 1946), 23-24.

44 *Ibid.*, June 6, 1863, to Owen Lovejoy, Princeton, Ill.

45 *Ibid.*, Mar. 17, 24; Apr. 13, 23; June 11, 1863, for Dorothea L. Dix.

46 *Ibid.*, Mar. 21; Apr. 7, 11, 15; May 12, 1863, for list of pamphlets sent to Gov. O. P. Morton of Indiana.

47 *MBBP*, Mar. 19, 1863 for Gov. Cannon of Delaware.

48 *Ibid.*, May 19; May 30, and June 3, 1863, for distribution of pamphlets to the Presbyterian clergy, and May 29, 1863, for distribution of pamphlets to the "Episcopal Convention." Chester F. Dunham, *The Attitude of the Northern Clergy Toward the South, 1860-1865* (Toledo, Ohio 1942), makes no reference to the winning of the clergy to the cause of the Union.

49 Erastus Corning, *President Lincoln's Views. An Important Letter on the Principles Involved in the Vallandigham Case.* . . . (Philadelphia, 1863). *PD,* June 19, 1863, for the approval of its publication in an edition not to exceed 100,000 copies.

50 Davis, *op. cit.,* 301, *passim.*

51 Andrew G. Curtin to Thomas Webster, Hbg., June 15, 1863 ALS, HSP.

52 Extracts from *Ferd. J. Dreer's 1863 Journal,* MS in Dreer's hand. *ULA.*

53 John Edgar Thomson (1808-1874) became a member of the League, Mar. 13, 1863, see *Chronicle,* 518.

54 George H. Crossman (1808-1882) was elected to membership in the League, June 10, 1869; see *Chronicle,* 479. Crossman was Quartermaster at the Depot and Office of Army Clothing and Equipage, at the Schuylkill Arsenal, Phila., Pa.

55 Bradley, *Henry Charles Lea,* 97-98.

56 *Ibid.,* 104-105. Scharf and Westcott, *op. cit.,* III, 808.

57 Taylor, *op. cit.,* 250, for the First Union League Regiment, or 45th Regiment Infantry, Ninety-Day Militia. Recruiting details are in the unpublished *Proceedings of the Military Committee of the Union League: 1863-1865, ULA.*

58 *Union League House* (July 6, 1863), Circular. Joseph R. Fry was in charge of the Military Committee until his death on July 5, 1865. He was succeeded by James H. Orne as chairman.

59 *ARULP* (Philadelphia, 1865), 21-22, for an accurate summary of the military affairs of the League.

60 Alfred M. Green, *Letters and Discussion on the Formation of Colored Regiments and the Duty of the Colored People in regard to the Great Slaveholders' Rebellion in the United States of America* (Philadelphia, 1862). Luis F. Emilio, *History of the Fifty-Fourth Regiment of Massachusetts Volunteer Infantry, 1863-1865* (Boston, 1891), 344-349.

61 George H. Boker, *The Black Regiment* (June, 1863), which appeared originally under the title *The Second Louisiana* on May 27, 1863. William D. Kelley, *The Conscription. Also Speeches of the Hon. W. D. Kelley, of Pennsylvania in the House of Representatives, on the Conscription; the Way to Attain and Secure Peace; and on Arming the Negroes, with a Letter from Secretary Chase* (Philadelphia, 1863). See note 64, *infra.*

62 *MBGM,* June 8, 1863.

63 Thomas Webster (and others) to Edwin M. Stanton, Philadelphia, June 10, 1863; Edwin M. Stanton to Thomas Webster, Washington, June 17, 1863, published in Lathrop, *op. cit.,* 151-152.

64 *Addresses of the Hon. W. D. Kelley, Miss Anna E. Dickinson, and Mr. Frederick Douglass, At a Mass Meeting, held at National Hall, Philadelphia, July 6, 1863, for the Promotion of Colored Enlistments* (Philadelphia, 1863), 1-2.

65 Lathrop, *op. cit.*, 75-81, provides the first account of the movement to enlist black troops by the League.

66 *Free Military School, for applicants for commands of Colored Troops, No. 1210 Chestnut Street, Philadelphia. Established by the Supervisory Committee for Recruiting Colored Regiments* (Philadelphia, 1863), final outside wrapper for a partial list of League members who belonged to the committee. *ARULP* (Philadelphia, 1906), 4-5, contains a praiseworthy report of Barker's activities in organizing black regiments.

67 *Philadelphia Supervisory Committee for Recruiting Negro Troops.* Undated broadside. For Colonel John H. Taggart, see Taylor, *op. cit.*, 74. In addition to the Chestnut Street recruiting station, according to the *Chronicle*, 305, another was located at Seventh and Emeline Streets in South Philadelphia.

68 *The Age*, Apr. 1, 3, 9, 10, and *passim*, showed its hostility even before the troops were officially organized.

69 *Negro History: 1553-1903. An Exhibition of Books, Prints, and Manuscripts from the Shelves of The Library Company of Philadelphia and The Historical Society of Pennsylvania* (Philadelphia, 1969), pictorial inserts, unnumbered.

70 The history of Camp William Penn is still unwritten. Land on which the barracks were built belonged to League members Edward M. Davis, Morris L. Hallowell, Frederick Fraley, and others; see S. F. Hotchkin, *The York Road, Old and New* (Philadelphia, 1892), 107.

71 Cheesman A. Herrick, *General Louis Wagner, An Appreciation* (Philadelphia, 1928). Taylor, *op. cit.*, 106, 187, 325.

72 *United States Infantry Tactics . . . for the Use of Colored Troops of the United States Infantry* (Washington, D. C., 1863).

73 Details of the organization of black regiments can be found in Taylor, *op. cit.*, 189-195. Lathrop, *op. cit.*, 78-80, and Samuel P. Bates, *History of Pennsylvania Volunteers, 1861-1865; prepared in compliance with acts of the Legislature*, V (Harrisburg, 1871), 925-1137, is still the only detailed account of the black troops trained at Camp William Penn.

74 *Chronicle*, 305-306.

75 Taylor, *op. cit.*, 190.

76 George H. Boker, *Union League House . . . The Union League has appointed a committee of its members for the purpose of obtaining employment for disabled Soldiers and Seamen who have honorably retired from the service of their country* (June 1st, 1863).

77 *ARULP* (1863), 9, for this and similar activities.

78 Mrs. Mary Rose Smith [a black woman] to George H. Boker, Phila., undated, 1863, and G. H. Crossman to George H. Boker, Phila., Nov. 30, 1863. The Crossman letter only is printed in *Chronicle*, 113-114. The record of visitation to blacks, Irish, and others is incomplete, but those recorded from Jan. 18, 1866 to Mar. 28, 1866 have survived. In these three months the League provided for 548 needy women.

79 *MBGM*, 16, 1863, for the first statement on this or any other election.

80 George McDowell Stroud (1795-1875) was the author of *A Sketch of the Laws Relating to Slavery* (Philadelphia, 1827). A revised and enlarged edition appeared in 1856. *MBBP*, Aug. 18, 1863 for the election of Lea to the Board of Publication, and *MBBP*, June 26, 1863 for *the Army and Navy Journal*.

81 William Elder (1806-1885), a physician, abolitionist and economist, wrote for the League, *The Debt and Resources of the United States* (Philadelphia, 1863), and Lorin Blodget (1823-1901), an editorial writer for McMichael's *North American*, wrote *The Commercial and Financial Strength of the United States as shown in the Balance of Foreign Trade and the Increased Production of Staple Articles* (Philadelphia, 1864). Both were early League members.

82 Ellis Yarnall (1817-1905) was the author of *Wordsworth and the Coleridges* (New York, 1899), and *Forty Years of Friendship as recorded in the correspondence of John Duke, Lord Coleridge and Ellis Yarnall* (London, 1911) which contains their Civil War correspondence.

83 Charles Dexter Cleveland (1802-1869) was elected to League membership on May 25, 1865: *Chronicle*, 477.

84 *ARULP* (1865), 22. Maceuen was secretary of the Board of Publication before he enlisted in the Sixth Union League Regiment (198th Regiment, Pennsylvania Volunteers).

85 Davis, *Pennsylvania Politics*, 305 and *passim*.

86 Alexander K. McClure, *Old Time Notes of Pennsylvania*, II (Philadelphia, 1905), 52-73, treats this election, which is useful for comparative purposes.

87 Based on *Address and Resolution of The Union League of Philadelphia. September 16, 1863* (Philadelphia, 1863), 3, 5-6, and *passim*.

88 Issac Wayne MacVeagh (1833-1917) was the author of *Address to the Union State Central Committee of Pennsylvania* (Philadelphia, 1863). *MBBP*, Sep. 12, 1863, resolved to place all pamphlets in its hands over 1,000 copies, and all stereotype plates of its publications at the disposal of the State Central Committee. McClure, *op. cit.*, II, 57-60, writes of MacVeagh's effectiveness.

89 See note 88.

90 Davis, *op. cit.*, 303.

91 *North American*, May 19, 1863.

92 Ronald Levy, "Bishop Hopkins and the Dilemma of Slavery," *Pa. Mag.* XCI (1967), 56-71, provides a concise and accurate study of the controversy; Wainwright, *op. cit.*, 305, is also very useful. Neither author related the controversy to The Union League.

93 See note 92.

94 *The True Issues Now Involved. Shall the Republic stand on the foundation laid by our Patriotic Fathers, or shall the Nation be sacrificed to the covetousness and knavery of the Confederates in Treason? The Loyal Northern Democracy abhor Secession, Rebellion, and Disunion* (Philadelphia, 1863).

95 Stroud's *Southern Slavery and the Christian Religion* was first published in the *North American*, Sep. 16, 1863. An earlier edition was printed as a circular. *Woodward on Foreigners* (Philadelphia, 1863), and its translation in German, *Woodward über die Fremden*.

96 George M. Stroud, *The Views of Judge Woodward and Bishop Hopkins on Negro Slavery at the South. Illustrated from the Journal of a Residence on a Georgian Plantation by Mrs. Frances Anne Kemble* (Philadelphia, 1863). The illustration of the whipped slave was not an artist's conception, but based on a photograph of "Slave Ben" which had reached the League. *MBBP*, May 14, 1863. It was first serialized in the *Public Ledger*, Oct. 2, 3, 6, 7, 8, 1863.

97 Lea's first two pamphlets, *A Few Words . . .* and *Democratic Opinions*, were approved for publication, *MBBP*, Sep. 18, 1863. *The Bible View of Polygamy* (Philadelphia, 1863) was first identified as a League pamphlet by Bradley, *Henry Charles Lea*, 92-93.

98 *The Voice of the Clergy* is an undated folio broadside, printed in bold type on one side only.

99 Wainwright, *op. cit.*, 305.

100 *Ibid.*

101 Goodwin's, *Southern Slavery* appeared shortly after the death of Gerhard in 1864. See note 12, *supra*.

102 Louis C. Newman, *The Bible View of Slavery Reconsidered. A Letter to the Right Rev. Bishop Hopkins* (Philadelphia, 1863) is significant because the author, a Jewish convert to Christianity, had knowledge of biblical Hebrew. *MBBP*, Dec. 17, 1863, records the recommendation by Colwell for the publication of 1000 copies.

103 The debate can be found in, *Soldiers Read!! Citizens Read!!! Address of the Democratic State Central Committee. Letter of Major Geo. A. Woodward. Letter of Judge Woodward* (Philadelphia, 1863).

104 Clement Mario Silvestro, *None But Patriots: The Union Leagues in Civil War and Reconstruction* (Ann Arbor, 1961), 66 and 215. Unpublished doctoral dissertation.

105 The manuscript of the *First Annual Report* in Boker's holograph is in the *ULA*, as is a full set of the annual reports.

106 The list of presentation medals is in the *Chronicle*, 540-543. More recently, the list of recipients is in the published membership roll which is issued from time to time.

107 *ARULP* (1863), 10-11.

108 *Ibid.*, 11.

Chapter III   From Amnesty to Assassination

1 *Amnesty Proclamation and Third Annual Message of Abraham Lincoln, President of the United States, read in Congress Dec. 9, 1863* (Philadelphia, 1864). Listed in Monaghan, *Lincoln Bibliography*, No. 191. It has not been previously identified with the League.

2 For details on Dougherty, see chap. I, note 42, and Appendix.

3 George H. Boker, *The Will of the People* (Philadelphia, 1864). The resolution to nominate Lincoln for a second term was introduced on Jan. 11 by William D. Lewis, one of the original founders of the Union Club, and Morton McMichael, who published it the following day in the *North American*. According to Sylvestro, *op. cit.*, 189-190, the New Hampshire League preempted this claim. The resolution was reprinted a number of times and published in David B. Williamson, *Life and Public Services of Abraham Lincoln* (Philadelphia, 1864), 180-183, an official campaign biography.

4 Henry Charles Lea, *A Democratic Peace Offered for the Acceptance of Pennsylvania Voters* (Philadelphia, 1864). A German translation also was published.

5 *Celebration of The Union League House, February 22, 1864. Presentation of a Flag by the Ladies of Philadelphia* (Philadelphia, 1864).

6 *The Planters Almanac for 1864* (No imprint), 12, for Lincoln's Amnesty Proclamation, and 16, for *General Orders No. 64*.

7 Col. Moses B. Walker to Brig. General William D. Whipple, near Atlanta, Ga., Aug. 23, 1864. The letter was forwarded promptly to Boker, describing the success of the *Almanac*.

8 James Russell Lowell, *The President's Policy* (Philadelphia, 1864), 2, was not noted previously as a Union League publication because of its original appearance in the *North American Review* (Nov. 1864). It was reprinted in Lowell's *Political Essays* (Boston, 1872), 177-209, but the text varies considerably.

9 Horace Binney, Jr. was a vice-president of the League from 1863 to 1868, and president from Dec. 1868 to Feb. 1870. He died in office.

10 The Boker-Leland friendship is described in Bradley, *George Henry Boker*, 66-69.

11 George H. Boker, *Poems of the War* (Philadelphia, 1864). James Murdoch, *Patriotism in Poetry and Prose* (Philadelphia, 1864) was reprinted in a pamphlet edition according to *MBBP*, Apr. 7, 1864. It was dedicated to James L. Claghorn, Ferdinand J. Dreer, and Joseph Harrison, Jr., three Union Club founders.

12 Ferdinand L. Sarmiento, *The History of Our Flag* (Philadelphia, 1864), was dedicated to The Union League of Philadelphia.

13 For bibliographical background on this edition of the Emancipation Proclamation, see *Our Daily Fare*, June 17, 1864, 70; *American Book Prices Current* (New York, 1864), 435-436, and *The New Colophon* (New York, 1950).

14 *The Age*, Nov. 13, 1863. One year later a response did come from H. C. Lea, *The Record of the Democratic Party, 1860-1865* (Philadelphia, 1865), 14-15.

14a James R. Fry to Abraham Lincoln, Apr. 26, 1864, inviting the president on behalf of the League and the Sanitary Commission to attend the Fair. Quoted in Basler, *op. cit.*, VII, 324.

15 Wainwright, *A Philadelphia Perspective*, 475, for Fisher's description.

16 *Ibid.*, and *Evening Bulletin*, June 17, 1864.

17 *Evening Bulletin*, June 17, 1864.

18 Other accounts of Lincoln's visit are in *Our Daily Fare*, June 17, 1864; Kenneth A. Bernard, *Lincoln and the Music of the Civil War* (Caldwell, Idaho, 1966), 216-218.

19 Captain S. Emlen Meigs provided an eyewitness account of the Lincoln visit to the League in June 1864 and presented it to the League Feb. 10, 1905; *ULA.*

20 Edward C. Knight (1813-1892), who ran on a local Republican ticket in 1856, was elected to League membership Jan. 10, 1863, *Chronicle*, 496; see Winslow, *op. cit.*, 46-49, for a contemporary sketch of Knight's commercial activity.

21 *Chronicle*, 542, for list of medal recipients, and honorary membership to the League.

22 Joseph Adams Smith, *An Address Delivered before The Union League of Philadelphia on Saturday Evening, January 20, 1906. At the presentation by the Art Association of the Painting Representing the Battle between the Kearsarge and Alabama* (Philadelphia, 1906).

23 *MBBP*, Dec. 6, 1864, is a retrospective statement by Lindley Smyth on canvassing the state prior to the election.

24 Henry Charles Lea, *To the Soldiers of the Union* (Philadelphia, 1864). An edition also appeared in German.

25 Lea, *The Democratic Times* (Philadelphia, 1864). An edition also appeared in German.

26 *Congressional Record of Geo. H. Pendleton* (Philadelphia, 1864). The author or compiler is unidentified in League records.

27 Henry Charles Lea, *The Great Northern Conspiracy of the "O.S.L."* (Philadelphia, 1864). Col. C. Carroll Tevis to George H. Boker, 8th Army Corps, Jan. 12, 1864, captured the following documents that appear to be unrecorded: *K.G.C. First or Military Degree—Named K.I.H.* (no place, no date). *K.G.C. Second or Final Degree—Named 18.* (no place, no date). Internal evidence suggests that they were published in Auburn, Ala., possibly between Mar. and Nov., 1860. For a note on Tevis see Dennis Clark, *The Irish in Philadelphia* (Philadelphia, 1973), 113.

28 Carl Schurz, *"For the Great Empire of Liberty, Forward!"* (Philadelphia, 1864), later reprinted in, *The Speeches of Carl Schurz* (Philadelphia, 1865), 269-320, a volume which Schurz dedicated to the League.

29 For Lowell see note 8, *supra*. William Whiting, *The Return of Rebellious States to The Union. A Letter from Hon. Wm. Whiting to The Union League of Philadelphia* (Philadelphia, 1864) and chap. II, note 22.

30 Frank Freidel, *Francis Lieber, Nineteenth-Century Liberal* (Baton Rouge, 1947), 352-353.

31 A comprehensive study of the attitude of the German-American press during the war would be useful. See *MBBP*, Sep. 10, 13, 1863, for subscription to the *Amerikaner*; Jan. 1, 1864 for Berks County, and Dec. 6, 1864, for Danville, Ky.

32 *Uncle Sam's Debts and his Ability to Pay Them* (Philadelphia, 1864); *The Old Continental and the New Greenback Dollar* (Philadelphia, 1864); and Lorin Blodget, *The Commercial and Financial Strength of the United States* (Philadelphia, 1864). In addition to these three, see the work of the Chief Justice of the Supreme Court of Pennsylvania, John Meredith Read, *Opinion in Favor of the Constitutionality of the Legal Tender Acts, May 24, 1865* (Philadelphia, 1865). See Appendix for Read, a founder of The Union Club.

33 Benjamin Franklin Reimer, *Permit a fellow-member of The Union League, to call your attention to the fact, that in this age of invention . . . there is no material improvement in the Infantry service in our Army . . .* (Philadelphia, 1864), circular, printed on recto and verso of the first leaf. Reimer was a photographer.

34 *ARULP*, (1863), 13; *MBGM*, May 12, 1864 for assignment of Gibbons and Joseph B. Townsend to receive members of the Methodist Episcopal Conference at the League. The author of *Christianity versus Treason and Slavery* is unidentified.

35 Sabato Morais (1823-1897) was born in Leghorn, Italy, and came to Philadelphia in 1851. He was associated with Congregation Mikveh Israel until his death in 1897. He was elected to the clerical roll of the League in 1887: *Chronicle*, 537, and Henry S. Morais, *op. cit.*, 66, *passim.*

36 *Christianity versus Treason*, 15-16.

37 Jeremiah Clemens (1814-1865) is described in *DAB* IV (New York, 1930) 191-192, as a soldier, novelist, and senator. For his prewar views, see *Speech of Mr. Clemens of Alabama* (Washington, D.C., 1851); the League pamphlet, *Letter from Hon. Jere Clemens* (Philadelphia, 1864) was printed in the *New York World*, Mar. 24, 1864. Walter L. Fleming, *Civil War and Reconstruction in Alabama* (New York, 1905), 144, *passim.*

38 Sidney George Fisher, *Address of The Union League of Philadelphia, to the Citizens of Pennsylvania, in favor of the re-election of Abraham Lincoln* (Philadelphia, 1864). Wainwright, *A Philadelphia Perspective*, 475, 487, where Fisher's authorship is made known.

39 A detailed account of the publication and distribution of *The Union League Gazette* is contained in the report of Charles C. Wilson to John Hanna, Phila., Oct. 22, 1864. MS. HSP, Society Misc. Collection. The *Gazette* is a foolscap folio, only seven copies of which have been located. All copies carry an October, 1864 date, and are numbered consecutively. *ARULP* (1864), 5-6, for the number of documents published.

40 See chap. II, note 57, and Lathrop, *op. cit.*, 71.

41 *Evening Bulletin*, May 5, 1865; *The Press*, May 11, 1865.

42 *Ibid.*

43 *Ibid.*

44 Scharf and Westcott, *op. cit.*, I, 823.

45 The telegram announcing Lee's surrender is in *ULA*, Scharf and Westcott, *op. cit.*, I, 823.

46 Maxwell Whiteman, *While Lincoln Lay Dying: A Facsimile Reproduction of the First Testimony Taken in Connection with the Assassination of Abraham Lincoln as Recorded by Corporal James Tanner* (Philadelphia, 1968), 13.

47 Broadside circular designating the League as the official pallbearer, *ULA.*

48 These memorial addresses were published as *Proceedings of The Union League of Philadelphia, Regarding the Assassination of Abraham Lincoln, President of the United States* (Philadelphia, 1865). Monaghan, *Lincoln Bibliography*, No. 800, describes them as vindictive. Charles Gibbons, *The Truth Plainly Spoken, At a Meeting of The Union League of Philadelphia, Held at Concert Hall, April 17, 1865, in seconding the Resolution offered by Horace Binney, Jr., Esq., the Hon. Charles Gibbons spoke as follows* (Philadelphia, 1865), and Leonard Myers, *Abraham Lincoln. A Memorial Address Delivered by Hon. Leonard Myers, June 15, 1865, before The Union League of the Thirteenth Ward* (Philadelphia, 1865).

49 Taylor, *op. cit.*, 276, 322-323.

50 Bradley, *George Henry Boker*, 224-227.

51 *Diary of Thomas Stewardson, Jr.*, April 23, 1865. MS. The *Diary* is presently in the hands of John Stewardson, a grandson of the diarist and a resident of Cape Cod, Mass. Stewardson was elected to League membership, Mar. 23, 1863; see *Chronicle*, 516.

52 Lea, *Record of the Democratic Party, 1860-1865* (Philadelphia, 1865), I.

53 Bradley, *Henry Charles Lea*, 96.

54 *ARULP* (1865), 16.

Chapter IV   Patriotism and Politics

1 Chronicle, 542; *ARULP* (1865), 8. MBGM, Dec. 6, 1865, and Jan. 9, 1866, on the official resolution for the support of Johnson.

2 *Senate Executive Document No. 2, 39th Congress, 1st Session* (1865-1866).

3 *ARULP* (1865), 4.

4 *ARULP* (1865), 4-5.

5 Carl Schurz, *The Condition of the South: Extracts from the Report of Major-General Carl Schurz, on the States of South Carolina, Georgia, Alabama, Mississippi and Louisiana: Addressed to the President* (Philadelphia, 1865). MBBP, Jan. 6, 1866 for the approval of an edition of 20,000 copies.

6 The bitter attack on Johnson, *ARULP* (1865), 6-8, was written by Boker.

7 *Ibid.*

8 *Ibid.*, 4-5. Benjamin Hunt, Abraham Barker, William Still, Philip P. Randolph, J. M. McKim . . . " to urge upon the public the justice and expediency of admitting all citizens to the Passenger Cars, without distinction in regard to color" (Philadelphia, Jan. 10, 1865). Circular letter printed on recto only, *ULA*. Still, a leader in the black community, was the author of *The Underground Railroad* (Philadelphia, 1872). Hunt, Barker and McKim were League members.

9 Walter Fleming, *Documentary History of Reconstruction: Political, Military, Social, Religious, Educational & Industrial, 1865 to the Present Time,* II (Cleveland, 1907), 7-29, laid the basis for these twentieth-century interpretations which influenced a whole school of historians.

10 Walter Fleming, *Civil War and Reconstruction in Alabama* (New York, 1905), 553-568. For a full understanding of this seemingly complex problem, a comparison of Fleming's statements with the documents of the New York and Philadelphia Leagues is important.

11 Fleming, *Documentary History,* 7-29, *passim.*

12 Guy James Gibson, *Lincoln's League: The Union League Movement During the Civil War* (Urbana, Ill., 1957), 511, properly separates the Union League of America from The Union League of Philadelphia.

13 Bruce Grant, *Fight for a City* (Chicago, 1955), 26-27, for the decline and rise of the Chicago club. Alexander W. Williams, *A Social History of the Greater Boston Clubs* (Barre, Vt., 1970), 24-28.

14 *ARULP* (1865), 18; *ARULP* (1866), 4-5.

15 For the first reorganization of this Board, see *MBBP*, Feb. 15, 1865, and later Feb. 19, 1866. J. Gillingham Fell (1816-1878), a coal merchant and railroad director, became a member of the League on Jan. 22, 1863, and served as president from 1865 to 1868; see *Chronicle,* 347-349; 461, 483.

16 Howard G. Gillette, Jr., *Corrupt and Contented: Philadelphia's Political Machine, 1865-1887* (Ann Arbor, Mich., 1971), 18-26. In this doctoral dissertation McMichael is summarized in a new light. See Appendix for McMichael. *ARULP* (1866), 14-15. Harry M. Tinkcom, *John White Geary: Soldier Statesman 1819-1873* (Philadelphia, 1940), 113-119.

17 Charles D. Cashdollar "Andrew Johnson and the Philadelphia Election of 1866," *Pa. Mag.* XCII (1968), 365-383, provides a good picture of the "swing around the circle." However, he repeats the myth that the League "was very careful on the Negro issue." *ARULP* (1866), 8, refers to Johnson's political tour as "indecent," and the annual report is courageously proNegro. Further, League vice-president Morton McMichael, who welcomed black leader Frederick Douglass as one of the campaign speakers is clear evidence of the conduct of League leadership.

18 *MBGM,* Aug. 14, 1866; *ARULP* (1866), 11.

19 E. Merton Coulter, *William G. Brownlow: Fighting Parson of the Southern Highlands* (Chapel Hill, 1937), 318-320.

20 See note 18, *supra.*

21 *ARULP* (1866), 12; *The Press,* Sep. 8, 1866.

22 *MBBP,* May 7, June 4, Aug. 6, and Nov. 12, 1866 provides the details on the distribution of gubernatorial campaign literature.

23 *MBBP*, May 7, 1866. *Platform of the National Union Party of Pennsylvania, Adopted in Convention, at Harrisburg, March 7th, 1866.* The English language edition consisted of 95,000 copies and a German language edition of 17,000 copies. For Cameron, see Erwin Stanley Bradley, *The Triumph of Militant Republicanism* (Philadelphia, 1964), 234; 261-262.

24 *Address of The Union League of Philadelphia to the Citizens of Pennsylvania, Sep. 6, 1866* (Philadelphia, 1866), 14. There are two editions of the *Address;* the later edition carries the additional title, *with Resolutions Adopted August 22, 1866.* Henry Charles Lea was the author of the *Address* and Lindley Smyth prepared the *Resolutions.* The latter were directed to the Southern Loyalists who convened in Philadelphia.

25 Lindley Smyth, *Is the South Ready for Restoration?* (Philadelphia, 1866), appeared without the author's name. At this time Smyth was chairman of the Board of Publication. He was a prominent sugar refiner, a founder of the Republican Party in Philadelphia, and an original signer of the Articles of Association. In 1868 he received the Gold Medal of the League for his patriotic activity. He was president of the Pennsylvania Company after the Civil War. President Grant offered him the post of Secretary of the Treasury which Smyth declined. See the *Evening Bulletin*, Oct. 17, 1896, and *ARULP* (1899), 64.

26 Edwin Percy Whipple, *The Johnson Party. From the Atlantic Monthly, September, 1866* (Philadelphia, 1866). The sheets of Whipple's polemic were obtained in advance of publication by Boker from Ticknor & Fields of Boston. The League edition deleted Whipple's name. See *ARULP* (1866), 14-15, and *Atlantic Monthly*, Sep. 1866, 374-381. George Sewall Boutwell *The Usurpation* (Philadelphia, 1866) was also obtained from the *Atlantic Monthly* where it appeared in October, 1866, 506-513.

27 Tinkcom, *op. cit.*, 116. *A Sketch of the Life and of the Civil and Military Services of Maj. Gen. John W. Geary, Candidate of the National Union Party for Governor of Pennsylvania, 1866* (Philadelphia, 1866); *MBBP*, May 7, 1866. A German translation appeared simultaneously.

28 *Record of Hiester Clymer; and Historical Parallel between Him and Major-General John W. Geary. Also Official Returns of Election on Constitutional Amendments Allowing Soldiers the Right to Vote* (Philadelphia, 1866).

29 Tinkcom, *op. cit.*, 119.

30 Fleming, *Civil War and Reconstruction in Alabama*, 553, and *passim*, bases his statements on the *Chronicle*, 5-8, and on Henry W. Bellows, *Historical Sketch of the Union League Club of New York. Its Origin, Organization, and Work, 1863-1879* (New York, 1879), 6-9. Neither of these allegations is found here. Fleming contradicts himself on page 555 in stating that they drew away from being "strictly political" and became strictly social clubs.

31 Fleming, *Documentary History*, II, 3, *passim*.

32 James Ford Rhodes, *History of the United States*, VI (New York, 1906), 180-181, 306-307, repeats the views of Fleming in an earlier period; E. Merton Coulter, *The South During Reconstruction, 1865-1877* (Baton Rouge, 1947), 127-129, ascribes the origin of the Loyal Leagues and the Union League of America to "Freedmen's Bureau agents and other Northern emissaries" who influenced Negroes to organize secret Leagues with bizarre rituals similar to those of the North in order to vote Republican. His source was Fleming. Avery Craven, *Reconstruction: The Ending of the Civil War* (New York, 1969), 225-226 repeats these errors. Craven cites Fleming but also historians like David Donald, *Journal of Southern History* X (1944), 447-460. Kenneth Stampp, *The Era of Reconstruction, 1865-1877* (New York, 1965), 156, writes that "The Negroes, ignorant and illiterate, played an essentially passive role, casting their votes as radical agents of the Union League and Freedmen's Bureau told them to." This is a sampling of an endless list of erroneous statements.

33 W. E. B. DuBois, *Black Reconstruction* (New York, 1935), 680, writes "There is no foundation for this." DuBois was the noted black revisionist.

34 *Report of the Proceedings of a Meeting Held at Concert Hall, Philadelphia on Tuesday Evening, November 3, 1863, to take into consideration the Condition of the Free People of the South* (Philadelphia, 1863). Stephen Colwell was president, and J. Miller McKim and Ellis Yarnall were secretaries. Of its 38 members, 27 have been identified as members of the Philadelphia League.

35 *ARULP* (1881), 8-9, for the appointment of Charles J. Stillé as the chairman of a committee for promoting the interests of education in the South.

36 *MBGM*, Feb. 27, 1866.

37 *Ibid.*, Apr. 9, May 14, 1867. *ARULP* (1867), 11.

38 James M. McPherson, *The Struggle for Equality: Abolitionists and the Negro in the Civil War and Reconstruction* (Princeton, 1964), 378-382; Fleming, *Civil War and Reconstruction in Alabama*, 509. Both refer to Kelley but make no mention of his League association.

39 *ARULP* (1868), 3.

40 *Ibid.*, 4.

41 DuBois, *op. cit.*, 680, clarifies this by writing "They [the Southern planters] chose instead force and secret revolution. It was not, then, the organization of The Union Leagues that caused the Ku Klux Klan, it was the determination to deprive Negroes, by force, of any real weapon for economic bargaining." Compare with the earlier writers, i.e., John Moffat Mecklin, *The Ku Klux Klan: A Study of the American Mind* (New York, 1924), 55-56, who states that the Klan was a product of the League; and J. C. Lester and D. L. Wilson, *Ku Klux Klan: Its Origin, Growth and Disbandment* (New York and Washington, 1905), 24, 29, 79-81, where the same unfounded claim is made.

42 *MBGM*, Sep. 8, 1867; Jan. 15, 1868, on carrying out Reconstruction laws.

43 *Ibid.*, Feb. 11, 1868 regarding a statement by the League on impeachment.

44 Edmund Gibson Ross to E. A. Stockton, Sante Fe, N.M., Mar. 21, 1897, MS, *ULA*. Ross, a Democratic Senator from Kansas, 1866 to 1871, voted not guilty in the impeachment proceedings. It was he who presented the document to Stockton, who was elected to League membership Apr. 12, 1905. *The Union League [Membership Book]* (Philadelphia, 1914), 113.

45 These points are best exploited by Brooks M. Kelley, "Simon Cameron and the Senatorial Nomination of 1867" *Pa. Mag.* LXXXVII (1963), 375-392, and John D. Stewart, II, "The Deal for Philadelphia: Simon Cameron and the Genesis of a Political Machine, 1867-1872," *Journal of the Lancaster County Historical Society*, 77 (1973), 43-45.

46 Membership Register, MS, *ULA*.

47 For the reactions to city government and the postwar rise of the political machines see *MBGM*, June 11, 1867; for the political defeat of the Republicans see *MBGM*, Oct. 9, 1867. *ARULP* (1867), 15 *passim*, comments on this setback in greater detail. Almost the entire report is devoted to the local and state political scene. Lea, *The Crisis* (Philadelphia, 1867); *MBBP*, Nov. 6, 1867.

48 Lea, *Democratic Frauds. How the Democrats Carried Pennsylvania in 1867* (Philadelphia, 1868). *MBBP*, July 29, 1868, reports that over 90,000 copies were published and distributed. A German translation, *Demokratische Betrügereien*, was published simultaneously. See *Declaration of Intent Records*, 1840, Archives, City of Philadelphia; *Supreme Court Naturalizations Judge John M. Read's Decision. November 2, 1868* (Philadelphia, 1868). Union League poster. See Appendix for Read.

49 *Essays on Political Organization, selected from among those submitted in competition for the prizes offered by The Union League of Philadelphia* (Philadelphia, 1868).

50 *MBGM*, June 11, 1867.

51 *MBGM*, May 1, 1868.

52 Galusha A. Grow, *Union League of America of Pennsylvania* (Philadelphia, 1868). In James T. DuBois and Gertrude S. Mathews, *Galusha A. Grow, Father of the Homestead Law* (Boston and New York, 1917), no mention is made of Grow's League association.

53 Lea, *Address of The Union League of Philadelphia, to the Citizens of Pennsylvania, with the Preamble and Resolutions, Adopted in General Meeting*, August 26, 1868 (Philadelphia, 1868), 1. *MBBP*, Sep. 30, 1868, reports that 90,112 copies were published and distributed. See also Bradley, *Lea, op. cit.*, 114.

54 *MBBP*, July 29, Sep. 30, 1868, gives a detailed account of the work of the campaign and publication committees.

55 Scharf and Westcott *op. cit.*, I, 835. *ARULP* (1868), 10, and (1869), 9-10.

56 *ARULP* (1869), 3, and (1868), 9.

57 *MBGM*, Nov. 10, 1868, *passim*, for the resolution of Lindley Smyth and the reaction of James L. Claghorn.

58 *MBGM*, Jan. 12 and May 11, 1869 for the Resolution and discussion which led to the Registry Act; Philip S. Klein and Ari Hoogenboom, *A History of Pennsylvania* (New York, 1973), 318; Erwin Stanley Bradley, *The Triumph of Militant Republicanism* (Philadelphia, 1964), 349-350, 365. Heretofore, the Registry Act was not known to have originated within The Union League. Frank B. Evans, *Pennsylvania Politics, 1872-1877: A Study in Political Leadership* (Harrisburg, 1966), 16, in an otherwise excellent book presents a distorted image of the League's political role.

59 *MBGM*, June 23, 1869 where it is reported that the Act is unconstitutional, and July 13, 1869 that it was upheld by the State Supreme Court.

60 *ARULP*, (1869), 7-9.

61 *Ibid.*, 17-18.

62 *MBGM*, Sep. 13; Oct. 18, 1870. *ARULP* (1870), 9-10. Mahlon H. Hellerich, *The Pennsylvania Constitution of 1873* (Ann Arbor, Michigan, 1956), 94-99, for other details. Evans, *op. cit.*, 77.

63 *Ibid.* For Frederick Fraley, see Appendix; for reference to Francis Jordon, see Brooks M. Kelley, *op. cit.*, 385.

64 *ARULP* (1870), 15.

65 Gillette, *op. cit.*, 50, for the founding of the Citizens Municipal Reform Association. Bradley, *Henry Charles Lea*, 184-196.

66 *Ibid.*, 51-52.

67 *Debates of the Convention to Amend the Constitution of Pennsylvania: Convened at Harrisburg, November 12, 1872; Adjourned, November 27, to meet at Philadelphia, January 7, 1873* (Harrisburg, 1873). 8 vol. The last working day was on Dec. 27, 1873.

68 For a recent summary of the convention, see Klein and Hoogenboom, *op. cit.*, 318-321.

69 *MBGM*, Nov. 25, 1873; Jan. 31, 1874, and Nov. 20, 1874.

70 *The Union League of Philadelphia to the Republican Voters of Pennsylvania* (Philadelphia, n. d.). Robert B. Corson was named secretary and Amos R. Little, chairman. *The Press*, Oct. 11, 1875, lists the names of 62 members of the Pilgrims; Gillette, *op. cit.*, 149-152.

71 The literature on the "Committee of Sixty-Two" consists of no less than 12 circulars and broadsides which are known to have survived. They provide in detail the basis of the controversy.

72 Amos R. Little and Robert T. Corson, *Union League House, Philadelphia, October 6th, 1875.* Circular attacking corruption among the "Mysterious Pilgrims" and their backers. Two important pamphlets on the subject, both with the same title: *To the Members of The Union League* (Philadelphia, Oct. 6, 1875) and Oct. 13, 1875, reveal the inner conflict.

73 *North American and Gazette,* Oct. 6, 1875; *Evening Bulletin,* Oct. 12, 1875; *The Press,* Oct. 14, 1875; and *The Times,* Oct. 7, 1875. *To the Members of The Union League: Philadelphia, October 13, 1875:* Circular on the "Committee of Sixty-Two." *To the Republican Members of Council,* undated circular. Untitled circular dated Oct. 13, 1875 attacking the "Committee." Evans, *op. cit.,* 163-164 writes that the League acted "surprisingly" in taking the initiative, when in fact it was a natural evolution in its search for clean politics.

74 *The Press,* Nov. 24, 1875; *ARULP* (1875), 9-10. *MBBD,* April 13; Nov. 30, 1875; Sep. 16, 1876.

75 *MBBD,* Sep. 12, 1876. The full resolution is in *MBBD,* June 28, 1880.

76 *Report of the Committee of The Union League on Municipal Government* (Philadelphia, 1878); Scharf and Westcott, *op. cit.,* I, 849; Klein and Hoogenboom, *op. cit.,* 323.

77 F. L. Sarmiento, *Historical Sketch of the Soldiers' Home in the City of Philadelphia* (Philadelphia, 1886), 15. Robert B. Beath, *History of the Grand Army of the Republic* (New York, 1889), and Beath collection of memorabilia in *ULA.*

78 *MBBP,* Aug. 26, 1869.

79 *Proceedings of a Meeting of The Union Club of Philadelphia, Held at The League House, December 27, 1870.* Only 55 copies were published. *Minute Book Union Club, 1865-1905,* MS, *ULA.*

80 For Barker, see Appendix. *Philadelphia Club* (announcement), *Jan. 28, 1869; The Saturday Club, Organized October 13, 1871:* this is evidently the first circular listing its officers and members.

81 Bradley, *Boker, op. cit.,* 245-246.

82 *Reception tendered by the members of The Union League of Philadelphia to George H. Boker, Minister of the United States to Turkey. . . .* (Philadelphia, 1872).

83 See Appendix for Rogers and Harrison.

84 James Reid Lambdin (1807-1889); *Chronicle,* 497, and *Catalogue of the Collection of Paintings belonging to The Union League of Philadelphia* (Philadelphia, 1940), 29-35.

85 Daniel Ridgway Knight (1839-1924) was elected to League membership in 1870, *Chronicle*, 496. J. Henry Haseltine (1833-1907) was elected to League membership in 1863: *Chronicle*, 490.

86 Peter F. Rothermel (1817-1895) signed the *Articles of Association* Jan. 12, 1863. See, *Articles*, printed copy, *ULA*. Edwin B. Coddington, "Rothermel's Painting of the Battle of Gettysburg" *Pennsylvania History* XXVII (1960), 1-27; *Prominent Pennsylvanians* I (Philadelphia, 1898), 402-404.

87 Augustus George Heaton (1844-1927) was elected to League membership in 1866: *Chronicle*, 490; *Catalogue . . . of Paintings*, 21-22.

88 Edward Dalton Marchant (1806-1887) was elected to League membership in 1865: *Chronicle*, 501. The portrait of Lincoln was painted from life in August, 1863. See *Catalogue . . . of Paintings*, 38-40. The Borie portrait is no longer in the possession of the League.

89 *Union League House, Philadelphia Nov. 7, 1870*. Circular letter calling for an "Art Reception." *Catalogue of the First Art Reception of The Union League of Philadelphia* during the evenings of Dec. 8th, 9th and 10th, 1870 (Philadelphia, 1870); *Catalogue of the Second Art Reception . . .* February 9th, 10th, and 11th, 1871 (Philadelphia, 1871).

90 *Catalogue of the Third Art Reception of The Union League of Philadelphia,* . . . April 26th, 27th, 28th, 29th, 1871 (Philadelphia, 1871), 3.

91 *Catalogue of Engravings, Etchings and Mezzotints, exhibited at the Third Art Reception, of The Union League of Philadelphia, October 1873* (Philadelphia, 1873); *Ledger and Transcript*, Nov. 1, 1873.

92 Evidence that the Eakins portrait of Hayes was rejected because it lacked social respectability is vaguely supported. The history of this minor episode is as follows: Lloyd Goodrich, *Thomas Eakins: His Life and Work* (New York, 1933), 55 *passim*; F. O. Matthiessen, *American Renaissance: Art and Expression in the Age of Emerson and Whitman* (New York, 1941), 609.

93 *Minute Book of the Art Association of The Union League* 1882-1915; *Chronicle*, 330.

94 *MBBD*, Sep. 13, 1870: musical programs and ephemera *ULA*, Document Cases, "Music and Musical Life." James Bellak was elected to League membership in 1865: *Chronicle*, 470.

95 Scharf and Westcott, *op. cit.*, I, 839-840; John Russell Young, *Memorial History of the City of Philadelphia*, I (New York, 1895), 540; William D. Kelley, *Speeches, Addresses and Letters on Industrial and Financial Questions* (Philadelphia, 1872), 415-426.

96 *ARULP* (1874), 8.

97 *ARULP* (1875), 12-13, and (1876), 17.

98 *ARULP* (1876), 18.

99 Henry Armitt Brown (1846-1879): *Chronicle*, 407-408; Henry Armitt Brown, *Oration at Valley Forge, June 19, 1878: The One Hundredth Anniversary of the Departure of the Army of the Revolution from Winter Quarters at that Place* (Philadelphia, 1911). For Francis M. Brooke see Young, *op. cit.*, II, 371-373.

100 Valley Forge Park Commission, *Valley Forge Park* (Philadelphia, 1950), 48.

101 *Chronicle*, 512, for Scovel's admission to the League; *The Sumter Anniversary, 1863. Opinions of Loyalists concerning the Great Questions of the Times* (New York, 1863), 57, where Scovel is described as "a member of the copperhead legislature of New Jersey."

102 Barnie F. Winkelman, *John G. Johnson Lawyer and Art Collector 1841-1917* (Philadelphia, 1942), 129-136.

103 For a full appreciation of these functions, consult the *Annual Reports* and the numerous programs issued for these occasions. A typical newspaper description of a New Year's day reception is in the *Public Ledger*, Jan. 2, 1896.

104 *MBBP*, Sep. 30, 1868, is the final entry of the original Board of Publication.

105 *ARULP* (1893), 5, for the last listing of the Board of Publication.

106 A study of the Constitution and the changes in the By-Laws, which were frequent, is essential for the comprehension of club government.

107 A full study of the Vare brothers is necessary for understanding the political life of Philadelphia. Useful, though partisan in context, is William S. Vare, *My Forty Years in Politics* (Philadelphia, 1943).

108 Henry Cohen (1810-1879) was elected to membership April 24, 1863: *Chronicle*, 477; Sulzberger, May 16, 1894: *Chronicle*, 517; Jacob Solis-Cohen, Dec. 10, 1881: *Chronicle*, 477; and Morais in 1887: *Chronicle*, 537.

109 Statistics on annual membership are published in the *Annual Reports.*

110 Tourgee was originally on the correspondents' roll, but on Dec. 14, 1881 he was transferred to the active roll: *Chronicle*, 518.

111 *MBBD*, April 18, 1870.

112 Scharf and Westcott, *op.cit.*, I, 836.

113 *Ibid.*, 837.

114 W.E.B. DuBois, *The Philadelphia Negro* (Philadelphia, 1899), 40-41.

115 *Addresses Upon the Occasion of the Reception of Henry M. Hoyt, Governor of Pennsylvania, by The Union League of Philadelphia, April 15th 1879*, 11. One of Boker's most forceful addresses on Reconstruction was delivered at this time.

116 *ARULP* (1881), 8-9, *MBBD,* Nov. 14, 1881.

117 John Eaton, *Illiteracy and its Social, Political and Industrial Effects. An Address delivered by invitation before The Union League Club of Philadelphia* (Philadelphia, 1893).

118 *ARULP* (1883), 11.

119 *ARULP* (1884), 14.

120 *ARULP* (1884), 15. *Twenty-Fifth Anniversary of the Organization of The Union League of Philadelphia* (Philadelphia, 1888), 1-6.

121 *Ibid.,* 10-20.

122 *Ibid.,* 24.

Chapter V   Transition and A New Crisis

1 Irwin Unger, *The Greenback Era. A Social and Political History of American Finance, 1865-1879* (Princeton, N.J., 1964), is a useful study that coincides with this period, and closes in the year that Carey died. Many of the figures dealt with here are discussed by Unger but their association with and influence upon the League has not been recognized.

2 Arnold W. Green, *Henry Charles Carey, Nineteenth Century Sociologist* (Philadelphia, 1951) covers certain aspects of Carey's far-flung activity but a broader study of his life seems imperative.

3 *Ibid.,* 35-37.

4 *MBBD,* June 28, 1880; *ARULP* (1880), 4.

5 Henry C. Lea, "The Third Term," in *National Republican League* (1880), 1-4.

6 The following circulars and handbills under the title *Union League of Philadelphia* were issued in favor of Garfield and are listed by date: Aug. 27; Sep. 21, 27, 28; and Oct. 30, 1880.

7 *ARULP* (1880), 10-19.

8 *ARULP* (1881), 13; (1882), 14-15.

9 *MBBD,* June 24, 1884; *ARULP* (1885), 11-12 and *ARULP* (1888), 13.

10 *ARULP* (1888), 14-16.

11 *Ibid.,* (1888), 10-11, for a resumé of the Cleveland administration. Robert D. Marcus, *Grand Old Party. Political Structure in the Gilded Age 1880-1896* (New York, 1971), 132-135.

12 See full text of *ARULP* (1892) and (1893) for the debate on the voting conduct of League members, and notes 14 and 18, *infra.*

13 *MBBD*, Jan. 18, 1894. The tariff discussion consists of 55 pages. *A Protest Against the Wilson Tariff Bill by The Union League of Philadelphia* (Philadelphia, 1894).

14 *ARULP* (1892), 14-21.

15 *Ibid.*, 21.

16 *Ibid.*, 25-26.

17 *Catalogue of the Library of The Union League. September 1, 1884* (Philadelphia, 1884). *ARULP* (1893), 80-83.

18 *ARULP* (1893), 8.

19 *Ibid.*, 8-42, for the full proceedings that led to the adoption of the compromise. According to *The Press*, Dec. 14, 1892 there were from 210 to 215 Democrats who were members of the League at this time.

20 Whiteman, *op. cit.*, 1-13.

21 *Chronicle*, 410; Oliver C. Bosbyshell, *The 48th in the War. Being a Narrative of the Campaigns of the 48th Regiment Infantry, Pennsylvania Veteran Volunteers, During the War of the Rebellion* (Philadelphia, 1895). A sketch of the life of Benson is in the *Chronicle*, 357-359. *ARULP* (1909), 25. For Lambert, see *In Memoriam: William Harrison Lambert* (Philadelphia, 1912), 12-21, and *Catalogue of the Library of the Late Major William D. Lambert of Philadelphia*, I (New York, 1914), iii-vii.

22 The Lincoln Monument Association was founded July 4, 1865; Mayor Alexander Henry was president, C. J. Stillé, secretary, and James L. Claghorn, treasurer. Certificate in *ULA.*

23 See *Special Committee on Memorial to the Regiments Recruited by The Union League of Philadelphia* (Philadelphia, May 1, 1901).

24 *The Pilgrims' Book Containing The Articles of Constitution of The Pilgrims to the Battlefields of the Rebellion and Other Matters of Interest to the Members of that Organization* (Philadelphia, 1911).

25 See note 13, *supra.*

26 For general background to this episode, see Maxwell Whiteman "The East European Jew in Philadelphia," in John E. Bodnar, *The Ethnic Experience in Pennsylvania* (Lewisburg, Pa., 1973), 296-297.

27 *Russian Refugee Meetings: Minutes*, Feb. 23, 27, 1882, for meeting in Wanamaker's office and the steps taken to publicize the resolution in the press. MS in possession of the author.

28 *Ibid.*

29 *ARULP* (1901), 49, 111, 124, 142, 167.

30 *ARULP* (1890), 16.

31 Young, *Memorial History*, I, 554-559.

32 *"Nothing is Good Enough that can be made Better."* Circular dated May 26, 1881, which launched the acquisition of the Moravian and Sansom Streets properties. *Circular to the Members of The Union League of Philadelphia* (Philadelphia, October 12, 1881), under the signature of Edwin N. Benson, chairman of the Union League Annex.

33 Leonard Blumberg of the Department of Sociology, Temple University, made available data on houses of prostitution which he obtained from the Society to Protect Children. Letter to author, June 26, 1974.

34 For a comparative examination of the decline and increase of the League membership, see *ARULP* for the years under discussion.

35 For the establishment of the Real Estate Advisory Board, see *ARULP* (1897), 59-60.

36 *ARULP* (1896), 57-63. For Blankenburg see Lucretia L. Blankenburg, *The Blankenburgs of Philadelphia* (Philadelphia, 1928), 14-28. For Clayton McMichael, see *Chronicle*, 413; for James Elverson, Jr., 482; for Isaac N. Solis, 513; for Edward T. Stotesbury, 256 and *passim;* for the Lippincotts, 498. Charles Emory Smith, who died Jan. 19, 1908, was U.S. Minister to Russia in the Harrison administration, and Postmaster General in the McKinley administration. *Chronicle,* 268, and *passim.*

37 Although Walter Davenport, *Power and Glory: The Life of Penrose* (N.Y., 1931), and Robert Douglass Bowden, *Boies Penrose: Symbol of an Era* (N.Y. 1937), provide the essential background of this politically enigmatic figure, an in-depth study of his career would be useful.

Chapter VI   From High Tide to World War I

1 *ARULP* (1896), 61. *Speech of General Daniel H. Hastings, Governor of Pennsylvania, at the opening of the Ohio Campaign at Canton, Ohio, September 18th, 1896* (Harrisburg, Pa. 1896). *Campaign Committee of 1896. The Union League of Philadelphia,* Circular.

2 Louis Filler, *Crusaders for American Liberalism* (N.Y., 1939), 137.

3 See McKinley Reception file, 1897, *ULA.*

4 *ARULP* (1897), 63, "In Memoriam."

5 *Minutes of a Special Meeting of The Union League of Philadelphia called to consider the Report of the Monetary Commission. January 29, 1898* (Philadelphia, 1898), and *The National Financial System. Addresses by Hon. George F. Edmunds and C. Stuart Patterson, Esq. of the Monetary Commission. The Union League, Philadelphia January 8, 1898* (Philadelphia, 1898).

6 Herbert Adams Gibbons, *John Wanamaker*, I (New York, 1926), 373-374.

7 See McKinley Reception file, 1898, *ULA*.

8 *ARULP* (1898), 38-39.

9 *Ibid.*, 40.

10 *Address of Mr. Joseph G. Darlington Introducing the United States Peace Commissioners delivered at the dinner given them by The Union League of Philadelphia February 4, 1899* (Philadelphia, 1899).

11 *Address Prepared by Mr. Booker T. Washington for delivery at a dinner given by members of The Union League Club on February 12, 1899 in commemoration of the birth of Abraham Lincoln* (Philadelphia, 1899). See *The Philadelphia Times*, Feb. 16, 1899.

12 Albert J. Beveridge, *For the Greater Republic, Not for Imperialism* (Philadelphia, 1899). See the *Philadelphia Inquirer*, Feb. 16, 1899.

13 *Founders' Day Annual Banquet November 25, 1899. Addresses by Hon. John D. Long, Secretary United States Navy. Hon. J. G. Schurman, President Philippine Commission and Cornell University. Hon. Dimner Beeber, Judge Superior Court of Pennsylvania. Silas W. Pettit, Esq., Ex-President The Union League. Joseph G. Darlington, Esq., President The Union League* (Philadelphia, 1899), 44-45, and 59-60. For a detailed description, see *The Press*, Nov. 26, 1899.

14 William P. Frye, *Expansion of Territory, Expansion of Trade* (Philadelphia, 1900), 18-20.

15 Lyman J. Gage, *Business Vicissitudes. A Backward Look* (Philadelphia, 1900), 7, and *passim*.

16 Joseph B. Foraker, *Puerto Rico* (Philadelphia, 1900), 9, and *passim*.

17 *ARULP* (1900), 28-32.

18 *Ibid.*, 22-25.

19 *Ibid.*, 28-29.

20 *ARULP* (1901), 148-161.

21 Details of McKinley's assassination were reported meticulously for the League by telegraph and telegram. All items are in *ULA*.

22 *Memorial Meeting of The Union League on the Assassination of the President September 20, 1901* (Philadelphia, 1901), the proceedings of which were reprinted in *Chronicle*, 418-439.

23 *Memorial Meeting*, 27. *ARULP* (1901), 49, on anarchists.

24 *Catalogue of the Collection of Paintings*, 36-37 for the MacCameron portrait.

25 For varying attitudes and conditions of membership, see *ARULP* (1901), 14, 15, 17, 140; (1904), 18, 25, 27, 32; (1906), 39; (1907), 10.

26 *ARULP* (1901), 49-50.

27 *Banquet in Honor of Founders' Day. The Union League.* (Philadelphia, 1902). Roosevelt Reception file, *ULA*. *ARULP* (1902), 88-105, for the addresses of Roosevelt, Root, and Lodge.

28 *ARULP*, 106-107.

29 *Ibid.*, 15.

30 *Daily News*, Nov. 26, 1900; *North American*, Nov. 27, 1900, for the attacks upon the League for not inviting Ashbridge to the McKinley celebration.

31 Lincoln Steffens, "Philadelphia: Corrupt and Contented," in *McClure's Magazine* (N.Y., 1903), 251.

32 *The Speeches of John Wanamaker on Quayism and Boss Domination in Pennsylvania Politics* (Philadelphia, n.d.).

33 *To the President and Board of Directors of The Union League of Philadelphia, Philadelphia, September 30th, 1905.* Typescript, *ULA*, defining the struggle against political corruption, and a response by League secretary William H. Lambert, October 16, 1905, disavowing the Committee of Twenty-One as representing the League. See correspondence between George D. McCreary and William Potter, Oct. 21, 1891, which says "that there be no deviation in his behalf (McCreary) from the unwritten law of the League, to take no action in the endorsement of candidates for municipal offices."

34 *ARULP* (1904), 43-44, and National Campaign Committee file for 1904, *ULA*.

35 *Ibid.*, 74-79, for the Roosevelt address.

36 For Clarence H. Clark (1833-1906) and Abraham Barker (1821-1906), the last of the original members of The Union Club, see Appendix.

37 *The Building Committee of The Union League of Philadelphia, Appointed January 29, 1906.* MS, *ULA*. This treasury of architectural data contains all of the details regarding the extension of the League House. The final entry is October 27, 1911.

38 *ARULP* (1908), 15, and for the general political outlook of the League, 81-134.

39 *Ibid.* 83.

40 *Program of the Ceremonies of the Laying of the Corner Stone of the New Building of The Union League of Philadelphia Sunday October 9th, 1909.* ARULP (1909), 123-135, for the report of the Building Committee, and ARULP (1913), 22-23, for necrology of Hope.

41 *ARULP* (1910), 103-123 under "Farewell Remarks."

42 *Ibid.*, 117.

43 *Catalogue of the Collection of Paintings*, 8 and 121.

44 *Catalogue of the Library of the Late Major William D. Lambert* III, 124, item 1161.

45 *The Freedom of the Press. Governor Samuel W. Pennypacker's Message Approving the Bill in Restraint of its Liberty and Charles Emory Smith's Editorial in Protest* (Philadelphia, 1903).

46 *ARULP* (1906), 103.

47 Sulzberger-Pennypacker-Penrose correspondence in possession of the author.

48 Blair Bolles, *Tyrant from Illinois: Uncle Joe Cannon's Experiment with Personal Power* (New York, 1951), 68-76.

49 *Ibid.*, 72.

50 *ARULP* (1911), 67-68.

51 *Ibid.*, 68.

52 *ARULP* (1912), 18-43, which comprises the published minutes of a special meeting. Other data have not survived and the record is based on this report.

53 *Ibid.*, 19.

54 *Ibid.*, 23.

55 *Ibid.*, 27.

56 *ARULP* (1912) which consists of 192 pages. Removal of the Roosevelt portrait is a common story told at the League. It was rehung before 1916. *ARULP* (1912), 37 gives reasons why the Republicans lost in 1912.

57 *Ibid.*, 108-109, 112. For the proceedings commemorating Grant's birthday, see 153-180. *ARULP* (1911), 25, for the creation of the Gettysburg Battlefield Commission by Gov. Edwin Stuart and the appointment of General Louis Wagner as chairman.

58 *ARULP* (1913), 52-57.

59 *Ibid.*, 22.

Chapter VII   War, Peace and Depression

1 *Souvenir of the Fiftieth Anniversary of the Opening of the League House May 11, 1915* (Philadelphia, 1915).

2 *ARULP* (1914), 51, for the first comments on the war in Europe. For problems of shipping and the expansion of the maritime industry, see 61-62. *ARULP* (1915), 12.

3 *An Account of the Reception Given to George P. Morgan, Chairman of the Committee on Membership 1898 to 1906; Member of Board 1907 to 1911; Secretary 1908 to 1911. Also a Condensed Statement of Mr. Morgan's War Record* (Philadelphia, 1915). *ARULP* (1915), 79-139, for Root and the fiftieth anniversary celebration.

4 *ARULP* (1916), 9-29, for the minutes of a special meeting to ratify the nominations of Charles E. Hughes and Charles W. Fairbanks.

5 *ARULP* (1917), 14, for the League resolution, and Woodrow Wilson to J. W. Hamer, Secretary, Union League of Philadelphia, Washington, February 12, 1917. LS, *ULA*.

6 *Ibid.*, 36-38.

7 *Ibid.*, 60, 75; *ARULP* (1918), 13. See World War I file, *ULA*, and *ARULP* (1919), 52, 57-58, for a summary of this war work.

8 *ARULP* (1917), 60, for subscriptions to the Liberty Loans. *ARULP* (1919), 37, gives a full account of the five Liberty Loans.

9 Major-General William G. Price, Jr. (1869-1960) in Charles J. Cohen, *The Penn Club* (Philadelphia, 1924), 289-290, and his necrology in *ARULP* (1960), 38-39. C. Brewster Rhoads (1893-1973), in *ARULP* (1973), 9-11.

10 *ARULP* (1918), 18, 35, 38.

11 The Lincoln Memorial Room concept was proposed by Governor Stuart, *ARULP* (1915), 63-64, at the reception to George P. Morgan.

12 *ARULP* (1917), 58.

13 *ARULP* (1916), 75. Although Meigs name is not on the printed list, he was active in its compilation. *Chronicle*, 411.

14 *Founders' Day. The Union League of Philadelphia: Dedication of the Memorial Room* (Philadelphia, 1917), 43.

15 *ARULP* (1919), 35.

16 *ARULP* (1918), 36.

17 Henry Starr Richardson, *The Story of Sproul: Being a broadly sketched History of the Life and uncommonly varied Activities of the Man elected Governor of Pennsylvania by an Overwhelming Vote on November 5, 1918* (Philadelphia, 1919), 3-4. *Public Ledger*, Mar. 22, 1928, and *Philadelphia Inquirer*, Mar. 23, 1928 for obituary and editorial notice.

18 *ARULP* (1919), 32, 49, 97.

19 *The Union League of Philadelphia November 5, 1921*. Amendment to the By-Laws, Section 12, Article I, substituting "male" for "person."

20 *ARULP* (1920), 47.

21 *Ibid.*, 31-60 for full text of the ratification of the nomination of Harding and Coolidge.

22 Klein and Hoogenboom, *op. cit.*, 399. *Chronicle*, 469, for the admission of Atterbury to the League June 15, 1900; 488 for the admission of Grundy Jan. 7, 1888; and 502 for the admission of Mellon Jan. 4, 1888.

23 George Wharton Pepper, *Philadelphia Lawyer, An Autobiography* (Philadelphia, 1944), 137-141. Pepper was elected to membership Nov. 13, 1931 and died May 24, 1961: League obituary notice, *ULA*.

24 Richardson, *op. cit.*, 33-34.

25 John W. Hamer, *To the Members, December 26, 1923*. Circular letter requesting League members to endorse the Mellon tax reduction plan.

26 Pepper, *op. cit.*, 196-199. The League with naive faith in Harding, undertook to raise a fund that would restore the house of the president in Marion, Ohio, or to erect a handsome mausoleum, or to found a chair of diplomacy in his name; see letter dated Jan. 21, 1924 over the signature of Horace C. Jones, Harding file, *ULA*.

27 *ARULP* (1925), 109-142 for the anti-immigrant address of Montaville Flowers.

28 *Address in Lincoln Hall by Major Vivian Gilbert*. Undated circular. Vivian Gilbert, *The Romance of the Last Crusade* (N.Y., 1923). *ARULP* (1926), 151-164, for the address of Robert von Moschzisker.

29 *ARULP* (1924), 81, and *passim*.

30 *Ibid.*, 119-152.

31 *ARULP* (1926), 47-68.

32 *Ibid.*, 137-148, for the "Reception to the Governors of the Thirteen Original States."

33 *ARULP* (1927), 72-84.

34 *ARULP* (1928), 65-72.

35 Club and social entertainments are described or summarized in each annual report.

36 *ARULP* (1928), 182-187, for the report of the Library Committee.

37 *ARULP* (1897), 45-46.

38 *The First Annual Dinner of the Kettle Club, January 21st, 1885:* Menu. *The Kettle Club II* (Philadelphia, 1923), 13. *"Lincoln Association of The Union League,"* Jan. 24, 1893, John Russell Young, secretary (circular) *ULA.* Richard H. DeMott and Maxwell Whiteman, *The Kindergarten Club: 1896* (Philadelphia, 1967) unpublished. Other data exists for most of the League clubs and tables.

39 *ARULP* (1924), 29-44, for background on these new approaches to membership.

40 *Ibid.*

41 For the controversy at the New York Club, see *New York Daily Tribune,* Apr. 14, 1893; *The Sun,* May 5, 1893.

42 *ARULP* (1928), 37.

43 *Ibid.*, 11-22, for minutes of a special meeting to ratify the nominations of Hoover and Curtis, and *passim.*

44 *ARULP* (1929), 21-22, and annual election records for 1929, *ULA. Evening Bulletin,* Nov. 26, 1929, and *The Philadelphia Inquirer,* Dec. 10, 1929.

45 C. Stuart Patterson was president during 1897-1898, and George Stuart Patterson from May 20, 1930 to the end of 1931. For the latter, see *Public Ledger,* May 21, 1930.

46 *ARULP* (1930), 63. *Evening Bulletin,* Feb. 12, 1930, and *Public Ledger,* Feb. 12, 1930.

47 *ARULP* (1931), 53-127, contains the published addresses of Julius Klein, James M. Beck, and David A. Reed, in addition to that of Herbert Hoover. For comment on Reed, see *Public Ledger,* and *Philadelphia Inquirer,* Nov. 28, 1931.

48 *New York Times,* Dec. 21, 1931; *Public Ledger,* Dec. 7, 1931, for background of Pilides Costa's portrait, and *ARULP* (1931), 105-107, for the brief Hoover address.

49 *Philadelphia Inquirer,* July 9, *Philadelphia Record,* Dec. 20, and *Evening Bulletin,* Dec. 20, 1930, all discuss various aspects of the League fund raising program for the unemployed. Also, see circulars issued by the League's *Committee for Unemployment Relief,* Jan. 19, Feb. 23, 1931, *ULA.*

50 All of these issues were discussed by League speakers: see note 47, *supra.*

51 *ARULP* (1932), 50-61.

52 *Ibid.*, 109. The statement was made by General J. G. Harbord.

53 *Ibid.*, 65-70, and *passim.*

54 *Ibid.*, 21-22.

55 *Public Ledger*, Apr. 8, 1930, and *ARULP* (1932), 48, for Raskob.

56 *ARULP* (1933), 21.

57 *Ibid.*, 20, for membership, and 33-39 for the financial report.

58 *Ibid.*, 52-66.

59 Joseph Dorfman, *The Economic Mind in American Civilization 1918-1933,* V (New York, 1959), 730-732, and *ARULP* (1934), 52, *passim.*

60 *ARULP* (1935), 76.

61 *ARULP* (1936), 15-38.

62 *Ibid.*, 80-91, and 99.

63 *Evening Bulletin*, Nov. 4, 1936.

64 Reported in the *Philadelphia Record*, June 8, 1943.

65 *Ibid.* See note 55, *supra*, for Raskob. Dates of resignation obtained from League membership records.

66 Ira Jewell Williams, *The Union League of Philadelphia. Constitution Day Observance "The Chief Pillar of the Republic"* (Philadelphia, 1937). *ARULP* (1937), 34, 61-71. *ARULP* (1938), 55-69, "Some Memories of a Lincoln Student." *ARULP* (1939), 69.

67 *Catalogue*, see chap. IV, note 84.

68 *ARULP* (1940), 72-73, describes the citywide movement of independent Republicans to recruit Judge Lamberton for the office of mayor.

69 *Chronicle*, 482.

70 *ARULP* (1940), 72-73.

71 Klein and Hoogenboom, *op. cit.*, 413.

72 *ARULP* (1940), 90-92.

73 *Ibid.*, 101-124, and *Evening Bulletin*, Nov. 6, 1940.

74 *ARULP* (1941), 79-95, for Donovan's full address. An earlier address of Donovan is in *ARULP* (1927), 50-56.

75 *ARULP* (1941), 99-111, for D'Olier's address, and 115-124, for Bullitt's address.

Chapter VIII   Turmoil and Reappraisal

1 *ARULP* (1941), 21-22.

2 *ARULP* (1942), 41-42, and 99-100, for report of the War Emergency Committee.

3 *Ibid.*, 91, and *ARULP* (1944), 21-22.

4 *ARULP* (1942), 70-91, for the address of John W. Hanes; 77-86, for address of Gov. Edward Martin, and 61-74, for Gov. John W. Bricker.

5 *Ibid.*, 82-83.

6 *ARULP* (1944), 25.

7 *ARULP* (1944), 24, 56-57.

8 *ARULP* (1945), 56; Ivan H. Peterman, *Milestones of Union League History* (Philadelphia, 1958), 46; John S. D. Eisenhower, *The Bitter Woods* (New York, 1969), 27-30.

9 See "Staff Profiles" in *Bulletin of The Union League:* Mar., Sep., Dec., 1970; Mar., Oct., Dec., 1971; Oct., 1973.

10 *ARULP* (1945), 37; for other reports of this committee, see *ARULP* (1946), 80-83, and (1947), 31.

11 *ARULP* (1946), 43.

12 *Ibid.*, 44, and *ARULP* (1948), 59-60, for its completion.

13 *Who's Who in America*, 38th ed. (Chicago, 1974), 1775.

14 *ARULP* (1948), 41-42, 65, for a list of that year's speakers.

15 *ARULP* (1946), 75.

16 *ARULP* (1947), 32-33, and documents in Boys' Work file for this and following years. *ARULP* (1949), 28.

17 *ARULP* (1949), 29.

18 *ARULP* (1958), 24.

19 *ARULP* (1955), 25.

20 Background information obtained from Daniel M. Layman, manager. *ARULP* (1948), 37-38.

21 *ARULP* (1961), 56-57, for Schmidt and Lerner; *ARULP* (1948), 40, for Jones.

22 See note 9, *supra; ARULP* (1950), 45, and (1959), 58.

23 See note 9, *supra*.

24 *ARULP* (1955), 28.

25 *ARULP* (1949), 49; *ARULP* (1956), 62-63.

26 *ARULP* (1957), 32. This observation was made by George W. Elkins, Jr.

27 *ARULP* (1955), 45, and *ARULP* (1960), 71, for the Oak Room; *Ibid.*, for the Meredith Room; *ARULP* (1961), 55, for the Old Cafe. With the exception of H. J. Harris' painting of Broad Street, which was acquired after 1940, all of the other paintings are briefly described in the *Catalogue.*

28 For the statistics used here, consult summaries in the annual reports for the period covered, especially *ARULP* (1946), 12-13. The statement on the Republican Party, *ARULP* (1940), 22, was made by W. Atlee Burpee, Jr., and the idea of a "father and son club" *ARULP* (1957), 34, came from Frederick H. Starling.

29 *ARULP* (1952), 44, 61-62.

30 See note 28, *infra*, and *ARULP* (1957), 34, and (1959), 19-20. On the conditions determining clerical membership see *ARULP* (1948), 18-21.

31 *ARULP* (1958), 45-46, and (1959), 54-56.

32 *ARULP* (1958), 58; and for comparison see the Lewis address (1942), 51; the cancelled address of Joseph Fort Newton (1950), 44. See also the addresses of Norman Vincent Peale (1951), 70, and George Wharton Pepper (1952), 62. Senator Hugh Scott delivered the Lincoln Day Address (1953), 73, and Major-General U. S. Grant III, chairman of the Civil War Centennial, spoke on Lincoln's birthday: *ARULP* (1961), 54.

33 The legacies of Walter T. Bradley (died 1929), Joseph H. Taulane (died 1931), W. Kirkland Dwier (died 1950), and John Louis Haney (died 1959), were activated shortly after their deaths.

34 For a contemporary discussion of Marquand's novels of social Boston, see *Current Biography* (April, 1942), 42-44.

35 Typical of O'Hara's novels, with passing references to the League, is *Ten North Frederick* (New York, 1955), 63, 216, and *passim.*

36 Arthur Lewis, *The Worlds of Chippy Patterson* (New York, 1960) provides an entertaining outsider's view of the Pattersons and of the League.

37 E. Digby Baltzell, *Philadelphia Gentlemen: The Making of a Philadelphia Upper Class* (Glencoe, Ill., 1958), and *The Protestant Establishment: Aristocracy and Caste in America* (New York, 1964), both contain numerous references to the League and its members.

38 Nathaniel Burt, *The Perennial Philadelphians: The Anatomy of an American Aristocracy* (Boston, 1963), 373-377. *Chronicle*, 475, for the admission of Nathaniel Burt to the League, Jan. 10, 1863.

39 See chap. IV, note 32, *supra*, for background on more recent studies. Avery Craven, "The Union League of America" in *Encyclopedia Brittanica,* 22 (Chicago, 1958), 702.

40 Gibson, *op. cit.*, and Sylvestro, *op. cit.*, in chap. II, note 104, and chap. IV, note 12.

41 *ARULP* (1960), 20-22; 60, 75-76.

42 *ARULP* (1962), 40, 46, 68.

43 *Ibid.*, 68, and *passim*, for a detailed account of the Centennial Celebration, and Centennial file, *ULA,* for announcements and programs.

44 *Ibid.*, 69.

45 *Ibid.*, 71.

46 *Ibid.*, 72

47 *Ibid.*, 19-20.

48 *ARULP* (1963) for the full proceedings of the 100th Annual Meeting.

Index

abolitionism, *see* antislavery movement

Abraham Lincoln. A Memorial Address . . . (Myers), 308n38

Adams Express, 84

Address of Mr. Joseph G. Darlington Introducing the United States Peace Commissioners . . . 329n10

Address Prepared by Mr. Booker T. Washington . . . 329n11

Address of The Union League of Philadelphia to the Citizens of Pennsylvania, Sep. 6, 1886 (Lea), 99, 319n24

Address of The Union League of Philadelphia to the Citizens of Pennsylvania, with the Preamble and Resolutions, Adopted in General Meeting, August 26, 1868 (Lea), 321n53

Address before The Union League in the 24th Ward, Philadelphia (Browne), 308n37

Address of The Union League (Fisher), 82, 100, 316n38

Africa, 34, 58, 173; World War II and, 246, 247, 252

African Slave Trade, The . . . *Judah P. Benjamin's intercepted instructions to L. Q. C. Lamar, styled commissioner* . . ., 307n29

age: employee service awards, 258; old age pensions, 235, 239, 259; Union League membership and, 228, 261, 263

Agnew, Daniel, 55, 63

agriculture, 151, 230, 238

airplanes, 209

Alabama, 15, 30, 79, 81-82, 174

Alabama (vessel), 76

Alabama League, 95, 100-101, 318n10

Alabama Militia, 81

Alessandroni, Walter E., 271

Allegheny County, Pennsylvania, 113

Allen, Henry J., 220, 229

Allentown, Pennsylvania, 39

Allibone, Thomas, 308n40

Alston, Rev. William J., 47, 61

Alton, Illinois, 39

Ambrose, Paul (*pseud.*, John Pendleton Kennedy), 35

"America Honoring Her Fallen Brave" (Haseltine), 122

"American Centennial March, The" (Wagner), 133

American Federation of Labor, 199

American Industrial League, 146

American Iron and Steel Association, 276

American Jewish Committee, 199

American Neutrality League, 207

American Philosophical Society, 5, 136, 274, 275, 276, 277

American Revolution, 5, 30, 49, 60, 223

339

"American Salute" (Gould), 268
American Steamship Line, 162
Amerikaner (newspaper), 80
Amnesty Proclamation (1863), 69, 70, 71
Amnesty Proclamation and Third Annual Message of Abraham Lincoln . . .
    (Union League of Philadelphia), 69, 313n1
Amor Patriae Ducit, motto, 184, 215, 272
anarchists, 162, 163, 180, 330n23
Anderson, James M., 263
Anderson, Robert, 8
Andrew, John, 46
"Andrew Johnson and the Philadelphia Election of 1866" (Cashdollar), 318n17
Anglo-Saxons, 138, 172-73
Antelo, Anthony J., 273
anti-Communism, 222, 235, 244, 246, 247; Cold War, 253-54; Roosevelt and,
    251
Antietam, battle of, 15, 160
antislavery movement, 23, 28, 91, 140, 300n17; gradualist, 4, 26; Lincoln re-
    election (1864) and, 69-70; Negro military service and, 45, 46-47; press
    attitudes on, 9, 30, 39; religious attitudes and, 12, 14, 41 (*See also specific
    sects*); Republican Party organization and, 1, 2, 3, 4, 5, 6, 7; slaveowner
    reimbursement issue and, 8; State elections of 1863 and, 55, 57, 58-62
anti-trust laws, 178, 183, 187
Apalachicola, Florida, 38
Appomattox, Virginia, 86, 215
Aquinaldo, 176
Ardennes, Belgium, 252
Argonne, battles of the, 213
Argus (newspaper), 11
Arkansas, 15
armaments, 14-15, 80-81, 172, 209, 252, 253; industry, 243-44
Army and Navy Journal, 54
art, 28, 121-22, 207, 271; catalogs, 242, 270, 323n84, 324nn89-91; dining room
    displays, 261, 337n27. *See also* music; paintings; sculpture
Arthur, Chester Alan, 149, 160, 162
Ashbridge, Samuel H., 184, 185, 330n30
Ashhurst, John, 273
Ashhurst, Richard L., 36
Ashhurst, Samuel, 38
Ashhurst, William H., 28, 273, 306n10; publications and, 32, 36, 38, 42
Ashmead, Henry B., 11, 303n57
Asia, 173, 236. *See also specific countries*
Associated Press, 180
athletics, 256
Atlanta, Georgia, 71
Atlantic Monthly, The, 319n26
atomic warfare, 252, 253

Atterbury, W. W., 220, 333n22
Attitude of the Northern Clergy Toward the South, 1860-1865 (Dunham), 308n48
Austria, 242, 277
Austria-Hungary, 169, 207
automobiles, 219, 221

Bach, Johann Sebastian, 268
Bailly, Joseph A., 129
Baily, Joel J., 116
Bailey, Banks and Biddle (firm), 169
Baird, Alexander, 303n59
Baird, Henry Carey, 11, 146
Baker, Melville G., 230, 231
Baker, Lt. General Milton G., 268
Baker, William S., 169
Baldi, Joseph M., 2nd, 253
Baldwin, Matthias W., 237, 305n8
Baldwin Locomotive Works, 277
Balkans, The, 160, 246
Baltimore, Maryland, 70, 74, 160
Baltimore American (newspaper), 84
Baltimore & Ohio Railroad, 51
Baltzell, E. Digby, 266, 337n37
banking, 5, 146, 147, 175, 186, 204; depression of the 1930's and, 234; Monetary Commission (1898) decisions on, 169, 171
Banks, General Nathaniel Prentiss, quoted, 46
Baptist Publication Society, 164
Baptists, 81
Barba, Horace M., 241
Bardo, Clinton L., 239
Barker, Abraham, 91, 120, 190, 273, 330n36; Negro troops and, 47, 187, 310n66; segregated transportation and, 317n8
Barkley, Alben W., 254
Barnard, Frederick A. P., 35, 307n32
Barnes, H. Edgar, 241
Barratt, Norris S., 229
Bates, Samuel P., cited, 310n73
Battle of the Bulge, 252
"Battle Hymn of the Republic, The" (Howe), 224
Beath, Robert Burns, 52, 117, 157-58
Beauregard, Pierre Gustave Toutant, 9
Beaver, General James A., 150
Beaver County, Pennsylvania, 55, 308n41
Beck, James M., 334n45
Bedell, George, 252

Beeber, Dimner, 177, 180, 192, 329n13; quoted, 194, 196
Beedy, Carroll L., 229
Belgium, 217, 243, 252
Bell, John, 56, 301n35
Bell, William Stewart, 307n26
Bellak, James, 131, 324n94
Bellefonte, Pennsylvania, 308n41
Bellows, Henry W., cited, 306n11, 319n30
Benham, Rear Admiral A. E. K., 297
Benjamin, Judah P., 34, 307n29
Benson, Edwin N., 115, 143, 190, 226, 327n21; League House Benson Annex and, 158, 163, 328n32; Union League medal and, 297
Benson Table, Union League, 226
Berks County, Pennsylvania, 80
Berlin blockades (1945), 254
Bethlehem, Pennsylvania, 308n41
Bethlehem Bach Choir, 268
Beveridge, Albert J., 174, 175, 222, 329n12
Bible, The, 12, 14, 30, 62; legal studies and, 154
Bible View of Polygamy, A (Lea), 60, 312n97
Bible View of Slavery (Hopkins), 58-59, 60-62
Bible View of Slavery Reconsidered (Newman), 62, 312n102
Biddle, Charles J., 26, 58, 59, 62
Biddle, Clement M., 132
Biddle, Craig, 114
Biddle, Thomas A., 273
Bierstadt, Albert, 129, 196, 270
Bingham, General H. H., 114, 239
Bingham, Hiram, 229
Bingham, Colonel Lafayette, 46
Binney, Charles C., 306n10
Binney, Judge Horace, 18, 136, 273, 302n49; on *habeas corpus*, 10-11, 303nn54, 56; portrait, 122
Binney, Horace, Jr., 26, 73, 88, 194, 273; civil rights and, 117; death of, 118, 314n9; Frederickson on, 307n20; library and, 136; memorial window, 158; military committee and, 43; sons of, 28, 306n10
biological warfare, 209
"Bishop Hopkins and the Dilemma of Slavery" (Levy), 312n92
Bispham, George T., 165
Bitter Woods, The (Eisenhower), 336n8
Bituminous Coal Consumers Counsel, 241
Black, Jeremiah S., 302n40
"Black Codes," 94
Black Reconstruction (DuBois), 320n32
"Black Regiment, The" (Boker), 39, 46, 309n61
Blaine, James G., 147, 150
Blair, Montgomery, 36

Blankenburg, Lucretia L., cited, 328n36
Blankenburg, Rudolph, 153-54, 165, 185, 205, 328n36
Blodget, Lorin, 54, 80, 311n81, 315n32
Blumberg, Leonard, cited, 328n33
Bodnar, John E., 327n26
Boies Penrose: Symbol of an Era (Bowden) 328n37
Boileau, Albert, 303n62
Boker, George Henry, 10, 12, 22, 28, 79, 105, 215, 273; Annual Reports, 64, 66, 93-94, 98, 313n105; biographers of, 265, 266, 314n10; branch Leagues and, 29, 38, 306n11; on freedmen, 102-103, 140-41; on Grant, 108; on Johnson, 94, 317n6; on League House, 66-67; Library gifts, 136; on Lincoln, 69, 70, 88, 313n3; Negro troops and, 39, 42, 46, 309n61; political activism of, 115, 145, 181; on the Registry Act (1869), 109-10; Russian ministry of, 133; Sanitary Fair (1864) and, 73, 74, 75; on Southern sympathizers (1861), 16, 18; speeches of, 71, 118, 143-44, 194, 325n115; Turkish ministry of, 120-21, 133; Union League Medal, 64, 297; on veterans' employment, 52-53
Bokum, Herman, 35, 307n32
Bolivar, William C., 140
Bolles, Blair, 331n48
Bombardment of Fort Sumter, The (Bierstadt), 196, 270
Booth, John Wilkes, 86, 88
Borie, Adolph E., 28, 273, 306n10
Borie, Charles L., 273
Borneman, Brigadier General John A., 271
Bosbyshell, Oliver C., 158, 327n21
Boston, Massachusetts, 16, 29, 46, 50, 160, 307n26; Marquand and, 265, 337n34
Boutwell, George Sewall, 99, 319n26
Bowden, Robert Douglass, cited, 328n37
Bowser, David B., 219
Bradley, Edward Sculley, 265, 303n60
Bradley, Erwin Stanley, cited, 319n23
Bradley, Walter T., 265, 337n33
Brandeis, Louis D., 39
Brazil, 133
"Breaking Up the Sleighing Party" (Krieghoff), 261
Breckenridge, John C., 56, 301n35
Brewster, Benjamin Harris, 23, 45
Bricker, John W., 241-42, 250, 251, 336n4
Bricks Without Straw (Tourgee), 139
Bright, John, 64, 133
Bristol, Pennsylvania, 220
Broad Street, Philadelphia, 66, 75, 85-86, 90, 201, 249; Armory, 140; Harris painting of, 337n27; League centennial parade (1962), 268; McKinley victory parade (1896), 169; Railroad Station, 163. *See also* League House
Brodhead, George M., 256, 267
Brooke, Francis M., 134, 325n99
Brooklyn Bridge, 146

Brooks, Reverend Phillips, 88
Brooks, Preston Smith, 2
Brotherhood, W., cited, 301n31
Brown, Alexander, 273
Brown, Henry Armitt, cited, 325n99; quoted, 134
Brown, John, 1, 4
Brown, Millard D., 255, 258
Brown, Susan C. (Mrs. Charles Ingersoll), 6
Browne, Nathaniel Borodaille, 38, 59, 308n37
Browne, William Garl, 130
Brownlow, Parson William G., 98
Bryan, William Jennings, 167, 177, 191
Bryans, Henry B., 256
Bryant, John E., 141
Bryant, William, 209
Bryant, William Cullen, 121
Buchanan, James, 2, 4, 150, 303n63
Buffalo, New York, 81, 182; McKinley death in, 178, 180
Building Committee of The Union League of Philadelphia, Appointed January 29, 1906, cited, 330n37
Bulletin of The Union League of Philadelphia, 264-65, 336n9
Bullitt, William C., 247, 335n75
Bullitt Charter (1887), 116, 165, 184
Bull Moose Party, *see* Progressive ("Bull Moose") Party
Bull Run, second battle of, 15
Burlington, New Jersey, 38, 308n40
Burpee, W. Atlee, Jr., 337n28
Burt, Arthur, 135, 156
Burt, Nathaniel, 266, 337n38
Busch, Miers, 230, 231
Bush-Brown, Henry K., 158, 201, 270
Business Vicissitudes. A Backward Look (Gage), 329n15
Business Week (periodical), 238
Butler, General Benjamin, 84
Bye, Arthur Edwin, 242

Cabeen, Robert B., 274
Cadman, Reverend S. Parkes, 231
Cadwalader, General George, 52, 274
"Cafe Royal" (Tissot), 261
Cairo, Illinois, 39
California, 100, 149, 254
Camden, New Jersey, 38, 84
Cameron, J. Donald, 104, 105, 166
Cameron, Simon, 4, 55, 84, 105, 112, 220; Boker tribute, 121; Bradley on, 319n23; Johnson and, 99, 104, 321n45

Campbell, John, 6, 11, 301n31, 303n56
Camp Curtin, 45
Camp Wheeler, 252
Camp William Penn, 38, 49-51, 52, 310n70
Canada, 117
Cannon, "Uncle Joe," 198-99, 331n48
Cannon, William, 41, 308n47
Canteen Club, Union League, 226
Canton, Ohio, 167, 328n1
Carey, Henry C., 2, 6, 8, 80, 136, 274, 326nn1-2; art collection of, 121; Catto and, 139; economic theories of, 145-47, 299n8; Pennsylvania Constitutional Convention and, 111; portraits, 122
"Carey Vespers," 147
carpetbaggers, 95, 100
Carson, Hampton L., 169
Carver, Dr. George Washington, 242
Casey, Silas, 50
Cashdollar, Charles D., cited, 318n17
Catalogue of the Collection of Paintings belonging to The Union League of Philadelphia (Lambdin), 323n84
Catholics, 30, 81, 138
cattle, 183
Catto, Octavius, 47, 139-40
Centennial of American Independence, 131-34, 146, 223
Centre County, Pennsylvania, 105
Chamberlain, Neville, 242
Chambersburg, Pennsylvania, 43
"Champion Single Sculls, The" (Eakins), 129
Chancellorsville, battle of, 160
Chandler, Joseph, 147
Chandler, Zachariah, 45
Charleston, South Carolina, 5, 8, 50, 52, 86
Chartist Movement, The (Hovell), 301n31
Chase, Salmon P., 147
Chattanooga, Tennessee, 64
Chauncey, Charles, 299n5
Cheltenham Township, Pennsylvania, 38, 49, 308n39
Chelten Hills, Pennsylvania, 49
chemical warfare, 209
Cherbourg, France, 76
chess, 196
Chestnut Street, Philadelphia, 43, 70; clubhouse, 28, 66, 75, 136, 305n8; Grant house on, 90; McKinley victory parade on, 168; military school on, 49
Chicago, Illinois, 39, 74, 151; Democratic Conventions in, 235, 245; Republican Conventions in, 106, 203, 204, 220, 299n6
Childs, George M., 112
China, 4, 236

Chinese, 149, 160

Chinese Exclusion Act (1882), 149

Christianity, *see* Catholics; Protestants; *and see specific sects*

Christianity versus Treason and Slavery: Religion Rebuking Sedition (Union League, ed.) 81, 316nn34, 36

Christian Observer, The (periodical), 11, 303n61

Christmas, 226, 264

Chronicle of The Union League, 137, 183-84

Churchill, Winston, 243

Cincinnati, Ohio, 81

Citizens Municipal Reform Association, 112, 116, 322n65

civil rights, 62, 93, 100, 102-103, 107, 120, 318n17; Democratic plank (1948) on, 254; *habeas corpus*, 9-11, 32, 42, 55, 122; Milliken on racial majorities, 144; Philadelphia black community and, 94-95, 139-41, 245; public facilities and, 94, 117, 139, 274, 317n8. *See also* education; labor; voting; women's movement

Civil Rights Act (1866), 94, 100

Civil Rights Act (1875), 142

Civil War, 1-91, 107, 116, 143, 182, 194, 222-23, 226, 250; battlefield tours, 160, 327n24; centennial, 264, 267-72; commemorative art, 121, 122, 158, 213, 215, 270, 327nn22-23; dissent in, 7, 8-9, 10, 11-12, 14-15, 16, 18, 20, 21, 22-23 (*See also* Copperheads); fiftieth anniversary, 201, 205-206; GAR library on, 219; naval battles, 76, 175; renewal fears (1866), 99; Southern surrender, 78-79, 82, 86-91, 215, 316n45; Spanish American War and, 172; unionist secret societies in, 95-96, 266; Union League Library on, 136, 264, 265, 271

"Civil War and Civil Rights" exhibition, 271, 272

Civil War and Reconstruction in Alabama (Fleming), 318n10, 319n30, 320n38

Claghorn, Charles Eugene, 152-53

Claghorn, James Lawrence, 28, 32, 109, 140, 274, 314n11, 327n22; art collection of, 121, 129-30; election of 1863 and, 57; on national political action, 115, 116, 145; troops and, 42, 43; Union League Medal, 297

Claghorn, Louise, 86

Clark, Clarence H., 187, 274, 330n36

Clay, Henry, 3

Clearfield County, Pennsylvania, 105

Clemens, Jeremiah, 81-82, 316n37

Cleveland, Charles Dexter, 54, 136, 311n83

Cleveland, Grover, 150, 152, 154, 156, 326n11; death of, 191

Cloak, William A., 225

Club Managers Association of America, 258

clubs, 5, 6, 12, 15-16, 18, 91, 301n23; "inner," 118, 120, 147, 225-26; sociological critiques of, 266 (*See also* social status); suburban development and, 259; Unionist secret societies, 95-96; Union League Charter view of, 209; of Union League employees, 258-59. *See also specific organizations*

Clymer, Hiester, 97, 98, 100, 319n27

"Coachman" (Hubbell), 261

coal industry, 239
Coatesville, Pennsylvania, 174
Cobden, Richard, 64
Cochran, Thomas, 132
Cohen, Charles J., cited, 332n9
Cohen, Henry, 138, 325n108
Colby, Bainbridge, 241
Coleridge, Lord John Taylor, 54
Collins, Herman L. ("Girard," pseud.), 197, 224
Collins, Ralph, 252, 259
colonization movement, 58
Columbia College, 307n32
Columbian Exposition (Chicago, 1893), 151
Colwell, Stephen, 22, 26, 91, 274; economic theories of, 21, 146; freedmen's relief and, 101, 117; League Library and, 136; publications of, 21, 32, 33, 42, 80, 312n102
Comegys, Norris, 225
Comfort, William Wistar, 251
Commercial and Financial Strength of the United States . . . (Blodget), 311n81, 315n32
Communist Party of America, 222, 235, 240, 249; Roosevelt and, 251
Conarroe, George M., 33
Concert Hall, Philadelphia, 79, 320n34
Confederacy, The, 6, 12, 15, 30, 64; formation of, 9; slave trade and, 34; surrender (1865), 52, 86, 90, 91, 93, 96, 101. *See also* secessionism; South, The
Confederate Army, 15, 81, 84, 86; Pennsylvania campaign (1863), 42-43, 45-46, 54, 56, 70; Union pamphleteering in, 30, 34, 71
Congregational Church, Princeton, 39
Congregationalists, 81
Congregation Mikveh Israel, Philadelphia, 81, 138, 316n35
Connecticut, 229
Connell, Joseph A., 258
Conscription Act, 42, 57, 62, 78
Constitution Day, 241, 335n66
Continental Army, 134. *See also* United States Army
Continental Hotel, Philadelphia, 74, 76
Convention of Southern Unionists (Philadelphia, 1866), 97-98
Cook, Joel, 180
Cooke, Jay, 252
Cooke & Company, Jay, 132
Coolidge, Calvin, 219, 220, 221-22, 333n21; election of 1928 and, 229, 230; Union League Medal, 223, 297
Cooper, James Fenimore, 35
Cooper Shop, Philadelphia, 36
Copeland, Aaron, 268
Copperheads, 9, 23, 26, 95, 97, 304n75; election of 1866 and, 99, 100; League House fire (1866) and, 98; Lincoln and, 7, 22, 42, 88; Negro civil rights and,

62; Union defeats and, 15; Union League publications and, 30, 33. *See also* Civil War, dissent in; South, The, Philadelphia relations with

Corcoran Gallery of Art, 270

Corn Exchange Bank, Philadelphia, 97

Corning, Erastus, 41-42, 309n49

Corregidor, Philippines, 271

Corrupt and Contented: Philadelphia's Political Machine, 1865-1887 (Gillette), 318n16

Corson, Robert B., 322n70, 323n72

Costa, Pilides, 334n48

cotton, 5, 8, 183, 238

Coulter, Merton, cited, 320n32

Coventry, England, 247

Cox, James M., 220

Cramp & Sons, William, 162

Craven, Avery, 320n32, 338n39

Cresswell, Robert, 252

Crossman, General George H., 43, 53, 309n54, 311n78

Crump, John, 85

Cuba, 12, 171, 172, 174, 175, 178; Roosevelt in, 182

Cummings, Alexander, 304n67

Cummings and Peacock (publishers), 304n67

"Curiosities of the Law, The" (Carson), 169

Curtin, Andrew G., 4, 7, 11, 42; quoted, 43; election of 1863 and, 55, 56, 63

Curtis, Charles, 229, 235, 334n41

Czechoslovakia, 242, 254

Czolgosz, Leon, 180

Daily Fare, The (newspaper), 73

Dalzell, John, 183

Danville, Kentucky, 80

Danville, Pennsylvania, 308n41

Da Ravenna, 130

Darlington, Joseph G., 165, 172, 180, 182, 329nn10, 13

Darlington, Pennsylvania, 308n41

Davenport, Walter, cited, 328n37

Davis, Edward L., 255

Davis, Edward M., 38, 49, 141, 299n5, 300n17, 308n39; Camp William Penn and, 49, 310n70; Whiting and, 307n21

Davis, Henry C., 174

Debates of the Convention to Amend the Constitution of Pennsylvania, 322n67

Debt and Resources of the United States, The (Elder), 311n81

Declaration of Independence, 276

Decoration Day, 158

Deerhound (vessel), 76

DeGange, Marie, 258

Delaware, 41, 73, 236
Delaware County, Pennsylvania, 217
Delaware River, 5, 256
Dembitz, Lewis N., 39
Democratic Frauds. How the Democrats Carried Pennsylvania in 1867 (Lea),
321*n*48
Democratic Opinions on Slavery (Lea), 60, 312*n*97
Democratic Party, 12, 42, 75, 91, 143; Catholics and, 81; depression (1930's)
and, 232, 234, 235-37; Lincoln's death and, 88, 90; municipal reform and,
112; national election (1864) and, 69, 76, 78, 84; national election (1868)
and, 107, 108, 109; national elections (1880's), 149, 150; national elections
(1890's) and, 151-52, 167-68, 177; national elections (1900-1936) and, 177,
191, 205, 223, 229-30, 240; national elections (1948-1960), 254-55, 266-67;
Negro labor and, 30; Negro voting rights and, 103, 142; Pennsylvania Constitutional Convention and, 111; Pennsylvania State election campaigns
(1863), 54, 55, 56, 57, 58-59, 60, 62; Pennsylvania State election campaigns
(1866-1867) and, 97, 98, 99-100, 105-106; Pennsylvania strength (1940),
244-45; Reconstruction attitudes of, 95, 110; Republican party-organization
and, 2, 3, 4, 5, 7; Roosevelt fourth term bid and, 251; secessionist issue and,
8-9, 10, 15, 22-23, 41, 55, 84; tariff views of, 147, 149, 152, 205, 300*n*9;
Union League members from, 26, 118, 120, 194, 236, 240-41, 302*n*42, 327*n*19;
Union League pledges of Republicanism (1893) and, 152-57; World War I
and, 208, 217, 220; World War II and, 247
Democratic Peace for the Acceptance of Pennsylvania Voters (Lea), 78, 313*n*4
Democratic Times, The (Lea), 315*n*25
Dennis, Kathlean A., 271
Depression of 1857, 3
Depression of 1873, 112, 147; the Centennial and, 132, 133, 134
Depression of 1893, 152, 164
Depression of the 1930's, 219, 230-39, 244, 245, 255; Coolidge warning of, 223
Dewey, Admiral George, 172
Dewey, Thomas E., 251, 254
Diary of Thomas Stewardson, Jr., 317*n*51
Dickinson, Anna E., 47, 310*n*64
Dillingham Bill, 199
dinner dances, 264, 270
Disston, Hamilton, 237
Dix, Dorothea Lynde, 39, 41, 308*n*45
Documentary History of Reconstruction . . . (Fleming), 318*nn*9, 11, 319*n*30
Dodge, Grenville M., 192
D'Olier, Colonel Franklin, 247, 335*n*75
Donald, David, 320*n*32
Dongo, Italy, 252
Donovan, Colonel William J. (Wild Bill), 246-47, 249, 335*n*74
Dorfman, Joseph, 335*n*59
Dougherty, Daniel, 26, 69, 91, 155, 274; quoted, 22; speeches, 8, 71, 75, 79, 121,
302*n*42; Union Club meetings and, 118

Douglas, Stephen A., 56, 301n35
Douglass, Frederick, 45, 46, 47, 310n64; Philadelphia visit (1866), 98, 318n17
Doylestown, Pennsylvania, 308n41
Dragon, Carmen, 268
Dreer, Ferdinand J., 136, 274, 306n9, 314n11; quoted, 43
Drexel, Anthony J., 97, 112, 116
Drexel & Company, 186
Drexel Institute, 163
Driscoll, Alfred E., 263
DuBois, W. E. B., cited, 325n114; quoted, 320nn33, 41
Duff, James H., 263
Dunbar, Paul Lawrence, 242
Dundas mansion, Philadelphia, 15
Dunham, Chester F., cited, 308n48
Dunkirk, battle of, 243
du Pont, Admiral Samuel Francis, 76
Durand, Asher B., 130
Dürer, Albrecht, 130
Dutch, 38
Dwier, W. Kirkland, 265, 337n33

Eakins, Thomas, 129, 130, 324n92
"Earl Cornwallis and the Siege of Yorktown, The" (Tower), 169
Earle, George H., 244
"East European Jew in Philadelphia, The" (Whiteman), 327n26
Easter, 264
Easton, Pennsylvania, 38, 39
Eaton, John, 141, 326n117
Eben, Carl Theodore, 39
Economic Mind in American Civilization, 1918-1933, The (Dorfman), 335n59
Edmunds, George F., 329n5
Edmunds Act (Pennsylvania, 1921), 221
education, 271, 310n66, 326n117; Civil War mementos and, 160; employee
    benefits for, 259; of Negroes, 101, 102-103, 139, 141-42, 174, 320n35; in
    Pennsylvania, 111, 166, 221; in Puerto Rico, 176; scholarships, 256, 258; of
    Southern whites, 141
Egan, Patrick J., 213
Eisenhower, Dwight D., 3, 263, 297; Union League centennial and, 267, 268, 270
Eisenhower, John S. D., 336n8
Elder, William, 54, 80, 146, 311n81
elections (Congressional and State), 153; *1860*, 6-7, 300n14; *1863*, 8, 54-63, 69,
    78, 81, 104, 311n86; *1866*, 97, 98-100, 318n22, 319nn23-28; *1867*, 104, 105;
    1875-1890, 114-15, 140, 166, 150, 151; *1918-1938*, 217, 220-21, 232, 240;
    1940-1962, 240, 244, 250-51, 254-55, 271
elections (Municipal), 112, 115-16, 143, 157; *1856*, 2, 300n11; *1853*, 3; *1866*,

97, 318 *nn*16-17; *1869*, 110; *1887*, 116; *1891*, 117; *1895*, 166; *1940*, 244, 335*n*68; Union League Republicanism pledges and, 153-54

elections (National), 115-16, 272; *1856*, 2; *1860*, 4, 5, 7, 56, 58, 301*n*35; *1864*, 69, 76-84, 203; *1868*, 106, 107-108, 109, 194, 203; *1872*, 203; *1876*, 116, 133, 134; *1880*, 147, 149; *1884*, 150; *1888*, 150-51; *1892*, 151-52; *1896*, 165, 166, 167-68, 328*n*1; *1900*, 176-77; *1904*, 186; *1908*, 191-92; *1912*, 201-206, 228, 331*n*56; *1916*, 208; *1920*, 219-20; *1924*, 221-22; *1928*, 223, 229-30, 334*n*43; *1932*, 235-36; *1936*, 116, 239-40, 241, 251; *1940*, 244-45; *1944*, 251; *1948*, 254-55; *1952*, 263; *1960*, 266-67

elections (Union League of Philadelphia), 139; *1863*, 28; *1918*, 217; *1930*, 230-31; *1961*, 267; non-voting memberships, 263

Elkins, George W., Jr., 337*n*26

Elverson, James, Jr., 165, 328*n*36

Emancipation Proclamation, 28, 33, 34, 41, 122; labor and, 30; Sanitary Fair (1864) edition of, 73-74, 215

Emmons, J. Grey, Jr., 267

Encyclopaedia Britannica, 266, 338*n*39

England, 33, 54, 64, 76, 133; colonialism, 172-73; Irish nationalism and, 117; labor conditions in, 160; World War I and, 207, 222; World War II and, 242, 243, 246, 247, 270

Episcopalians, 18, 41, 58, 59, 60-61, 81, 308*n*48; Methodist-Episcopal Conference, 316*n*34

Era of Reconstruction, 1865-1877, The (Stampp), 320*n*32

Erie, Pennsylvania, 308*n*41

Ethnic Experience in Pennsylvania, The (Bodnar), 327*n*26

ethnic groups, *see* specific groups

Europe, 163, 217, 220; Cold War and, 253-54; depression of the 1930's in, 234, 242. *See also specific countries*

Evans, Frank B., cited, 322*n*58

expansionism, 172-76, 177, 181

Expansion of Territory, Expansion of Trade (Frye), 329*n*14

ex parte Merryman (case), 302*n*48

Fairbanks, Charles W., 208, 332*n*4

Fairmount Park, Philadelphia, 132-33, 158, 215, 270

Falmouth, Virginia, 36

Farragut, Admiral David G., 97, 201

Fast Implies a Duty, A (Porter), 307*n*26

Father and Daughter Night, Union League, 264, 270

Father and Son Night, Union League, 264, 270, 337*n*28

Federal Bounty Commission, 43

Fell, E. Lawrence, 231, 232, 237, 246; quoted, 236, 244

Fell, J. Gillingham, 88, 139, 158, 194, 274; League presidency, 97, 318*n*15

Felton, Samuel Morse, 274

Ferguson, Donald R., 252

Few Words for Honest Pennsylvanians, A (Lea), 60, 312n97
Fields, Arthur T., 252
Fifteenth Street, Philadelphia, 135, 164-65, 190, 192
Fight for a City (Grant), 318n13
Fillmore, Millard, 2, 300n14
Fisher, John S., 229
Fisher, Joseph A., 267
Fisher, Sidney George, 6, 94; 316n38; quoted, 10, 74, 75, 82
fishing, 150
Fitler, Edwin H., 116, 132, 297
flags, 143, 306n9; election (1936) incident, 240; Pennsylvania battleflag collection, 219; Philadelphia Negroes and, 139; Union Club, 20; Union League, 28
Fleming, Walter, 318nn9-11, 319nn30-31, 320nn32, 38; quoted, 102
Flowers, Montaville, 333n27
Fool's Errand, The (Tourgee), 139
Foote, Andrew Hull, 15
Foraker, Joseph B., 176, 329n16
Foraker Act (1899), 176
Force Acts, 142
Ford's Theater, Washington, D.C., 86
Forest Club, Boston, 16
"For the Great Empire of Liberty, Forward!" (Schurz), 315n28
For the Greater Republic, Not for Imperialism (Beveridge), 329n12
Forney, John Wien, 12, 23, 58, 63, 84, 86, 198, 303n64; Boker tribute (1871), 121; Buchanan and, 2, 303n63; Cameron machine and, 105; at Catto funeral, 140; Johnson and, 97
Fort Delaware, 46
Fort Le Boeuf, 122
Fort Mifflin, 49
Fort Preble, 15
Fort Sumter, 8, 9, 41, 122, 143
Fort Wagner, 52
Fortress Monroe, 52
48th in the War, The . . . (Bosbyshell), 327n21
Forty Years Among the Old Booksellers of Philadelphia (Brotherhead), 301n31
Founders' Day, 135, 169, 178, 329n13; *1902*, 182, 183, 330n27; *1904*, 186-87; *1919*, 219; *1924*, 222; *1927*, 223; *1962*, 271
Founders' Day. The Union League of Philadelphia: Dedication of the Memorial Room, 332n14
Fountain Society, 277
Fourteen-Point Program, 220
Fraley, Frederick, 88, 111, 132, 274, 310n70
France, 33, 54, 183; Civil War prisoner exchange in, 76; Confederate overtures to, 35, 64; World War I and, 207, 209, 213; World War II and, 242, 243, 251, 252, 270
Francis Ferdinand, Archduke of Austria, 207

Francis Lieber, Nineteenth-Century Liberal (Freidel), 315n30
Frankford Arsenal, 43
Franklin, Benjamin, 264, 273; portrait sculpture of, 196
Franklin Institute, Philadelphia, 131, 146, 274, 276, 277
Fraser, John, 85, 136, 190
Frederickson, George M., cited, 307n20
freedmen, *see* Negroes
Freedmen's Bureau, 94, 99, 100, 101, 320n32
Freedmen's Bureau Bill (1866), 99
Freedom of the Press, The. Governor Samuel W. Pennypacker's Message Approving the Bill in Restraint of its Liberty and Charles Emory Smith's Editorial in Protest, 331n45
Free Military School for Applicants for Commands of Colored Troops, 49
Free Soil issue, 1, 3, 5
Freidel, Frank, cited, 306n14, 315n30
Frémont, John Charles, 2
French, 138
Frick, Henry C., 162
Frothingham, Theodore, 274
Fry, Joseph Reese, 1, 43, 299n4, 309n58; quoted, 45
Frye, William P., 175, 329n14
Fugitive Slave Law (1850), 1
Fulton, Samuel E., 256, 259, 263; Union League centennial and, 267, 268, 271
Furness, Horace Howard, 136, 154
Future of the North-West. In Connection with the Scheme of Reconstruction without New England, The (Owen), 41

Gage, Lyman J., 175, 329n15
Gallagher, Joseph M., 241
Garfield, James A., 147, 149, 180, 326n6
Garner, John Nance, 235
Gary, Colonel William M., 46
Gasparin, Comté Agenor de, 64
Gates, Thomas Sovereign, 297
Geary, John W., 109, 110; elections of 1866 and, 97, 98, 100, 318n22, 319nn27-28
Georgia, 6, 30, 71, 94, 141
Georgia State Convention, 71
Gerhard, Benjamin, 18, 26, 275; death of, 118, 306n12, 312n101; publications and, 32, 61
Germans, 165; Civil War appeals to, 30, 35, 38-39, 57, 59, 79-80, 306n16, 315n31; election of 1866 and, 98, 319n23; election of 1867 and, 105, 321n48; Haymarket bombing and, 162; World War I and, 207
Germania Orchestra, 143
German-Russian Nonaggression Pact (1939), 243, 246
Germany, 80, 160, 183; Allied occupation (1945), 254; World War I and, 207, 208, 217; World War II and, 242-43, 245-47, 250, 252

Gettysburg, battle of, 43, 45, 47, 49, 62, 143; battlefield tours, 160; battle paintings of, 122; cemetery, 63; fiftieth anniversary, 205

Gettysburg Battlefield Commission, 331n57

Gibbons, Charles, 1, 10, 28, 155, 255, 275; antislavery activism of, 3-4, 6, 91; art and, 129; Catto award and, 139; election of 1868 and, 108; guest speakers and, 135; on Lincoln's assassination, 88, 317n48; Lincoln visit (1864) and, 74, 75; Negro troops and, 46; New Jersey visit (1863), 308n40; on Pennsylvania Constitutional reform, 110-11; Pennsylvania Senate term, 3, 299n5; resolution on voter registration reforms, 109; Richmond victory and, 86; Union Club founding and, 18; Union League Articles of Association and, 21-22, 23, 26; Union League branches and, 29, 38

Gibbons, John, 3

Gibbs, Jonathan C., 47

Gibson, Guy James, 318n12, 338n40

Gilbert, Major Vivian, 222, 333n28

Gilchrist, Alexander, 225

Gillette, Howard G., Jr., cited, 318n16, 322n65

Gilmore, Adelaide T., 264

Gilpin, Charles, 2, 8, 302n41

Girard (pseud., Herman L. Collins), 197, 224

Girard College, 224

Girard Will (case, 1830's), 11

Godey, Louis Antoine, 12, 304n65

Godey's Lady's Book (periodical), 12

gold, 152, 167, 177, 181; depression of the 1930's and, 234, 238

Goltzius, Hendrik, 130

Goodwin, Daniel R., 61-62, 312n101

Gorman, Arthur P., 152

Gould, Morton, 268

Gradual Emancipation Act (Pennsylvania, 1781), 4

Grady-Salus Libel Act (Pennsylvania, 1903), 197-98

Grafters Club, Union League, 226

Graham, George S., 220, 229

grain, 163, 183

Grand Army of the Republic, 52, 53, 117, 168; George G. Meade Post, 219; veterans' claims and, 157-58

Grand Old Party. Political Structure in the Gilded Age 1880-1896 (Marcus), 326n11

Grant, Bruce, cited, 318n13

Grant, Major-General U.S., 337n32

Grant, Ulysses S., 15, 84, 90, 97, 191, 306n10; at Appomattox, 86, 215; centennial celebrations and, 133; election of 1868 and, 106, 107-108, 109, 194, 203; League House memorial room, 201; re-election (1872), 112, 137; Smyth and, 319n25; third term proposals, 147; Turkey and, 120

Grant's Birthday, 135, 172, 205, 331n57

Grant's Cabin, Philadelphia, 215

Grassi, Peter, 258, 259

Gray Reserves, 43, 201
Great Northern Conspiracy of the "O. S. L.," The (Lea), 315n27
Greeks, 160
Green, Arnold W., cited, 326n2
Greenback Era, The. A Social and Political History of American Finance, 1865-1879 (Unger), 326n1
Gribbel, John, 211, 215, 232
Ground Hog Club, Union League, 226
Grow, Galusha, 107, 321n52
Grundy, Joseph R., 220, 231, 333n22
Grützner, Edward, 261
Guam, 171
Guiteau, Charles J., 149

habeas corpus, 9-11, 32, 42, 55, 122; Taney on, 302n48
Haddonfield, New Jersey, 38, 308n40
Hallowell, Morris L., 310n70
Hamer, John W., 204, 332n5, 333n25
Hamlin, Hannibal, 45, 84
Hancock, General W. S., 302n42
Hanes, John W., 250, 336n4
Haney, John Louis, 265, 337n33
Hanna, Marcus A., 176-77
Harbord, Major General J. G., 236, 335n52
Harding, Warren Gamaliel, 219, 220, 221, 333nn21, 26
Hare, John Innes Clark, 18, 23, 26, 43, 275; resignation, 143
Harper's Ferry, Virginia, 4, 160
Harper's Weekly, 98
Harr, Luther A., 241
Harris, H. J., 337n27
Harrisburg, Pennsylvania, 43, 45, 46, 122, 272
Harrisburg *Telegraph* (newspaper), 84
Harrison, Benjamin, 150-51, 154, 157, 194, 328n36
Harrison, Joseph, 112
Harrison, Joseph, Jr., 121, 275, 314n11
Hartranft, John F., 114
Harvard University, 88, 165, 235
"Harvest Home: When the War Was Over" (John), 270
Haseltine, J. Henry, 122, 324n85
Haseltine, Ward B., 275
Hastings, General Daniel H., 167, 328n1; quoted, 239
Havana, Cuba, 171
Haverford College, 251
Hawaii, 171, 175
Hawthorne, Nathaniel, 137

Hayes, Rutherford B., 116, 138; Philadelphia visit (1876), 133-34, 194; portraits, 130, 324n92
Haymarket bombings, 162
Hayne, Paul H., 120
Hearst, William Randolph, 167
Hearth Club, Union League, 226
Heaton, Augustus George, 122, 129, 324n87
Heiligman, Otto Robert, 231; quoted, 241
Heilman, Wesley M., 255
Henderson, Joseph W., 256, 259
Henry, Alexander, 3, 9, 74, 88, 327n22
Henry Charles Carey, Nineteenth Century Sociologist (Green), 326n2
Henry Charles Lea (Bradley), 303n60
Herrick, Cheesman A., 224
Hershey, Pennsylvania, 251
Heuer, Russell P., 263
Hiroshima, Japan, 252
Historical Sketch of The Union League Club of New York . . . (Bellows), 306n11, 319n30
Historical Society of Pennsylvania, 136, 274
History of Municipal Development, A (Penrose), 165-66
History of Our Flag, The (Sarmiento), 73, 314n12
History of Pennsylvania Volunteers, 1861-1865 (Bates), 310n73
History of The Union League of Philadelphia (Lathrop), 137, 302n43, 303n58, 310nn65, 73
History of the United States (Rhodes), 320n32
Hitler, Adolf, 242-43, 244, 246, 252
Hobart, Garret Augustus, 165, 176, 194
Hollidaysburg, Pennsylvania, 308n41
Holmes, Leroy, 225
Holmes, Oliver Wendell, 88, 121
Holmesburg, Pennsylvania, 308n41
Holy Trinity Church, Philadelphia, 88
Homer, Winslow, 130, 270
Homestead Act (1862), 23, 107
Homestead Strike (1892), 162
Homiller, William F., 225
Hooker, Joseph, 84
Hoover, Herbert, 217, 221, 229, 334nn41, 47; depression of the 1930's and, 230, 232, 234-35, 236, 237, 239; portrait, 232, 334n48
Hoover, Lou Henry (Mrs. Herbert Hoover), 229
Hope, Bob, 297
Hope, James F., 192
Hopkins, Bishop John Henry, 58-59, 60-62, 312n92
Horstmann Table, Union League, 226
Hovell, Mark, cited, 301n31
How A Free People Conduct A Long War (Stillé), 14, 33, 304n71

Howard, General Oliver Otis, 101, 168, 192
Howard University, 101
Howe, Julia Ward, 224
Hoyt, Henry M., 140, 325n115
Hubbell, Henry S., 261
Huey, Samuel B., 150, 297
Hughes, Justice Charles Evans, 208, 221, 236, 332n4
Hunt, Benjamin, 317n8
Huntsville, Alabama, 81-82
Huston, Joseph M., 190

Illinois, 39, 41, 84, 267
illiteracy rates, 141, 326n117; Dillingham Bill on, 199; in Puerto Rico (1890's), 176
immigrants, 2, 30, 59, 80, 145, 333n27; education and, 141, 199; exclusion laws, 149, 160, 180-181, 199, 222, 223; increase in immigration, post-Civil War, 151, 160, 162, 207; melting pot theory and, 173, 183; voting irregularities (1867), 105-106, 109, 321n48. *See also specific groups*
imperialism, 172-76, 177, 181
Independence Hall, Philadelphia, 86, 88, 98, 122, 168, 215
Independence Square, Philadelphia, 7, 45, 59, 63
India, 163, 183
Indiana, 30, 39, 41, 79, 149; Beveridge and, 174, 222
Indianapolis, Indiana, 169
Indians, 224
industry, 96, 99, 145, 146, 149, 151, 222, 223; anti-trust laws and, 178, 183, 187; depression (1930's) and, 230, 232, 234, 237-40; foreign export and, 177-78; Southern, 102; suburban movement of, 259
Infantry Tactics (Casey), 50
influenza, 211, 213
Ingersoll, Charles, 6, 8, 10, 14, 18, 56, 304n70
Ingersoll, Charles Jared, 6
Ingersoll, Edward, 8
Ingersoll, Joseph R., 8, 304n71
Ingersoll, Susan C. Brown (Mrs. Charles Ingersoll), 6
Inglenook Club, Union League, 226
Inner Civil War (The), Northern Intellectuals and the Crisis of the Union (Frederickson), 307n20
insurance: employee, 225, 239, 259; old age, 235, 239
Ireland, 30, 117
Irish, 105, 117, 245; Civil War appeals to, 30, 59, 81, 306n17; labor, 53, 311n78
Irish Patriot (The). Daniel O'Connell's Legacy to Irish Americans, 306n17
Iron Age, The (periodical), 146
iron and steel industry, 146, 151, 183; naval expansion and, 177
Iron and Steel Association, 146
Island Number Ten, battle of, 15

Is the South Ready for Restoration? (Smyth), 319n25
Italians, 138, 160, 181, 244, 316n35; Union League exclusion of, 229
Italy, 147, 154; World War II and, 243, 245, 250, 252

Jackson, Andrew, 33, 35, 39, 57
Jahncke, Ernest Lee, 234
James, Arthur H., 240, 244
James, David B., 256
James, David B., Jr., 265
James River, 15
Janvier, Francis, 73
Japan, 171, 234; World War II and, 236, 243, 245, 247, 249, 250, 252, 254, 271
Jerusalem, 222
Jessup, Alfred D., 275, 276
Jews, 81, 138, 160, 165, 244-45, 316n35, 325n108; Dillingham Bill (1906) and,
    199; European persecution of, 162, 327nn26-28; Union League exclusion of,
    229
Jews of Philadelphia, The (Morais), 305n6
John, Joseph, 270
Johnson, Andrew, 96, 102, 317n1; Freedmen's Bureau and, 94, 99, 100, 101;
    impeachment movement, 104, 317n6, 321nn43-44; Philadelphia visit (1866),
    97, 98, 318n17; Reconstruction Act vetoes, 103; Union League expulsions for
    support of, 135, 153; Union League Medal for, 93, 297
Johnson, John G., 156, 325n102
Johnson, Lyndon Baines, 266
Johnson, Robert L., 255
Johnson Party, The (Whipple), 319n26
Johnson-Reed Act (1924), 222
John White Geary: Soldier Statesman 1819-1873 (Tinkcom), 318n16
Jones, Horace C., cited, 333n26
Jones, Ifor, 268
Jones, J. Levering, 163, 184; quoted, 172-73
Jones, Tom, 225, 258, 259, 336n21
Jordan, Francis, 111
Jordan, Virgil, 239; quoted, 238
Journal of a Residence on a Georgian Plantation (Kemble), 59, 60
Journal of Southern History (periodical), 320n32
Judaism, 81, 138; scholarly collections, 198

Kalinowski, Edward A., 252
Kansas, 100, 220, 229, 239, Free Soil issue and, 1, 3
Kansas City, Missouri, 229
Kearney, General Philip, 306n9
Kearsarge (vessel), 76
Kelley, Brooks M., cited, 321n45

Kelley, William D. ("Pig-Iron"), 1, 2, 99, 299n6, 320n38; Alabama visit (1866), 102; at Catto funeral, 140; centennial celebrations and, 131-32; Negro troops and, 46, 47, 309n61, 310n64; tariffs and, 146-47

Kelly, John B., 240, 245

Kemble, Frances, 59, 60, 312n96

Kennedy, John F., 266, 267

Kennedy, John Pendleton, 35

Kensington, Pennsylvania, 129

Kentucky, 15, 39, 79

Kettle Club, Union League, 225-26, 334n38

Keyser, Dr. Peter P., 169

Kindergarten Club, Union League, 226, 334-38

King, Horatio C., 192

King, Robert P., 303n59

King, Samuel, 162

King and Baird (publishers), 303n59

Knight, Daniel Ridgway, 122, 129, 324n85

Knight, Edward C., 76, 111, 297, 314n20

Knights of the Golden Circle, 12, 14, 33, 35; Tevis on, 79, 315n27

Knights of the White Camelia, 103

Knox, Colonel Frank, 239

Knox, Judge John C., 88

"Know Nothing" (American) Party, 2, 5, 300n14

Knox, Philander C., 192

Kolb, Colonel Louis J., 224, 230, 231

Korean War, 259

Krieghoff, Cornelius, 261

Kuhn, Hartmann, 28, 305n8

Ku Klux Klan, 103, 320n41

Ku Klux Klan: Its Origin, Growth and Disbandment (Lester and Wilson), 320n41

Ku Klux Klan: A Study of the American Mind, The (Mecklin), 320n41

Kunzig, Judge Robert L., 254

labor, 143, 144, 204; black, 30, 53, 174, 311n78; contract, 149; immigrant, 160, 162-63, 199, 222, 223, 333n27; insurance benefits, 225, 239, 259; in League clubhouse construction (1864), 85; Roosevelt fourth term and, 251; service awards, 258; strikes, 152, 162; unemployment (1930's) and, 230, 232, 234, 235, 239; of veterans, 35, 52-53, 64, 70, 157, 224, 252-53; wage levels, 151, 232, 238; war recruitment (Civil War), 43; of women, 224, 250, 264, 311n78; World War I and, 213; World War II and, 244, 250

Laboulaye, Edouard de, 64

Ladies' Night, Union League, 136, 224, 242, 251

Lafayette College, Easton, 264

LaFollette, Robert Marion, 222

Lafore, John A., Jr., 253

Lamar, Lucius Q. C., 34

Lambdin, James Reid, 121-22, 129, 323n84

Lambert, William H., 158, 197, 327n21, 330n33

Lamberton, Judge Robert E., 244, 245, 335n68

Lancaster, Pennsylvania, 103

Landon, Alfred M., 239, 240, 241

Lane, David H., 114

Lathrop, George Parsons; quoted, 51-52; Union League history, 137, 302n43, 303n58, 310nn65, 73

Lautenbach, Kurt, 225

Lawrence, David, 231

Layman, Daniel M., 225, 252, 258, 270, 336n20

Lea, Henry Charles, 11, 30, 38, 60, 91, 146, 303n60, 312n97; on anti-Union societies, 79, 315n27; Bradley biography, 265; election of 1867 and, 105, 321nn47-48; Johnson and, 99, 319n24; Lincoln and, 70, 78-79, 90, 313n4, 314n14, 315nn24-25; medieval studies of, 154; municipal reform and, 112, 113, 117, 321nn47-48; on Reconstruction goals, 107, 321n53; resignation of, 147, 326n5; troops and, 42, 43, 45, 54

League House, 66, 75, 85-86, 90, 134-36, 209, 330n37, 331n40; Armistice celebration (1918), 217; art collection, *see* art; Benson Annex, 158, 163, 328n32; Boker reception (1871) at, 120-21; Coast Guard use (1942) of, 250; concerts, *see* music; Fifteenth Street extension, 135, 164-65, 190-91, 192, 194, 196-97, 226; fire (1866), 98; formal opening, 117-18; Garfield campaign (1880) and, 149; governors' conference (1944) at, 251; improvements (1950's), 259, 261, 263, 337n27; League anniversary celebrations, 143, 207-208, 332nn1, 3; League centennial celebrations (1962), 268-72; library, 28, 136, 154, 190, 196-99, 219, 224, 264-65, 271, 327n17; Lincoln Hall, 122, 131, 199, 201, 229, 236, 333n28; Lincoln Memorial Room, 213, 215, 217, 270, 332nn11-14; McKinley receptions, 168-69, 172, 181; memorial window, 158; operating costs (1933), 237; Pearl Harbor attack news (1941), 249; Republican Convention (1900) guests, 176; Roosevelt receptions, 182-83, 184, 186-87; Union Club meetings at, 118, 120; United States centennial celebrations (1876), 133; United States sesquicentennial reception (1926), 223; veterans' employment service in, 252-53; World War memorials, 253

League of Nations, 220, 222, 223

Leary-Stuart & Company, Philadelphia, 197

Lebanon, Pennsylvania, 308n41

Leclere, Joseph, 308n40

Lee, Alfred, 196, 225, 265

Lee, Robert E., 15, 42, 45, 56; surrender (1865), 86, 316n45

Legal Tender Acts, 42, 62, 80, 315n32

Legardeur de Saint Pierre, Jacques, portrait, 122

Leland, Charles Godfrey, 73, 74, 215, 314n10

Lend-Lease Program (1940), 245-46

Leonardo Da Vinci, 265

Lerner, Michael, 258, 336n21

Lester, J. C., cited, 320n41

Letter to a Friend in a Slave State (Ingersoll), 14, 304*n*70
Letter to the President of the United States, by a Refugee (Barnard), 307*n*32
*Letters from General Rosecrans! To the Democracy of Indiana. Action of the
Ohio Regiments at Murfreesboro, Regarding the Copperheads* (Union League
of Philadelphia), 33, 36
Levy, Ronald, 312*n*92
Lewis, Abraham J., 275
Lewis, Arthur, 265-66, 337*n*36
Lewis, Edwin M., 275
Lewis, Henry, 116
Lewis, Jimmy, 252, 261
Lewis, William David, 46, 147, 275; Lincoln nomination (1863), 313*n*3
Lewis, William Mather, 264, 337*n*32
Lewisburg, Pennsylvania, 308*n*41
Lexington, Kentucky, 5
Libel Act (Pennsylvania, 1903), 197-98
Liberty Loan Program, 211, 332*n*8
Liberty Statue, Philadelphia, 211
Library Company of Philadelphia, 136, 154
"Library Nights," 224
Lieber, Francis, 80, 315*n*30
Life of Horace Binney, (Charles Binney), 306*n*10
Life and Public Services of Abraham Lincoln (Williamson), 313*n*3
Lincoln, Abraham, 14, 20, 22, 23, 57, 107, 135, 147, 267, 304*n*71; Amnesty
Proclamation (1863), 69, 70, 313*n*1; assassination of, 86-90, 93, 116, 140,
143, 180, 217, 264, 316*nn*46-47, 317*n*48; Corning correspondence, 41-42,
309*n*49; election (1860), 3, 4, 5, 7, 56, 58, 301*n*35; Emancipation Proclamation, 28, 33, 73-74, 122, 174, 215, 314*n*13; Gettysburg Address, 63, 215, 268;
habeas corpus suspension by, 9-10, 11, 32, 42, 122, 302*n*48; Heiligman on,
241; historical perspectives on, 222-23, 264, 337*n*32; Inaugural (1861) Address, 9, 302*n*44; memorial collections on, 158, 196, 197, 215, 224, 226, 241;
monetary policy of, 146; Pershing on, 224; Philadelphia visit (1864), 74-76,
194, 314, 14*a*-19; portraits of, 122, 324*n*88; press censorship of, 303*n*61;
Reconstruction plans of, 103, 104; re-election (1864) campaign for, 70, 76-84,
116, 203, 313*n*3; State elections of 1863 and, 54, 62, 63; Taft and, 191, 206;
Union League Medal, 64, 297; Union League Memorial Room, 213, 215, 217,
332*nn*11-14
Lincoln, Mary Todd (Mrs. Abraham Lincoln), 74
Lincoln, Robert Todd, 135
Lincoln Association, Union League, 226, 334*n*38
Lincoln Club, Union League, 226, 231
Lincoln Hall, Philadelphia, *see* League House, Lincoln Hall
Lincoln oder McClellan (Lieber), 80
Lincoln Monument Association, 327*n*22
"Lincoln Portrait, A" (Copeland), 268
Lincoln's Birthday, 169, 172, 205-206, 222-23, 241; *1899,* 174, 329*n*11; *1928,*
223-24; *1953,* 337*n*32; Civil War Centennial and, 264, 268

Lincoln's League: The Union League Movement During the Civil War (Gibson), 318n12
Lippincott, Craige, 165, 328n36
Lippincott, Joshua Ballinger, 11, 112, 116, 118, 275, 303n58, 328n36; economic publications, 146; Union League library and, 136
Lippincott, Robert, 165, 328n36
Lippincott's Magazine, 120
List of Pamphlets Distributed by the Board of Publication of The Union League of Philadelphia, 306n16
Little, Amos R., 132, 322n70, 323n72
Littleton, Arthur, 263
Liverpool, England, 5
Lockwood, E. Dunbar, 112
Lodge, Henry Cabot, 176, 182, 199, 266, 330n27
Logan Circle, Philadelphia, 73
London, England, 54, 270
London *Guardian* (newspaper), 54
Long, John D., 175, 329n13
Longfellow, Henry Wadsworth, 121
Louisiana, 94
Louisiana Purchase, 186
Louisville, Kentucky, 39
Lovejoy, Elijah P., 39
Lovejoy, Owen, 39, 308n44
Lowell, James Russell, 39, 71, 79, 121, 313n8
Loyalists' Ammunition, The (Union League of Philadelphia), 33
Loyal Leagues, 95-96, 100, 320n32; racial violence and, 103
"Loyal Opposition in Civil War Philadelphia, The" (Wainwright), 303n62
Loyal Publication Society, 80, 308n36
Lucas van Leyden, 130
Luce, Clare Boothe, 251
Lusitania (vessel), 208
Lutherans, 81
Lynchburg *Virginian* (newspaper), 142

McAdoo, William G., 213, 217
MacArthur, General Douglas, 268
McCabe, Thomas B., 267, 268
McCall, Peter, 58, 61
MacCameron, Robert Lee, 181, 330n24
McCarter, Richard T., 160
McClellan, George B., 15, 50, 76, 84; Lea on, 78-79
McCloskey, Matthew H., Jr., 240, 245
McClure, Alexander K., 4, 55, 84, 99, 105, 311n86; at Catto funeral, 140; Republicanism pledges and, 154
McClure's Magazine, 184

McCreary, George D., quoted, 330n33
Maceuen, Charles Izard, 54-55, 122, 311n84
McDonald, Harl, 268
Mack, Connie, 256
McKim family, 38, 300n17
McKim, James Miller, 3, 4, 6, 46, 91, 300n17, 320n34; freedmen's relief and,
    101; segregation and, 317n8
McKinley, William, 146, 151, 191, 244, 328n36, 330n30; assassination of, 178,
    180-81, 183, 184, 329n21, 330nn22-23; election of 1896, 165, 166, 167-68;
    Roosevelt and, 176-77, 183, 187; Spanish American War and, 171, 172, 173;
    Union League reception for, 168-69, 194
McKinney, Cornelius, 252
McMichael, Clayton, 165, 328n36
McMichael, Morton, 4, 8, 10, 12, 165, 185, 194; at "Carey Vespers," 147; at
    Catto funeral, 140; on Civil War, 57, 79; Godey and, 304n65; Lincoln re-
    election (1864) and, 69, 82; machine politics and, 105, 106-107, 116; mayoral
    election (1866) and, 97, 318nn16-17; memorial window, 158; Sanitary Fair
    (1864) and 74, 75; speeches, 71, 88, 98, 118; tariff issues and, 2, 6, 300n9;
    troops and, 43; Union Club organization and, 18, 275; Union League organi-
    zation and, 26, 29
McNary, Charles L., 245
McPherson, James M., cited, 320n38
MacVeagh, Wayne, 56-57, 63, 104, 165, 311n88; Pennsylvania Constitutional
    Convention and, 112; Turkey ministry, 120, 121
Maine, 147, 175, 229, 240
Maine (vessel), 171
Manchuria, 236
Manila Bay, 171, 194
Manufacturers Club of Philadelphia, 151
Marchant, Edward Dalton, 122, 324n88
Marcus, Robert D., cited, 326n11
Marion, Ohio, 333n26
Market Street, Philadelphia, 163
Marne, battle of The, 213
Marquand, John P., 265, 337n34
Marshall, General George C., 253
Marshall, Justice John, 122, 222
Marshall Plan, 253
Martin, David, 114
Martin, Edward, 250, 336n4
Marx, Karl, 197
Maryland, 30
"Mass in B Minor" (Bach), 268
Massachusetts, 46, 103, 176, 199, 205, 220, 266
Massachusetts Militia, 46
Mawson, Edward S., 305n6

Meade, General George G., 45, 84, 97, 201; portrait, 122; Union League Medal, 297

Mecklin, John Moffat, cited, 320n41

Meigs, Dr. John Forsyth, 6, 21

Meigs, Captain S. Emlen, 215, 314n19, 332n13

Mellon, Andrew W., 220, 221, 333nn22, 25

Mellon Plan, 221, 333n25

Melville, Herman, 197

Memorial History of Philadelphia (Young), 197, 328n31

"Memories of America" (Dragon), 268

Mercer, George Gluyas, 152, 156

Mercer, Singleton A., 275

Merchants' Exchange, Philadelphia, 97

Meredith, 6, 111, 194, 300n10; Catto funeral and, 139; *habeas corpus* issue and, 11; memorial window and, 158; Registry Act and, 109; Union League Medal, 297; Union League presidency, 2, 28, 261

Meredith Room, League House, 261

Merrick, Samuel Vaughan, 118, 276, 277

Messchert, Matthew Huizinga, 32, 39, 46, 54, 129, 307n23

Methodists, 41, 81, 316n34

Methodist Episcopal Conference, 316n34

Mexican War, 100

Mexico, 12, 35, 208

Midvale Steel Company, 146

Milestones of Union League History (Peterman), 265, 336n8

Milhous, Thomas, 300n16

Military Order of the Loyal Legion, 88, 117, 157, 158, 268; memorial for, 253

Mill, John Stuart, 64

Miller, E. Spencer, 276

Milliken, James, 276; quoted, 144

mining, safety issues, 100

Mississippi, 6, 34, 94

Mississippi, University of, 35

Mississippi River, 15

Missouri, 79

Mitchell, General, 15

Mobile, Alabama, 102

Monetary Commission (Indianapolis, 1898), 169, 171, 329n5

money, 135; art collection costs, 130, 242; bequests to the Union League, 196; boys' citizenship awards, 255, 256; campaign contributions, 147, 151, 236, 267; for centennial celebrations, 132-33; 267; clubhouse costs, 66, 85, 190, 191; deflation (1930's), 232; for employee retirement, 259; foreign policy and, 175; gold standard, 152, 165, 167, 169, 171, 177, 181, 238, 329n5; hoarding (1930's), 235; interest rates and, 146, 171; paper, 42, 62, 80, 146, 147, 171, 238; for publications, 32, 57, 91, 306n13; public funds management, 112-13, 114; for public works, 234; regimental costs, 43, 45, 47, 84-85; scholarships, 256, 258; servicemen's center costs, 211; slaveowner reimbursement issue, 8; for unemployment relief (1930's), 232; Union League dues, 28, 164, 209,

237, 250, 261, 263; war bonds, 211; World War I contributions, 209, 332n8;
World War II contributions, 250
Montfaucon, France, 213
Montrose, Pennsylvania, 308n41
Moore, Bloomfield H., 276
Moore, J. Hampton, 220
Morais, Henry S., 305n6
Morais, Reverend Sabato, 81, 138, 316n35, 325n108
Moran, Edward, 129
Moran, Peter, 129
Moran, Thomas, 129
Moraski, John J., 265
Moravian Street, Philadelphia, 88, 164, 196, 328n32
Morgan, George P., 160, 208, 297, 332nn3, 11
Morgan, J. P., 186, 187
Mormons, 1, 60
Morris, Clayton, 225, 259
Morton, Oliver Perry, 41, 308n46
Moschzisker, Robert von, 222, 229, 232, 333n28
Mother's Day, 264
Mott family, 38, 299n5
Mott, Lucretia, 3, 41, 49, 141, 299n5, 300n17
Mount Holly, New Jersey, 38
moving pictures, 207, 224
Munich Conference (1938), 242, 243
Murdoch, James, 73, 314n11
Murfreesboro, Tennessee, 38
music, 129, 131, 224, 264, 324n94; Union League centennial, 268, 270, 271;
United States centennial, 133
Mussolini, Benito, 252
Myers, John B., 7-8, 28, 276, 306n10
Myers, Leonard, 38, 308n38, 317n48
My Forty Years in Politics (W. S. Vare), 325n107

Nagasaki, Japan, 252
Naples, Kingdom of, 147
Nashville, Tennessee, 38
National American (periodical), 146
National Cemetery, Gettysburg, 63
National Hall, Philadelphia, 310n64
National Industrial Conference Board, 238
National Manufacturers Association, 239
National Recovery Act (NRA, 1932), 239
National Union Party, 56, 98-99. See also Republican Party
Nation's Business (periodical), 237
Nation's Sins and the Nation's Duty, The (Bell), 307n26

Nazism, 242, 243, 246, 247; war crimes trials, 254
Nebraska, 1, 3
Negroes, 11, 21, 62, 242, 271, 318n17; "colonization" proposal, 58; disfranchise-
    ment of, 113, 142-43, 144; education of, 101, 102-103, 139, 141-42, 174,
    320n35; labor and, 30, 53, 174; military service, *see* United States Army,
    Negro troops; Northern migration of, 140, 141, 163; Philadelphia health
    center program, 245; public facilities and, 94, 117, 139, 274; Republican
    Party voting support by, 100, 101, 102, 103, 106, 117, 142, 244, 320n32;
    Roosevelt (Theodore) and, 182; violence against, 103, 139, 140, 320n41. *See
    also* antislavery movement; civil rights; slavery
Negromania (Campbell), 11
New Castle, Pennsylvania, 308n41
New Deal, 238-39
New England, 32, 41, 223, 236, 307n20. *See also specific states*
New Jersey, 29, 73, 205, 259, 263, 308n40; pamphleteering in, 38, 84
New Jersey State Legislature, 135, 325n101
Newman, Lewis C., 62, 312n102
New Mexico, 15
New Orleans, Louisiana, 5
Newton, A. Edward, 224
Newton, Reverend Joseph Fort, 222-23, 241, 337n32
New York City, New York, 16, 29, 35, 50, 58, 160, 230; Irish Regiment, 246
New York State, 191, 208, 307n20; governors of, 107, 176, 182, 223, 235
New York *Sun* (newspaper), 334n41
New York Times, The (newspaper), 84
New York *Tribune* (newspaper), 81, 307n32, 334n41
Nichols, Roy F., 264
Nicolay, John G., 73
Nixon, James, 300n16
Nixon, Patricia (Mrs. Richard Nixon), 263
Nixon, Richard Milhous, 3, 263, 266-67, 300n16
Nixon, Will P., 300n16
Nolan, Thomas, 151
Normandy, France, 76, 251, 252, 270
North Africa, 246, 252
North American (newspaper), *see* Philadelphia *North American* (newspaper)
North American Review (periodical), 313n8
Northampton County, Pennsylvania, 80
Northern Interests and Southern Independence (Stillé), 34
Northern Securities Company, 187
Northumberland, Pennsylvania, 308n41
Norton, Charles Eliot, 90, 308n36
Norway, 243

Oak Room, League House, 259, 337n27
Ober, Thomas K., 226

Ober, Thomas K., Jr., 249, 264
"O Captain, My Captain" (Whitman), 197
O'Connell, Daniel, 30, 306n17
O'Hara, John, 265, 337n35
Ohio, 176, 191, 219, 241, 242, 254; anti-Union sentiment in, 79, 100; German
    settlers of, 30; McKinley and, 151, 167; pamphleteering in, 39, 149; Union
    League branches in, 29
Ohio (vessel), 178
Ohio Day (1876), 133
oil industry, 231
Old Cafe, League House, 261, 337n27
Old Time Notes of Pennsylvania (McClure), 311n86
One Hundredth Anniversary Catalogue of Scarce and Interesting Books (Campbell), 301n31
On Our Way (Roosevelt), 238
Ontario Supreme Court, 215
"Open Door" trade policy, 236
Open Table, Union League, 213, 226
Opinions of a Man Who Wishes to Be a Governor of Pennsylvania (Woodward), 59
Order of the Sons of Liberty, 79
Ormandy, Eugene, 297
Orne, James H., 309n58
orphans, 35, 53, 117, 158
Osler, Sir William, 164
Our Continent (Tourgee), 197
"Our Heroic Themes," (Boker), 88
Owen, Robert Dale, 41
Owlett, G. Mason, 251
Oyster Bar Table, Union League, 226

paintings, 28, 86, 181, 196, 306n9, 323n84; Civil War commemorative, 66, 76,
    121-22; Hoover portrait commission, 232, 334n48; League House dining room
    displays, 261, 337n27; Union League exhibitions, 129-31
Paludan, Phillip S., cited, 308n34
pamphlets, 29-42. See also specific titles
Pan-American Exposition (Buffalo, 1901), 178, 180
Panay (vessel), 243
Pancoast, Dr. William H., 169
Paris, France, 243
Paris Peace Treaty (1898), 173, 329n10
Passmore, L. Alan, 256
Patriotism in Poetry and Prose (Murdoch), 73, 314n11
Patterson, C. Stuart, 201, 203, 204, 231, 334n45; Harding nomination (1920),
    219-20; at Monetary Commission (1898), 169, 329n5
Patterson, George Stuart, 230, 231, 334n45

Patterson, Joseph, 116, 132
Patterson, Robert, 146
Paul, James W., 276
Peace Congress (1861), 28
Peacock, Gibson, 12, 97, 304n67
Peale, Norman Vincent, 337n32
Peale, Rembrandt, 129
Pearl Harbor, Hawaii, 249
Pedro II, emperor of Brazil, 133
Pemberton, New Jersey, 38, 308n40
Pendleton, George H., 79, 315n26
Penn, William, 1, 3, 131; tricentennial, 251
Penn Club, The (Cohen), 332n9
Pennsylvania, 149; bicentennial, 131; elections, *see* elections (Congressional and State); electorate research (1864), 78; ethnic groups in, 30, 38, 80; Roosevelt (Franklin) administration and, 236, 240, 244-45; Sanitary Fair (1864), 73; Union League development in, 29, 308n41; United States centennial celebrations, 132-33; voter registration, 105-106, 109-10, 116. *See also specific place-names*
Pennsylvania, University of, 141, 264; Medical College, 164; School of Veterinary Medicine, 275
Pennsylvania Academy of Fine Arts, 121, 122, 131, 187, 274, 276
Pennsylvania Company, 319n25
Pennsylvania Constitution, 59, 192; revision (1874), 110-13, 116, 322nn67-68
Pennsylvania Democratic State Central Committee, 59, 61, 63
Pennsylvania Executive Council, 4
Pennsylvania Freedmen's Relief Association, 101
Pennsylvania Freeman (periodical), 3, 300n17
Pennsylvania Highway Bureau, 221
Pennsylvania House of Representatives, 112
Pennsylvania Legislature, 3, 109, 165; Constitutional reforms (1874), 112; Gibbons on, 111
Pennsylvania Manufacturers' Association, 220, 251
Pennsylvania Militia, 23, 42-43, 91; black recruitment, 47, 49-52 (*See also* United States Army, Negro troops); Bucktails, 26; Charleston fall and, 86; Chasseurs, 88; Fourth, Fifth and Sixth Union League Regiments, 84; Ninth Union League Regiment, 90; 45th Regiment, 45; 52nd Regiment, 46; Second Reserves, 62
Pennsylvania National Guard, 213; inner Union League club of, 226; reorganization (1921), 221; Veterans Corps, First Regiment Infantry, 158, 168, 172, 201, 268, 270-71; World War II and, 250
Pennsylvania Politics, 1872-1877: A Study in Political Leadership (Evans), 322n58
Pennsylvania Railroad, 43, 163, 187, 220, 276
Pennsylvania Senate, 3, 112, 165, 299n5
Pennsylvania Society for the Prevention of Cruelty to Animals, 277
Pennsylvania State Constitutional Convention (1837), 59

Pennsylvania Supreme Court, 55, 62, 63, 271, 276; voter registration and, 106, 322n59

Pennsylvania Union Central Committee, 56, 107, 311n88

Pennypacker, Samuel W., 197-98, 199, 331n45

Penrose, Boies, 165-66, 180, 198, 328n37; immigrant literacy requirement and, 199; national election (1912) and, 204; national election (1920) and, 219, 220; Senate campaign of, 185

People's Party, 3, 7. *See also* Republican Party

Pepper, George S., 196

Pepper, George Wharton, 221, 228, 239, 249, 333nn23, 26, 337n32

Perennial Philadelphians (Burt), 266, 337n38

Pershing, John J., 223-24, 297

Pétain, Marshall Henri-Philippe, 243

Peterman, Ivan H., 252, 265, 336n8

Petersburg, Virginia, 55, 84

Petersen House, Washington, D. C., 86

Peterson, Charles Jacobs, 12, 276, 304n66

Peterson & Brothers, T. B. (publishers), 304n66

Peterson's Magazine, 12, 304n66

Pettit, Henry, 132

Pettit, Silas W., 329n13; quoted, 156

Pew, J. Howard, 231, 232

Phi Beta Kappa, 88

Philadelphia, Pennsylvania, 1-2, 5-6, 301n23, 302n41; artists resident (1870's) in, 129, 130; civil rights movements and, 95, 101, 139-41; Civil War military threats to, 15, 42-43, 45, 56; Hoover (Lou) visit (1928), 229; immigrants in, 160, 162, 163, 166, 207; Johnson visit (1866), 97, 98, 318n17; Lee surrender news (1865) in, 86; Lincoln assassination and, 88, 140; machine politics in, 106-109, 112-16, 138, 151, 166, 182, 184-86, 267, 318n16, 321n47, 323nn72-73, 76, 330nn32-33; McKinley victory parade (1896), 168; municipal elections, see elections (Municipal); national election (1860) and, 7, 301n35; Negro health services in, 245; Negro troop training in, 49, 50-51, 52; population (1890), 163; Republican Party conventions in, 176-77, 245, 254; Roosevelt re-election (1936) and, 240; Sanitary Fair (1864), 71-76, 132, 314n14a; servicemen's center, 209, 211; suburban shifts, 259; Union League reflection of, 265-66, 267; United States centennial celebrations in, 131-33, 134, 146, 223; United States sesquicentennial celebrations in, 223; ward Union Leagues of, 29, 38, 75; youth organizations, 255

Philadelphia Academy of Music, 66, 162, 168, 192, 220, 274; Civil War centennial (1962), 268, 270, 272

Philadelphia Academy of Natural Sciences, 66, 276, 277

Philadelphia *Age, The* (newspaper), 42, 49, 98, 310n68; election of 1863 and, 57; on Emancipation Proclamation sales, 74; Negro civil rights and, 95

Philadelphia *Argus* (newspaper), 11

Philadelphia Armory, 140

Philadelphia Athenaeum, 136

Philadelphia City Council, 75, 88, 110

Philadelphia City Hall, 211, 261
Philadelphia Civil War Centennial Committee, 270
Philadelphia Club, 5, 6, 10, 20; Boker presidency, 120; Southern sympathizers in, 16
Philadelphia Committee of One Hundred, 116-17
Philadelphia Committee of Seventy, 117
Philadelphia Committee for Unemployment Relief, 232
"Philadelphia: Corrupt and Contented" (Steffens), 184, 330n31
Philadelphia County, Pennsylvania, 113
Philadelphia Court of Common Pleas, 299n6
Philadelphia *Evening Bulletin* (newspaper), 12, 97, 304n67, 334nn44, 46, 49, 335nn63, 73
Philadelphia *Evening Journal* (newspaper), 11-12, 303n62
Philadelphia *Evening Star* (newspaper), 305n3
Philadelphia Gentlemen: The Making of a Philadelphia Upper Class (Baltzell), 266, 337n37
Philadelphia Inquirer, The (newspaper), 197, 333n17, 334nn44, 47, 49
Philadelphia Lawyer, An Autobiography (Pepper), 333nn23, 26
Philadelphia Municipal Reform League, 185
Philadelphia Museum of Art, 132, 158
Philadelphia Navy Yard, 256
Philadelphia Negro, The (DuBois), 325n114
Philadelphia *North American* (newspaper), 2, 4, 6, 10, 12, 18, 107; on Chestnut Street clubhouse, 305n8; on Johnson (1866), 97; Lincoln re-election (1864) and, 69, 313n3; State election of 1863 and, 58; Wanamaker purchase of, 185
Philadelphia *Palmetto Flag, The* (newspaper), 9, 11, 302n45
Philadelphia Peace Jubilee (1898), 172
Philadelphia Perspective, A (Wainwright), 314nn15-16, 316n38
Philadelphia *Press* (newspaper), 12, 58, 84, 86, 305n8; on Johnson, 97; Libel Act protest (1903), 197-98; on Mysterious Pilgrims, 322n70; on Union League Republicanism, 155, 327n19
Philadelphia *Public Ledger* (newspaper), 60, 333n17, 334nn45-48
Philadelphia *Record* (newspaper), 241
Philadelphia School of Design, 121
Philadelphia *Union League Gazette* (newspaper), 82, 84, 316n39
Philippines, 171, 174, 175, 176, 178; Taft in, 191; World War II and, 271
Phillips, Henry M., 120
Phillips, Herbert L., 253
Piatkowski, Edward L., 251
Pilgrims to the Battlefields of the Rebellion, 160, 327n24
Pillsbury, Harry N., 196
Pinchot, Gifford, 220, 221, 231
Pirates' Crew Table, Union League, 226
Pittsburgh, Pennsylvania, 162, 220, 308n41
Pittsburgh Courier (newspaper), 84
Planter's Almanac, The (Union League of Philadelphia), 71

Platform of the National Union Party of Pennsylvania, Adopted in Convention, at Harrisburg, March 7th, 1866, 319n23
Poe, Edgar Allan, 39
Poems of the War (Boker), 73
Poland, 243
Poles, 160, 180, 181
political parties, 2-3, 18, 26. *See also specific parties*
polygamy, 1, 60
Pope, John, 15
Populism, 151, 167
Porter, Reverend Charles Summerfield, 33, 307n26
Porter, William W., quoted, 191, 209
Port Hudson, Louisiana, 46
Portland, Maine, 38
Port Royal, South Carolina, 101
Portuguese, 138
Potter, Bishop Alonzo, 59, 60-61, 312n98
Pottstown, Pennsylvania, 307n26
Power and Glory: The Life of Penrose (Davenport), 328n37
Presbyterians, 41, 100, 146, 162, 271, 300n17, 308n48; unionism and, 21, 33, 81
President Lincoln's Views. An Important Letter on the Principles Involved in the Vallandigham Case . . . (Corning), 309n49
President's Policy, The (Lowell), 313n8
press, the, 3, 15, 29, 32; censorship and, 11-12, 55, 56-57, 197-98, 303nn61-62, 331n45; ethnic, 30, 39, 57, 79-80, 140, 306nn16-17, 319n23, 321n48; Hearst chain, 167; on Jewish persecutions, 162; McKinley assassination and, 180; political corruption and, 115, 184-85; pro-slavery, 9, 11-12, 14, 20, 42, 49, 62, 71, 303n61; Southern, post-Civil War, 142; Spanish American War and, 171, 172; on The Union League of New York, 229. *See also specific journals*
Price, General William G., Jr., 213, 220, 230, 232, 332n9; Union League Gold Medal and, 224, 297
Princeton, Illinois, 39
Princeton University, 73, 205, 239
prisons, 100
Privilege of the Writ of Habeas Corpus under the Constitution, The (Binney), 11, 303n54
Proceedings of The Union League of Philadelphia, Regarding the Assassination of Abraham Lincoln, President of the United States, 317n48
Progressive ("Bull Moose") Party, 201, 204, 205, 208, 220, 228, 231; LaFollette and, 222
Prohibition (Volstead Act, 1920), 219, 221, 230, 235
protectionism, *see* tariff
Protest Against the Wilson Tariff Bill by The Union League of Philadelphia, A, 327n13
Protestant Episcopal Church of Vermont, 58, 59, 60

Protestant Establishment (The): Aristocracy and Caste in America (Baltzell), 337n37
Protestantism, 138; slavery and, 12, 14, 18, 58-62, 81, 308n48, 312nn92, 95-98. *See also specific sects*
Protest of the Bishop and Clergy of the Diocese of Pennsylvania Against Bishop Hopkins' Letter of African Slavery, 61
Publication Distribution Records (Union League of Philadelphia), 306n15
Pueblo Indians, 224
Puerto Rico, 171, 176, 178
Puerto Rico (Foraker), 329n16
Purposes for which The Union League of Philadelphia was founded . . . (Boker), 306n11
Pushkin, Alexander, 275

Quaker Road, battle of, 55
Quakers, 3, 81
Quay, Matthew S., 105, 138, 151, 166, 185, 330n32
Quinn, Arthur Hobson, 232
Quisling, Vidkun, 243

radio, 219, 229, 236, 249
railroads, 100, 102, 151, 169, 204; antitrust movement and, 187; locomotive manufacture, 237; subsidies, 234
Raimondi, Marcantonio, 130
Randolph, Philip P., 317n8
Raphael Sanzio, 130
Rashevsky, Samuel, 196
Raskob, John J., 236, 241, 335nn55, 65
Rathbone, Basil, 268
Rawle, Henry, 114
Rawle, William Henry, 276
Rawlings, James, 225
Read, John Meredith, 276, 315n32, 321n48
Reading, Pennsylvania, 39
"Reading the Declaration of Independence" (Rothermel), 122
Reading Railroad, 151, 163
Rebuke of Secession Doctrines by Southern Statesmen (Union League of Philadelphia), 34
Reconstruction, 82, 93-96, 98, 100, 101-102, 320n32; black migration and, 141; Lea on goals of, 107, 321n53; racial violence in, 103, 104; reversals of policy (1880's), 142-43, 157, 325n115; secessionist re-entry terms, 93, 99; Tourgee on, 139
Reconstruction Acts (1867), 103-104
Reconstruction: The Ending of the Civil War (Craven), 320n32
Reconstruction Finance Corporation, 234

Record of the Democratic Party, The (Lea), 90, 314n14
Record of Hiester Clymer; and Historical Parallel between Him and Major-General John W. Geary. Also Official Returns of Election on Constitutional Amendment Allowing Soldiers the Right to Vote, 319n28
Red Cross, 250
Redmond, David J., 259, 261
Reed, David A., 231, 334n45
Reed, George, 276
Reed, Joseph, 4
Reed, Thomas B., 73
Reed, William B., 4, 56
Reeves, Samuel J., 276
Reform Club, 112, 116
Registry Act (Pennsylvania, 1869), 109-10, 112, 116, 322nn58-59
Reimer, Benjamin Franklin, 315n33; quoted, 80-81
religion, 138, 141, 228-29, 334n41; Lincoln and, 264, 337n32. *See also specific faiths*
Rembrandt van Rijn, 130
Remagen Bridge, 252
Reply to Mr. Charles Ingersoll's "Letter to a Friend in a Slave State," A (Thayer), 304n72
Report of the Proceedings of a Meeting Held at Concert Hall, Philadelphia on Tuesday Evening, November 3, 1863, to take into consideration the Condition of the Free People of the South, 320n34
Republican Club of Philadelphia, 1, 32, 299nn1, 7
Republican Invincibles, 3, 300n16
Republican Party, 47, 120, 272; centennial (1954), 263; Committee of Sixty-Two and, 114-15; economic attitudes of, 117, 145-47, 167, 171, 177, 181, 203, 208, 230, 232, 234, 235-37, 238, 239-40, 244-45; founding of, 1-23, 55, 299nn1, 7, 319n25 immigration and, 163, 166; Jubilee (1904), 186; National Convention (1856), 1, 2, 299n8; National Convention (1860), 299n6; National Convention (1900), 176-77; national election (1864) and, 69, 70, 74, 76, 82, 84, 203; national election (1868) and, 106, 107-108, 109, 203; national elections (1880's) and, 147, 149, 150-51; national elections (1890's) and, 151-52, 165, 167-68; national elections (1908-1928) and, 191, 192, 219-20, 223, 229-30; national elections (1940's) and, 245, 254-55; national election (1960), 266-67; naval power and, 175, 177-78; official art and, 130; Pennsylvania Constitution (1874) and, 110, 111, 112, 113; Reconstruction attitudes of, 79, 93, 94, 95, 96, 99, 100, 101, 102, 103-104, 110, 142, 320n32; Roosevelt-Taft split (1912) and, 201-206; State election platforms (1863), 56-57, 59, 62, 63; State elections (1866), 97, 98-100, 104-105; State elections (1918) and, 217; State elections (1940), 244; State elections (1962), 271; Teapot Dome and, 221; Union League official identification issue, 22-23, 26, 91, 116, 138, 152-57, 182, 194, 196, 204, 228, 240-41, 244, 261, 266, 327n19; World War I and, 208; World War II and, 247, 250-51
Republican Party Pennsylvania State Central Committee, 56, 107, 311n88
Republican Party Veterans Committee, 167-68

Return of Rebellious States to The Union. A Letter from Hon. Wm. Whiting to The Union League of Philadelphia, 315n29
Rhineland, 242
Rhine River, 252
Rhoads, C. Brewster, 213, 267, 268, 332n9; quoted, 272
Rhodes, James Ford, 320n32
Richards, J. Permar, Jr., 256, 263, 267
Richards, William T., 196
Richardson, Henry Starr, cited, 333nn17, 24
Richmond, Virginia, 15, 102; Union capture, 86
Ridgway, John J., 112
Riddell, William Renwick, 215
Right Angle Table, Union League, 226
River and Harbor Bill, 149
Roanoke Island, 15
Roberts, Justice Owen J., 220, 221
Roberts, Samuel J., 271
Rochester Station, Pennsylvania, 308n41
Roden, Frank van, 297
Rogers, Fairman, 121, 129, 276
Romance of the Last Crusade, The (Gilbert), 333n28
Roosevelt, Franklin Delano, 220, 235-37, 238-39, 243, 244; re-elections, 240-41, 245, 251; World War II and, 243, 245-46, 252
Roosevelt, Theodore, 146, 171, 194, 220, 330n27, 331n56; antitrust action, 184, 186-87; death of, 219; election of 1904 and, 186; election of 1916 and, 208; Taft and, 191, 201-206, 228; Vice Presidency, 176-77, 181, 182
Root, Elihu, 182, 208, 297, 330n27
Rosengarten, Joseph P., 154
Ross, Edmund Gibson, 321n44
Rothermel, Peter F., 122, 129, 324n86
Rough Riders, 182
Rowand, Jacob L., 308n40
Russia, 183; American legation in, 73, 104, 133, 151, 162, 328n36; Cold War and, 253-54; emigration from, 160, 162, 327nn26-28; Soviet government of, 217, 222, 235, 244; World War I and, 207, 217; World War II and, 243, 246, 247, 250, 251
Russian Revolution, 217

St. Louis, Missouri, 165
St. Thomas African Church, Philadelphia, 61
Salem, New Jersey, 308n40
San Francisco, California, 39, 178
Sanitary Fair (Philadelphia, 1864), 71-76, 132, 314n14a
Sansom Street, Philadelphia, 66, 85, 196; land purchases, 154, 164, 191, 328n32
Sansom Street Hall, Philadelphia, 43
Santiago, Cuba, 171, 172, 194

Sarajevo, Bosnia, 207
Sarmiento, Ferdinand L., 73, 314n12
Sartain, John, 130
Sartain, Samuel, 118
Saturday Club, 120
Savannah, Georgia, 5
Savannah River, 15
Schmidt, Eli C., 258, 336n21
scholarships, 256, 258
Schongauer, Martin, 130
Schurman, Jacob Gould, 175, 329n13
Schurz, Major General Carl, 93, 94, 315n28; quoted, 79
Schuylkill Arsenal, 53, 309n54
Schuylkill River, 132
Schweizer, John Otto, 213, 215
Scotland, 160
Scott, Hugh, 268, 337n32
Scott, Warwick Potter, 252
Scovel, James, 135, 153, 325
Scranton, William W., 271
sculpture, 129, 196; Civil War themes, 122, 158, 201, 213, 215
Secession as a Folly and Crime (J. Ingersoll), 8
secessionism, 11, 20, 21, 267, 301n28; class attitudes toward, 5, 6, 16, 18; compromise efforts and, 7-8, 9, 14, 28, 41, 55, 78-79; Democratic Party dissent from, 22-23, 55, 57, 78, 84; elections of 1863 and, 56-57; Southern dissenters from, 34, 35, 81-82, 97-98; Union re-entry terms, 93, 99
Sellers, William, 131, 132, 146, 277
Semmes, Captain Raphael, 76
Sesquicentennial of American Independence (1926), 223
Seven Days Battle (1862), 15
Seward, William H., 73
Seymour, Horatio, 107, 108
Shafer, Raymond P., 271
Shakespeare, William, 154, 265
Shapley, Rufus E., 155
Sherman, James Schoolcraft, 191, 192
Sherman, General William Tecumseh, 160, 192
Shiloh, battle of, 15
shipbuilding industry, 177, 208
Shippen, Edward, 106, 109
Sicily, 252
Sickles, Daniel E., 168
Silvestro, Clement Mario, cited, 312n104, 313n3, 338n40
Simms, William Gilmore, 120
Sketch of the Laws Relating to Slavery, A (Stroud), 311n80
Sketch of the Life of the Civil and Military Services of Maj. Gen. John W. Geary, Candidate of the National Union Party for Governor of Pennsylvania, 1866

Sketch of the Wistar Party of Philadelphia, A, 301n24

Skinner, Cornelia Otis, 242

slavery, 1, 2, 8, 9, 23, 26; church attitudes toward, 12, 14, 18, 33-34, 41, 58-62, 78, 81, 308n48, 312nn92, 95-98; emancipation from, 28, 30, 33, 34, 41, 46, 57, 79, 90, 91, 93-94, 96, 101, 103, 122, 140-41, 144, 307n27. *See also* antislavery movement; Negroes

Slavery the Mere Pretext for the Rebellion (Kennedy), 35

Smith, Alfred E., 223, 229-30

Smith, Charles Emory, 151, 165, 172, 173, 328n36; Libel Act protest, 197-98, 331n45

Smith, Daniel, Jr., 277

Smith, Joseph Adams, cited, 314n22

Smith, Lloyd P., 154

Smith, Mary Rose, cited, 311n78

Smith, Xanthus R., 76, 129

Smyth, Lindley, 32, 78, 82, 99, 315n23; resolution on political involvement, 108-109; Southern Loyalists and, 319nn24-25; Union League Medal, 297

Snowden, A. Louden, 180

social status, 15-16, 18, 20, 137-38, 181, 301n23; Civil War and, 107; Republican Party organization and, 1, 5, 6; Roosevelt (Franklin) and, 235; Union League membership and, 228, 265-66, 306n11, 337nn37-38

Social History of the Greater Boston Clubs, A (Williams), 318n13

Socialism, 167

Socialist Party of America, 205, 222, 240

Society of Mysterious Pilgrims, 113-14, 322n70, 323n72

Society to Protect Children, 328n33

Soldiers' and Sailors' Annex of the Union League, 211

Solis, Isaac N., 165, 328n36

Solis-Cohen, Dr. Jacob, 138, 325n108

Somerset (vessel), 38

Somerset Club, Boston, 16

Somme, battle of The, 243

Sons of the Revolution, 268

South, The, 140, 141; education in, 101, 141, 142, 320n35; Lincoln death and, 88, 90; national election (1864) and, 78-79, 81-82; Pennsylvania state elections (1863) and, 54, 56-57; Philadelphian relations with, 5-6, 7, 8-9, 15, 16, 18, 20, 22, 35, 56, 97, 301n28; Prohibition issue in, 230; Reconstruction, 82, 93-96 (*See also* Reconstruction); Republican Party in, 102, 103, 104, 150; state secessions, *see* secessionism; States Rights Party (1948), 254; Union League propaganda and, 30, 34, 35, 71, 167. *See also* Confederacy, The; *and see specific states*

South Carolina, 120; emancipation in, 46, 101; secession of, 9

South During Reconstruction, 1865-1877, The (Coulter), 320n32

Southern Advance Association, 141

Southern Slavery and the Christian Religion (Stroud), 59, 312n95

Southern Slavery in its Present Aspects . . . A Reply to a Late Work of the Bishop of Vermont on Slavery (Goodwin), 61-62, 312n101

South (The): A Letter from a Friend in the North. With Special Reference to the Effects of Disunion Upon Slavery (Ingersoll), 304n70
Spain, 171, 172, 176, 178
Spanish, 141
Spanish-American War, 171-72, 194; imperialist doctrine and, 172-76, 177, 178; Roosevelt in, 182
"Speech," (Stephens), 71
Speech of Hon. Charles Gibbons, delivered at National Hall, Philadelphia, October 5th, 1860, 4, 301n21
Spottsylvania Court House, battle of, 84, 160
Springfield rifle, 80, 172
Sproul, William C., 217, 219, 220, 221, 333n17; sesquicentennial (1926) and, 223
Stalin, Joseph, 235
Stampp, Kenneth M., cited, 301n28, 302n40, 320n32
Stanton, Edwin M., 46, 47, 86, 104
Starling, Frederick H., 337n28
State in Schuylkill, 5
Stauffer, William H., 258
steam power, 177, 178
Stearns, George L., 46
steel, *see* iron and steel industry
Steffens, Lincoln, 184-85, 186, 330n31
Stephens, Alexander H., 71
Stetson, John B., 237
Stevens, Thaddeus, 84, 99; portrait, 122; Reconstruction and, 93, 103
Steward, Reverend William B., 34
Stewardson, Thomas, Jr., 317n51; quoted, 88
Stewart, John D., II, cited, 321n45
Stewart, John R., 255
Still, William, 317n8
Stillé, Charles Janeway, 73, 154, 307n27, 327n22; Bryant (John) and, 141; Frederickson on, 307n20; education and, 320n35; League library and, 136; pamphleteering of, 14, 33, 34, 79, 304n71
Stimson, Henry L., 236
Stockton, E. A., 321n44
"Story of David Copperfield, The" (film), 207
Story of Sproul, The (Richardson), 333nn17, 24
Stotesbury, Edward T., 165, 186, 203, 232, 328n36
Strong, George Templeton, 308n36
Stroud, George McDowell, 54, 59-60, 311n80, 312nn95-96
Struggle for Equality (The): Abolitionists and the Negro in the Civil War and Reconstruction (McPherson), 320n38
Stuart, Edwin S., 192, 197, 198, 199, 331n57; League presidency, 217; Lincoln Memorial Room and, 332n11
Stump, Admiral Felix B., 268
submarines, 208, 209

Sudetenland, 242
sugar interests, 171
Sully, Thomas, 28, 66, 86, 306n9
Sulzberger, Judge Mayer, 138, 154, 197, 198, 325n108; Dillingham Bill and, 199
Sumner, Charles, 2, 103
Sumter Anniversary, 1863. Opinions of Loyalists concerning the Great Questions of the Times, 325n101
Swann, Wilson Cary, 277
Swayne, Noah H., 2nd, 224

Taft, Robert A., 254, 255, 263
Taft, Robert A., Jr., 271
Taft, William Howard, 146, 187, 191, 192, 194; election of 1912 and, 201-206, 228
Taggart, Colonel John H., 49
Taney, Justice Roger Brooke, 302n48
tank warfare, 209
Tanner, James, 86, 168, 215, 217; Lincoln assassination reports and, 88, 316n46; veterans' claims and, 157
Tariff Act of 1890, 151
tariffs, 3, 21, 23, 222, Carey theories and, 145-46, 147; depression (1930's) and, 234; labor conditions and, 160; Republican Party views on, 2, 6, 99, 117, 145, 149, 150, 151, 165, 167, 177, 181, 203, 230, 300n9; Wilson (Woodrow) and, 205, 208; Wilson-Gorman Bill and, 152, 327n13
Tatham, Henry B., 112
Taulane, Joseph H., 265, 337n33
taxes, 240; Mellon Plan and, 221, 333n25; poll taxes, 105
Taylor, Bayard, 73, 121, 147
Taylor, H. Birchard, 255
Taylor, Zachary, 2
Teapot Dome, Wyoming, 221
technology: military, 209, 252; steam, 177, 178
telegraphy, 180
Temple of Music, Buffalo, 178, 180
Temple University, 255, 328n33; Athletic Association, 256; Chorus, 268
Tener, John K., 205
Tennessee, 15, 35, 98
Ten North Frederick (O'Hara), 337n35
Tenure of Office Act (1867), 104
Testimony of a Refugee from East Tennessee, The (Bokum), 307n32
Tevis, Colonel Carroll, 315n27; quoted, 79
Texas, 235
Thackeray, William M., 197
Thanksgiving Day, 264; *1863*, 64, 70
Thayer, Judge M. Russell, 14, 28, 108, 304n72

"Third Term, The" (Lea), 326n5
Thomas, Major General George H., 38
Thomas, William B., 2, 43, 300n11
Thomson, John Edgar, 43, 309n53
Thorpe, Merle, 237
Thurston, John M., 175
Ticknor & Fields (publishers), 319n26
Tiffany, Charles Lewis, 130
Tilden, William J., 204
Tilghman, Colonel Lloyd, 50
Tilghman, William M., 277
Tinkcom, Harry M., cited, 318n16
Tissot, Jacques Joseph, 261
Titanic (vessel), 205
To the Members of the Union League, 323n72
To the Soldiers of the Union (Lea), 315n24
Tourgee, Albion, 139, 197, 325n110
Tower, Charlemagne, Jr., 154, 169, 203, 204
Towne, John Henry, 277
Townsend, Joseph B., 277, 297
trade, 5-6, 7, 8, 183; arms embargo (1940) repeal, 243; Asian, 236, 243; depression (1930's) and, 234, 237; grain export, 163; imperialist doctrine on, 175; interstate commerce control, 187; merchant marine expansion and, 177, 178, 183, 208; price controls, 236, 239; Puerto Rican, 176; reciprocal treaties, 178; in slaves, 34, 307n29; tariff protection, 147 (*See also* tariffs); Union League Articles on, 22
transportation: automobiles, 219, 221; mass, 245; segregated, 94, 117, 317n8. *See also* railroads
Trescher, Robert L., 267
Tripoli, 172
Triumph of Militant Republicanism, The (Bradley), 319n23
Trott, George, 277
Truman, Harry S., 252, 254-55
Trumbauer, Horace, 190, 191
Turkey, 120, 133
Turpin, Dick, 74
Turner, William Jay, 203, 220; quoted, 204
Tuskegee Institute, 174
Twenty-Five Year Club, 258-59
Tyndale, Hector, 1, 4, 299n3
Tyrant from Illinois: Uncle Joe Cannon's Experiment with Personal Power (Bolles), 331n48

Uhle, Albert, 196
Ukrainians, 160
Underground Railroad, The (Still), 317n8

Unger, Irwin, cited, 326n1
Union Army, see United States Army
Union Club of New York City, 16
Union Club of Philadelphia, 6, 18, 20, 21, 26, 47, 225, 306n12; Barker death (1906) and, 187; founders, listed, 273-77; meetings of, 118, 120
Union Club of Philadelphia Articles of Association, 20, 21
Unionism, 1-91. See also Civil War; secessionism
Union League of America, 95-96, 100-101, 107, 318n12
Union League of America of Pennsylvania (Grow), 321n52
Union League of Boston, 29, 36, 96, 102, 318n13; Marquand on, 265
Union League of Chicago, 39, 96, 102, 318n13
Union League Gazette (newspaper), 82, 84, 316n39
Union League House, see League House
Union League House, Philadelphia, October 6th, 1875 (Little and Corson), 323n72
Union League of New Hampshire, 313n3
Union League of New York, 21, 29, 36, 306n11, 308n36; Germans and, 80; Reconstruction attitudes of, 95, 96, 101, 102; religious discrimination in, 228-29, 334n41
Union League of Philadelphia: clubhouses, 28, 29, 41, 46, 52, 64, 66-67, 75, 76, 136, 305n8 (See also League House); dues, 28, 164, 209, 237, 250, 261, 263; employees, 224-25, 250, 251-52, 258-59, 261, 270, 271, 336n9; expulsions, 135, 152-53, 155, 156, 241; "inner clubs," 225-26; membership numbers, 66, 138, 164, 165, 213, 226, 231, 232, 237-38, 261, 263, 325n109, 328n34; membership qualifications, 22-23, 26, 137-38, 152-57, 181, 219, 226, 228-29, 231, 240-41, 261, 263, 305n3, 327n19, 330n25, 333n19, 337n30; motto, 184, 215, 272; organization of, 1, 12, 20, 21-28, 96, 134-39, 308n41; publications of, 11, 12, 14, 28 (See also Union League of Philadelphia Board of Publication); Union League centennial (1962), 224, 226, 265, 267-72, 338n43; Union League semicentennial (1913), 205-206. See also League House; and see specific boards and committees, e.g., Union League of Philadelphia Board of Directors
Union League of Philadelphia (Mawson), 305n6
Union League of Philadelphia Advisory Real Estate Board, 164-65, 328n35
Union League of Philadelphia Annual Reports, 184; 1863, 64, 66, 313n105; 1865, 66-67, 93-94; 1866, 98, 318n17; 1887, 142; 1898, 172; 1912, 205
Union League of Philadelphia Art Association, 129-31, 196, 205, 207; catalogue (1940), 242; Lincoln Memorial Room and, 213
Union League of Philadelphia Articles of Association, 28, 38, 122, 144, 302n41, 303n58, 319n25, 324n86; on political commitment, 22-23, 26, 55-56
Union League of Philadelphia Board of Directors, 66, 225; Constitutional reform and, 110-11; elections of 1875 and, 114-15; Fifteenth Street land purchase, 135; on League House reconstruction (1896), 165; library and, 136; Lincoln re-election (1864) resolution and, 69, 82; military recruitment (1942) drive, 250; Negro community of Philadelphia and, 139-40; Roosevelt (Franklin) administration and, 237, 241; Union League centennial and, 267;

Union League membership candidates and, 138; United States centennial
  celebration plans and, 133; voter registration reform and, 109
Union League of Philadelphia Board of Finance, 134, 135, 167; centennial celebration costs and, 132, 133
Union League of Philadelphia Board of Publication, 29-42, 43, 45, 76, 303*n*59,
  307*n*27, 318*n*15; Amnesty Proclamation (1864) and, 70, 71, 313*n*1; announcement of, 306*n*13; economic texts, 146; elections of 1863 and, 54, 57-58, 59-
  62; elections of 1866 and, 97, 98, 318*n*22, 319*nn*23-28; elections of 1868 and,
  107-108; elections of 1880 and, 149; elections of 1896 and, 167; library and,
  136, 137; Lincoln re-election (1864) campaign and, 70, 76-84; Minute Book
  discovery, 306*n*14; Negro troops and, 46, 47; printing volume (1863-1864),
  64, 82, 303*n*57, 306*nn*15-16; Sanitary Fair (1864) and, 73-74, 314*n*13; Schurz
  report (1865) and, 94
Union League of Philadelphia Boys' Work Committee, 256, 258, 336*n*16
Union League of Philadelphia Building Committee, 163, 330*n*37
Union League of Philadelphia *By-Laws*, 26, 28, 134, 137, 139, 325*n*106; on
  League presidency, 231; on political action (1875), 115-16; Republicanism
  pledge proposal (1893), 153-57; women's exclusion by, 219
Union League of Philadelphia Campaign Committee of 100 (1944), 251
Union League of Philadelphia Centennial Committee, 267, 268
Union League of Philadelphia *Charter*, 66, 181-82, 209, 252, 272; on member-
  ship qualifications, 137, 153, 155, 228-29. *See also Union League of Philadel-
  phia Articles of Association*; Union League of Philadelphia *By-Laws*
Union League of Philadelphia Constitution, 137, 219
Union League of Philadelphia Employment Committee, 53, 64, 70
Union League of Philadelphia Entertainment Committee, 263
Union League of Philadelphia Finance Committee, 237
Union League of Philadelphia Guest Committee, 134, 135-36, 231
Union League of Philadelphia House Committee, 129, 134-35, 267; concerts, 131.
  See also League House
Union League of Philadelphia Library Committee, 134, 136, 137, 154, 224, 232;
  Civil War centennial and, 264-65. *See also* League House, Library
Union League of Philadelphia Medal, 64, 76, 194, 319*n*25; Coolidge and, 223;
  Eisenhower and, 268; Johnson and, 93; Pershing and, 223-24; recipients,
  listed, 297
Union League of Philadelphia Membership Committee, 137-39, 208, 229; Re-
  publicanism pledge demand, 153, 155, 228
Union League of Philadelphia Military Committee, 42-47, 64, 70, 84-85, 88, 90;
  Fry and, 43, 45, 309*n*58; *Proceedings*, 309*n*57
Union League of Philadelphia National Activities Committee, 217
Union League of Philadelphia National Campaign Committee, 192, 229
Union League of Philadelphia Patriotic Action Committee, 217
Union League of Philadelphia Political Activities Committee, 217, 255, 263
Union League of Philadelphia Public Affairs Committee, 231, 237, 239
Union League of Philadelphia Public Meetings Committee, 167
Union League of Philadelphia to the Republican Voters of Pennsylvania, The,
  322*n*70

Union League of Philadelphia. Sixty-Two, Committee of, 114-15, 323*nn*71, 73, 76
Union League of Philadelphia Supervisory Committee on Enlistment of Colored Troops, 49, 51-52, 70, 187, 310*n*67; Sanitary Fair (1864) and, 75; Webster and, 47, 307*n*21
Union League of Philadelphia. Twenty-One, Committee of, 185, 330*n*33
Union League of Philadelphia Unemployment Relief Committee, 334*n*49
Union League of Philadelphia War Emergency (1941) Committee, 249-50, 336*n*2
Union League of Philadelphia War Veterans Committee, 253
Union League of San Francisco, 39
Union Pamphlets of the Civil War (Freidel), 306*n*14
Union Party, 3. *See also* Republican Party
Union Volunteer Refreshment Saloon, Philadelphia, 36
Unitarians, 81
United Nations, 253; Security Council, 254
United Service Organization, 211
United States Army, 16, 64, 106, 168, 215; arms of, 14-15, 80-81, 172, 209, 252, 253; Civil War participation by Union League members, 91, 122; conscription, 42, 57, 62, 78; Huntsville occupation (1863), 81-82; Negro troops, 32-33, 35, 38, 39, 42-53, 70, 75, 94, 117, 139, 153, 174, 187, 219, 268, 309*nn*60-61, 310*nn*64-73; scorched earth policy, 79; slave liberation, 101; Spanish American War and, 172; Union League publications and, 29, 30, 33, 34, 36, 38, 41, 54, 70, 71, 78; volunteer calls (1864), 84; voting rights, 62; World War I and, 209, 211, 213. *See also* veterans' aid
United States Army Clothing and Equipage Office, 53
United States Army Department of the Cumberland, 71
United States Army Department of the Potomac, 84
United States Central Intelligence Agency, 247
United States Coast Guard Reserve, 250
United States Commissioner of Education, 141
United States Congress, 11, 14, 26, 299*n*6, 300*n*14; abolitionist influence (1863) in, 55; arms embargo repeal (1940), 243; art commissions, 28; Arthur vetoes and, 149; centennial celebrations and, 131-32, 133; Czarist Russian pogroms and, 162; Democratic majority (1948) in, 255; depression (1930's) and, 231, 232, 234, 237; elections, *see* elections (Congressional and State); *habeas corpus* suspension and, 302*n*48; immigrant literacy tests and, 199; Johnson impeachment efforts, 104; Monetary Commission (1896) and, 171; Negro civil rights and, 94, 101, 103-104, 142; Presidential Message (1863) to, 69; Republican losses (1890) in, 151; secessionist states' re-entry and, 99; Southern education funds and, 141; Southern Republicans (1884) in, 150; Spanish American War and, 171, 178; tariff repeal efforts (1870's) in, 147; war declaration (1941), 249. *See also* United States House of Representatives; United States Senate
United States Constitution, 14, 57, 97, 102, 192, 241; Amendment Eighteen, 219, 221, 230, 235; Amendment Fifteen, 139, 142; Amendment Fourteen, 103, 142; Amendment Nineteen, 219; *habeas corpus* and, 9-10, 11, 42; National Recovery Act and, 239; slavery and, 34, 58; territorial expansion and, 176, 177

United States Department of Agriculture, 245
United States Department of Commerce: Hoover Secretaryship, 221, 229
United States Department of the Navy, 171, 175, 176, 182, 234, 306n10, 329n13;
  Wyoming oil lands and, 221
United States Department of State, 9, 221, 236, 253
United States Department of War, 35, 46, 47, 79, 104, 182, 191, 307n21
United States Farm Board, 234
United States Federal Bounty Commission, 43
United States Federal Land Bank System, 234
United States Federal Reserve, 232
United States Home Loan Discount Bank, 234
United States House of Representatives, 107, 147, 198, 232, 237, 243, 251
United States Marine Corps, 38, 215, 268
United States Merchant Marine Fleet, 177-78
United States Mint, 158
United States Navy, 38, 76, 91, 215; expansionism and, 175, 177-78; Spanish
  American War and, 171, 172; Union League youth projects and, 256; World
  War I and, 209; World War II and, 249
United States Office of Strategic Services, 247
United States Peace Commission (1899), 173, 329n10
United States Pension Bureau, 157
United States Philippine Commission, 175
United States Post Office Department, 36, 84, 328n36
United States Public Lands Committee, 221
United States Sanitary Commission, 33, 36, 53, 304n71; Fair (1864), 73-76
United States Senate: Cameron seat, 4, 105, 166; Forney Secretaryship, 12;
  imperialist influences (1899) in, 174-75; Johnson impeachment trial, 104;
  Penrose seat in, 166, 185, 220-21; Republican majority (1918) in, 217;
  Republican minority (1930's) in, 232, 251; Roosevelt (Franklin) and, 237,
  243; Schurz report (1865), 94; Sumner assaulted in, 2; tariff bill (1894) in,
  152
United States Senate Military Affairs Committee, 246
United States Soldiers' Claim and Pension Agency, 53
United States Supreme Court, 9-10, 39, 62, 208, 220, 221, 236; Beveridge on,
  222; Force Acts and, 142; Philippine annexation and, 176; Roosevelt
  (Franklin) and, 239, 240, 241
United States Treasury Department, 2, 141, 147, 175, 213, 220, 319n25
United States Unemployment Relief Organization, 234
United States War Savings Bonds, 250
United States Works Progress Administration (WPA), 239
United War Chest (1942), 250
Universalists, 81
Usurpation, The (Boutwell), 319n26

Vallandigham, Clement L., 42, 100
Valley Forge, Pennsylvania, centennial, 134

Valley Forge Military Academy, 268
Valley Forge National Memorial Arch, 134
Valley Forge Park Commission, 325n100
Vandalia, Illinois, 217
Vare, Edwin H., 138, 166, 220
Vare, George A., 138, 166, 220
Vare, William S., 138, 166, 220, 325n107
Verree, John P., 2, 277, 300n14
Vermont, 58, 59, 61, 240
veterans' aid, 35, 52-53, 64, 70, 84, 91, 117; pensions, 150, 157, 235; World War
    II, 252-53
Veteran Corps First Regiment Infantry, National Guard of Pennsylvania, 158,
    168, 172, 201, 268, 270-71
Vichy, France, 243
Virginia, 98, 102, 160
Voice of the Clergy, The (Potter), 60-61, 312n98
Volstead Act (1920), 219, 221, 230, 235
voting, 59; of blacks, 94, 100, 103, 113, 117, 139, 141, 142, 143; post-depression
    (1930's) pattern changes, 244-45; registration, 105-106, 109, 112, 116, 185,
    321n48, 322nn58-59; secret ballot, 117; of soldiers, 62; of women, 197, 219,
    221, 224, 333n19

Wagner, General Louis, 49-50, 51, 140, 204, 205, 331n57; Republicanism pledge
    and, 153, 154, 155-56, 157
Wagner, Richard, 133
Wainwright, Nicholas B., cited, 303n62, 312n92, 314nn15-16, 316n38
Walcott, "Jersey" Joe, 256
Walker, Colonel Moses B., 71
Wallace, Henry A., 245
Wallis, M. Roos, 263
Wanamaker, John, 116, 132, 151, 166, 237; quoted, 162; political reform and,
    185, 330n32; Spanish-American War and, 172
Wanamaker, Thomas, 185
Warburg, James P., 239
War of 1812, 47
War Powers of the President (Whiting), 32, 307n22
Warren, Earl, 254
Warsaw, Poland, 243
War Veterans' Club, 168
Washington, Booker T., 174, 182, 329n11
Washington, George, 32, 264; Baker collection on, 169; Lea on, 90; portraits,
    28, 66, 86, 122, 196, 306n9; Valley Forge and, 134, 325n99
Washington, D. C., 101, 149; Lincoln assassination in, 86, 88
Washington (D. C.) *Chronicle* (newspaper), 84; *Sunday Chronicle*, 12
Washington, Pennsylvania, 308n41
Washington Grays, 268

Washington's Birthday, 36, 70-71, 135, 169, 199
Waterford, Pennsylvania, 308n41
Watts, Henry Miller, 277
Waugh, Samuel B., 129
Ways and Means of Payment, The (Colwell), 146
Webster, Thomas, 32, 47, 307n21
Weeks, John W., 205
Welch, Howard, 259
Welsh, John, 132
Welsh, 105
West, The, 129, 149, 167; expansion, 151, 172-76, 177; Southern Reconstruction and, 95. *See also specific states*
West Indies, 6
West Middletown, Pennsylvania, 308n41
Westmoreland, General William G., 297
West Philadelphia, Pennsylvania, 38
Wetherill, John Price, 132
Wetter, John S., 114
Wharton, George M., 56, 58, 61
Wharton, Joseph, 146, 151
Wheeler, Charles, 112, 116
"When Johnny Comes Marching Home" (song), 268
Whig Party, 2, 5, 15, 275; Gibbons and, 3, 6, 299n5
While Lincoln Lay Dying . . . (Whiteman), 316n46
Whipple, Edwin Percy, 99, 319n26
Whipple, Colonel William D., 45, 71
White, Jacob C., 47
Whiteman, Maxwell, cited, 316n46, 327n26
Whiteman, Paul, 256
Whiting, William, 32, 79, 307nn21-22, 315n29
Whitman, Walt, 197
Whitney, George, 277
Whittier, John Greenleaf, 133, 300n17
Widener, George and Harry, 205
widows, 35, 53, 117; employment, 224, 225, 311n78
Wiedersheim, Colonel Theodore W., 168
Wilderness, battle of The, 160
Wilderness Club, Union League, 226
William Penn Memorial Museum, Harrisburg, 122, 272
Williams, Alexander W., cited, 318n13
Williams, Ira Jewell, 231, 335n66
Williams, John, 146
Williamson, David B., 82, 313n3
Willkie, Wendell L., 245, 247
Will of the People, The (Boker), 69-70, 313n3
Wilmot, David, 147
Wilmot Proviso, 147

Wilson, D. L., cited, 320n41
Wilson, William L., 152
Wilson, Woodrow, 205, 332n5; World War I and, 207, 208-209, 213, 217, 220
Wilson-Gorman Bill (1894), 152, 327n13
Winchester, battle of, 160
"Wine Tasters, The" (Grützner), 261
Winslow, John A., 76
Wisconsin, 30, 39
Wishbone Club, Union League, 226
Wistar, Caspar, 5
Wistar Party, 6, 16, 20, 118, 120, 267; social status and, 5, 301n24
Wister, William Rotch, 1, 47, 299n2
Wittman, Fred, 258
women's rights movement, 3, 154; suffrage, 197, 219, 221, 224, 333n19
Wood, William, 116
Wood Street, Philadelphia, 140
Woodward, George A., 62-63
Woodward, George Washington, 55, 100; pamphleteering (1863) of, 57, 59-60, 61, 62-63, 312nn95-96, 103; pro-slavery statements of, 8, 23, 59, 302n40
Wordsworth, William, 54
Worlds of Chippy Patterson, The (Lewis), 337n36
World War I, 152, 160, 187, 207-17, 222, 226, 246, 332nn2, 7-8; Belgian neutrality in, 217, 243; European reconstruction after, 220; industrial regulation in, 239; naval power in, 178; Pershing and, 223-24; Union League memorial plaque, 253; veterans' benefits, 235
World War II, 211, 236, 238, 242-47, 255; United States involvement in, 249-52, 253, 270, 271
Wyoming, 221

Yale University, 239
Yarnall, Agnes, 270
Yarnall, Ellis, 54, 311n82, 320n34
Yellowstone National Park, 129
Yeomans, Earl R., 256
York, Pennsylvania, 38, 308n41
York River, 15
Young, John Russell, 155, 156, 165, 183; Forney and, 12, 63, 303n64; Lincoln Association and, 226, 334n38; Philadelphia history, 197, 328n31; on Union League founding, 305n3
youth organizations, 255-56

Zalinski, Edmund L., 270
Zell, Lieutenant Colonel T. Ellwood, 88